Shared Sp[ace and] the New Nonprofit Workplace

SHARED SPACE AND THE NEW NONPROFIT WORKPLACE

China Brotsky + Sarah M. Eisinger + Diane Vinokur-Kaplan

OXFORD
UNIVERSITY PRESS

Oxford University Press is a department of the University of Oxford. It furthers
the University's objective of excellence in research, scholarship, and education
by publishing worldwide. Oxford is a registered trade mark of Oxford University
Press in the UK and certain other countries.

Published in the United States of America by Oxford University Press
198 Madison Avenue, New York, NY 10016, United States of America.

© Oxford University Press 2019

Library of Congress Cataloging-in-Publication Data
Names: Brotsky, China, author. | Eisinger, Sarah M., author. |
Vinokur-Kaplan, Diane, author.
Title: Shared space and the new nonprofit workplace / China Brotsky,
Sarah M. Eisinger, Diane Vinokur-Kaplan.
Description: New York, NY : Oxford University Press, [2019] |
Includes bibliographical references and index.
Identifiers: LCCN 2018051604 (print) | LCCN 2018053828 (ebook) |
ISBN 9780190940478 (updf) | ISBN 9780190940485 (epub) |
ISBN 9780190940461 (pbk. : alk. paper)
Subjects: LCSH: Nonprofit organizations—Management. | Office buildings. |
Shared services (Management)
Classification: LCC HD62.6 (ebook) | LCC HD62.6 .B7534 2019 (print) |
DDC 658/.048—dc23
LC record available at https://lccn.loc.gov/2018051604

9 8 7 6 5 4 3 2

Printed by Marquis, Canada

Cover photos:
- Top left: Leddy Maytum Stacey Architects
- Top middle: Nonprofit Centers Network
- Top right: TSNE MissionWorks
- Bottom left: Tim Benson Photography, © 2015
- Bottom middle: NEW, Inc.
- Bottom right: Saul Ettlin

This book is dedicated to all the nonprofit center champions who have had the vision to employ real estate to realize their missions, and who work daily to keep their spaces animated and lively.

For all their support, love, and patience—

To my husband Amiram, my children and their families, and my own family, both here and gone—Diane Kaplan Vinokur

For Jonathan and Micah—Sarah M. Eisinger

For Dan and Corey—China Brotsky

"Space has always been the spiritual dimension of architecture. It is not the physical statement of the structure so much as what it contains that moves us."
—Arthur Erickson, Architect, Vancouver, BC, 1924–2009

Contents

A Personal Reflection from China Brotsky—And the Beginning of a Movement

In the early 1990s, when I entered the building that was to become my first non-profit center, I couldn't believe my eyes. It had formerly been an army hospital but sat unused after the last earthquake in San Francisco, and the army had done only minimal repairs. Wires were hanging down the walls, and dust and pebbles covered the terracotta floors. One whole wing was painted black—all the walls. We figured that must have been their X-ray department. Ugly yellow tile covered the hallways.

But the ceilings were high, it had beautiful arches over an internal driveway, and the setting in the new Presidio National Park with a view of the Golden Gate Bridge was spectacular. Our developer told me the building had "good bones," and the fact that it was an historic building from the 1890s would help us with the financing. I decided my boss wasn't crazy after all, and we set to work. Four years, 150,000 square feet, and seventy tenants later, the Thoreau Center opened!

And this was just the beginning. Tides went on to help pioneer the concept of office condominiums for nonprofits in New York City. This time we started with an old stone skyscraper and a group of organizations that had to work very hard, with lots of legal work, to figure out how to work together well over time. Meanwhile, across the US and Canada, other practitioners were creating significant shared space projects.

After that came conferences and workshops and consulting engagements as those of us creating and studying centers did our best to answer the steady stream of questions from nonprofits, governments, and even for-profits throughout the US and Canada about how to create their own community assets. We even created a network to help us spread the word—and Diane and Sarah, my coauthors of this book, were leaders in that work.

Sometimes the people involved in this work felt like evangelists, sometimes it felt like a movement. The concept of nonprofit shared spaces began to emerge across North America, and as momentum built, this field of practice was born. Not only were these efforts creating effectiveness and efficiency through shared resources, they were also bringing people together to collaborate. As a collective whole of nonprofit leaders, real estate experts, academics, and funders, we shared a vision that all nonprofits should have the quality, stable, and affordable space they needed for their work—helping others and transforming society. As I've visited so many nonprofit centers in the years that followed, I see the seeds of this vision in action.

Preface

Shared Space and the New Nonprofit Workplace is a collaborative effort by three experts in the *shared space* and *nonprofit real estate* fields—written to bring attention to the nonprofit workplace and the dramatic changes it is undergoing. In particular, we focus on the way space and other services are being increasingly shared by nonprofits. At a time of growing numbers of nonprofits and uncertain funding, sharing space is a financially sound approach. But it is more than economics that is creating these changes. It is also an emerging trend for nonprofits to be more collaborative in their programs and their work in general. There is also appreciation that solving deep social problems and enlivening communities in the US and Canada takes many organizations and programs. The synergy that comes from the cooperation among nonprofits, often in concert with government or business, can help us reach our societal goals and democratic ideals.

This book was written in the spirit of the new collaboration that we discuss in the book. Even though we were dispersed across the US, the authors' equal contributions, discussions, and synergy were enlivening, and we all feel that the book is much better through this collaborative team effort than it ever would have been without it. We've listed our names alphabetically by last name as a symbol of this collaboration.

The lessons in this book are a product of the hard-earned experience of the authors and hundreds of organizations, partners, and colleagues with whom we have worked. Nowhere is this truer than in the recommendations of what *not* to do. If we didn't make the mistake, then we knew someone who did and who was willing to tell an entire workshop about it.

Within this book, the authors have included relevant, available research, as well as our own experiences and knowledge, to create a road map for everyone, no matter their sector, to help organizations realize their visions. We have also included the stories of others who have succeeded in creating effective nonprofit centers, and have fresh lessons to add to our collective knowledge. We call these *Stories from the Field*. Not least are the lessons about how social innovation and social enterprise can thrive in nonprofit and multi-sector centers.

The shared space field is now comprised of the operators of nonprofit centers and shared service programs, the tenant organizations that occupy these centers and the allied fields that champion them: government agencies, philanthropies, real estate leaders, and academics. The field is undergirded by the support organization, the Nonprofit Centers Network (NCN). The ideas presented in this book are an outgrowth of all of these groups and their collective field-building work.

NCN, an organization that provides training, consulting, peer learning opportunities, and research for the nonprofit real estate field in the US and Canada, continues to exist and thrive and answer queries large and small. For that reason, the authors are donating all our net proceeds from the sale of this book to NCN.

Whether you're already underway on a shared space and have specific challenges, you're looking to articulate the benefits of nonprofit centers to potential funders, you currently operate a center and are looking for new approaches, or you're just considering this model, *Shared Space for a New Nonprofit Workplace* has something to meet your needs and those of your communities.

China Brotsky + Sarah M. Eisinger + Diane Vinokur-Kaplan

Overview of the Book

To date, little attention has been paid to how nonprofit organizations are physically housed and programmatically integrated to do the work they do. In *Shared Space and the New Nonprofit Workplace*, we look at new physical and social configurations occurring among these organizations to help them fulfill their missions. This book addresses the *shared space infrastructure model*—a model that works for people, organizations, and communities.

Shared Space and the New Nonprofit Workplace is the first time such information has been presented in one, cohesive whole, and our goal is to see ambitious growth in the field and ongoing documentation of the breadth and reach of nonprofit centers. This book is geared toward practitioners—those wanting to start new centers or enhance existing centers. Nonprofit leaders and board members will find the book especially instructive. However, academics and students focusing on nonprofits and social change will also find useful information, research, and stories. Local government, philanthropy, community development specialists and social entrepreneurs, as well as commercial real estate practitioners will find the book helpful for understanding the model and supporting its growth in their communities.

This book addresses several central themes from the practical how-to, to an overview of the field, and research supporting the model. It ends with a call to action to support new shared spaces. These themes provide the basis for getting a nonprofit center off the ground. Chapter 3: Mission Comes First offers a conceptual model and an overview of the process. Chapter 6: The Development Process delineates the financial requirements of these unique real estate projects and more detail on real estate considerations. Chapter 7: Finding a Home covers site selection. Chapter 10: Who Drives Decisions outlines information on multiownership structures and how centers are governed. And, Chapter 13: The Design Process shares the design tools to enhance the mission of the space.

To address operations and programming, Chapter 15: Facilities That Facilitate provides practical information on day-to-day operations, while Chapter 18: Creating Collaboration in Nonprofit Centers shows how nonprofit centers can support collaboration goals.

Chapter 21: Deepening the Shared Space Model highlights approaches to deepening the nonprofit center model, such as replication and more ambitious shared services programs. Chapter 24: Partnering with Allies demonstrates how allied fields of government, philanthropy, social enterprise, and community development can support shared spaces. Chapter 29: It Takes a Network to Build a Field documents the development of the shared space field and the lessons learned from the growth of the Nonprofit Centers Network.

On research and evaluation, Chapter 5: Making the Case presents detailed research on the impacts and benefits of nonprofit centers. These empirical results can be useful and influential in gaining support and resources for new or existing projects. Chapter 28: Key Lessons to Learn from Earlier Nonprofit Centers provides a history of nonprofit centers and provides lessons learned through their experiences that are still valuable today. Chapter 30: Thinking Forward looks at trends that could support the growth of more nonprofit centers.

Each section is enhanced with *Stories from the Field*, living examples of the challenges and triumphs of the shared space field. Creators and leaders of thirteen organizations from across the US and Canada, representing each of the four main types of nonprofit centers, have contributed to this book. Their stories and photos bring the history, research, recommendations and analyses to life while communicating important lessons. We also invited experts, including an architect and a developer, to contribute chapters reflecting their special knowledge.

The nonprofit center model is presented here in book form to document the successes in the field, highlight the challenges in developing the model, and shed light on winning templates that can be applied in other communities. This book provides a road map to creating the space to house nonprofit organizations and the programs and collaboration to nurture them.

PART 1
INTRODUCTION

1 A New Model for Nonprofits

Shared Space and the Nonprofit Center

Imagine a young mother who works at a low-wage job. With her earnings she still needs nonprofit services to support her children—a fifth-grade daughter who is having academic trouble at school and a preschool son with serious medical issues. Accessing these vital services, however, requires her to cobble together programs from various providers across the county in which she lives. So every month she must travel many miles: weekly trips with her daughter to a nonprofit tutoring program and frequent visits with her son to a nonprofit medical clinic. She also tries to attend a weekly nonprofit job skills program so she can get a better job. These trips are in addition to her commute to her full-time job across town and visits to a food bank.

What if we erased that barrier? Instead of this mother driving or taking the bus to multiple places, often missing appointments or being late to work, we bundle many of the services she needs in one place. What if medical, social, and educational professionals could collaborate as a unit to help this family?

Such co-locations of nonprofit service organizations working and collaborating in one site exist in the United States and Canada and have for decades. For example, in Redmond, Washington, a one-story retail strip mall that was no longer a productive asset became Together Center (originally named the Family Resource Center). It was incorporated in 1990 and purchased property for the Center in 1993. Today, more than twenty organizations provide human services in this centrally located facility, offering access to childcare referral, mental health services, cultural navigation (including translation services), dental and medical services, and more. Many are nonprofits, but there are also some outreach and access offices from county government services.[1]

Similarly, in Canada, the Saskatoon Community Service Village in Saskatchewan is a vibrant, collaborative center attached to the local YWCA. It "exists to enhance the quality of life and services for the community."[2] Through collaboration, cooperation, sharing of resources, social responsibility and mutual respect, its member agencies seek effective and sustainable means to provide quality community services.[3] Together they provide a wide array of services for families, crisis intervention, parenting education, sexual assault treatment and information, and various YWCA temporary residence programs, as well as the area's United Way office.

These Direct Service Centers are just one of four organizational types of the *nonprofit center,* or shared space, model (for the purposes of this book, we use these terms interchangeably). This model also includes three other types discussed in detail later in the chapter. These types are: Theme Centers, where all residents are related to a particular focus, such as the environment, health, or the arts; Generalist Centers, where nonprofits working on a variety of issues co-locate for the shared space benefits; and Flexible Space Centers, such as coworking and incubator sites.

The shared space model is versatile, applicable to many nonprofit organizations with different missions and concerns. Take, for example, a small nonprofit organization whose executive director wants to grow from working at the kitchen table and professionalize the organization's operations. It moves into the newly built (c)space in Louisville, Kentucky, a membership-based coworking space for nonprofits and socially minded businesses operated by the nonprofit Foundation for a Healthy Kentucky.[4] Here, members pay a fee for space and have access to a shared reception area, conference rooms, workroom, and a kitchen. More important, they gain an address, a community, and new networks to advance their mission.

In Ottawa, Canada, a courthouse was repurposed to become Arts Court, now housing more than twenty arts organizations. Galleries, dance and theater companies, administrative offices of festivals, and the Ottawa Arts Council all share space, bringing new visibility and audiences to these organizations.

The Together Center, Saskatoon Community Service Village, Arts Court, and (c)space are all examples of the nonprofit center, an important infrastructure model in the nonprofit sector that has grown in prominence over the last twenty years and is built on the pioneering work of nonprofit organizations during the early 20th century. In its simplest form, nonprofit centers are buildings that provide quality, affordable space and shared services to multiple nonprofits while providing opportunities for collaboration and program enhancement. These centers sometimes house government and commercial tenants as well, promoting cross-sector collaboration. More recently, the nonprofit center model has also incorporated coworking spaces to help individuals, social entrepreneurs, and small organizations who may need more flexible, affordable space. At their best, organizations in nonprofit centers work together in support of a common mission, tackling complex issues in a variety of ways: through joint marketing campaigns, program delivery, legislative agendas, or sharing staff.

These nonprofit centers, hubs of innovation and collaboration, replace outmoded and substandard spaces housing nonprofits in cities and rural areas across the US and Canada. Too often nonprofit organizations operate in unsuitable space: they are crammed into church basements or office buildings and spaces that are not equipped to meet the technology-driven, collaborative-oriented office and program space of today. Or organizations move from place to place when rents rise, leading to disruption in their operations. The problems of nonprofit displacement and lack of satisfactory space intensifies in areas undergoing rapid gentrification. In particular, small and emerging organizations are forced to make do with inefficient, rundown, or temporary space.[5] Their staff are often overworked and underpaid[6] and isolated from their professional peers and new learning opportunities.

The nonprofit center addresses all of these concerns: the needs of a constituent population, the scarcity of affordable real estate, and the lack of quality space to foster collaboration and enhanced programs and services. As of mid-2018, more than 475 nonprofit centers are located across the United States and Canada, with another 230 in development or exploration,[7] and nonprofits and social entrepreneurs are flourishing in these mission-enhancing workspaces by sharing space and resources.

Common features of nonprofit centers include two or more nonprofits[8] located in the same building or campus with shared resources and amenities. They are an innovative way for nonprofits to enhance the quality of their workspaces and promote well-being for tenant organizations, their staff, and the people, movements, and communities they serve.[9]

CREATING OUTCOMES: BENEFITS AND IMPACTS

The impacts for the organizations housed within these shared spaces and for the clients and people served by them are compelling. Rich anecdotes on the success of shared space have emerged over time. A limited number of field studies have documented the benefits and impacts of nonprofit centers to substantiate these anecdotal impacts. Nonprofit centers became a recognized topic of academic interest in the early 2000s in the US[10] and soon after in Canada.[11] The most comprehensive research study of nonprofit centers and their tenants in the US and Canada was carried out in 2011 by Mt. Auburn Associates under the auspices of the Nonprofit Centers Network (NCN), an intermediary organization that supports the field. Its report is entitled *Measuring Collaboration: The Benefits and Impacts of Nonprofit Centers.* An overview of the outcomes is presented here in brief while Chapter 5: Making the Case and Chapter 29: It Takes A Network offer much more detail.

Benefits

For tenant organizations in nonprofit centers, the benefits are seen in both improved organizational efficiency and effectiveness. One of the most important benefits is occupancy cost savings. Box 1.1 shows financial savings to tenants in nonprofit centers.

Substantial savings resulted not just from lower rents but also from the relative stability of rents in nonprofit centers, even in cities with an exploding real

> ### Box 1.1 Cost Savings from Nonprofit Center Tenancy
>
> The 2011 NCN study looked at tenants' reduction in operating costs from being in a nonprofit center. Savings resulted from lower lease costs, as well as savings from shared services, shared spaces, and staffing provided through the center. The average annual cost savings is about 7% of annual operating costs. Overall, "resident organizations rank low cost as the most critical benefit of locating in a nonprofit center."

estate market. As an example, Figure 1.1 shows the trajectory of rental rates paid by tenants at a pioneering nonprofit center in San Francisco, the Thoreau Center for Sustainability (now Tides Converge), compared to market-rate rents over sixteen years, a period correlated to huge market upswings due to successive tech booms. Although rents increased over time at the Thoreau Center, it was able to maintain stable and affordable rent for its nonprofit tenants while the wider commercial real estate market saw dramatic rent spikes. Predictability is critical to nonprofit financial planning so this long-term stability is highly valuable.

Tenants operating in nonprofit centers also found measurable improvement in a variety of organizational effectiveness categories including increased organizational capacity, visibility in the community, information technology capacity, improved access to funders, and improvements in coordinated service delivery. Some centers offer free or low-cost technical assistance workshops and seminars for their tenants and others. For example, TSNE MissionWorks (formerly Third Sector New England) offers education on a wide range of topics, such as executive succession planning, strategic communications, and workplace culture.[12] The 2011 survey also found staff morale among tenant organizations was measurably higher in nonprofit centers compared to their previous locations outside of the nonprofit center.[13]

Communities benefit from nonprofit centers, too. Nonprofit centers provide amenities like community rooms, conferences centers, resource libraries, performance spaces, art exhibits, recreational facilities, and educational programs that benefit the surrounding community—services that can be scarce in low-income, high-need communities. These new community spaces create opportunity for increased civic engagement.

Impacts

Centers create significant social impacts as well, on people, place and society. They influence the well-being of people who come to them for services and who work in them. By having an impact on the financial health, efficiency, and effectiveness of the tenant organizations, nonprofit centers stretch the private and public-sector funds committed to their operation. The result is improved services, education, and advocacy that reach more people.

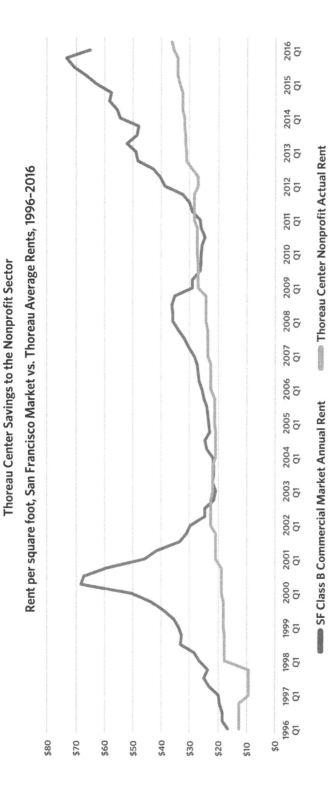

FIGURE 1.1 This figure depicts the rent rates charged by Tides' Thoreau Center Sustainability (now Tides Converge) in San Francisco as compared to the general market and thus *the rent savings that resulted for the nonprofit tenants.* While the Thoreau Center's rents continue to escalate, they do so at a steady and predictable rate, two key factors for nonprofit organizations. At the same time, the general market sees massive rent fluctuations corresponding to the dot-com booms and busts. These wide fluctuations are difficult for nonprofit organizations to weather making nonprofit centers a better alternative. *Source: Tides.*

Note 1: Actual rents and square footage between 1996 and 2003 are estimated from rent invoices, as the actual rent rolls are unavailable. Thus they may be incomplete and may contain slight errors.

Note 2: SF Class B Market Rates obtained from Colliers International.

Thoreau Center Savings to the Nonprofit Sector

Rent per square foot, San Francisco Market vs. Thoreau Average Rents, 1996–2016

In addition to the wealth of community services and spaces they bring, nonprofit centers can have a variety of positive impacts on their neighboring communities. Centers established in abandoned or decommissioned buildings can contribute positively to community-centered economic development, as was seen with Together Center and Arts Court. The Jessie Ball duPont Fund renovated and moved into a decommissioned mid-century modern library that was vacant and in disrepair in downtown Jacksonville, Florida. Moreover, newly constructed rural nonprofit centers like the Common Roof™ centers in Ontario have spurred ancillary development around them.

Some centers have leveraged their internal collaboration to create societal impacts that go beyond their direct constituents. This includes creating hubs for advocacy and legislative work, creating cultural spaces for communities, and carrying out policy advocacy to strengthen public support in the environmental and human services arenas. Both the benefits and impacts are further quantified in Chapter 5: Making the Case.

INNOVATION OPPORTUNITIES

The nonprofit center is an excellent incubator for innovation, bringing diverse people and organizations together in flexible space for new kinds of discourse and collaborations. It provides creative solutions to major issues facing the US and Canadian charitable sectors. According to a recent essay from the National Council of Nonprofits,[14] nonprofit managers face a shifting environment, one of fewer government grants and declining donor loyalty and corporate support. Therefore, they must increase their organizations' efficiencies and implement effectiveness to its maximum. Sharing space and resources offers innovative ways of managing activities toward those goals.

Support for Small Nonprofits

While large institutions, such as hospitals, universities, and big museums, dominate the headlines on nonprofits, the majority of charities and nonprofits are small in terms of their annual expenditures. In the US, almost two-thirds of the nonprofits that report annually to the Internal Revenue Service expended less than $500,000 in annual budget in 2013[15] as shown in Figure 1.2.

To meet their missions, small organizations must perform all the major functions of a larger organization but in the most cost-effective way. Such organizations are often undercapitalized, with limited access to—and knowledge of—investment capital resources for further building or enhancing their infrastructure[16]. Nonprofit centers can assist small nonprofits in their overall operations. They can provide an attractive home where managers enjoy stable rents and function more successfully through shared equipment and shared back-office services, such as accounting. Collectively, the tenants represent a critical mass

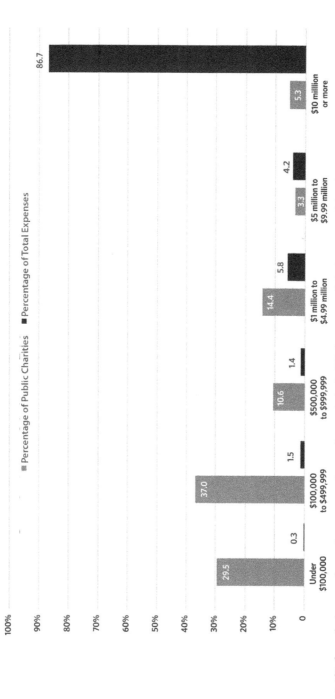

Number and Expenses of Reporting Public Charities as a Percentage of All Reporting Public Charities in the US

■ Percentage of Public Charities   ■ Percentage of Total Expenses

FIGURE 1.2 This figure depicts annual operating expenses of nonprofit agencies in the US, the majority of which operate with less than $500,000 in reported expenses. These smaller orga-
nizations are well served by nonprofit centers and shared resources, which help them professionalize their operations and leverage limited organizational capacity. *Source: Adapted from
Brice McKeever. The Nonprofit Sector in Brief 2015: Public Charities, Giving, and Volunteering. Washington, DC: Urban Institute-National Center for Charitable Statistics, October 29, 2015,
Figure 1, p. 4. Urban Institute, National Center on Charitable Statistics, Core Files (Public Charities, 2013). Reprinted with permission.*

that can pursue discounts on such necessary resources as supplies and telecommunications. Thus, they can devote more of their resources to mission. Their proximity facilitates their planning and collaborating on joint projects and grants. Small organizations can benefit from the expertise of the leaders of a nonprofit center. Finally, the nearby presence of other nonprofit professionals helps leaders and their staff avoid the social isolation of being tucked away in a single business office, with no nearby peers.

The Nonprofit Village in Rockville, Maryland, for example, which opened its doors in 2009 in a 10,000-sq. ft. space, is uniquely designed to meet the needs of small organizations. After starting with providing fixed offices and desks for rent to small and emerging nonprofits, the Village expanded to provide an ongoing series of nonprofit management and fundraising classes and other support for their tenants. They have launched a Virtual Office program for nonprofits in the community, providing mail services, conference rooms, and "hot desks" (drop-in space that can be rented through a monthly membership fee) in a convenient, transit-friendly location.[17]

A Counter-Balance to Nonprofit Displacement and Gentrification

Over the last decade and a half, major cities such as Vancouver, San Francisco, Los Angeles, Seattle, New York, and Boston have all seen massive booms in both commercial and residential real estate due to growth in the technology and biotech sectors, in-migration back to cities resulting in significant residential construction, favorable lending rates and increased foreign investment. These market factors have had ripple effects on nonprofit organizations as they navigate the real estate market. As an example, a regional report on nonprofit displacement in six counties of California's Bay Area published in 2016 found that most nonprofit respondents (82%) were concerned about sustaining their work in the face of rising office space costs in the region.[18] Those nonprofits serving communities of color and low-income communities showed an especially high level of concern. The survey found that steady increases in the rental rates of commercial real estate had pushed office prices to 122% above where they were five years earlier. Nearly two out of every three nonprofits said they would have to make a decision about moving within the next five years. In the face of massive displacement, nonprofit centers, like the Thoreau Center (now Tides Converge), referenced in Figure 1.1 and shown in Figure 1.3, with their stable rents and priority on housing nonprofits become an important alternative to the commercial market.

Nonprofit organizations have an intrinsic and often overlooked value in the real estate market. Nonprofits can be a stabilizing influence in the market because of the large number of charitable organizations needing space over time. Even if they cannot pay the same speculative rates as for-profits, nonprofits will be there through tech bubbles and the normal real estate booms and busts. If their funding

FIGURE 1.3 *Thoreau Center for Sustainability, San Francisco, California.* This photo depicts the exterior of the Thoreau Center for Sustainability (now Tides Converge) in San Francisco. Founded in the mid-1990s, this center houses more than sixty organizations in what was formerly Letterman Army Hospital in the Presidio National Park. *Photo credit: Saul Ettlin.*

sources are stable and diversified, nonprofits can be reliable, financially sound tenants and owners, who should be taken seriously by landlords or those selling real estate.

Nonprofit centers can provide a solution to successive waves of nonprofit displacement. Nonprofits often need to be in specific locations to serve the target populations specified in their missions. With the cost efficiencies of shared space and services, nonprofit centers can provide part of the solution for keeping nonprofits in the neighborhoods they serve. See the story of the Children and Families Center in Charlotte, North Carolina, in Chapter 3: Mission Comes First for an example.

Long-term, community-centered solutions for addressing gentrification that often push out nonprofits (and residents and small businesses) remain a challenge across North America. One approach is underway in San Francisco where the second tech boom wave in this century is hitting nonprofits. Shared space projects are again reaching the philanthropic and city agendas: the City of San Francisco has partnered with the local Northern California Community Loan Fund to create grant funds to help nonprofits weather displacements and the regional association of grantmakers, Northern California Grantmakers, has held sessions on the problem. Individual foundations and corporations have sponsored trainings on creating shared spaces and created new conference spaces for nonprofits. As other places across North America encounter the forces of gentrification, shared spaces are one strategy, and opportunity, to serve as a meaningful counter-balance.

Integrated Services for Better Outcomes

One of the opportunities nonprofit centers provide is the ability to integrate services to improve outcomes for community residents. Especially in the health, human service, and legal areas, multiple nonprofits under one roof allows local residents to efficiently access co-located programs. The staff of the tenant organizations can use their proximity to develop better and more effective interventions for their clients. Most nonprofit agencies do not have the staffing capacity to keep up with all the services that most people seeking help require. By placing mental health, legal services, and other providers within reach of one another, staff are able to brainstorm and develop comprehensive solutions for clients. The United Way Greater Toronto's Community Hubs profiled in Chapter 11: Building Community, Not Just Buildings illustrate how shared space can also reach beyond services to community development and empowering communities.

Resource Sharing

Resource sharing encourages greater collaboration among nonprofits. "For most people, sharing resources—whether it be office space, accounting staff, or a common kitchen—is a new way to work."[19] This trend provides opportunities to actualize the millennial generation's emphasis on collaboration and transparency, and it dovetails with new shared resource approaches—every organizations does not need its own building to be successful. Such collective motivation opens all kinds of opportunities for nonprofit centers and their design. Figure 1.4 of the NEW Center in Michigan shows a training underway in a shared conference room.

FIGURE 1.4 *NEW Center in Ann Arbor, Michigan.* This photo depicts a training at the NEW Center in Ann Arbor. NEW has a second center in Detroit and offers space, consulting, and shared back-office services to its tenants. *Photo credit: NEW Inc. (Nonprofit Enterprise at Work).*

Cross-Sector Tenancy

In practice, nonprofit centers attract tenants from all sectors. While the majority of the nonprofit centers discussed here will have tenants or owners that are US or Canadian charities (or non-profits), there are multiple instances where occupants include other types of tax-exempt entities, government offices, or for-profit organizations complementary to the center's mission (see, e.g., The Posner Center for International Development, Denver, Colorado, where for-profit tenants involved in international development are also housed).

Sometimes, the for-profit tenants are new forms of social enterprises (e.g., LC3s or B corporations) or professionals whose work might include serving the nonprofits (e.g., accountants, graphic artists, and information technologists). In other cases, nonprofit centers are owned and operated by for-profit companies or developers (see The Union Mill, operated by Seawall Development Company in Baltimore, Maryland, which provides workforce housing for teachers and space for a community of education nonprofits). Whatever the configuration, these situations create opportunities for cross-sector synergy.

Public–Private Partnerships

Innovation comes in the public–private partnerships forged between government and nonprofits to create or operate nonprofit centers. One example is the Magnolia Place Community Initiative in Los Angeles, California. Magnolia Place serves as a community hub for local families serving 35,000 children living in two nearby neighborhoods. The Center's services help to strengthen families with young children by focusing efforts on economic stability, good health, nurturing parenting, and school readiness. It co-locates needed community services, covering healthcare to banking to Headstart to County satellite offices. "This is an innovative collaborative effort of over 70 faith-based and community groups, organizations and public agencies, dedicated to improving outcomes for children in a five-square mile (500 blocks) area." [20]

BEYOND BUILDINGS: A FRAMEWORK FOR NONPROFIT CENTERS

In order to best understand the nonprofit center model, there are three important dimensions to explore (see Figure 1.5). The first is to look at the building as an asset, with all the accompanying work to make it financially sustainable and to preserve it for ongoing community use. The second dimension is the building as a workplace where design and operations come together to create a place that supports the activities and mission of the tenant organizations and the people who work there and visit. Finally, there is the building as a program providing shared resources, affordable rents, service to the community, and collaboration opportunities. The most successful nonprofit centers maximize all three aspects to benefit their communities. The use of a building as an asset, a quality workplace, and a

Overview of Nonprofit Shared Space

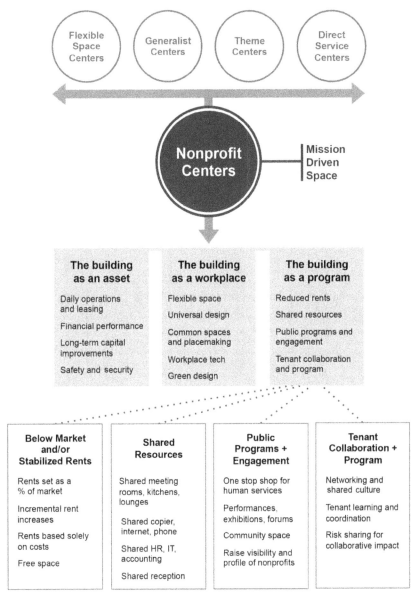

FIGURE 1.5 This graphic represents an overview of nonprofit centers. These mission-minded real estate projects are categorized across four different types: Flexible Space, Generalist, Theme, and Direct Service Centers. Nonprofit centers have several dimensions to them: they treat the building as an asset, a workplace, and a program. There are more than 475 known nonprofit centers across North America. *Source: The Nonprofit Centers Network, as adapted by Saul Ettlin.*

program expands the concept of facilities to spaces that can advance a mission, promote social change, and improve the stability of the nonprofit sector. Figure 5.1 shows this framework in a graphic that illustrates the detailed components of each aspect.

Types of Nonprofit Centers

One of the most important decisions in creating a nonprofit center is what kind of center to create. Many variations of nonprofit centers create the impacts and benefits as previously outlined. They are as diverse as the wide range of organizations who run them—nonprofits, foundations, local governments, and for-profit companies. To distinguish the different types of nonprofit centers, this book utilizes a basic typology developed by NCN and the research firm, Mt. Auburn Associates, as part of the 2011 field survey of existing nonprofit centers, with some small changes.[21] There are four types of nonprofit centers that can be differentiated by their mission and purpose: *Generalist Centers*[22], *Direct Service Centers, Theme Centers, and Flexible Space Centers.*[23] [24] See Table 1.1 with examples of each type at the end of this chapter.

(1) *Generalist Centers.* These centers include a mixture of nonprofits that focus on different issues, program areas, and constituencies. Often, the mutual objective of these nonprofits is seeking quality, stable and affordable workspace. This "catch-all" center works well in urban centers where rents are high or in rural areas where nonprofits are isolated and the opportunity to co-locate with other nonprofits creates visibility and mitigates isolation. The center's leasing criteria focuses mainly on offering affordable space. One might find arts, social service, advocacy, and environmental nonprofits all together in the same building but serving different constituencies. Examples include NEW (Nonprofit Enterprise at Work) Center in Ann Arbor, Michigan (profiled in Chapter 17: From Grants to Earned Income) and Midland Shared Spaces in Midland, Texas.

(2) *Direct Service Centers.* Here, various organizations provide direct services to a clientele, like Together Center, as previously described. These are sometimes known as "one-stops" in which arrays of integrated services are co-located and available to the consumers (or clients). One-stops are a long-standing model in the nonprofit sector dating back to the late 1960s. Direct Service Centers are often staffed by professional social work, medical, or educational staff and supplemented by volunteers. They may have a large number of visitors who receive services from several different

agencies. Examples include integrated services for children and families, health homes for seniors (Tanglewood Park in Muskegon, Michigan), youth centers (Partnership for Children, Fayetteville, North Carolina), or centers like the Ed Roberts Campus dedicated to disability rights and universal access in Berkeley, California (profiled in Chapter 14: Universal Design).

While there can be some overlap between a theme center and a Direct Service Center, the Direct Service Center is distinguished by the presence of professionals and volunteers who directly interact with the many clients who come to the center for services. Leasing in such a center focuses on the mission compatibility, interest in collaboration, and efficiency of sharing common spaces.

(3) *Theme Centers.* Here, tenant organizations are connected by a unified theme and are often involved in distinct but related activities. There are centers focusing on environmental sustainability (the Alliance Center by the Alliance for Sustainable Colorado, Denver, Colorado), international development (The Posner Center, Denver); health and wellness (The Wellness Center, Los Angeles, California), the arts (the Torpedo Factory Art Center, Alexandria, Virginia and Spaces@520 managed by the Alliance of Resident Theatres/New York), advocacy (the Syracuse Center for Peace and Social Justice, Syracuse, New York), or faith-based communities (The Hope Center, Plano, Texas). Synergies in Theme Centers can magnify the impact of each individual organization. Tenants in the Alliance Center in Denver, for example, support each other in passing environmental legislation through the Colorado Legislature.

Leasing for a Theme Center focuses on how new tenants complement the activities carried out by the existing community of tenants as well as on ability to pay the asking rents. Some Theme Centers think expansively about how tenants fit together. For example, some environmental centers have brought in health-related nonprofits as a bridge between these interrelated fields.

(4) *Flexible Space Centers.* There is another distinctive type of space that exists either on a stand-alone basis or as a feature within a larger center. Flexible spaces are primarily aimed at start-up organizations but are also used by individual consultants, for-profits, or small organizations. This category includes the increasingly popular coworking spaces, adapted from the earlier model of office suite businesses. These often provide more flexible "licenses" for space rather than longer-term leases. Whether focused on rotating or fixed desks and offices, these spaces usually provide shared amenities such as advanced technology, kitchens, and conference rooms as well as staff committed to animating the space through events and other activities. They are known for their open office plans and design that fosters interaction and collaboration. Many nonprofit centers today operate

FIGURE 1.6 *(c)space, Louisville, Kentucky.* This photo depicts a coworking space available at the (c)space in Louisville, Kentucky, a coworking space developed by the Foundation for a Healthy Kentucky in Louisville. Coworking spaces are available to organizations and individuals on a monthly basis and offer a solution for smaller organizations and social entrepreneurs. *Photo credit: Foundation for a Healthy Kentucky.*

both coworking spaces and more standard office offerings. This encourages growth and innovation in the nonprofit and social enterprise fields. For instance, TSNE MissionWorks'[25] building in Boston, The NonProfit Center, has space reserved for emerging social entrepreneurs. Similarly, The Center for Change in Madison, Wisconsin, has reserved space for new social change organizations. The Foundation for a Healthy Kentucky's (c) space in Louisville gives nonprofit "members the opportunity to interact and collaborate with other nonprofit organizations and community-minded businesses and professionals." [26] Figure 1.6 shows (c)space's professional coworking space. See Chapters 16 and 23 for examples of nonprofit centers in this category.

Some Flexible Space Centers are nonprofit incubators, like business incubators, which provide space for a limited amount of time. They may provide support services that are most relevant to new nonprofit organizations, such as legal counsel, business planning, and fundraising. Freestanding nonprofit incubator centers can be found in a variety of sectors, including the arts. The goals of arts incubators can vary, however. Some seek "to produce successful firms that will leave the program financially viable and freestanding, while others pursue such diverse goals as supporting individual professional development, providing gallery space, or advocating for social change." [27]

Not all nonprofit centers fit neatly into one category. Some centers flow across categories like The Community Service Building in Wilmington, Delaware, which is a Generalist Center but requires all its tenants to be Delaware-serving, its theme. Regardless of type, shared spaces succeed because they can be infinitely customized to meet the actual needs of the organizations involved, their missions, and the communities they serve.

BUILDINGS FOR PEOPLE

While organizational efficiency and effectiveness are meaningful outcomes, the inspiration for the model remains the people who are served: the young mother seeking services and finding a welcoming place in a nonprofit center, or the dance company that can find an affordable studio to create new work (see Figure 1.7 from the Liberty Station in San Diego, California), or the community activists who now have a place to meet and organize. These people and their organizations are the heart of nonprofit centers.

FIGURE 1.7 *Liberty Station, San Diego, California.* This photo depicts Liberty Station in San Diego, a shared nonprofit arts complex built on a former naval base. The campus is home to arts organizations including theaters, dance companies, and ground-floor retail. *Photo credit: Dave Roberts.*

Table 1.1 The Shared Space Model: Examples of Nonprofit Centers in the United States and Canada

	West	Midwest	South	East	Canada
			GEOGRAPHIC LOCATION		
			GENERALIST CENTERS: Nonprofits with distinctly different missions		
Mixed Missions	Under One Roof, Hutton Parker Foundation, Santa Barbara, CA	NEW-Nonprofit Enterprise at Work, Ann Arbor, MI	Midland Shared Spaces, Midland TX	Community Service Building, Wilmington, DE	Community-Wise Resource Center, Calgary AB
			SERVICE CENTERS: Nonprofits providing direct services to clienteles		
Education	Z Place, Denver, CO	The Children's Campus of Kansas City, KS	Jefferson School City Center, Charlottesville, VA	Miller's Court, Baltimore, MD	The Orange Hub, Edmonton, Alberta
Health or Multiservice including Health	Magnolia Place, Los Angeles, CA	Health 360, Lincoln, NE	Jackson Medical Mall, Jackson, MS	Harbor House Community Service Center, Southwest Harbor, ME	Access Alliance, Toronto, ON
Human Services	Harry and Jeanette Weinberg Kukui Center, Honolulu, HI	Fairhill Partners, Cleveland, OH	Children and Family Service Center, Charlotte, NC	Samaritan Center, Detroit, MI	Richmond Caring Place Society, Richmond BC

(continued)

Table 1.1 Continued

	THEME CENTERS: Nonprofits have similar missions around an overall theme				
Arts and Culture	The Dairy Center for the Arts, Boulder, CO	Athenaeum Theatre, Chicago, IL	Torpedo Factory Art Center, Alexandria, VA	Spaces at 520, New York, NY	The Arts Factory, Vancouver, BC
Religion and Community	The Hope Center, Plano, TX	Genesis of Ann Arbor, Ann Arbor, MI	The Commons on Merton, Memphis TN	Interchurch Center, New York, NY	Joseph & Wolf Lebovic Jewish Community Campus, Maple, ON
Public Affairs/ Social Justice/ Change	The Lab at CEL, Berkeley, CA	Social Justice Center, Madison, WI	Buncombe County Family Justice Center, Ashville, NC	Syracuse Center for Peace & Social Justice, NY	Centre for Social Innovation, Toronto, Ontario
	FLEXIBLE SPACE CENTERS: Incubators and Coworking Spaces				
Coworking and Social Enterprise	Wilson Historic District Incubator Program Dallas, TX	The Summit in Fort Wayne, Indiana	(c)space, Louisville, Kentucky	Centre for Social Innovation New York, NY, NY	HIVE, Vancouver, BC

Notes: This table provides a snapshot of nonprofit center examples across geography and typography. There are examples of all four categories of nonprofit centers in North America: Generalist, Direct Service, Theme, and Flexible Spaces. While there is overlap among these categories, this chart illustrates the breadth of diversity of the field.

Source: Brotsky, Eisinger, and Vinokur-Kaplan.

1. To see the various types of nonprofit and governmental organizations housed at Together Center, consult its website. Accessed March 27, 2018. http://www.together-center.org/how-we-partner/our-agencies/.

2. Quoted from the website donation form of Saskatoon Community Service Village Inc., a registered charity. Accessed March 27, 2018. https://www.canadahelps.org/en/dn/12329.

3. For descriptions of the partner agencies' services, see Saskatoon Community Service Village Inc. Accessed March 27, 2018. http://www.villagesaskatoon.com/village-agencies.

4. The Foundation for a Healthy Kentucky's mission is "to improve the health of Kentuckians through policy changes and community investments. We are a non-profit philanthropic organization created with assets from a settlement agreement following the merger of Anthem, Inc. and Kentucky Blue Cross Blue Shield. Since its inception, the Foundation has invested more than $27 million in health policy research, training and grantmaking." Accessed March 2018. www.healthy-ky.org/about-us/mission.

5. GrØnbjerg, K. A. and Nagle, A. E. "Structure and Adequacy of Human Service Facilities: Challenges for Nonprofit Managers." *Nonprofit Management & Leadership*, Winter, 5(2):117–140, 1994 AND Salamon, L. M. and Geller, S. L. "Investment Capital: The New Challenge for American Nonprofits." *Listening Post Project Communiqué No. 5*. Baltimore: Johns Hopkins University Center for Civil Society Studies at the Institute for Policy Studies, 2006.

6. Reisch, M. & Sommerfeld, D. "Welfare Reform and the Future of Nonprofit Organizations." *Nonprofit Management and Leadership* 14(1): 19–46, 2000 AND Cohen, R. "Nonprofit Salaries: Achieving Parity with the Private Sector." *Nonprofit Quarterly*, June 21, 2010.

7. These centers, known as emerging centers, fall into two categories. In development, it means doing a capital campaign and/or under construction. In exploration, it can be any early stage—groups doing feasibility studies, building partnerships, or other planning phases.

8. A note on terminology: Throughout this book, we use the term "nonprofit" spelled without a hyphen (sometimes called nongovernmental organizations [NGOs] internationally) to talk about a broad category of charitable and social welfare civil society organizations. In the United States, these are commonly also known by their tax designation as 501(c)(3)s or 501(c)(4)s; in Canada, they are commonly referred to as registered charities or non-profits. However, in Canada, as laid out in the text, non-profit (with a hyphen) refers to a certain type of nonprofit organization similar to the 501(c)(4) in the United States. You will notice these different usages especially in Chapter 10: Who Drives Decisions. Nonprofit centers are also sometimes referred to as nonprofit co-locations.

9. Vinokur-Kaplan, D. and McBeath, B. "Co-Located Nonprofit Centers: Tenants' Attraction and Satisfaction." *Nonprofit Management and Leadership*, 25: 77–91, 2014.

10. Vinokur-Kaplan, D. *"Shall We Dance?" Government and For-Profit Community Development Partnerships with Co-Located Nonprofit Sectors*. International Society for Third Sector Research (ISTR), Dublin, Ireland, July 2000.

   Vinokur-Kaplan, D. *Nonprofit Landlords Leasing to Nonprofit Tenants: Legal and Managerial Strategies Used at Nonprofit Co-Location Enterprises in the U.S.* International Conference on Nonprofit Enterprises: Governing Development and Funding Innovation. Faculty of Economics and Institute for the Development of Nonprofit Organizations (ISSAN). University of Trento, Italy, July 8–9, 2001.

   Vinokur-Kaplan, D. *Shared Services: Creating Collaborative Solutions for Nonprofits*. Annual Meeting of ARNOVA, Arlington, VA, November 2010.

   Vinokur-Kaplan, D. *New Workspace for Small Nonprofits: Real Estate Innovations by American Foundations*. Annual Meeting of ERNOP (European Research Network on Nonprofits and Philanthropy). WU Vienna University of Economics and Business, Vienna, Austria, June 7, 2011.

Vinokur-Kaplan, D. and Dobbie, D. S. *Nonprofit Co-Locations as Capacity Building Tools for Communities*. Association for Research on Nonprofit Organizations and Voluntary Action (ARNOVA) 31st Annual Conference. Montreal, Canada, November 2003.

11. Keough, N. Gismondi, M., and Swift-Leppäkumpu, E. "Sustaining Social Democracy Through Heritage-Building Conservation." Chapter 9 in Gismondi, M., Connelly, S., Beckie, M., Sean Markey, S., and Roseland, M. (Eds.), *Scaling Up: The Convergence of Social Economy and Sustainability*. Toronto: Athabasca University Press, 2016 (Distributed by UBC Press c/o UTP Distribution, 5201 Dufferin Street, Toronto, ON M3H 5T8).

12. Third Sector New England. Accessed October 16, 2016. http://tsne.org/about-us.

13. Nonprofit Centers Network. *Measuring Collaboration: The Benefits and Impacts of Nonprofit Centers (Executive Summary)*. San Francisco: Nonprofit Centers Network, 2011, 11–12.

14. Chandler, Jennifer. "Five Predictions for 2014," *Bisnow*. Accessed April 19, 2018. https://www.bisnow.com/archives/newsletter/association/five-predictions-for-2014/. Reprinted at National Council for Nonprofits. https://www.councilofnonprofits.org/article/five-predictions-2014

15. McKeever, B. S. and Pettijohn, S. L. *The Nonprofit Sector in Brief: Public Charities, Giving, and Volunteering*. Washington, DC: The Urban Institute, October 2014. https://www.urban.org/research/publication/nonprofit-sector-brief-2015-public-charities-giving-and-volunteering.

16. Salamon, L. M. and Geller, S. L. "Investment Capital: The New Challenge for American Nonprofits." *Listening Post Project Communiqué No. 5*. Baltimore: Johns Hopkins University Center for Civil Society Studies at the Institute for Policy Studies, 2006.

17. Nonprofit Village. website, https://www.thenonprofitvillage.org/about/history/. *n.d.*

18. Harder & Company. Harder & Company Community Research, March 2016. *Status of Bay Area Nonprofit Space & Facilities*. https://harderco.com/areas-of-impact/#equityplace.

19. Edwards, Katie. "A New Way to Work: Six Takeaways on Nonprofit Resource Sharing," October 31, 2016. Accessed April 16, 2018. https://www.nonprofitcenters.org/new-way-work-six-takeaways-nonprofit-resource-sharing/.

20. U.S. Children's Bureau. Programs: Magnolia Community Initiative. Accessed February 25, 2016. https://www.all4kids.org/ program/magnolia-community/.

21. The authors have updated the basic typology of the NCN to include a fourth category, the Flexible Space. The authors have also renamed the categories to make them clearer as to the use of the space.

22. In the original typology reported by Mt. Auburn Associates, the preparers of the survey's report, this first category was called "multi-sector centers." However, the term "multi-sector" is often used to refer to combinations of nonprofit, for-profit, and government organizations. Therefore, we use "Generalist" to refer to centers housing nonprofit organizations focused on a diverse set of issues.

23. We have replaced the original terminology of "incubators" with Flexible Space Centers to take into account the enormous growth in coworking space in this decade.

24. Nonprofit Centers Network. *Measuring Collaboration: The Benefits and Impacts of Nonprofit Centers (Executive Summary)*. San Francisco: Nonprofit Centers Network and Thoreau Center for Sustainability (now Tides Converge), 2011, 5–6.

25. Formerly Third Sector New England.

26. See https://www.healthy-ky.org/about-us/(c)space).

27. Essig, Linda. "Arts Incubators: A Typology," *The Journal of Arts Management, Law and Society*, 44(3): 169–180, July 3, 2014.

2   *Stories from the Field*

Once Upon a Time
The Story of the Literacenter

Stacy Ratner

Literacenter, Chicago, Illinois

In the spring of 2009, in a classroom a few miles from one of Chicago's least resourced neighborhoods, the directors of two literacy-focused organizations struck up a conversation about the challenges of working in a nearby school, Schiller Elementary. They thought they were just filling time until the other seventeen invitees arrived, all executive and program directors of similar literacy nonprofits. But as more and more people came into the room, the discussion grew. "How many of us are there?" someone finally asked. Nineteen hands went up. With the exception of the original two speakers, no one in the room had had any idea that the other organizations were working at Schiller. Some students were participating in supplementary literacy programs multiple times every day. And yet, despite (or, as subsequent investigation would suggest, perhaps because of) so much accumulated literacy support, reading scores at Schiller were going down.

IN THE BEGINNING

Schiller Elementary closed later that year. However, the nineteen participants in the meeting kept in close touch. They began to do small projects together, like community Literacy Nights and an online map to track who was working where; they organized themselves as the Chicago Literacy Alliance (CLA). In 2010, thirteen of them collaborated to offer coordinated services to another elementary school, making sure to offer programs for students in each grade as well as professional development opportunities for educators and adult literacy support services for families. Within two years of this work together, reading scores had gone up, and the school came off probation. It was time to explore collaboration more seriously and to commit time and resources to its potential to change the literacy landscape of Chicago.

The idea of a shared workspace dedicated to literacy, the first of its kind in the country, came in part from these early experiences, and in part from CLA's co-founders' experience in the technology start-up sector, where such spaces are the expectation. If we co-founders could make it easier for CLA's growing member list to interact with one another more often than our bimonthly meetings, we knew they would find ways to collaborate and accelerate the pace of change.

But we were still an all-volunteer organization with no budget, financial history, or official legal status, and with preexisting commitments to our own organizations. To turn the dream of shared workspace into an actual place would require major work on multiple fronts: finding a location, securing legal incorporation and financial support, and convincing our broad and informal coalition that workspace was a legitimate project on which to focus. So, we filed for our 501(c)(3), engaged the pro bono support of a visionary real estate firm and an experienced space planner, and started looking at properties, meeting with funders, and talking to our members about what such a space might mean to them. We developed a mission statement as shown in Figure 2.1.

Member conversations and a feasibility study during the first few months told us we were looking for at least 35,000 sq. ft. of centrally located space near public transportation. It would need retail frontage (one of our founding members runs a bookstore that would locate there), a loading dock (many of our members handle and distribute large quantities of heavy books), multiple meeting rooms of varying sizes (including one that could seat over one hundred people), private offices or cubicles (cubes) for at least ten organizations with two to five staff members, connected but separable office suites for two organizations with a combined total of forty more, and outside signage opportunities to promote the space to passersby.

But there were not many available spaces that met these criteria, and we were competing with a rising tide of well-funded, well-known tech companies who wanted the same kinds of features in the same neighborhoods and could pay triple the amount that our most optimistic funding projections suggested we could afford. Worse, as time went on, the initial excitement and belief among our members and prospective funders began to wane. We walked a fine line between sharing our progress (promising the new location's initial term sheet looks good!) and limiting our announcements (major national company made an offer for the whole building, so our six months of work on the deal is over!), and we did not always get the balance right.

Then, nearly three years after first proposing the Literacenter idea, our luck finally changed. A major Chicago nonprofit was vacating one of its locations early and needed to find a replacement tenant. The opportunity had not been made public, but thanks to our real estate representative's constant scouring the market on our behalf, the landlord thought of us and made the call. Ninety days later, after a whirlwind of negotiations with ownership, our two anchor tenants, and the private foundations we had been cultivating all during the search, we were finally ready to go. On New Year's Eve of 2014, we signed a lease for the Literacenter. In January 2015, having made our first full-time team hires, we started building the space we'd been promising for so long.

FIGURE 2.1 *Mission of the Literacenter.* The Literacenter's mission statement is on full display in the space and emphasizes collaboration among services to improve literacy in Chicago. *Photo credit: Tim Benson.*

Into the six months that elapsed between signature and opening day, we crammed an amount of work that would normally have taken at least twice that. Without the strong relationships we'd formed during the prolonged exploration phase, it would not have been possible. But since we'd spent so much time going over the vision with our architects, furniture vendors, and other key partners, we were able to adapt to the specifics of our new home and move fast to implement execution. The lease-breaking payment owed to the building by our predecessors covered our remodeling and buildout costs. A major loan from IFF, (the largest nonprofit Community Development Financial Institution [CDFI] in the Midwest) negotiated over the year before, funded the fixtures and furnishings. As we camped in the Starbucks across the street and gave hard-hat tours to prospective members, we incorporated their questions and suggestions into the coalescing layout and our supply orders. In May 2015, our two anchor tenants and sixteen additional member organizations began working from the space. One month later, we held a day-long grand opening party. And in summer 2016, we celebrated our first anniversary with more than ninety member organizations of all sizes.

In total, CLA and our 124 member organizations now serve more than 18 million people annually. Our collective programs span the literacy lifespan from early childhood education and book grants through K–12 programs, literary enrichment offerings, and adult literacy services. Though we differ widely in size and specifics, all of us are working to make Chicago a more literate place, and all of us share the core principles of collaboration, commitment, and collegiality. The Literacenter, recognized in 2016 with a Library of Congress award for best practices in literacy, is not only our workspace. It is our physical manifestation of our commitment to our cause, to each other, and to our city.

The current Literacenter comprises 41,000 sq. ft. spread across three floors of space in Chicago's burgeoning West Loop neighborhood. As shown in Figure 2.2, every detail of the space builds on our shared cause of literacy, from magnetic letters in the bathrooms and stacks of books in the welcome area, to book-pun names of every meeting room, the five Literascooters zipping around the second floor, and the Spiny Staircase, which links all the spaces together and features a different book's spine design on each step.

The main elements of the Literacenter's space are:

- First floor: Anchor tenant's Open Books' retail bookstore, offices, and classrooms.
- Second floor: Fourteen meeting rooms (all painted different colors, equipped with phones, whiteboards, and projection monitors, and ranging in capacity from three to one hundred people); offices and cubes for thirteen organizations; a connected wing of offices for anchor tenant Working in the Schools, which empowers students as readers through volunteer literacy programs and teacher development; coworking desks and tables of varying sizes; a kitchenette with free coffee, tea, and hot chocolate; mailboxes (every member gets one), storage lockers (ditto), and informal social spaces; a wall featuring all members' logos; a central monitor with information on upcoming events; and the Welcome Desk.
- Lower level: Two meeting rooms and the LitLounge (featuring kitchen facilities, comfortable furniture, foosball, shuffleboard, ping-pong, video games, movie screens, board games, and two pianos).

FIGURE 2.2 *Interior of the Literacenter.* Literacenter's inviting open floor plan is not only a good place for reading, but also allows the "literascooters" parked on the left side to roam. *Photo credit: Tim Benson.*

- Wi-Fi everywhere: This lets members book rooms online and share needs, questions, and ideas through the member web portal. Rooms can also be booked directly from the iPads outside them, which show reservations for the day. A connected app texts members to alert them to visitor check-ins at the Welcome Desk.
- Keycard scanners at all doors: This provides 24/7 access for members. Peak use tends to occur between 8:30 AM to 5 PM on weekdays, when the CLA team staffs the Welcome Desk and provides support of all kinds, but it is a rare evening or weekend that does not include at least one member event.

On an average day, activity at the Literacenter likely includes a CLA-sponsored workshop, unconference, seminar, meetup circle, book club, or movie night. Members hold their own meetings and events throughout the space, which also can be transformed into a party venue for major fundraisers. In addition to tracking organic interactions that happen as a result of sharing space, the CLA team makes active introductions and connections across the member base to encourage collaboration. We also handle all basic maintenance, though members agree to a set of shared space principles (booking rooms in advance, cleaning up after themselves, and being open to collaboration) upon joining.

Everyone is welcome to join CLA's steering committees, the most popular of which centers on programs and improvements for the space. And members also benefit from an ever-increasing array of discounted offerings negotiated by CLA, ranging from back-office services (e.g., payroll, HR, insurance) and everyday items (e.g., desk supplies, telephone setups) through professional programs (e.g., executive education at Northwestern University's Kellogg School of Management) and local providers (e.g., restaurants, gyms, retail establishments).

The Literacenter's current rate of occupancy for offices and cubes, all leased on a month-to-month basis at heavily subsidized rates, is 100%, except for the major spaces occupied by our two anchor members. As more organizations join, the wait list for dedicated space grows. In the meantime, members without assigned places cowork across the facility, reserving small meeting rooms for focused sessions whenever necessary.

Some member groups have moved out of their former locations to be exclusively here: Literacy Chicago, the city's oldest provider of adult literacy services, reduced its rent expenses by more than 70% by relocating to the Literacenter, saving the organization from shutdown and giving its adult learners a supportive, colorful, welcoming new place to pursue their goals. Others have adopted the space as their first-ever outside workplace: Literacy Works, which operated from its staff's homes for fifteen years, credits their Literacenter tenancy with accelerating their work, improving their fundability, increasing their capacity, and unifying their team. A growing contingent of one- to two-person start-ups share tables with representatives from major regional organizations who use the space as a satellite downtown location or an auxiliary place for events that do not fit at their usual offices. Perhaps most inspiring of all, many member groups have begun to use the Literacenter for their program offerings, so meeting rooms frequently host adults learning to read in the mornings, teens attending creative writing classes in the late afternoons, and college applicants coming to mentoring sessions at night.

WHAT WE TALK ABOUT WHEN WE TALK ABOUT COLLABORATION

On a main wall at the Literacenter, in multicolored text ten feet high, is the statement:

We are dedicated to our mission of increasing the combined impact of our community's literacy organizations by providing opportunities for creative and effective collaboration.

Collaboration, like any other human relationship, is unique to its participants and impossible to replicate with precision. Our job at the CLA is not to design collaborations and instruct groups to engage in them. Rather, we make introductions, publicize examples, and provide contexts so that everyone can form partnerships that work for them and that can, in turn, inspire others. Some of our regular programs, like our monthly Confab and Coffee Hour, have no agenda other than to introduce people to one another and discover what they have in common. Others, like Literaskills and Literaself, bring members together for presentations on topics of shared interest that lead to related discussions. A few, like Unconferences and our annual Symposium, focus on a specific area where collaboration would be valuable and finish with follow-up actions for the groups who participate. All of them build on our perpetual conversations with everyone at the Literacenter (beginning with their answers to question #2 on our short application form: "How do you hope to contribute to the CLA community?"), our talks with people who reach out to CLA to find help with their own literacy needs, and our ongoing engagement with our city.

Since the opening of the Literacenter, member collaborations sparked by interactions in the space have included everything from basic sharing of information through the creation of new ventures. Each month, we feature them in our Literatales podcast series and our newsletter. A few examples include:

- Chicago HOPES for Kids, the CLA, and Open Books joining forces to source hundreds of high-quality books, match them to specific requests, gift-wrap them for the holidays, and deliver them to students in homeless shelters.
- Bookwallah and Kids Like Us finding ways to cross-refer Indian storybooks for their programs.
- Infiniteach and Smart Chicago partnering to get iPad apps for students with autism into schools and libraries.
- Cabrini Connections and Emerald City Theatre sharing resources to introduce students to the wonders of live performance.
- The Viola Project and WITS (Working in the Schools) connecting networks to start a new after-school program.
- Communities in Schools Chicago and Literacy Works teaming up to offer parent and professional development workshops to partner schools.

- Poetry Center of Chicago, Free Write, and Chicago Books to Women in Prison joining forces for a poetry exhibition event and shared book drive.

What we talk about when we talk about collaboration, then, is not a set of best practices or a checklist of actions to be taken. We are committed to making collaboration possible and attractive, to encouraging it as a creative and efficient solution for challenges of time and resource, and to championing it as the best way to accelerate change in our community towards our shared goal of a 100% literate Chicago. Within those guides, we revel in learning from our members and in being inspired by what they do together.

NOW WE ARE ONE

In the twelve months since Literacenter's opening, CLA has learned an immense amount about what works, what could be better, what attracts members to the community, and what they find most valuable once they are part of it. Despite the years of preparation, we knew there would be challenges and learning opportunities aplenty once our beautiful dream of idyllic cooperation met the realities of hundreds of people sharing a kitchen, using the HVAC system, and needing rooms at identical times for varying purposes. What follows are among the most valuable things we know now.

The Bottom Line Is Not Always Financial

In our initial projections, keen to show momentum and make the space available to as many groups as possible, we built in rent subsidies of up to 50% of market rates and set membership fees well under those of comparable groups. Although this financial structure and our other quantifiable benefits (e.g., discounted access to back-office services, special deals at local providers, etc.) are appealing to many members, they are not what attracts new groups or what keeps members happy about their decision.

Rather, what members value most are the advantages of being part of a community and the opportunities we foster to make deep connections within it. Many a membership has been silently sold by a visit to the welcome area and a view of all the member logos on the wall, well before we got to the fees and perks stage of the conversation, and many others have been upgraded to a higher-cost tier once the group began participating in CLA programs, finding partners in the space, and settling into the community web.

Space Use Is a Delicate Balance

Because meeting facilities were a priority for everyone in our pre-opening conversations, we designated most of our small rooms as meeting places and not offices. When, within ninety days of opening, demand for dedicated space exceeded the small number of offices available, we repurposed all our cubes (originally meant to be touchdown stations for coworkers needing a semiprivate desk for the day) into assigned space for resident tenants. Even this fix was short-lived, though, and now we have a growing wait list for cubes and offices. From a revenue standpoint, converting a few of the meeting rooms into offices (or dedicated storage rooms, another frequent request) would increase our earned income and boost our financial sustainability. But, since doing so would limit the greater utility of the space for everyone, we have kept things as they are and vowed to add more offices and storage rooms if we get the chance to expand.

Similarly, as our member groups began inviting guests to the Literacenter and hosting events there, we started to receive requests for individual memberships and day passes from visitors with little or no connection to literacy who loved the space and wanted to be part of it. As with repurposing meeting rooms into offices, the financial implications of making these changes were tempting; by offering individual memberships and day passes at even a fraction of other local coworking space rates, we could have added substantially to our earned income and lessened the need to raise money from other sources. In the end, however, we once again put mission first. Our members count on the fact that the people next to them at the table, in the lounge, or on a couch in the welcome area are vested in our shared cause and could be potential partners.

As a compromise for our financial prospects, we instead invested some marketing resources into promoting the Literacenter as a venue for event rental, charged at close-to-market rates and subject to availability (member reservations always come first). Dozens of cocktail parties, board meetings, corporate retreats, and special events later, we've found good ways to balance these income generators with the needs of our community and delight in the opportunity to let Chicago's event planners support literacy by using our space.

No Two Snowflakes Are the Same

Since our members offer such a broad span of innovative programs and approaches to literacy, many of them bring individual challenges to the Literacenter space. A few such changes we've made to accommodate unique needs and wants include altering the lease to allow for program-trained dogs, creating an express check-in process for adult learners that doesn't require written/typed sign-in, and installing a book drop box in the back parking lot. Because our space is leased rather than owned, there have been requests we couldn't accommodate. On balance, though, we've managed to meet the critical needs of most members, even ones we couldn't have foreseen.

One Plus One Plus One Equals Power

Although CLA membership is open only to organizations, engaging every individual person who uses the space is a top priority. By keeping track of who is at the Literacenter, when their birthdays should be celebrated (which we do once a month, with cake and singing for everyone), what brought them to their positions, and which parts and features of the space they use most, we're able to make sure they get involved in appropriate professional development opportunities like our Literaskills, Literaself, Literaleaders, and Unconferences programs. We also make sure that they feel comfortable sharing their skills and experiences with the community so that we benefit from the accumulated talents, experience, and passions of several hundred people.

Overhead's Not Dead

The Literacenter was made possible by the extraordinary starting support of a private family foundation and IFF's loan. Total earned income from membership fees, external rentals, paid programs, and other avenues covers a third of our annual financial needs, leaving us tasked with finding the rest from traditional sources like charitable foundations, corporate social responsibility partners, and individual donors. Because CLA's budget is overwhelmingly Literacenter-related, most traditional funders do not consider us a fit with their giving guidelines, which prioritize programs and direct service above the "overhead" expenses of space and team. Having been in the Chicago nonprofit sector for many years, we knew this would be an issue, but we thought that demonstrable success in accelerating the work, productiveness, and innovation of literacy groups across the city would make a compelling case for support. To date, however, we have been disappointed (though unsurprised) to discover that most funders remain uninterested in changing their criteria to support models like ours.

THE STORY AHEAD OF US, THE STORY BEHIND

The CLA, and by extension the Literacenter, came from the shared passion of a group of energetic and entrepreneurial people bound together by the cause of literacy. Our story to date is one of readiness to take risks, enjoyment of experimentation, and commitment to creativity. Now, with a year of real-life operating experience to draw on, we are looking ahead to the next chapters and the challenges we know they will present.

We were the first shared workspace in North America to focus on literacy. Now, groups in other cities have asked us to consider expansion to their communities, and we must decide whether such projects are within our scope. We have been fortunate in finding funding to cover the difference between our costs and our earned income. But we live and work in a city whose public schools are in flux and whose social service agencies are suffering from an ongoing state budget impasse. Therefore, we must find ways to assure our financial sustainability so that our members can continue relying on our support.

We opened the Literacenter with a small team willing to assume multiple roles. As our membership and program offerings expand, we must add new colleagues who share our energy and vision without increasing our budget beyond our means.

And we must make all of these decisions, from small details of space upgrades through major considerations of national growth, in ways that stay true to our founding principles and the realities with which they sometimes come into conflict. Our involvement with the Nonprofit Centers Network gives us perspectives from hundreds of other shared spaces who have faced similar situations, and we are perpetually grateful for the opportunities they provide to benefit from the experience of our peers nationwide.

No story worth writing deals solely in success. We know that, even with the best intentions and phenomenal support, we won't get everything right, and that the memories we share on our upcoming anniversaries will include regrets along with triumphs. From the level of the team in the trenches who took the Literacenter from idea to operations, though, the last year has been an epic experience. We can't wait to discover what the next many years have in store for us and to continue growing from the experience of building them every day.

PART 2
HOW TO CREATE A NONPROFIT CENTER

3 Mission Comes First
How to Create a Nonprofit Center

This next section of this book begins to tackle the practical aspects of developing nonprofit centers. We begin the discussion with a look at the organizational readiness elements that are necessary to get a project off the ground. We then discuss the mission and vision of the nonprofit center—key elements in making the case for support for the project, followed by a brief case study. We end by covering an overview of the development process and discuss the important strategic considerations for nonprofit center development.

ORGANIZATIONAL READINESS

Organizational readiness is the most important aspect of creating a successful nonprofit center. As we show in Figure 3.1, there are five basic elements to focus on in

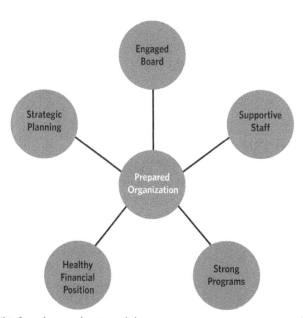

FIGURE 3.1 This figure lays out the essential elements an organization must assess, and, if necessary, strengthen to carry out a successful shared space project. *Source: Nonprofit Centers Network, as adapted by authors.*

evaluating readiness—do you have an engaged board? Supportive staff? Up-to-date strategic planning? A healthy financial position and strong programs? Let's consider them one by one.

Strategic Planning

The decision to create a nonprofit center should never be made in isolation. Organizations should be clear on their overall mission and direction and understand clearly how the real estate project will advance their overall program. An updated strategic plan and/or a business plan for the organization can help ensure that congruence exists and help to explain the project to potential funders and lenders.

Engaged Board

An engaged board of directors is the key backbone to a successful project. Too often, staff embark on shared space, or really any real estate project, without a thorough discussion with their board of directors and a supportive mandate to proceed. This can result in time and money wasted when the efforts are vetoed by the board as too risky or off mission. But beyond simple support, an engaged board will have board members ready to help raise money as needed for the project. In addition, the board should consider adding board members with some knowledge of real estate and finance who can help guide the project. if they don't already have them. An alternative is to set up a board committee with outside members with that expertise. Finally, in shared space collaboratives, having board members who will engage with the board members of partner organizations is very useful in building the collaboration.

Supportive Staff

Although the prime movers in the project may be senior staff and board members working with the project managers and other outside consultants, doing such a project will affect all members of the organization's staff. They will have to move offices, possibly change their commute, contend with less attention from senior staff, or even see changes in their programs because of new configurations in the space and new collaborative partnerships. Getting staff's buy-in very early in the project is important to avoid morale problems—staff who are on board with the vision will gladly accommodate the inconveniences. Staff input is also key in making the best decisions. For example, when it comes to the design process, staff in the trenches often understand work flow and what layout would be most effective far better than architects who have never done the work of the organization. Any good design process (and architect) will incorporate this input in creating a successful design.

Healthy Financial Position

As we outlined in Chapter 6: The Development Process, real estate projects of any kind, and especially shared space projects, take time and money—sometimes more than originally imagined. It can be dangerous to embark on such a project unless an organization is in a healthy and stable financial position. Good financial reporting and controls, strong board oversight, competent fundraising professionals on staff, and healthy reserves are all important components of a strong financial position. This criterion can be especially hard to meet in areas where steeply rising real estate costs are leading to nonprofit displacement. But doing advanced financial and business planning can make even rapid change easier to financially navigate. The authors strongly recommend the assessments, tools and financial tips provided in the Resources section of the Nonprofit Finance Fund website as a way to get started.[1] Local community loan funds can also help in the readiness process.

Strong Programs

As you enter a program collaboration with other organizations, having your own program in a stable position is very important. Is the organization meeting its program goals both for its mission and its funders? Is there stable, competent staff carrying out the work? If the new real estate doubles your program space, can you fill that extra space with financially sustainable programs? Are the organization's programs a compatible fit with those of your contemplated partners? These are all important questions to review in assessing your organizational readiness.

Coordinate the Readiness of All the Partners

Finally, the authors recommend that all the organizations integral to a collaborative space or services project do an organizational readiness assessment before the collaboration is finalized to prevent uneven levels of readiness creating difficulties for the partnership.

MISSION, VISION, AND PURPOSE

Many people ask what the right answer is for choosing what model their center should follow. Should they be a Theme Center or serve all nonprofits in the community? Should they raise all the funds through a capital campaign, or does debt have a role to play in financing their center? Should they create a condominium with partners or create a new nonprofit to own and manage their center? The reality is that nonprofit centers are as varied as the communities where they are located. It's a powerful model because its infinitely customizable to meet the needs of your organizations and community while drawing on best practices along the way.

The answer to all those questions starts with the mission and vision of the center you want to create. Clarify that, and many of the other answers fall into place. What is the social impact you aspire to achieve, now and in the future? Can you spell it out in a clear, concise, and compelling fashion? Who are partners, members, and/or tenants who can help you achieve that impact? What is your purpose, and how will this center achieve that purpose? As you go along, add to that mission and vision some of the feasibility research outlined in the following chapters, and many of the answers you need will fall into place. Before we go on to the road map for creating a shared space the next section tells the story of how the mission and goals of the Children and Family Service Center (CFSC) in Charlotte, North Carolina, shaped the development of their center over time.

Mission: Making Children Safe

The CFSC is a five-story office building in the Uptown neighborhood of Charlotte, North Carolina, that was built though a public/private collaboration aimed at serving children and families.[2]

The initial impetus for this nonprofit center, as it is many places, was the real estate boom and rapid gentrification of downtown Charlotte. Corporations were moving to Charlotte, and developers were buying rundown buildings in Uptown and replacing them with condominiums. But many low-income people still lived in Uptown and surrounding areas. Every month another nonprofit was dislocated and pushed to a location far from their core clients.

Watching this, a group of direct service executive directors began to discuss the idea of moving in together. They involved key board members who loved the idea and volunteered to help. They began looking for a location while also laying the groundwork for their fundraising drive.

After two years, they finally found a location. The hot real estate market meant real difficulties in finding a suitable building. So, they decided to build new. They secured a fifty-year ground lease from local government for a site near the government sector in Uptown. The site was near their client populations and one block from a transit hub.

The organizations all served children and families including a focus on domestic violence and child abuse. The police's child and family service unit initially co-located in the building. Their mission's all fit together. But they needed to raise millions of dollars, and donor support was essential. Donors cared a great deal about the nonprofits, and their clients who were struggling with transportation to get their needs met. But their eyes really lit up when they heard about the potential for collaboration among the organizations. The final criteria for member agencies included a commitment to build collaboration with other building agencies as well as a financial commitment from agency board members and executive directors.

As donors joined the volunteer effort, their vision helped shape the project. A local foundation provided funding for an executive director for the project and the structure evolved. CFSC became a new nonprofit to develop and own the building. The board was composed of one board member from each of the member agencies and an equal number of community representatives. They wanted to make sure member's voices were at the table on policies that affected them. But the team also wanted the community voice because the building wasn't just for the members. And community members provided expertise for the real estate process and shared services programs.

The final construction plans were shaped by the member agencies. Since social services has more women involved than men, the women's restrooms were larger with baby changing areas in both the men and women's restrooms. The team initially built shared meeting space but also set aside a large area for computer servers. This provided room to implement the shared IT services that came along when the members decided to centralize technology. They created intentional and common entry ways with a single point of entry and sign-out.

The board members understood from their experience with the agencies the daily cost of poor-quality space. They persevered in raising $9 million, enough money not just for a Class A building but also for new furniture and technology for all the occupants. A $3 million loan completed the project. The 100,000 sq. ft. building shown in Figure 3.2 opened in 2003 after five years of work.

Collaboration evolved over time at CFSC. It started with two and three organizations working together on a project. The Executive Directors Council met monthly. Eventually the executive directors began to plan shared services, urged along by donors and community members. Today, CFSC has shared accounting, HR, and IT functions available to tenants as well as shared space and shared security and building management. The combination of below-market rent and these shared services have resulted in $11 million in savings to the agencies over the first ten years of operations.[3]

FIGURE 3.2 *Children and Family Services Center, Charlotte, North Carolina.* This is the lobby of the 100,000 sq. ft. Children and Family Services Center building in Charlotte that houses a consortium of partner agencies working together to improve the lives of children and families. *Photo credit: Children and Family Services Center.*

Executive directors of the member agencies and of CFSC itself have changed as have some of the agencies but community service continues. The building now houses a coworking space. The mission has broadened to include the eradication of poverty in the Charlotte area while working together to serve families and children with housing, health, safety and economic advancement.[4] The nonprofits at CFSC serve almost 200,000 children and families annually in the county and the state.

STRATEGIC CONSIDERATIONS IN NONPROFIT CENTER DEVELOPMENT

So, you've done your organizational readiness assessment and so have your partners. You've clarified your mission, vision, and purpose. Now what? What are the steps in creating a nonprofit center, and what is involved in each step? What follows is a very short road map of the process of developing a center and a summary of the most important strategic considerations. These items are covered in detail in the remainder of the chapters in the book. Look at Figure 3.3 for the first overview.

What immediately becomes clear is that creating a nonprofit center is not a linear process. Assessing how much a capital campaign could raise is crucial in understanding how much space your project can afford to buy or lease. Similarly, understanding your ownership and governance model and finding your partners helps determine how much space you'll need. At the same time, the realities of the real

Road Map to Creating a Nonprofit Center

FIGURE 3.3 Developing a real estate project requires planning and then implementing the sequential steps laid out here while continuing to evaluate and adapt your planning as conditions change. *Source: Nonprofit Centers Network, as adapted by authors.*

estate market will allow you to understand what rent levels might be feasible for nonprofit tenants, which will, in turn, define the size of your cohort of potential tenants. So, the three tasks of finding the resources (financing and fundraising) and finding the real estate as well as figuring out your ownership and governance structure must be taken on together to move your project forward.

Leadership is an important aspect of this process. One key need is often a team or committee to oversee and guide the whole project. Typically, it would include board members, staff, and consultants from one or more of the partner organizations. This team should be given a formal mandate by the boards of directors in the form of a resolution or committee charter laying out responsibilities, expected outcomes, membership, reporting responsibilities, etc.

Establishing building operations and programs and services obviously can't commence until the building is either leased or bought and renovated. But carrying out those functions requires planning and implementation that can start as soon as the site is under control, or even before that, in terms of making sure that the real estate meets the spatial requirements for all tenants' shared programs and services.

Two other activities are threads that run through project creation from beginning to end. As shown on the top of Figure 3.3, the first is Planning and Feasibility, and at the bottom is Self-Evaluation. The authors' experience is that, as with many complex projects, changing conditions often dictate creative changes in direction. Keeping flexibility in your planning and being open to the implications of new data through feasibility studies will be key to a successful project. Similarly, opening the building is only the first step. The ability to candidly self-evaluate the work to date and in subsequent phases of the center's development is another essential measure of success; listening carefully to the feedback from partners, tenants and the community can provide invaluable information.

What follows in Figure 3.4 is an expanded version of Figure 3.3, aimed at filling out the content in each of the strategic considerations. Again, this figure is a preview of the rest of the book, which will explore these topics in detail.

Chapter 4: A Profile of Existing Nonprofit Centers, can provide important data as creators begin their exploration and planning. Understanding the variety of sizes and structures of established nonprofit centers will hopefully expand the possibilities a team can imagine. The research on the benefits of nonprofit centers outlined in Chapter 5: Making the Case, can help make the case to partners and donors on the reasons for funding new or existing centers. The complexities of obtaining financing and fundraising as well as building a Real Estate team and feasibility planning are included in Chapter 6: The Development Process. Chapter 7: Finding a Home focuses on finding the real estate. Establishing Building Operations (see Chapter 15: Facilities That Facilitate) and Programs and Services are covered next (see Chapter 18: Creating Collaboration in Nonprofit Centers and Chapter 21: Deepening the Shared Space Model). *Stories from the Field* are case studies that fill out important lessons. At each stage creativity and flexibility can help guide practitioners through even the most complex situations.

FIGURE 3.4 This figure presents in more detail some of the components of the strategic considerations shown in the road map in Figure 3.3. These elements and others are discussed more fully in the rest of the book. *Source: Nonprofit Centers Network, as adapted by authors.*

NOTES

1. See in particular this material from the Nonprofit Finance Fund. 2017, "Fundamentals for Nonprofits," https://www.nonprofitfinancefund.org/learn#learn-fundamentals.
2. The authors want to thank Peggy Eagan, first Executive Director of CFSC, for information about CFSC's history. Personal communication with China Brotsky, August 2017.
3. Children and Family Services Center. "About Us." 2018. http://www.childrenfamily.org/about-us/.
4. Children and Family Services Center. "Our Agencies." 2018. Accessed December 26, 2017. http://www.childrenfamily.org/agencies/.

4 A Profile of Existing Nonprofit Centers

Chapter 1: A New Model for Nonprofits introduced the concept of nonprofit centers and gave a sense of their numbers, including over seven hundred existing and in-development centers. This chapter gives a more graphic picture of the wide diversity of centers that exist throughout the US and Canada.[1] In each case, there is agreement that combining nonprofits in one site and sharing services is more financially sustainable, as well as better at serving the community and organizational missions.[2] One of the beauties of the nonprofit center field, as revealed in this chapter, is the wide variation in profile that can realize these results. Organizations planning centers often ask about the ideal size and model for their project. A review of this chapter makes clear that any number of configurations can succeed and meet the mission and goals of its planners.

A study done in 2011 of 130 existing centers demonstrates the scale of this field. It found that the centers already represented 9.3 million sq. ft. of space and close to 2,600 tenant organizations. A subset of approximately a hundred nonprofit centers in the survey earned $80.2 million in revenues annually, had 17,600 staff people working in the facilities, and hosted close to 67,000 visitors each week.[3]

Nonprofit centers vary on many demographic dimensions including location, size, and number of tenants. As shown in Figure 4.1, when surveyed in 2011 almost 80% of centers were in cities while 20% were in suburban and rural locations.[4]

Where Centers Are Located

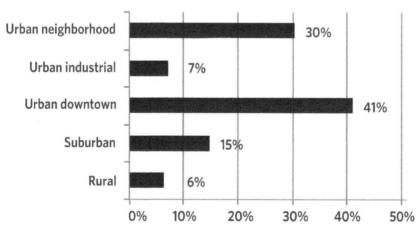

FIGURE 4.1 Although most nonprofit centers are in urban areas, over 20% are in rural or suburban locations. *Source: Nonprofit Centers Network.*

An analysis of 342 centers was done by a Senior Community Development Specialist at the Federal Reserve Bank of St. Louis in early 2017. Michael Eggleston matched center addresses to their respective census tract income level.[5] Almost exactly 50% percent of them were in either a low- or moderate-income census tract while the rest were in middle- or upper-income tracts, almost exactly 25% in each. Although this statistic affirms the usefulness of these projects in lower-income areas, depending on its goals, a variety of locations can meet project needs.

Nonprofit centers can be found in newly constructed buildings, as well as in renovated buildings, including former train stations, remodeled schools, repurposed historic hospitals, houses of worship, and office buildings. One of the most striking renovations is The Women's Building in San Francisco shown in Figure 4.2.[6]

Nonprofit centers range from a building with two or three nonprofit organizations co-located together to a very large office building or a campus filled with more than seventy tenants. The Al Sigl Community of Agencies has six campuses, over 650,000 sq. ft. and over thirty tenants. They have collaboratives on fundraising and marketing and joint ventures for shared services.[7] The Milwaukee Environmental Consortium provides space, accounting services, fiscal sponsorship, office services, and collegiality out of a leased office floor. Surveyed centers in 2011 had a median center size of 35,000 sq. ft., and 15% with a size of 100,000 sq. ft. or more. Figure 4.3 gives more detail on the size range.[8]

FIGURE 4.2 *The Women's Building San Francisco.* Originally an historic immigrant athletic club, The Women's Building became the first US women-owned community center and nonprofit hub. It is also the home to one of San Francisco's largest and best-known murals, painted in 1994 by some of the Bay Area's finest muralists. *Photo credit: "Maestrapeace" (1994 and 2000) by Juana Alicia, Miranda Bergman, Edythe Boone, Susan Kelk Cervantes, Meera Desai, Yvonne Littleton, and Irene Perez. All rights reserved.*

Size of Centers

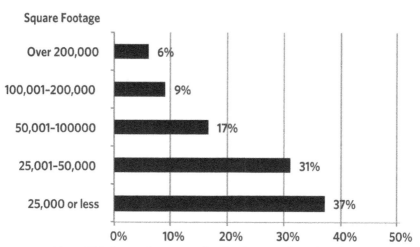

Square Footage

FIGURE 4.3 Almost 70% of nonprofit centers are less than 50,000 sq. ft. in size, with 32% greater than 50,000. Most of the larger centers are stand-alone buildings or campuses with multiple buildings. *Source: Nonprofit Centers Network.*

The number of tenants or partners in the building affects a number of operating factors from the budget available for building staff to the complexity of maintaining good internal communications and building collaboration. "The median number of resident organizations is eleven," but some centers surveyed had more than fifty tenants.[9] This is shown graphically in Figure 4.4. Some centers have consciously provided services and membership to the wider nonprofit or social enterprise community to build their impact.

A 2015 survey found 67% of nonprofit centers were in space owned for that purpose, and 33% were in leased space.[10] Many centers offer below-market rents and have waiting lists. As elaborated on in Chapter 15: Facilities That Facilitate, their income sources are varied including grants, personal and corporate donations, and multiple streams of earned income including rent. Many include sustainable (green) building features, and some are built to the highest environmental standards.

These buildings and sites have been developed through the planning efforts of individual organizations, nonprofit collaborations, foundations, government, and corporate entities. See Figure 4.5 for a breakdown based on research from the 2011 study.

Nonprofits in these centers benefit from the presence of other organizations, but centers allow each nonprofit to maintain its own mission, identity, and governance structure. Regardless of their configuration, they all meet the previously discussed definition: they all have a collection of individual nonprofit organizations or other entities located together under one roof with a social purpose. That purpose can vary widely while still preserving the benefits of this collaborative infrastructure model.

Number of Tenants

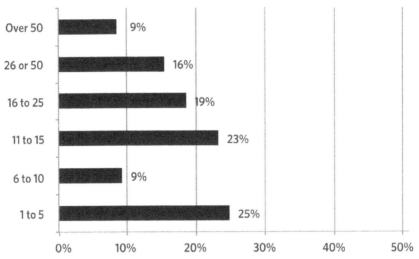

FIGURE 4.4 Over half of all nonprofit centers have fifteen or fewer tenant or partner organizations, but almost 10% have over fifty tenants. *Source: Nonprofit Centers Network.*

Who Develops Nonprofit Centers?

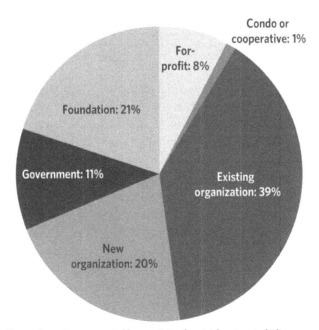

FIGURE 4.5 Nonprofit centers are created by a variety of societal sectors including nonprofits and foundations, government bodies, and for-profit companies. New organizations created are often the result of a collaborative effort among several nonprofits and community stakeholders to create a community asset. *Source: Nonprofit Centers Network.*

NOTES

1. Centers currently exist in multiple other countries worldwide, especially when including mission-based coworking centers, but a broader survey was outside the scope of this book.

2. Nonprofit Centers Network. *State of the Shared Space Sector Survey 2015: Changing How Nonprofits Work*. Denver: Nonprofit Centers Network, 2015 and Sullivan, P. "Sharing Spaces, Costs." *The NonProfit Times*, December 2, 2014. Accessed October 16, 2016. http://www.thenonprofittimes.com/news-articles/sharing-spaces-costs/.

3. Nonprofit Centers Network. *Measuring Collaboration: The Benefits and Impacts of Nonprofit Centers (Executive Summary)*. San Francisco: Nonprofit Centers Network, 2011, 5.

4. Nonprofit Centers Network. *Measuring Collaboration: The Benefits and Impacts of Nonprofit Centers (Executive Summary)*. San Francisco: Nonprofit Centers Network, 2011, 6.

5. Personal communication with Michael Eggleston, Senior Community Development Specialist, Federal Reserve Bank of St. Louis, 2017.

6. The Women's Building. "Maestra Peace Mural." 2015–2017. https://womensbuilding.org/the-mural/.

7. Personal communication with Thomas M. O'Connor, President, Al Sigl Community of Agencies, January 28, 2018. The Milwaukee Environmental Connection. "Milwaukee Environmental Consortium/About." 2017. https://meconnect.us/directory/member/milwaukee-environmental-consortium.

8. Nonprofit Centers Network. *Measuring Collaboration: The Benefits and Impacts of Nonprofit Centers (Executive Summary)*. San Francisco: Nonprofit Centers Network, 2011, 6.

9. Nonprofit Centers Network. *Measuring Collaboration: The Benefits and Impacts of Nonprofit Centers (Executive Summary)*. San Francisco: Nonprofit Centers Network, 2011, 6.

10. Nonprofit Centers Network. *State of the Shared Space Sector Survey 2015: Changing How Nonprofits Work*. Denver: Nonprofit Centers Network, 2015.

5 Making the Case

Gaining Support for Your Center with Data-Driven Results

Whether it is one individual or a group, people who want a nonprofit center must gain support and resources from a wide variety of sources. Once these advocates have defined its mission and vision (as outlined in Chapter 4: A Profile of Existing Nonprofit Centers), they must be able to make their case; they must be able to clearly express the many benefits a center can give to (i) its nonprofit tenants, including their associated clients, staffs, and volunteers; (ii) its physical neighborhood; and (iii) the community it serves. So, whether the project's leaders direct their message to funders, neighbors, the city government, or potential tenants, it must be *compelling, persuasive,* and *data-driven.* The need for such a message also applies to existing centers whose leadership seeks to expand its current building or develop an additional site.

This chapter helps you prepare your message by summarizing the positive benefits that nonprofit tenants have gained by being in a nonprofit center, and the center's own positive impact upon the greater community. Such convincing, data-driven results, based on empirical research, can help you gain support for your case.

"What good would such a nonprofit center do?" You're likely to encounter this or similar questions from potential supporters along the journey to develop your nonprofit center. This chapter provides you with results from recent surveys in the US and Canada to bolster your case for support and to dispel concerns. They show the success of nonprofit centers in helping to increase nonprofits' efficiency, effectiveness, and community impact. These results can help you influence potential supporters to donate their resources and to use *their* influence to support your center's cause.

RESEARCH ON THE BENEFITS OF NONPROFIT CENTERS

There are many ways in which nonprofit centers can strengthen nonprofit organizations and the nonprofit sector, as well as help their communities and society. For many years, practitioners have told compelling anecdotes from their own experiences in shared space. But only in the last twenty years have researchers tried to systematically capture the wide range of benefits associated with nonprofit centers and to document them for the public. Their results are organized and summarized in this chapter, and they provide valuable information that can be used by advocates of nonprofit center to make their case.

The first-known published study of tenant organizations at US nonprofit centers was conducted by University of Michigan professor, Diane Vinokur-Kaplan, who assisted by Bowen McBeath, then a doctoral student and now himself a professor. They studied three, large nonprofit centers as part of their Under One Roof Project, which investigated the benefits and challenges of nonprofit centers. They surveyed the directors of the nonprofit tenant organizations that were co-located in these three nonprofit centers regarding their initial attraction to—and their current level of satisfaction with—being in their centers. The results were published in the journal *Nonprofit Management and Leadership*[1] and are also summarized herein.

Subsequent research on tenant organizations and on the directors of nonprofit centers flourished because of the initiatives of the Nonprofit Centers Network (NCN). In 2011, the firm of Mt. Auburn Associates[2] conducted a study for NCN on nonprofit centers, in which they surveyed known nonprofit centers in the US and Canada. Its results are reported in *Measuring Collaboration: The Benefits and Impacts of Nonprofit Centers (Executive Summary)*, and were based on questionnaires and interviews with both the directors of nonprofit organizations (called "tenant directors") and the directors of their respective nonprofit centers (called "center directors"). A subsequent survey of nonprofit centers in the US and Canada was conducted by NCN in 2015, and its resulting report is entitled *State of the Shared Space Sector Survey 2015: Changing How Nonprofits Work*. Both the 2011 and 2015 reports are available from NCN, and the surveys' methodologies are summarized herein.[3] This chapter draws results mostly from the two 2011 surveys, given their particular emphasis on the benefits and impacts of nonprofit centers as seen by their tenants' CEOs and center directors.

GENERAL IMPROVEMENTS IN TENANT ORGANIZATIONS FROM LOCATING IN A NONPROFIT CENTER

There are many ways that locating in nonprofit centers can help improve tenants' organizations. The tenant directors evaluated how much their locating in the center helped to improve thirteen different aspects of their organization, as shown in Figure 5.1. Their results showed moderate to significant improvement in all these different aspects of their organizations, and none indicated "no effect" or "a negative effect." So, tenant organizations gained many positive benefits by locating in their nonprofit center.

One result of locating in a nonprofit center that helped to *significantly improve* the tenant organizations was "the awareness and credibility of our organization within the community." They gave this aspect the highest possible rating, "significant improvement"—as shown in Figure 5.1. Such awareness and credibility are very important when contacting potential sponsors, donors, and clients.

A second result showed *significant improvement* in tenants' "overall ability to achieve our organizational mission"—thus reflecting major improvement in the key

Tenants' Rating of Degree of Improvements for Organization from Location in a Nonprofit Center

Scale: 1 = No Improvement   2 = Minor Improvement   3 = Moderate Improvement   4 = Significant Improvement

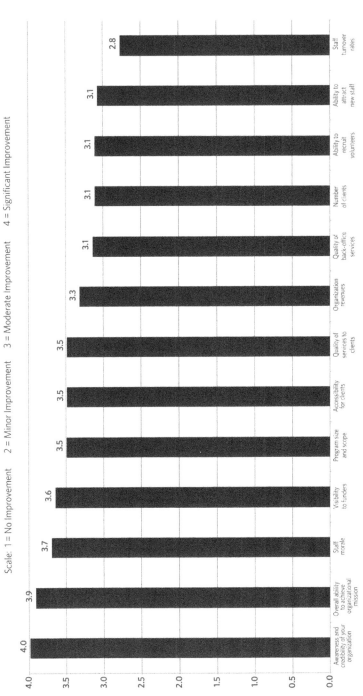

FIGURE 5.1 Responding tenant directors indicated that, on average, their location in a nonprofit center helped their organizations to have moderate to significant improvement in 13 important aspects. This analysis uses the 4-point improvement scale above, and the bars show each aspect's average improvement. (0%–4% noted location's "negative effect" on any aspect and were excluded.) *Source: Nonprofit Centers Network (2011) and additional data analysis.*

imperative of any organization. The tenants also indicated *significant improvement* in their organizations by being in a nonprofit center in five other aspects: "staff morale," "visibility to funders," "program scope and size," "accessibility to clients," and "quality of services to clients." Tenants also indicated *moderate improvement* in the six other organizational aspects: "organizational revenues," "quality of back office services," "number of clients," "ability to recruit volunteers," "ability to attract new staff," and "staff turnover rates." In sum, the tenants indicated that their location in a nonprofit center helped to moderately or significantly improve all of these key organizational aspects listed in Figure 5.1.

When the tenants were asked further whether their being in their center improved their organization's overall effectiveness and efficiency, "86% indicated improvement of either substantial or moderate effect."[4]

The NCN 2011 survey of tenant directors also found that they were very impressed with their *current space* at their nonprofit center. More specifically, the great majority (84%) stated that the quality of their current space was *better* than their previous space; only 14% said it was the same, and only 2% said it was worse. (Earlier, Vinokur-Kaplan, and McBeath also had found that the tenant directors at the three co-located sites were satisfied being there.)

THE RANGE OF BENEFITS CREATED BY NONPROFIT CENTERS

The NCN 2011 study "found a very broad range of benefits associated with nonprofit centers."[5] It classified the centers' benefits into three categories in which specific improvements in tenants' organizations or communities could be found: (1) "organizational efficiencies, (2) organizational effectiveness, and (3) community impact."[6] This categorization is summarized in Table 5.1. In the following pages, each of these three categories is briefly defined and applied to examples of specific benefits that a tenant organization can find through being at a nonprofit center. Then, more detailed results found for each of these three types of benefits are presented.

Organizational Efficiency

Organizational efficiency is increased when an organization can produce services or products while using less resources than before; by the same token, such efficiency is increased when it uses the same amount of resources, but it is able to accomplish more. This term, also has been more specifically defined as "an organization's degree of success in using the least possible amounts of resources, time, and costs (often called 'inputs'), to produce the greatest possible outputs (such as completed tasks or products)."[7]

For example, imagine a tenant organization located in a nonprofit center, which provides direct counseling services to individuals. As part of its lease, this tenant's staff now have easy access to the center's shared computer network, one that is faster and easier to use than the system they had used *before* they moved to the center. The

Table 5.1 Benefit Types and Range of Benefits

Benefit Type	Range of Benefits					
Organizational efficiencies (outputs)	Reduced and more stable rental costs	Reduced costs through shared services and spaces	Increased productivity through staff retention and staffing capacity			Improved service delivery
Organizational effectiveness (outcomes)	Increased organizational capacity	Increased knowledge	Increased IT capacity	Improved access to funders	Improved quality of back office services	
Community impact (impacts)	New community spaces and opportunities for civic	Higher quality space through new or renovated facility	Community access to technology	Learning and capacity building assets	New environmental and sustainability practices	Better location or access for staff and clients

Note: Nonprofit centers can provide many different types of benefits to their tenants and their communities. They are shown grouped into three categories: organizational efficiencies, organizational effectiveness, and community impact.

Source: Adapted from the graphic "Range of Benefits," Nonprofit Centers Network (*2011, p. 9*).

staff could now complete their record-keeping and correspondence in less time than before. So, this tenant organization would increase its efficiency in handling paperwork and thus receive an important benefit from being at the center—that saved time can now be devoted directly to its mission.

Organizational Effectiveness

Organizational effectiveness, the second category of benefits shown on Table 5.1, measures an organization's degree of success in accomplishing its stated aims or goals. For example, a tenant organization could seek such annual goals as improving the quality of its services, hiring a more diverse workforce, improving its level of environmental sustainability, or having a more supportive work environment for all its employees. Often, tenant organizations' attainment of their goals is helped by the tenant-focused programs of the nonprofit center. These programs and services can include group meetings, training sessions, workshops, shared services, and/or advice from the center's community animator staff.[8] Thus, the nonprofit tenant organizations benefit from the center's resources and are aided in increasing their effectiveness.

Community Impact

Community impact, the third category in Table 5.1, measures the degree to which a nonprofit center increases or improves the long-term functioning of its community. Community impact can refer to changes in the physical and economic environment of a geographical community. For example, the community could be a deteriorating neighborhood whose environment is improved by the presence of an attractive nonprofit center and the services the center offers for the community's benefit. Examples of such services may include free access to meeting rooms or to office equipment for neighborhood volunteer groups or free entry to training sessions in which neighborhood residents can gain new skills for better jobs.

IMPROVED ORGANIZATIONAL EFFICIENCIES

Cost savings are often associated with nonprofit centers, and they are an important way to increase a nonprofit's efficiency. "These savings result from both lower lease costs as well as savings from shared services, spaces, and staffing provided through the center."[9] As previously mentioned in Chapter 1: A New Model for Nonprofits, among the tenant organizations responding to the NCN 2011 survey, "the average annual cost savings is about 7 percent of annual operating costs."[10]

The NCN 2015 survey also looked at tenants' savings in operating costs through the same sources. It found:

Of those who could quantify their savings, the average annual costs savings was nearly $25,000. Many executive directors in shared spaces also recognize the time-savings in time to their staff, which is much more difficult to quantify. One respondent stated,

"For an organization of our size it is really critical not to have any unnecessary overhead costs. The shared copy machines, phones, and conference rooms all keep our costs down and decrease staff time dedicated to dealing with these issues."[11]

Lowered Costs for Tenants' Space

In the 2011 NCN study, over three-fourths (78%) of the executive directors of tenant organizations reported that "the cost of the space was a critically important characteristic" of cost savings for them.[12] Indeed, nonprofit centers' reputation for lower lease rates is very important for recruiting and attracting nonprofits as tenants. In an earlier study of three large US nonprofit center, Vinokur-Kaplan and McBeath asked directors of tenant organization how important nine items were in influencing them to co-locate at their nonprofit center. Among the 118 responding tenants, the most important influences were leasing price, along with free parking and safety.[13] One of the most compelling benefits that nonprofit centers provide to tenants is affordable leasing costs, ones that are frequently below local market rates.

In NCN's 2011 survey of the directors of nonprofit centers, around a quarter (26%) noted that their center's lease rate for nonprofit tenants was 50% or less than market rate; almost a third (31%) mentioned that it was between 51% and 75% of market rate; and about another quarter (27%) indicated that it was between 76% and 95% of market rate;[14] "only a very small number, six percent, reported lease rates that were higher than their market rate in their community."[15]

How do nonprofit centers have below-market rents? There are at least two reasons: (i) foundations, corporations, and individuals may make donations that cover the center's own rental costs or mortgage, as one way to philanthropically support the nonprofit center for all its does for the nonprofits, the community, and society, and (ii) the nonprofit center itself may be exempt from some taxes that for-profit landlords must pay, such as local or state property taxes or other taxes in force in its locale. Thus, the rent that a nonprofit center charges its nonprofit tenants does not have to cover such tax costs, while for-profit landlords routinely include covering such taxes in their leasing rates.

Improved Quality and Location of Space

Not only were rents and other operating costs lower for the tenants, they also received better quality, more accessible space in which to work. In 2011, many tenant directors and center directors noted that the quality and the location of the space for the cost are major benefits. "It is not just that the rent is less expensive, but for the price, resident organizations are getting a much higher quality space in a much more accessible location than would otherwise be the case."[16]

In addition, "38% report moderate to significant improvements in the quality of back-office services, with centers most frequently providing telephone, internet, IT support, and office equipment use."[17]

Improved Tenant Access to Shared Resources

The shared resources that tenant organizations can use at a nonprofit center reduce their costs as well as enhance their convenience. Shared resources usually include access to meeting rooms that they can use for free or a low cost. Such access provides them with another important benefit: without adequate, convenient meeting rooms, staff cannot easily talk together as a group and develop together as an organization, nor can they collaborate face-to-face with other tenant organizations, much less any other organizations with whom they wish—or need—to meet. Shared resources also can facilitate the involvement and work of tenants' volunteers. As shown in Figure 5.2,[18] the 2011 NCN survey found:

Tenants reported that they made regular use of meeting rooms, with two-thirds using them at least once a month. Over one-third utilized shared office equipment, and over one-quarter used networking opportunities and management assistance at least once a month. Case studies provide strong evidence that these services translate into direct benefits for resident organizations through reducing their operating costs and increasing their capacity.[19]

IMPROVED ORGANIZATIONAL EFFECTIVENESS

Nonprofit centers also offer a variety of benefits to tenant organizations that help them progress toward their goals, such as financial sustainability, and thus they become more effective.

Improved Financial Status

Organizations in nonprofit centers enjoy improved finances including greater revenue generation, financial stability, and cost savings.

Greater Revenue Generation

Tenants' location in a nonprofit center has a positive impact on their funding and revenue. In NCN's 2011 survey of tenant directors, 59% of resident organizations reported moderate to significant improvement in their "visibility to funders," and 45% reported improvement in their organization's revenue.[20]

Financial Stability and Operational Savings

Nonprofit centers also help ensure the financial stability of their tenants. This stability is especially important given considerable fluctuations in various real estate markets. One way that centers can further bolster the cost-efficiency of the rents is by providing tenants with multiyear leases with the same yearly rate or with moderate, gradual increases. These extended arrangements free tenants from facing rental rates

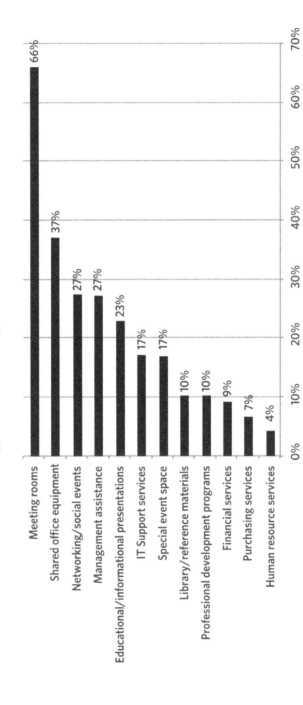

Percentage of Tenants Using Center's Services at Least Once a Month

- Meeting rooms — 66%
- Shared office equipment — 37%
- Networking/social events — 27%
- Management assistance — 27%
- Educational/informational presentations — 23%
- IT Support services — 17%
- Special event space — 17%
- Library/reference materials — 10%
- Professional development programs — 10%
- Financial services — 9%
- Purchasing services — 7%
- Human resource services — 4%

0% 10% 20% 30% 40% 50% 60% 70%

FIGURE 5.2 Nonprofit Centers provide a variety of shared services to their tenants. Such shared resources reduce their costs and enhance their organizational capacity. *Source: Nonprofit Centers Network (2011).*

that rise abruptly due to market forces, and they also give tenants a greater sense of financial stability.

Good Use of Cost-Savings

Given tenants' usual reductions in costs when they reside in a nonprofit center, the 2011 NCN study found that the tenant organizations then put their savings to good use. In 2011, one-third of resident organizations reported using their cost savings from locating in the center to increase program and operational spending, which can enhance mission-related activities and the office environment; 20% reported using their savings to develop new programs and services, which fosters innovation, and about 10% reported using their savings to increase staffing, thereby creating new jobs in the community[21] or to enhance their capacity.

The later 2015 NCN survey also examined how the nonprofits spent their savings from locating in shared space. Nearly a third (32%) spent them on "increasing existing program-related spending," while others used them for "increased staffing" (19%); "developing new service programs" (17%); "increased existing operations-related spending" (16%), which might include upgrading their technology; and "increased financial reserves" (16%).[22] In both periods in which the survey was conducted, the savings that tenant organizations realized from being in lower-rent environments with shared resources were generally spent pursuing their organization's mission.

Greater Programmatic Impact

Nonprofit centers can also have a beneficial effect on tenants' own programs. Over half of the 2011 tenant organizations (53%) reported "moderate to significant improvements in the size and scope of their programs" as a result of the formal and informal collaboration with other resident organizations and the shared services they receive.[23] In 2015, those reporting moderate to significant improvement in the scope of their programs went up to 63%, and 61% reported a similar improvement in program size.[24]

In terms of serving clients in 2011, there were some differences among the different types of centers that indicated moderate to significant improvement in 2011. Generally, the service centers reported the highest levels of improvement, as shown in Figure 5.3. About three-quarters of the service centers reported such improvement in accessibility for clients, and nearly 70% indicated such improvement in the quality of services for clients. Moreover, at least the majority of Generalist (multi-sector) Centers also enjoyed moderate to significant improvements in accessibility for clients and quality of services, and the Theme Centers were not far behind.[25]

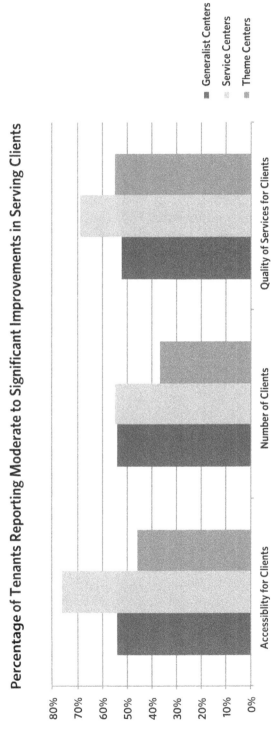

FIGURE 5.3 More than half of the tenants from Direct Service Centers and Generalist Centers noted moderate to significant improvements for their center's accessibility to clients, number of clients, and quality of services for clients, and more than a third from Theme Centers also reported such improvements. *Source: Nonprofit Centers Network (2011).*

The tenant organizations in nonprofit centers see wide-ranging benefits regarding their personnel, including improved staff morale, better staff attraction and retention, and improved staff satisfaction with their location.

Improved Staff Morale

Nonprofit work is often intense, especially for those providing direct services to clients such as social workers, healthcare providers, and educators. Morale can decline, given the emotional burden of working with clients in distress, usually living on lower salaries than their peers in the for-profit sector and not having adequate staff development resources. Nonprofit centers can help improve staff morale through at least two important benefits they provide: space for joint learning and training and proximity to peers for social support.

A significant number of nonprofit organizations located in the centers believe that these features have helped them, their staff, and volunteers, as shown in Figure 5.4.[26] One of the greatest impacts of nonprofit center tenancy has been on staff morale, with 65% of tenants in 2011 and 75% in 2015 reporting moderate to significant improvement.[27]

Better Staff Attraction and Retention

In 2015, one executive director of a tenant organization clearly stated the positive impact of its nonprofit center on the organization's attraction and retention of personnel: "We are able to attract and retain volunteers and staff because our office is so beautiful and pleasant to work in. Having a café on site also increased the attractiveness to our employees and increased their productivity."[28]

Such impact of the center was also found among many of the tenant executive directors surveyed in 2015; the majority (55%) of respondents reported moderate to significant improvement in their ability to attract new staff members, and almost half (47%) of executive directors surveyed reported an improvement in staff retention.[29]

Improved Satisfaction with Their Location

In their study of nonprofit tenants at three large US nonprofit centers, Vinokur-Kaplan and McBeath[30] probed a more psychological aspect among tenant directors: How satisfied were the executive directors of the residing nonprofits with being at their respective nonprofit centers? Their response choices went from "1=Not at All Satisfied" to "6=Very Satisfied." On average, the three groups of tenants indicated that they were quite satisfied with being at their centers (scoring 5.9, 5.3, and 5.2 on the six-point scale).[31]

These tenant directors at three centers also indicated how satisfied they were with nine specific aspects of their center, as shown in Table 5.2. The tenants at two centers were "satisfied" to "very satisfied" with seven aspects of their center: the leasing price, the physical layout, meeting rooms, free parking, safety and security,

Benefits of Centers on Staffing

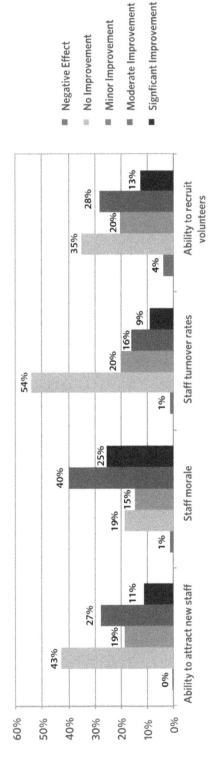

Legend:
- Negative Effect
- No Improvement
- Minor Improvement
- Moderate Improvement
- Signficant Improvement

Ability to attract new staff: 0%, 19%, 27%, 11%, 43%

Staff morale: 1%, 19%, 15%, 40%, 25%

Staff turnover rates: 1%, 54%, 20%, 16%, 9%

Ability to recruit volunteers: 4%, 35%, 20%, 28%, 13%

FIGURE 5.4 Location in a nonprofit center creates benefits for tenants in terms of staffing: 65% of executive directors reported moderate to significant improvement in staff morale, 41% in ability to recruit volunteers, and 39% inability to attract new staff. Only 25% reported improvement in staff turnover rates. *Source: Nonprofit Centers Network (2011).*

Table 5.2 Current Satisfaction of Tenants with Three Dimensions and Nine Items at Their Nonprofit Centers

	Downtown Center	Restoriana	Greenhouse	F-test	Significance
Financial Arrangements					
Leasing price	4.5	5.0	3.3	35.36	***
Physical Environment					
Physical layout	4.1	4.5	3.5	10.92	***
Meeting rooms	4.1	4.1	3.0	16.45	***
Break room facilities	3.6	4.1	3.0	10.25	***
Free parking	4.8	4.9	4.7	1.14	ns
Safety and security	4.3	4.9	4.5	5.65	**
Average	4.2	4.5	3.7		
Professional Environment					
Type of organizations at site	4.3	4.3	4.1	1.18	ns
More professional environment	4.0	4.6	3.7	7.83	***
Further develop organization	3.6	4.5	3.3	16.68	***
Average	4.0	4.5	3.7		
Overall average of nine items	4.3	4.7	3.6		

Note: Scale: 1 = very dissatisfied; 2 = dissatisfied; 3 = neutral; 4 = satisfied; 5 = very satisfied. Statistically significant differences between centers' ratings on each item were calculated using an F-test. ($*p < .05; **p < .01; ***p < .001$).

Source: Table 3, Current Satisfaction of Tenants with Three Dimensions and Nine Items at Their Nonprofit Centers. In Diane Vinokur-Kaplan and Bowen McBeath. "Co-Located Nonprofit Centers: Tenants' Attraction and Satisfaction." *Nonprofit Management and Leadership, 25*(1), 85, 2014. *Credit:* © Wiley Online Library. doi:10.1002/nml.21110. Used with permission of Copyright Clearance Center.

the types of other organizations at the site, and a more professional environment; one or the other was neutral regarding the "further development of their organization (e.g., in its management, skills, or knowledge base) and the "break room." At the third center, tenants were neutral to satisfied on the nine aspects of their center.

These tenant directors' overall satisfaction with being at their three centers is also reflected in their desire to stay there in the future. When asked how long they wished to stay at their current nonprofit center (irrespective of their leasing arrangements), the three groups of tenants overwhelmingly wanted to remain. Seventy percent stated they would want to stay indefinitely, and 13% wanted to stay from seven to twenty years; 11% planned to stay five years or fewer, and only 6% were planning to move immediately,[32] perhaps because they needed a larger space.

Greater Collaboration

Many nonprofit centers emphasize collaboration among tenants as one of their goals, and tenants are often interested in pursuing collaborations. The 2011 NCN study stated that "Tenants of nonprofit centers believe that their overall organizational capacity is enhanced as a result of the formal and informal collaboration with other resident organizations and the shared services they receive."[33] For example, in 2011, more than six in ten resident organizations responding to the 2011 survey (62%) "reported that collaboration with other tenants led to moderate to significant improvements in their effectiveness and efficiency."[34]

That survey also found that the most common ways in which nonprofit organizations housed in centers collaborated was regarding programs and services and client referrals:

Forty-six percent of the resident organizations reported that they collaborated at least on a monthly basis around their programs and services, and 34% collaborated with this frequency around client referrals. As one would expect, collaboration around client referrals was much more prevalent in service-type centers where 32% of the tenants reported that they collaborate at least once a week, as compared to 19% in multi-sector centers.[35]

NONPROFIT CENTERS' IMPACTS ON PEOPLE AND COMMUNITIES

What impacts can a nonprofit center have on their community? The research shows a range of positive impacts, and here they are organized according to their impact on people, place, and society, as shown in Table 5.3.

Improved Community Functioning

More People Served

Perhaps the clearest impacts are on the people involved with tenant organizations that provide direct services to clients (such as counseling, social and medical services, day care, and education). Based on their research, NCN reported in 2011:

The economies associated with nonprofit centers basically stretch limited private, foundation, and public-sector funds by reducing operating costs for nonprofit organizations residing in the center. These increased efficiencies lead to the ability to serve more clients (people) and to provide new and increased services that impact more people.[36]

Thus, more people in the community than before can benefit from the services nonprofits deliver and improve or enhance their lives in various ways. Some people can also get to the nonprofits more easily and in shorter time because these organizations are now located in more accessible locations; for example, the nonprofits they want to visit may now be near a bus stop, and the buildings can better accommodate

Table 5.3 Range of Impacts

Impact Type			
People	Increased number served due to greater access	Improved outcomes for clients due to better services and referrals	Human capital development through participation in Center activities and services	
Place	Revitalization of surrounding area	Enhanced quality of life through amenity development	Increased revenues for surrounding retailers	Fiscal benefits to the community
Society	Environmental improvements	New policies and approaches	Field building and knowledge creation	Increased social capital and civic engagement

Note: Research has shown that nonprofit centers create a range of positive impacts on individuals and groups, their locations, and the broader society.

Source: Nonprofit Centers Network.

their personal mobility situations, such as facilitating people in wheelchairs or providing childcare.

In the 2011 NCN survey, the clearest impacts were for the people involved with tenant organizations that provide direct services to clients (such as counseling, social and medical services, daycare, and education). Tenant directors in service centers reported "a direct connection between the benefits of being in the center and their ability to serve people."[37] Over 70% of service centers reported moderate to significant improvements in accessibility for clients, over 50% reported improvements in the number of clients, and nearly 70% reported such improvements for quality of services for clients.[38]

There is also anecdotal evidence available from case studies of service centers:

Many resident organizations of service centers interviewed for case studies note in particular the role of co-location with complementary organizations in bringing more clients to their organization by facilitating client referrals, enabling transportation-challenged clients to meet with multiple providers in a single visit, and reducing other barriers that individuals face who are in need of services.[39]

Two other major types of nonprofit centers have also illustrated improvements in serving their clients and stakeholders. Generalist Centers reported that over 50% have moderately or significantly improved their accessibility, number of clients, and quality of services for clients; and Theme Centers reported that more than 40% have improved their accessibility for those served and involved, more than 30% have increased their number of clients and stakeholders, and over 50% have improved the quality of services.[40]

Increased Human Capital Development

As shown in Figure 5.5, the 2011 NCN survey found many nonprofit centers provide facilities and services to the broad community beyond their resident organizations. The majority, 56%, provide meeting space that is available to the general public. In many communities, this type and quality of space was not previously available.[41] Thus, nonprofit centers serve to promote citizen engagement and voluntary action.

In addition, as illustrated in Figure 5.5, over 60% of the centers provide educational programs for the general public; over 30% provide performance space or exhibition space, and almost 20% provide recreational facilities. Thus each center often becomes an important place in their communities' cultural life; and a smaller group, over almost 20% provide recreational facilities.[42] "Many also provide ". . . educational services, computer resources, and meeting spaces to nonprofit organizations that are not residents of the facility."[43]

In summary, some of the positive impacts that nonprofit centers have on the people in the community and on nonresident nonprofit organizations occur through serving more people with improved services (including referrals to co-tenants and others), facilitating their participation in center activities, and encouraging them to meet, to learn, and to discuss critical issues within their facilities.

Impacts on the Community as Place

There are several additional ways that a nonprofit center may have an impact on a community, including changing and reviving its physical environment and enhancing the quality of life of the community's residents.

Revitalization of Surrounding Area

Oftentimes, the presence of a nonprofit center seems to have a positive impact on locations close by that spurs additional investment in the surrounding areas. For example, in 2011, "many center directors report that their investment has led to new property development and property renovation in the surrounding area. About one-third report moderate to strong impacts related to new property development and property renovation in the surrounding neighborhood."[44]

Also, while proving it is the sole cause of property renovation would require more research, there are examples such as NEW Center in Ann Arbor, Michigan, to consider. (NEW Center is the focus of Chapter 17: From Grants to Earned Income: Changing the Financial Profile at NEW Center.) Its cleanly designed presence on a remediated junkyard site, which had been was an eyesore for years may well have encouraged some of its commercial neighbors who later improved the appearance of their own nearby properties.

Nonprofit Center Contributions to Human Capital Development in Communities

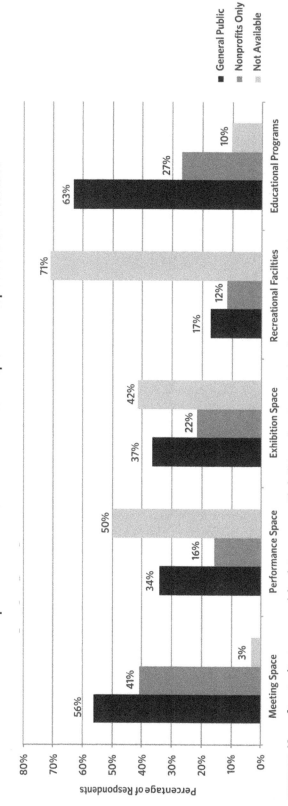

FIGURE 5.5 Nonprofit center directors reported that their centers provide facilities and services to the broader community beyond their resident organizations. They contributed most prominently to the general public through educational programs (63%) and meeting space (56%). Some *non-resident* nonprofits also benefited by accessing centers' spaces and educational programs. *Source: Nonprofit Centers Network (2011).*

The 2011 NCN survey of center directors found that 30% or more believed their nonprofit centers, once built, had a moderate to strong impact on new property development, property renovation, new businesses, expansion of existing businesses, and public infrastructure or amenities investments in the surrounding community,[45] as shown in Figure 5.6.

For instance, examples cited by center directors (in 2011) include "the development of new transit stops, roads, sidewalks, and public parks. Almost forty percent of center directors report moderate to strong impacts on public infrastructure investments."[46] In addition, nonprofit centers' own capital funding from a variety of sources has been used to renovate existing buildings in communities or to construct entirely new buildings. These investments bring about the infusion of many millions of dollars into the local economy for construction activities. Moreover, the presence of the center and its visitors and staff often bring new customers to neighborhood's retail establishments, thus strengthening small local businesses.

Such impacts are stronger in economically distressed areas. For the NCN 2011 study, Mt. Auburn Associates used a measure of "formally designated economically distressed areas." They found that "[a] relatively large number of centers, about 40 percent, on average, are located in such areas; in the case of service centers, over 60 percent are located in areas formally designated as distressed"[47] There,

[a] major investment in the renovation of a vacant building or the development of a new building on a long vacant lot has been a catalyst for further investment. In some cases, the nonprofit center has become a critical "anchor" property that has changed perceptions about a neighborhood.[48]

This impression was shared by many center directors in 2011:

Fifty-five percent of center directors in formally designated distressed areas report that their centers have had a moderate to strong impact on surrounding property renovation and 47% report a moderate to strong impact on new property development. This compares to 24% and 18%, respectively, for centers in economically stronger areas.[49]

In sum, the beneficial impacts of a nonprofit center can go beyond its own walls and provide many benefits to its surrounding environment.

Societal Impacts

There are also societal impacts that can be influenced by nonprofit centers. Such impacts go beyond the people and community directly involved in, or served by, a center. The NCN 2011 Survey stated: "These impacts result when a center and its resident organizations alter the civic and policy environment for their field."[50]

Perhaps societal impacts are the most complex and thus most difficult to quantify. However, the interviews and case studies gathered by Mt. Auburn Associates in

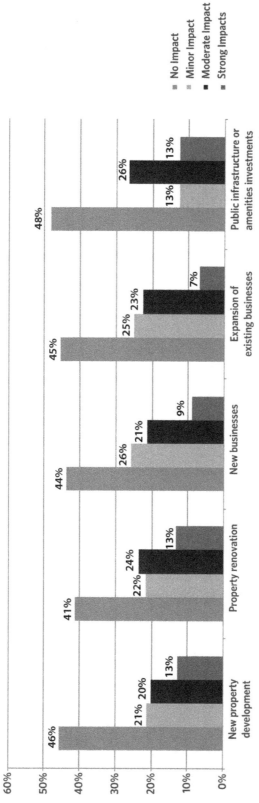

Center Economic Impacts on the Community

New property development
- 46%
- 21% 20%
- 13%

Property renovation
- 41%
- 22% 24%
- 13%

New businesses
- 44%
- 26% 21%
- 9%

Expansion of existing businesses
- 45%
- 25% 23%
- 7%

Public infrastructure or amenities investments
- 48%
- 13% 26%
- 13%

Legend:
- No Impact
- Minor Impact
- Moderate Impact
- Strong Impacts

FIGURE 5.6 The 2011 NCN survey of center directors found that 30% or more believed their nonprofit centers, once built, had a moderate to strong impact on new property development, nearby property renovation, new businesses, expansion of existing businesses, or public infrastructure or amenities investments in the surrounding community. *Source: Nonprofit Centers Network (2011).*

2011 provide some evidence of "how, through the use of collaboration and the creation of new spaces for civic engagement, nonprofit centers can spark new innovative
ideas, become a catalyst for organizing and advocacy, and lead directly to changes in
policies that have a beneficial impact on society."[51]

So, while there is not yet research done on this topic, there are interesting examples
and trends among nonprofit centers regarding environmental improvements,
increased social capital and civic engagement, and development of new policies and
approaches.

Environmental Improvements

For example, the environmental improvements that many centers bring are
increasing, and they set an example to the wider society. Some nonprofit centers
have formalized green practices and are green-certified buildings. As illustrated
in Figure 5.7, "43% of tenants reported moderate to substantial improvement in
adopting green practices due to their location in their nonprofit center."[52] The range
of centers' actions go from instituting composting and recycling programs in their
buildings to nonprofit centers dedicated to promoting sustainability.

Increased Social Capital and Civic Engagement

Nonprofit centers not only look inward to meet the needs of their tenants. They
also hold events that can increase their communities' social capital. These can include guided tours of their sites for the public and demonstrations of how collaborative workplaces can be successful. They recruit volunteers who build social capital.
Some offer their meeting rooms to other groups in the community, encouraging
more civic engagement in their communities. Finally, they are sites where the many
individuals who are trying to address complex social problems can meet, exchange
views, and build agendas for society's future.

Development of New Policies and Approaches

Societal impacts also occur when a center and its tenant organizations have a substantial impact on the civic and policy environment for their field. Beyond creating
green buildings and performing green practices, these impacts are difficult to quantify. However, Mt. Auburn Associates found examples through their research that
"provide evidence of how, through collaboration and the creation of new spaces for
civic engagement, nonprofit centers can spark new innovative ideas, become a catalyst for organizing and advocacy, and lead directly to changes in policies that have a
beneficial impact on society.[53]

A few of these examples of impacts on systems and policies include:

- Several centers with sustainability or environmental themes have become hubs for
  advocacy and policy around environmental issues. The resident organizations in
  these centers have collaborated on the passage of a wide range of legislation and

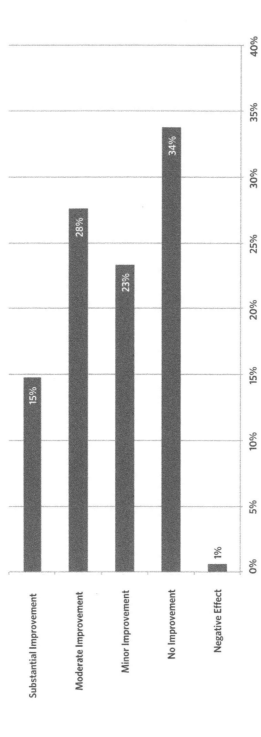

Percentage of Tenants Reporting Changed Green Practices Due to Location in Center

FIGURE 5.7 A total of 43% of tenants reported moderate or significant improvement in their adoption of green practices due to their location in a nonprofit center. *Source: Nonprofit Centers Network (2011).*

have used the centers to educate the broader community about community issues. One of these centers is profiled in Chapter 8: The Alliance Center.

• In many communities, arts centers have become strong focal points for the creative economy in the larger community. These centers have strengthened the cultural community and built creative skills in the community.

• Service centers targeted to specific groups such as the disabled or the elderly have become engaged in policy and advocacy effort to strengthen and support the support and services for their constituencies.[54]

Nonprofit centers also serve as visible symbolic landmarks and concentrated examples of care, concern, beauty, and engagement in community landscapes, which could inspire community members to share these same characteristics with their neighbors.[55]

CONCLUSION

As people embark on developing shared space projects, or growing their existing project, they should be emboldened by the research demonstrating the many positive benefits of nonprofit centers. These data-driven findings illustrate that nonprofit centers improve their tenant organizations' efficiency and effectiveness, while also offering many benefits to their staff, volunteers, and governing bodies. In some cases, the cost savings and shared services that resident organizations enjoy in nonprofit centers make all the difference in their ability to exist and continue their work for the public good; in many cases, they allow tenants to significantly enhance their skills and their services.

Moreover, such centers and their resident organizations have a beneficial impact on their communities and society. Advocates for nonprofit centers can communicate these accomplishments, backed by relevant research from this chapter, to make their case and gain support and resources from funders, local governments, boards of directors, real estate developers, and other potential partners.

Nonprofit centers offer both financial and social benefits to these organizations, their staffs, and their volunteers. There is high nonprofit demand, especially from smaller nonprofits, to move to these co-located sites, and once there, one study found that nearly all tenants are eager to stay there for years. Whether their type is Generalist, Theme-Based, Flexible Space, or Direct Service, nonprofit centers provide a way for nonprofits to become more efficient and effective in pursuing their missions. They also can have a positive impact on their communities; they provide benefits by enhancing the physical environments, and by giving knowledge, skills, and space to nurture the positive development of communities, and even of society.

NOTES

1. Vinokur-Kaplan, D. and McBeath, B. "Co-Located Nonprofit Centers: Tenants' Attraction and Satisfaction." *Nonprofit Management and Leadership, 25:* 77–91, 2014. The number of responding tenants at each site in this study follow, with the response

rates in parentheses: Restoriana, 27/27 (100%); Downtown Nonprofit Center, 49/54 (91%); and The Greenhouse, 42/52 (81%). The overall response rate is 118/133 (89%).

2. Mt. Auburn Associates is a US-based economic development consulting firm with over thirty years of experience in the design, implementation, and evaluation of strategies to promote the economic well-being of individuals, communities, and regions. See www.mtauburnassociates.com. Accessed December 17, 2017.

3. This 2011 study was led by Mt. Auburn Associates, and it was conducted between August 2010 and May 2011 for the NCN. Following is the report's description of the study's design, methodology, and response rates: "The research included a survey of the directors of nonprofit centers (146 responses)[1] [footnote appears following this quote], a survey of tenants of 16 nonprofit centers (167 responses, a 57% response rate), interviews with center directors in 15 centers, four focus groups of center directors, and, finally, five in-depth case studies. The research focused on "intentional" nonprofit centers, facilities that were established with the explicit mission of providing shared spaces and services for nonprofit organizations in the community." Nonprofit Centers Network. *Measuring Collaboration: The Benefits and Impacts of Nonprofit* Centers (Executive Summary). San Francisco: Nonprofit Centers Network, 2011, 3. The following footnote describes this survey's methodology on page 3 of that report: "A total of about 390 surveys were delivered to a very broadly defined universe of centers. The overall response rate was, thus, approximately 43%. However, the total population of operating, intentional nonprofit centers has been calculated by NCN to be about 212 of the 390 surveyed. Of the 146 responses to the survey, 133 were from established centers (the remaining thirteen were from centers in the planning or construction phase). Thus, information on established centers in the survey actually represents closer to 63% of the population of intentional nonprofit centers." NCN itself conducted a second study by email in early 2015, entitled *State of the Shared Space Sector Survey 2015: Changing How Nonprofits Work*. Denver: Nonprofit Centers Network, and its report was written by Katie Edwards and Ryan Long. Some questions were the same as in the 2011 surveys, and others were new. The 2015 results discussed in this chapter are drawn from a survey of executive directors of tenant organizations located in 19 nonprofit centers. The authors wrote that these nineteen nonprofit centers represented "a broad cross-section of buildings both in the US and Canada." Of the 260 executive directors of tenant organizations who received questionnaires, a total of 141 replied, rendering a response rate of 54%. At least one of this volume's authors also had access to an earlier, longer draft of this report, which is noted when appropriate.

4. Nonprofit Centers Network. *Measuring Collaboration: The Benefits and Impacts of Nonprofit Centers (Executive Summary)*. San Francisco: Nonprofit Centers Network, 2011, 10.

5. Nonprofit Centers Network. *Measuring Collaboration: The Benefits and Impacts of Nonprofit Centers (Executive Summary)*. San Francisco: Nonprofit Centers Network, 2011, 9.

6. Nonprofit Centers Network. *Measuring Collaboration: The Benefits and Impacts of Nonprofit Centers (Executive Summary)*. San Francisco: Nonprofit Centers Network, 2011, 9.

7. Adapted from Li, A. "What Is the Organizational Efficiency Factor?" *Houston Chronicle–Small Business*, 2018. Accessed February 26, 2018. https://smallbusiness.chron.com/organizationalefficiency-factor-37839.html .

8. For further details on the role of community animators in nonprofit centers, see Chapter 16: Creating Social Innovation Through Shared Space, Social Bonds, and Community Animation, by Toronto's Centre for Social Innovation.

9. Nonprofit Centers Network. *Measuring Collaboration: The Benefits and Impacts of Nonprofit Centers (Executive Summary)*. San Francisco: Nonprofit Centers Network, 2011, 10.

10. Nonprofit Centers Network. *Measuring Collaboration: The Benefits and Impacts of Nonprofit Centers (Executive Summary)*. San Francisco: Nonprofit Centers Network, 2011, 10.

11. Nonprofit Centers Network. *State of the Shared Space Sector Survey 2015: Changing How Nonprofits Work*. Denver: Nonprofit Centers Network, 2015.

12. Nonprofit Centers Network. *Measuring Collaboration: The Benefits and Impacts of Nonprofit Centers (Executive Summary)*. San Francisco: Nonprofit Centers Network, 2011, 10.

13. Vinokur-Kaplan, D. and McBeath B. "Co-Located Nonprofit Centers: Tenants' Attraction and Satisfaction." *Nonprofit Management and Leadership 25*: 77–91, 2014, 84, Table 2: Importance of Three Dimensions and Nine Items in Influencing Nonprofit Tenants to Co-Locate at Their Nonprofit Centers. The importance ratings mentioned are found on Table 2 therein.

14. The NCN 2011 report notes some differences in the tenants' evaluation of their lease rates: "Interestingly, tenants may be less likely to perceive their rent levels as concessionary than the center director. All but one of the centers from which tenants were surveyed reported that their lease rates were 95 percent or less of market rate and about two-thirds reported that they were 75 percent or less. Yet, only 60 percent of the tenants from these centers who reported knowing about their relative lease rates thought that their rates were lower than current market rates." Nonprofit Centers Network. *Measuring Collaboration: The Benefits and Impacts of Nonprofit Centers (Executive Summary)*. San Francisco: Nonprofit Centers Network, 2011, 11.

15. Nonprofit Centers Network. *Measuring Collaboration: The Benefits and Impacts of Nonprofit Centers (Executive Summary)*. San Francisco: Nonprofit Centers Network, 2011, 11.

16. Nonprofit Centers Network. *Measuring Collaboration: The Benefits and Impacts of Nonprofit Centers (Executive Summary)*. San Francisco: Nonprofit Centers Network, 2011, 11.

17. Nonprofit Centers Network. *Measuring Collaboration: The Benefits and Impacts of Nonprofit Centers (Executive Summary)*. San Francisco: Nonprofit Centers Network, 2011, 12.

18. Percentages were drawn from further analysis of data collected for NCN's 2011 survey but not included in the report. The data was provided by NCN.

19. Nonprofit Centers Network. *Measuring Collaboration: The Benefits and Impacts of Nonprofit Centers (Executive Summary)*. San Francisco: Nonprofit Centers Network, 2011, 8.

20. Nonprofit Centers Network. *Measuring Collaboration: The Benefits and Impacts of Nonprofit Centers (Executive Summary)*. San Francisco: Nonprofit Centers Network, 2011, 12.

21. Nonprofit Centers Network. *Measuring Collaboration: The Benefits and Impacts of Non profit Centers (Executive Summary)*. San Francisco: Nonprofit Centers Network, 2011, 14–15.

22. Nonprofit Centers Network. *State of the Shared Space Sector Survey 2015: Changing How Nonprofits Work*. Denver: Nonprofit Centers Network, 2015, 4.

23. Nonprofit Centers Network. *Measuring Collaboration: The Benefits and Impacts of Nonprofit Centers (Executive Summary)*. San Francisco: Nonprofit Centers Network, 2011, 12.

24. Nonprofit Centers Network. *State of the Shared Space Sector Survey 2015: Changing How Nonprofits Work*. Denver: Nonprofit Centers Network, 2015, 4.

25. Nonprofit Centers Network. *Measuring Collaboration: The Benefits and Impacts of Nonprofit Centers (Executive Summary)*. San Francisco: Nonprofit Centers Network, 2011, 14.

26. Nonprofit Centers Network. *Measuring Collaboration: The Benefits and Impacts of Nonprofit Centers (Executive Summary)*. San Francisco: Nonprofit Centers Network, 2011, 12.

27. Nonprofit Centers Network. *Measuring Collaboration: The Benefits and Impacts of Nonprofit Centers (Executive Summary)*. San Francisco: Nonprofit Centers Network, 2011, 11 and Nonprofit Centers Network. *State of the Shared Space Sector Survey 2015: Changing How Nonprofits Work (Final Report)*. Denver: Nonprofit Centers Network, 2015, 4.

28. Nonprofit Centers Network. *State of the Shared Space Sector Survey 2015: Changing How Nonprofits Work (Final Report)*. Denver: Nonprofit Centers Network, 2015, 4.

29. Nonprofit Centers Network. *State of the Shared Space Sector Survey 2015: Changing How Nonprofits Work (Final Report)*. Denver: Nonprofit Centers Network, 2015, 4.

30. Vinokur-Kaplan, D. and McBeath, B. "Co-Located Nonprofit Centers: Tenants' Attraction and Satisfaction." *Nonprofit Management and Leadership, 25*: 77–91, 2014, 85, Table 3.

31. This score represented the average of two different measures of tenants' level of satisfaction with being at their nonprofit center.

32. Vinokur-Kaplan, D. and McBeath, B. "Co-Located Nonprofit Centers: Tenants' Attraction and Satisfaction," *Nonprofit Management and Leadership, 25*: 77–91, 87.

33. This quote and the following statistics in this paragraph are from Nonprofit Centers Network. *Measuring Collaboration: The Benefits and Impacts of Nonprofit Centers (Executive Summary)*. San Francisco: Nonprofit Centers Network, 2011, 12.

34. Nonprofit Centers Network. *Measuring Collaboration: The Benefits and Impacts of Nonprofit Centers (Executive Summary)*. San Francisco: Nonprofit Centers Network, 2011, 10.

35. Nonprofit Centers Network. *Measuring Collaboration: The Benefits and Impacts of Nonprofit Centers (Executive Summary)*. San Francisco: Nonprofit Centers Network, 2011, 8.

36. Nonprofit Centers Network. *Measuring Collaboration: The Benefits and Impacts of Nonprofit Centers (Executive Summary)*. San Francisco: Nonprofit Centers Network, 2011, 14.

37. Nonprofit Centers Network. *Measuring Collaboration: The Benefits and Impacts of Nonprofit Centers (Executive Summary)*. San Francisco: Nonprofit Centers Network, 2011, 15.

38. Nonprofit Centers Network. *Measuring Collaboration: The Benefits and Impacts of Nonprofit Centers (Executive Summary)*. San Francisco: Nonprofit Centers Network, 2011, 14.

39. Nonprofit Centers Network. *Measuring Collaboration: The Benefits and Impacts of Nonprofit Centers (Executive Summary)*. San Francisco: Nonprofit Centers Network, 2011, 15.

40. Additional analysis of 2011 Nonprofit Centers Network Tenant Survey. Data provided by NCN.

41. Nonprofit Centers Network. *Measuring Collaboration: The Benefits and Impacts of Nonprofit Centers (Executive Summary)*. San Francisco: Nonprofit Centers Network, 2011, 13.

42. Nonprofit Centers Network. *Measuring Collaboration: The Benefits and Impacts of Nonprofit Centers (Executive Summary)*. San Francisco: Nonprofit Centers Network, 2011, 13.

43. Nonprofit Centers Network. *Measuring Collaboration: The Benefits and Impacts of Nonprofit Centers (Executive Summary)*. San Francisco: Nonprofit Centers Network, 2011, 13.

44. Nonprofit Centers Network. *Measuring Collaboration: The Benefits and Impacts of Nonprofit Centers (Executive Summary)*. San Francisco: Nonprofit Centers Network, 2011, 15.

45. Nonprofit Centers Network. *Measuring Collaboration: The Benefits and Impacts of Nonprofit Centers (Executive Summary)*. San Francisco: Nonprofit Centers Network, 2011, 15.

46. Nonprofit Centers Network. *Measuring Collaboration: The Benefits and Impacts of Nonprofit Centers (Executive Summary)*. San Francisco: Nonprofit Centers Network, 2011, 16.

47. Nonprofit Centers Network. *Measuring Collaboration: The Benefits and Impacts of Nonprofit Centers (Executive Summary)*. San Francisco: Nonprofit Centers Network, 2011, 15

48. Nonprofit Centers Network. *Measuring Collaboration: The Benefits and Impacts of Nonprofit Centers (Executive Summary)*. San Francisco: Nonprofit Centers Network, 2011, 15–16.

49. Nonprofit Centers Network. *Measuring Collaboration: The Benefits and Impacts of Nonprofit Centers (Executive Summary)*. San Francisco: Nonprofit Centers Network, 2011, 16.

50. Nonprofit Centers Network. *Measuring Collaboration: The Benefits and Impacts of Nonprofit Centers (Executive Summary)*. San Francisco: Nonprofit Centers Network, 2011, 16.

51. Nonprofit Centers Network. *Measuring Collaboration: The Benefits and Impacts of Nonprofit Centers (Executive Summary)*. San Francisco: Nonprofit Centers Network, 2011, 16.

52. Nonprofit Centers Network. *Measuring Collaboration: The Benefits and Impacts of Nonprofit Centers (Executive Summary)*. San Francisco: Nonprofit Centers Network, 2011, 17.

53. Nonprofit Centers Network. *Measuring Collaboration: The Benefits and Impacts of Nonprofit Centers (Executive Summary)*. San Francisco: Nonprofit Centers Network, 2011, 15.

54. Nonprofit Centers Network. *Measuring Collaboration: The Benefits and Impacts of Nonprofit Centers (Executive Summary)*. San Francisco: Nonprofit Centers Network, 2011, 16.

55. See Vinokur-Kaplan D. and Dobbie, D. S. "Nonprofit Co-Locations as Capacity-Building Tools for Communities." Paper presented at the 31st Annual Conference of Association for Research on Nonprofit Organizations and Voluntary Action, Montreal, Quebec, November 20, 2003.

PART 3
REAL ESTATE, FUNDING, AND FINANCING

6 The Development Process

Nonprofit real estate projects face a chicken-and-egg problem: How does a project get off the ground without a site but how can an organization find a site and launch a project without money? Shared space projects confront the same difficulty: the need to raise money before a project is fully formed to fuel the early stages of planning. Having sufficient resources to begin a real estate project provides legitimacy; it inspires confidence, builds momentum, and allows the project partners to advance to implementation.

This chapter looks at the real estate development process through the lens of how the money—grants, debt, and investments—come together to get a project done. While seemingly daunting at first, many nonprofit centers go on to success. Indeed, look at the fact of more than 475 centers operating across North America with 230 in the pipeline. Organizations of all sizes and budgets—in rural, suburban, and urban places alike—make shared space projects happen, from small leased space to larger, stand-alone buildings. While every shared space project doesn't need its own new ground-up construction building or a substantial renovation, that is the general model that we employ here to illustrate how all the financial components come together.

This chapter outlines how new projects come to fruition and the importance of early money to seed the planning process and feasibility analyses. It outlines the steps in the purchase or lease and renovation process as well as the range of expertise needed. It then discusses the capital campaign, debt tools, and other recent financial products that organizations employ to achieve their projects. Nonprofit shared space projects benefit from a wide variety of sources of capital, both commercial and nonprofit, which positions them to raise the necessary funding and implement financially sustainable projects.

REAL ESTATE AND MONEY: HOW SHARED PROJECTS ARE DIFFERENT

How are shared space projects different from other nonprofit facility development? Nonprofit facility development for individual organizations is a well-documented field with trained consultants, support organizations, foundations, real estate developers, and even real estate brokers with specialized nonprofit practices.[1] Real estate academic programs, historically focused on traditional commercial real estate development, are also now entering the sphere of community development real estate, of which nonprofit facilities are a component. And the affordable housing field has a well-developed infrastructure with an academic backbone, research, tax incentives at the federal and state levels (in the US), dedicated funding channels, and special financing tools.

Nonprofit centers are a subset in this wider real estate development field and have been underdocumented as a trend in the field. Indeed, this book is a first start to memorialize the methodology of the nonprofit center. The development of nonprofit centers is both unique and at times more complicated than conventional single-organization projects because of how they come together. While much of this chapter can apply to general nonprofit facility development, we have highlighted considerations unique to shared space projects.

Two areas that particularly distinguish shared space projects from standard nonprofit real estate projects are (i) the capitalization strategy—how the project raises money—which is dictated, in part, by the ownership structure, and (ii) the design, which aims to foster collaboration and interaction among staff, clients, and other users. The design elements are dealt with separately and in detail in Chapter 13: The Design Process.

HOW ARE SHARED SPACE PROJECTS FUNDED?

Nonprofit centers average around 30,000 sq. ft.[2] Capitalizing a project of this scale is a major undertaking. How are shared space projects funded? The answer, in short, is in myriad of ways. In its study completed in 2011, and updated in 2015, the Nonprofit Centers Network examined how nonprofit centers are created. Figure 6.1 illustrates the diversity of resources that shared space projects draw on. These include charitable equity investments (grants and donations), financing (conventional and soft debt, discussed in more detail in the following text), and existing assets (organizations draw on their own organizational resources such as unrestricted funds, current real estate portfolio, or endowments), or a combination of these sources.

All nonprofit real estate, including shared space projects, is funded by a combination of three types of capital: *equity, soft debt,* and *debt. Equity* is money that is a long-term investment in the building, and, unlike a loan, there is no interest paid on it. Equity does not get repaid until the building is sold. Equity is only repaid after all debt is repaid. If the building is ever sold in the future, the equity is only repaid if the sales price is enough to pay all debt and have excess to repay the equity. Any such repayment above the equity amount invested is the organization's return on investment (ROI) or profit. Since a sale is rarely anticipated for community facilities because of the long-term mission of the space this ROI calculation is generally not a significant part of the feasibility process.

Equity

Equity includes donated assets. Therefore, the market rate value of a donated building is considered to be equity. For example, if a foundation donates a building

Sample Shared Space Project, Capital Stack, $7 million project (purchase and renovation)

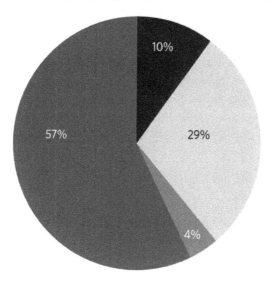

■ Organizational Reserves, 10%, $700,000

Conventional Debt, 29%, $2,000,000

■ Soft Debt, 4%, $300,000

■ Grants and Contributions, 57%, $4,000,000

FIGURE 6.1 This pie chart illustrates the sample sources for a shared space project (the capital stack) including organizational reserves, conventional debt, soft debt, and grants and contributions. While each project is different, this shows a reasonable proportionate share of each source including debt, organizational reserves, and contributions. *Source: Sarah M. Eisinger and China Brotsky.*

with an appraised value of $1 million dollars, then the project has $1 million in equity. Note that if this hypothetical project cost $4 million for total development costs, then you will have raised 25% of the project as equity. If the organization raises grants for the project, or in the cases that an organization has reserves that it can invest in the project, these funds would also be considered the organization's equity in the project. For their equity investment, some donors seek a return on their investment in the form of social returns, expecting the building to produce some sort of social outcome.

Debt

Debt is loaned to the development project and repaid from net operating income (NOI). NOI is the excess funds projected after subtracting operating expenses from income. NOI is the most important calculation for determining financing capacity because it dictates how much debt the project can support. There is both conventional debt and soft debt that comes into the project. Payments for conventional debt (e.g., bank debt) are made before payments on soft debt. Soft debt is debt that does not need to be repaid until after the conventional debt is repaid. Types of soft debt include subordinate loans and tax credit-backed debt, which will be discussed later in this chapter in the section The Role of Debt in Shared Space Projects.

Creating a new shared space requires capital to galvanize partners and pursue real estate. While it is true that some shared space projects don't rely on capital-intensive real estate projects, the focus here is on the projects that do require resources for a new building or to expand or renovate an existing space.

WHERE THE MONEY GOES: PHASES OF A REAL ESTATE PROJECT

Real estate projects have distinct phases that all require capital at varying levels. The phases of the shared space project are summarized in Figure 6.2: predevelopment, the real estate transaction, design and construction, operational planning, and occupancy and operations, all sequential phases that build on one another. Similar to all types of commercial real estate projects, capital expenditures start slowly and ramp up over time, tapering off as the space opens and stabilizes. The largest expenditures for any real estate project, for-profit or nonprofit, is the real estate acquisition and the design and construction phases.

Predevelopment

The predevelopment phase is the starting point for the real estate project when the concept is developed, and the feasibility is tested. Feasibility comes in various forms—testing the market for need for the project, financial feasibility in terms of how much the project will cost and the probability of reaching that goal, and design feasibility in terms of how the project will look and how large it should be.[3] Thorough feasibility work touching on each of these aspects is critical to test the viability of the project and to rally support. Feasibility analysis should be a formal process, led by a third party, either a consultant, board member, or other volunteer. Resources are required for this phase to pay for feasibility as well as team assembly, bringing on the team—consultants, lawyers, real estate experts, designers, and others.

The Real Estate Transaction: Site Acquisition

The real estate transaction is the process to secure a site, which is thoroughly discussed in Chapter 7: Finding a Home. In brief, shared spaces can pursue several kinds of sites including sites that are on the open market, called "market-rate" sites, advertised within the normal channels of commercial real estate. More unique sites and often the ones that will most suit nonprofit real estate projects are the "off-market" opportunities. These off-market opportunities are comprised

Shared Space Development Process

Phase I Predevelopment	Phase II Real Estate Transaction	Phase III Design & Construction	Phase IV Operational Planning	Phase V Occupancy & Operations
Concept, market feasibility, team assembly, ownership/ partnership development, capital campaign planning, preliminary design	Identify site and assume site control, secure funding and financing, capital campaign implementation, finalize construction team	Oversee construction team, secure donors with site visits and hard hat tours, finalize leases with anchor tenants	Vendor procurement, property management, staffing, organizational development to support program delivery and collaboration	Doors open! Working out the kinks and construction punch list; tenants move in

Design Phases

Concept Design	Schematic Design	Design Develop- ment	Con- struction Docu- ments and Bidding	Construction Documents and Bidding	Close Out

FIGURE 6.2 This figure shows an overview of the development and design process including the five phases of a shared space project from inception to opening. From a cash perspective, resources for a purchase and capital project are front-loaded to the early phases and then even out over time. As discussed in the chapter, a lease arrangement will be less capital intensive. Parallel to the development process are the industry-standard design phases to highlight what will be going on in the design and construction side of the project. *Source: Design phases adapted from AIA materials by authors.*

of decommissioned public-sector buildings (fire houses, schools, hospitals, etc.), sacred spaces (churches, rectories, etc.), and other properties owned by private developers who are seeking nontraditional buyers and uses. For the financial component of site acquisition, market-rate projects follow the same timeline as all other commercial projects: if it is a hot commercial market, the site could move quickly, and therefore, sufficient resources need to be lined up to secure the purchase or lease.

Off-market opportunities have a generally more forgiving timeline, particularly if it's a public-sector building that may be put out for an open application process (through a Request for Proposals or Qualifications). Off-market opportunities are not necessarily better than those in the traditional market as transactions for these sites can often move slowly. Additionally, off-market sites can be complicated to develop (think of the example of reusing a school building and its attendant challenges). However, these sites can be more exciting and interesting and are an excellent source for shared spaces.

An early decision that any nonprofit center project will need to make is to determine whether it is going to lease a property or buy land or a building. Leasing is advantageous financially in that projects don't necessarily need to conduct a major capital campaign to raise money for a down payment and construction. On the other hand, a lease will require a sizable security deposit, and the lease rate will most likely escalate annually. Leases often require the lessee to contribute to fixing up the space for their needs. Leasing can require ongoing cash year over year. Moreover, leasing space makes it harder for organizations to attract donors and supporters as the lease feels more temporary.

On the other hand, a lease offers organizations flexibility and the opportunity to test a space and the shared space model. The lease is a valid and appealing opportunity for these reasons. Buying is more complicated, involving raising funds to acquire the site and renovate or construct the space. Buying generally necessitates a capital campaign, described in more detail in the following paragraphs. This option, of course, provides permanence and stability, and after the initial capital raise, operating costs should be evident and stable.

Each option – leasing or buying -- presents both challenges and opportunities, and no one option is better than the other. The nonprofit center partners will need to decide which option is right for them and which option affords the most site opportunities in their local market.

Design and Construction

On the design and construction side, even if an organization inherits a building or leases space, it will likely require some upgrades or renovation and therefore financial resources. Think of the common example of the decommissioned public school that will now become a nonprofit center: the entire use of the building will need to change from classrooms to the new nonprofit center use—either offices or program space—and the space will need to be reimagined to accommodate the new users. Many older repurposed buildings require environmental remediation or abatement, upgrades to comply with updated building code requirements—seismic regulations, the Americans with Disabilities Act (ADA) (or equivalent), replacement of obsolete building systems, and other modernization required to comply with new laws. These modifications all require substantial capital resources.

For more on the design criteria and the unique design considerations of shared space projects, see Chapter 13: The Design Process.

Operational Planning and Occupancy

The last two phases of the project, operational planning and occupancy, take place once the site is acquired and the construction project is underway. From a resource-mobilization stand point, these phases are not as resource-intensive as the first phases. Often, a capital campaign will still be actively underway, but the main spike in expenses is earlier in the project. During operational planning, the project is spending monies on staffing up, purchasing technology, and planning to open. Leasing also takes place during this time as early commitments, particularly from anchor tenants (the major, larger tenants who will occupy the majority of the space), are important for cash flow as well as to secure any financing. During the early occupancy period, there are many start-up costs, but these ongoing expenses should level out. For more on the operations of shared spaces, see Chapter 15: Facilities That Facilitate.

IMPLEMENTATION: THE DEVELOPMENT PRO FORMA

Now that the phases of the project and the categories of expenses associated with each phase are understood, this next section discusses the project implementation—how the project is financially viable and the sources of money that fuel it.

The real estate development pro forma is a financial document that portrays the entire project and includes sources and uses of funds, operating expenses, and projected multiyear cash flow. It generally includes the following real estate development categories:

- Acquisition: purchase or lease;
- Capital budget: construction budget; and
- Operations: revenues and expenses.

Each of these three categories have many subcategories, and elements that are unique to shared space projects, described in Table 6.1. The proforma is a set of spreadsheets detailing the entire project costs: the acquisition, construction, and operations.

Nonprofit center financial projections are different than traditional real estate projects because they have added expenses including staff to manage collaboration and other programming expenses, which is illustrated in Figure 6.3. Even though nonprofit shared spaces have extra costs for programming, the use of nonprofit sources of capital, along with commercial debt and lower property taxes, mean that nonprofit centers can often cost less to run than commercial property. Nonprofit centers can therefore usually support a mission focus and lower, more stable rents.

FIRST MONEY IN—SEED MONEY FOR PREDEVELOPMENT

The hardest money to identify in a shared space project is the early money, the money that an organization may need to raise before there is a site and a defined set of project partners or tenants. This fact is largely true in all commercial real estate projects but harder in the shared spaces arena because of the complexity of governance and ownership and because shared space projects don't normally attract traditional real estate investors who seek an ROI. Before a project can attract money,

Table 6.1 Sample Proforma Categories in a Shared Space Project

Category	General Description	How Shared Spaces Projects Are Different
Acquisition	Purchase price or Lease obligation (rent, security deposit)	Shared space projects may not have any acquisition expenses if a building or space is acquired through a donor, foundation, or public entity or if a lease receives an ongoing rent subsidy.
Capital	Hard costs—construction costs bricks and mortar items + Soft costs—architecture and engineering team, legal counsel, capital campaign consultant, real estate consultant, etc. + Furniture, fixtures, and equipment—nonfixed items like technology equipment, kitchen appliances, conference room furniture, etc.	The construction budget includes general costs including hard and soft costs and furniture, fixtures and equipment. Shared space projects typically have additional consultants and advisors to implement the capital campaign, support real estate services, secure public sector dollars and advance organizational goals for the ownership structure and develop programmatic plans. These additional expenses add both more cost and complexity to the project.
Operations	Revenues—rent Expenses Reserves	Operations include revenues such as rental income from tenants. Shared space projects can enjoy varied revenue streams including from events, conference facilities, and shared services (information technology, reception, shared staff, etc.). Expenses are typically utilities, rent (if applicable), taxes (if applicable), insurance, property, management, maintenance contracts, etc. Other expenses include shared space staff such as center directors, program, marketing and administrative staff. Reserves—both operating and replacement—are funds set aside after debt has been serviced and all other expenses have been paid. Reserves can be placed in "restricted funds" or set aside in other vehicles to help bridge cash flow crunches, pay for deferred maintenance, improve tenant spaces when leases expire and make major capital investments (new boilers, etc.)

Notes: The financial model is broken out into three categories: Acquisition, Capital, and Operations. This sample pro forma outline includes all of these categories and many of the expected expenses in each. The chart also explains how shared space projects are different in each of the categories from purely commercial real estate.

Source: Sarah M. Eisinger and China Brotsky.

Shared Space vs. Conventional Real Estate
How the Revenues and Expenses Stack Up

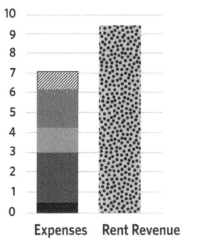

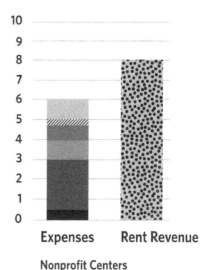

Traditional Commercial Real Estate

Nonprofit Centers

- Organizational and sharing management
- Property & business taxes
- Debt
- Building management
- Facility operating expenses
- Reserves
- Rent revenue

FIGURE 6.3 This figure shows the different revenues and expenses of traditional commercial real estate versus that of shared space projects. On the revenue side, commercial properties have the ability to charge market rate rents and to escalate rents more aggressively over time, especially in strong markets. Revenue potential is more modest for shared spaces as they seek to provide stable rent to nonprofit organizations. Escalations, while common, may be more modest as shared spaces often have a mission to provide affordable space. On the expense side, while both types of real estate have normal property expenses, shared spaces have added expenses to cover program activities and additional staffing. But nonprofit centers often have lower debt and property tax costs. *Source: Shelley Hamilton, MarinSpace, adapted by Sarah M. Eisinger and China Brotsky*

the first hurdle to figure out is: *Who will buy (or lease) the property?* In other words, *Who will bear the risk on the project?* Without a clear sense of the ownership structure and the partnership agreement among the key players, no project can get off the ground. These ownership and governance questions are dealt with in detail in Chapter 10: Who Drives Decisions.

Assuming there is a lead organization or entity who is championing the project, the endeavor needs seed capital to sustain itself. Typically, seed capital for shared

Table 6.2 Sources of Funding: Seed Money and Beyond

Sector	Sources of Funding
Public	• Mayoral and other municipal offices (local economic development or housing agencies) • State or provincial sources (economic development agencies, dedicated facilities funds) • Federal sources
Private	• Individual philanthropists or small donors • Family foundations • Community foundations • Charitable foundations • United Ways and other nonprofit granting entities • Loans from nonprofit community development intermediaries and Community Development Corporations • Business Improvement Districts or other local partnerships • Corporate gifts • Organizational reserves

Notes: Shared space projects enjoy the ability to identify funds from many different sources, not just traditional sources like banks. Sources can come from the public sector at all levels and from the private and philanthropic sectors including foundations and other donors. They can also access traditional sources like banks. Most shared space projects need to pursue funding from multiple sources.

Source: Sarah M. Eisinger and China Brotsky.

space projects comes from public, private, and internal organizational sources. Table 6.2 summarizes sources for seed capital and beyond. Support is generally from local sources as nonprofit centers typically serve a local audience and real estate is inherently local. It has been our experience that it is difficult to attract national funding unless there is a previous relationship with a funder, if the mission of the nonprofit center reaches beyond a local area, or if the organization has a broad geographic footprint.

Seed money for shared space projects is used for a variety of purposes, notably to build the project infrastructure, including bringing on a paid project team. It is also used to make the case for a project including the cost of preparation of a business plan, feasibility study, or concept plan. While there is no precise ideal amount of seed money, projects can get off the ground with grants or investment of as little as $15,000 to $50,000. Ongoing financial support is key to fueling the project advancement, and a clear sense of where the resources will come from over time is critical to a project's success.

Uses of Seed Money: Feasibility Study

One of the first uses of seed money is to cover the commissioning of a case of support including a feasibility study. Making the case for a project is critical and requires money to pay for staff or consultants. Projects that skip the step of testing feasibility can fail because they haven't taken the time to identify the demand for the project, a compelling social purpose and potential funding sources. The feasibility process also serves a secondary purpose of building consensus and momentum for a project; if the feasibility process is thorough, varied stakeholders have input and therefore gain some "ownership" over the project. Finally, understanding the demand for space and services in a given community gives a project its purpose. Feasibility studies should answer several core questions across three main areas.

Market Feasibility

At the early stage, the market feasibility looks at the need for the new space, who will use it, and why they need the new space. It should answer the following questions:

1. Who needs space, how much space do they need and when will they need it?
2. Who are the main interested parties in creating and occupying the space?

Financial Feasibility

At this stage, the financial feasibility should paint a broad-stroke, high-level financial picture including how much the project might cost to build and how much it might cost to operate including income from rents and operational expenses.

1. How much do these organizations or individuals currently pay for the space that they inhabit?
2. How much could these potential tenants/users pay for space?
3. How much will the project cost to purchase, build/renovate?

Design Feasibility

At this early stage, the design feasibility should illustrate how large the project might be, where it might ideally be located, and what how it might "look and feel."

1. What should happen inside the building (uses and functions)?
2. What is the desired location for the project?
3. What are other design requirements expressed by the potential users?

Figure 6.4 defines the three kinds of plans that an organization can commission. There is significant overlap in these plans but there are differences, and organizations should determine which plan is best for their project.

A feasibility study can cost anywhere from $15,000 to $50,000 or more depending on the scope and depth of analysis, who is conducting the study (a firm, individual consultant, or volunteer), and the geographic market (regional, city, town, etc.). Alternatively, projects can develop a concept plan that might come before a true feasibility test or a business plan, which provide detailed analysis on the business

Feasibility Study, Concept Plans and Business Plans—What's the Difference?

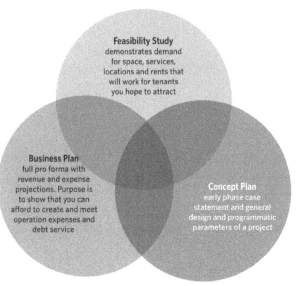

Feasibility Study demonstrates demand for space, services, locations and rents that will work for tenants you hope to attract

Business Plan full pro forma with revenue and expense projections. Purpose is to show that you can afford to create and meet operation expenses and debt service

Concept Plan early phase case statement and general design and programmatic parameters of a project

FIGURE 6.4 There are many ways to test to the viability of a nonprofit shared space project. Feasibility studies, concept plans, and business plans, while all different, generally all lay out the case for the project and show how it can be viable, based on the mission, the program goals and the financial model. *Source: Sarah M. Eisinger and China Brotsky.*

model and financial projections for the project. Business plans follow a similar cost range. As always, intrepid nonprofit organizations have succeeded in securing pro bono support for feasibility studies from graduate school teams, volunteer board members or other community advocates. With any pro bono services, it is important to set clear guidelines and deadlines and to ensure that researchers have relevant experience in the nonprofit sector and with the complexity of the shared space model.

Finally, the feasibility study should be considered a living document, and it should be added to and refined over time as more information is gathered on the project. For example, description of the core tenants, detailed financial projections, or design renderings and site information could be added as they come into focus.

Uses of Seed Money: Build the Team

A second cost area in the predevelopment phase is the assembling the external team to support the internal management team. The core business of a nonprofit organization is to carry out its nonprofit mission whether it is to provide direct services, training, education, advocacy, or something else. Real estate projects require a completely different set of skills and competencies and these are often best acquired through external help. The consultants in real estate projects vary, but having an exceptional team who is brought on at the right time, usually early in the project, is absolutely essential to a project's success. One of the biggest mistakes is to try to "go it alone" without the right team in place. Even organizations whose board of directors has relevant real estate expertise often need unbiased outside paid counsel to propel the project forward.

So, what does the right team mean? And how much does it cost? The following list summarizes the range of functions in a commercial[4] real estate project. It is important to note that not all these roles need to be filled on every project nor does every project require help in each of these areas. Some projects are simply less complex. As a general rule, however, projects will need to address all of these functions either internally or externally through hired consultants or volunteers. The core team functions are as follows:

- Legal: If there is any kind of real estate transaction as part of the project (purchase, lease, sale, condominium, transfer of deed, sublease, or assignment), legal counsel with credible, relevant real estate experience is highly recommended, if not required. Nonprofit experience is also important.
- Real Estate Procurement and Leasing: Projects require real estate services that can be addressed by a variety of providers including brokers and real estate consultants. Bringing on these team members will depend on whether the project already owns or controls a site[5] or if a search for a new site is required. It is recommended to solicit professional real estate services if any exploration of a real estate purchase or lease will be undertaken.
- Project Management: If any design and construction is required for the project, a best practice is to hire a third-party project manager or fee-developer.
- Design Team: An architect, interior designer, and engineer to provide design services including space programming, test fits, and concept drawings and construction documents.
- Others: As the project advances, there may be other project members required including a capital campaign consultant to develop and manage the campaign, Leadership in Energy and Environmental Design (LEED) consultant to manage environmental sustainability components as part of the design team, and a consultant to manage public-sector grant procurement. Other consultants include a commissioning agent, cost estimator during the construction phases, and specialty consultants, usually subcontractors to the architect.

We offer special guidance on two key roles. A best practice is to hire third-party project management at the outset—this role oversees the entire project: site acquisition, overall team assembly, and budgeting. They should have general real estate experience and ideally experience in the unique complexities of nonprofit real estate where cash management is challenging due to many funding streams and the overall timing of funding. A common pitfall is to forego hiring an external project manager for the project, and projects can get into trouble without this expertise. Other important early hires include a real estate attorney to evaluate the transaction and possibly a developer, who can serve in the project management role.

Organizations can fall into a common trap of hiring an architect or designer at the outset of the project. While architects have excellent experience in evaluating buildings and designing the space, and they become integral to the project eventually, approaching the overall project from the design perspective is not the right place to start. Because of the social mission of these projects, the driver must be the overall purpose or mission of the project; the architecture and site should ultimately *support* the mission, not the other way around. An architect, broker, or a real estate developer can help determine the ideal size and locational criteria. The design team can help with site evaluation but should not play a driving role until after site control.

RAISING THE EQUITY: THE CAPITAL CAMPAIGN

Once the feasibility test is met and the project team is hired, it is time for the project to turn its attention to the capital campaign, another cost center but also the main revenue generator of the equity portion of the project. Again, it is assumed here that a building is not gifted to the project and that the project partners will have to raise some level of capital to execute the project. This section addresses the following: setting targets, making the case, how to do it jointly, and who leads capital campaigns.

How much equity is required for the project depends on many factors—how large the facility will be, if the project requires substantial renovations or construction costs, who the owners are, and what the revenue sources will be. It is hard to say that there is a rule of thumb for how much equity is needed as it varies from project to project. Suffice to say, the more equity a project can raise, the better positioned it will be for long-term sustainability. With more equity, the project can afford the capital improvements, and it can avoid becoming overleveraged with debt which is ultimately a savings to tenants. At a minimum for a purchase scenario, a project will need money for a down payment and additional funds available for the ongoing project team costs. A best practice is to identify 25% to 50% of a project's total cost to purchase property and seek financing. Of course, there are many exceptions to this rule: Is the property gifted to the shared space owners? Is it a donated building from the public sector? Is there a benevolent developer involved who may subsidize the development? Organizations must have sufficient liquid funds to pursue a site; without funds, the project loses momentum and credibility. Capital campaigns are the main method for raising these equity funds.

Capital campaigns for shared spaces run a standard arc of activity including assessing feasibility and prospecting, setting goals, cultivation, the quiet phase, and then the more public phase. In a shared space project, the capital campaign structure is similar but with the added complexity of sometimes being executed jointly by multiple organizations. Setting aside the constraints of joint campaigns for the time being, shared space projects have several key questions to address in a capital campaign.

Setting a capital campaign target is a first task, which involves understanding the entire capital project costs. The tool for determining the capital campaign goal is the development pro formas previously discussed and detailed in Table 6.1. Capital project budgets encompass the acquisition of the property, the renovation or building of the space, outfitting the space, and an endowment or operating reserve fund to help with ongoing operational sustainability and to help maintain affordable rents.

Setting a Capital Campaign Target

Once the capital budget is determined, a capital campaign advisor (either internal or an external vendor) can conduct a feasibility study to set a reasonable campaign goal given the advisor's analysis of the organization, the project partners, the case for the project, the community, and competing local priorities. Digging in, capital project budgets are made up of hard and soft costs and furniture, fixtures, and equipment. Hard costs are "tangible assets that you need to acquire to complete your construction project."[6] These include land costs or the purchase of a building, site preparation work, and renovation or construction costs. Soft costs are personnel, and financing costs, including predevelopment due diligence, legal and financing fees, design and engineering, and permitting fees, among others, as outlined in Table 6.1. The third category, furniture, fixtures and equipment, is just that—the depreciating, nonattached items in the space (e.g., conference room tables and audio-video equipment). Together, these costs constitute the total capital budget. Capital campaigns are difficult to execute without site control although some organizations succeed in raising initial resources based on a good concept and clear project mission.

Case for Support

A central goal of a well-organized capital campaign is to establish a "case for support" or a "case statement." This written piece (or manifesto) establishes the language and messages of the project and clearly communicates the outcomes that the project will achieve. Cases for shared space projects are sometimes difficult to make; after all, a shared space project can be perceived as simply an umbrella organization that houses the organizations who help people. The shared space is seemingly removed from direct impact. However, shared spaces can serve as an important part of the ecosystem of a local social sector, stabilizing nonprofit occupancy in high-quality space and providing opportunities for direct service coordination, shared services, and collaboration. Making this case in a compelling way is a central step in setting up the campaign. Additional resources on this topic are in Chapter 5: Making the Case.

Joint Capital Campaigns

Running joint capital campaigns is complicated with lots of potential upside. In fact, the Stanford Social Innovation Review recently featured a piece on joint collaboration, citing the opportunity for joint campaigns:

Fundraising together, charities can reach goals and create the sort of impact they might never be able to achieve by themselves. Through collaboration, they can expose their organizations to new potential donors and supporters, and experience heightened public awareness around their mission and work. Meanwhile, donors are looking for organizations to work together and bring in more of the community so that their support can have more far-reaching impact.[7]

It goes on to discuss the keys pillars of successful joint campaigns: trust and shared values and culture; with these considerations in place, organizations can achieve "transformative results."

While shared space projects have the benefit of mining a deeper well of potential donors, they also have the challenge of participating organizations tripping over one another, especially in smaller markets. Some project partners even fear that other organizations will poach donors from each other. Additionally, shared space projects have the difficulty of overcoming a perception that they do not create direct impact, as previously discussed. While the data prove this wrong (see the impact research in Chapter 5: Making the Case), it remains challenging to clearly articulate the potential benefits. Organizations like the Al Sigl Community of Agencies in Rochester, New York, and the Children and Family Services Center in Charlotte, North Carolina, have successfully conducted joint campaigns and ably surmounted these challenges. Best practices include writing clear agreements between partners before launching a capital campaign that articulate rules for how to approach shared donors and how to avoid the poaching issue. These agreements also establish fundraising goals for each organization.

The critical decisions in a joint campaign include: Is there a relationship between funds raised and percentage of ownership in the facility, especially in the case of shared equity ownership? If organizations do not raise the amount agreed on, what will be the consequences? If one of the joint campaign organizations goes out of business or leaves the venture, what happens to their contributions? Finally, clearly articulating community benefits from the outset can rally supporters. Many organizations have overcome these issues and gone on to manage successful joint capital campaigns.

Who Manages Capital Campaigns

A thoughtful capital campaign managed by a professional fundraiser gives donors and other community members confidence in the project. While it's not always necessary to have a third-party vendor, having someone to keep the campaign on track, set key milestones, and maintain consistent messaging positions the campaign for success. Employing the use of an external capital campaign advisor is a best practice. Unless an organization has in-house development staff with capital project development experience, the authors recommend consultation with a consultant. Both national consulting firms and local consultants can provide excellent services for a shared space capital campaign and ideally should have some demonstrated experience in raising funds in the shared space arena.

MONEY FOR SITE ACQUISITION AND DESIGN AND CONSTRUCTION PHASES

Following the concept development phase, hiring the team and developing the capital campaign, the financial requirements for the project explode and rapidly accelerate. Organizations need money readily available to pursue a site—a lease or purchase of a real estate site as previously discussed. They also need to have an-chor tenants lined up before pursuing any financing as banks and other lenders want to see a demonstration of the ability to pay back debt through secured leases. (Anchor tenants are the larger tenants who make the early commitment to the pro-ject. Owners secure this "commitment" through a memorandum of understanding [MOU] or letter of intent [LOI] process; a formal lease obligating all parties comes later on in the process when the project is further underway).

Organizations will then need resources to pay for the improvements to the pro-perty, whether it is new construction or a renovation. The design and construction period can be long, intense, and demanding of resources. There is no rule for how long projects can take, but the more complex the project is, the more expensive and time consuming it will be. The old adage "Time is money" is never truer than in real estate. The following section outlines the possible sources of funds besides the equity raised through a capital campaign that shared space projects have utilized.

Financing: The Role of Debt in Shared Space Projects

Debt financing often plays an important role in facility projects. As in traditional commercial real estate, debt can be utilized at many stages of the project for working capital, construction, bridge, and long-term mortgage financing. Bond financing is also a form of debt financing often utilized in the nonprofit sector for real es-tate projects. Debt is an especially important tool when nonprofit organizations rely on the public sector or other sources of contributions to fund their projects and when the timing of this infusion of resources doesn't match up to the timing needs of the project. Bridge financing can be critical in that circumstance. On the other hand, nonprofit facility projects and shared space projects must demonstrate the ability to service debt through revenues (rent and other income) to acquire any debt and mitigate risk. Debt financing for the nonprofit sector is a well-documented subsector of the nonprofit field.[8] This section will only touch on the typical sources employed by shared space projects as well as emerging new sources and the unique considerations for shared space projects. Key terms (from the Nonprofit Finance Fund) are defined as:

- Working Capital: The amount of liquidity (unencumbered cash and cash equivalents such as donated services) an organization has on hand or accessible (e.g., through a line of credit). Working capital covers predictable periods when cash outflows exceed cash inflows due to seasonal or cyclical volatility.
- Construction Loan: A loan, usually short-term, which is made to finance construction.
- Bridge Loan: Loan made on a short-term basis in anticipation of being paid out by permanent or long-term funding.
- Mortgage: Security instrument by which the borrower (mortgagor) gives the lender (mortgagee) a lien on property as collateral for the repayment of a loan.
- Bond: A bond is a debt investment in which an investor loans money to an en-tity (typically corporate or governmental) that borrows the funds for a defined

period of time at a variable or fixed interest rate. Bonds are used by companies, municipalities, states, and sovereign governments to raise money and finance a variety of projects and activities.

- Debt Service: Payments on debt incurred by the project.
- Operating Expenses: Day to day facility operating expenses not including debt services.
- Reserves: Resources that are regularly set aside every year for repairs, tenant improvements, and the possibility of future cash flow shortfalls.
- Debt Service Coverage Ratio: The ratio of projected annual operating income to operating expenses before debt service that is available to pay for debt service. Note that lenders will require that the project be able to generate an excess of income over operating expenses and debt service.

Financing Source: Community Development Financial Institutions

A program of the US Treasury Department, a certified Community Development Financial Institution (CDFI) is a

specialized financial institution that works in market niches that are underserved by traditional financial institutions. CDFIs provide a unique range of financial products and services in economically distressed target markets, such as mortgage financing for low-income and first-time homebuyers and not-for-profit developers, flexible underwriting and risk capital for needed community facilities, and technical assistance, commercial loans and investments to small start-up or expanding businesses in low-income areas. CDFIs include regulated institutions such as community development banks and credit unions, and non-regulated institutions such as loan and venture capital funds.[9]

The Nonprofit Finance Fund, Local Initiatives Support Corpration (LISC), Seedco, Illinois Facilities Fund (now IFF), the Northern California Community Loan Fund (NCCLF), and countless other local CDFIs should be a first stop for any shared space project. While CDFIs provide lending, some also offer grants, technical assistance, and other real estate and capacity-building services that can benefit a shared space project, along with deep local knowledge and networks.

Financing Source: Traditional Banks

Especially in this prolonged period of low interest rates (though changing now), debt financing from more traditional sources can be attractive for shared space projects. Many nonprofit organizations already maintain banking relationships, and these relationships can grow to support a shared space project through debt financing. Local banks might compete to finance a project because of a pre-existing, trusting relationship and they may offer more attractive terms than other sources.

Any organization pursuing financing, whether conventional or otherwise, will have to demonstrate creditworthiness, thresholds that an organization will have to pass to qualify for a loan. Box 6.1 illustrates the key criteria that lenders use to determine an organization's creditworthiness as they are pursuing debt. In sum, organizations will need to have the adequate organizational resources to pay back its debts as demonstrated by stable revenue and project feasibility. An organization should borrow money from a position of strength rather than seeing debt as a resource of last resort.

Box 6.1 Determining Creditworthiness

♣ Stable revenue sources

♣ Financial feasibility of project

♣ Debt of service coverage

♣ Strong financial position

♣ Market need

♣ Service delivery capacity

♣ Cash reserves or assets

♣ Successful fundraising history

Source: Capital Incubator. http://www.capitalincubator.org/

New Funding Vehicles—Emerging Sources of Funding

One of the strengths of nonprofit real estate projects is the ability to draw on a range of funding tools available to them. This section touches on impact investing products as well as tax credits. The maturing impact-investing field has some applicability to shared space projects and requires advanced financial acumen. These tools are typically useful for larger projects, projects in the $1 million-plus capital project.

Social bonds or *pay for success* are relatively new in the US and Canada and may have some relevance going forward for shared space projects especially in the human services field.

Pay for Success is a creative approach to funding social services, with potential to bring new, significant, and reliable resources to proven preventative programs. In a Pay for Success deal, private investors pay for preventative or interventional social services up front. Should these services deliver their intended results, governments then reimburse the investors with a return on their investment, while saving money on what they otherwise would have spent. It is a model designed to both improve outcomes and reduce costs.[10]

The first social bond was made in New York City in 2013 focused on recidivism among juvenile offenders[11]; in Canada, Alberta completed the first social investment bond in 2014.[12] A similar model is a community bond, which offers a large number of small investors the opportunity to participate in the financing of a project. A successful application of this tool so far in the shared space arena is in Toronto with the Centre for Social Innovation (see Chapter 16: Creating Social Innovation Through Shared Space, Social Bonds and Community Animation). This tool is only now available in Canada. It remains to be seen if these tools become more widespread in the shared space arena, though the idea of quantifying the outcomes of a direct services shared space could be compelling.

Program-Related Investments

Program-related investments (PRIs)[13] provide

a well-established mechanism for foundations to use different forms of financing, in addition to grants, to achieve their programmatic goals. Like grants, PRIs are used to make inexpensive financing available to non-profit or for-profit enterprises to address social and environmental challenges. Unlike grants, PRIs are expected to be repaid, generally with a modest rate of return. Once repaid, these funds can be used by the foundation for subsequent charitable investments.[14]

PRIs have supported shared spaces and continue to be an underutilized resource for organizations. (See Chapter 8: The Alliance Center: Colorado's Hub of Sustainability, on the Alliance Center's capitalization strategy and the use of a PRI from the Denver Foundation to support its renovation.)[15] Many local community foundations and family foundations are increasingly making PRIs to nonprofits. Organizations should consider this debt tool as a potential excellent source for the project as local foundations look to creatively leverage their funds.

Tax Credit Backed Financing

Unique to the United States, tax credits are a dollar-for-dollar credit that investors can claim on their tax returns in exchange for investing in projects that provide specified community benefits. Examples of tax credit backed financing at the national level in the US include the New Markets Tax Credit, and Historic Tax Credit. Certain states also have similar tax credit programs. New Market Tax Credits have been used very successfully in community economic development and arts projects as well as nonprofit centers. Historic Tax Credits give benefits for investing in the renovation of historic structures. A field unto itself, each credit has specific requirements and thresholds for applicability. Additionally, these are sophisticated tools and complex to apply to real estate projects. Projects that seek to utilize these tools should solicit the advice of professional financial experts such as nonprofit financial intermediaries or banks.

The most recent development in the US on tax incentives was the 2017 Tax Cuts and Jobs Act inclusion of a new economic development tool, Opportunity Zones, a tax incentive designed to encourage long-term private capital investment in America's low-income communities. There are more than 8,700 Opportunity Zones now in the US eligible to tap into over $6 trillion dollars of unrealized capital gains to support redevelopment projects and new businesses. According to the *Novogradac Journal of Tax Credits,* the Opportunity Zone incentives "allow investors to defer (up to nine years) paying tax on gains if those gains are invested in qualified opportunity funds (QOFs) that in turn invest in Opportunity Zones." As a new tool coming on-line, interested projects should evaluate these incentives for applicability to shared space projects and how they work in concert with other tax incentives.[16]

PULLING IT ALL TOGETHER

Employing all of the sources discussed here requires sophisticated projects and partners. Two *Stories from the Field* share different experiences in pulling together complex funding and financing structures in support of shared space projects. Chapter 8 on The Alliance Center in Denver, Colorado shows the use of multiple tax credits. Chapter 9 on the David Brower Center in Berkeley, California, also shares the story of its funding mix, which includes public money, tax credits, and private sources. In particular, the charts in this chapter are instructive in understanding the breadth of sources. Not all projects need to use these sources, of course; some projects are smaller and simply less complicated, but the shared space universe has examples of utilizing these tools with great sophistication and success.

CONCLUSION: MONEY MAKES THE WORLD GO ROUND

When a shared space begins operations, cash flow from tenants and other projected revenue begins. Nonprofit shared spaces typically get to cash flow positive in three to five years; others enjoy full capacity right away and create NOI immediately, which can then be funneled back to programming or reserves. Others still have capital campaign pledges still to collect, or debt to pay off, sometimes over several years. Others still may need ongoing subsidization to pay for additional staff or special programming at the space. In all cases, careful planning for capital and operating needs is critical to the survival of a shared space.

Shared space projects require substantial resources to implement successfully. As this chapter has discussed, resources are available at all phases of the project development and from multifold sources. Ultimately, bold and tenacious leadership is required to execute these complex projects and to mobilize the necessary resources to make them happen. Despite the complexities of assembling the resources and designing the space, hundreds of projects across North America have surmounted these hurdles and operate successfully in their communities. The wide range of resources available to nonprofits should give confidence to organizational leaders that raising the funds and realizing the dream of a new space is possible.

1. See organizations like the Nonprofit Finance Fund, Illinois Facilities Fund (now IFF), Northern California Community Loan Fund, Enterprise Foundation, LISC, and Low Income Investment Fund, among others.

2. See Nonprofit Centers Network. "State of the Sector." In *State of the Shared Space Sector Survey 2015: Changing How Nonprofits Work*. Denver: Nonprofit Centers Network, 2015.

3. One of the main ways to do this with a nonprofit center is a survey of nonprofits in the field or city to assess interest, need for space, and how much they will be willing to pay in rent.

4. Commercial real estate is defined as any property owned to produce income. For the purposes of this book, we use the term "commercial real estate" to distinguish it from residential real estate, which is an entire field in its own right. Commercial real estate can be owned or leased and can be operated by a for-profit or nonprofit entity. It can be office, performance/exhibition, program, warehouse, or retail space.

5. A "site" can refer to a building, campus of buildings, a suite or floor in an office building, or a plot of land.

6. See http://construction.about.com/od/Cost-Control/a/Hard-Costs.htm.

7. Lee, J. "The Next Wave in Fundraising Collaboration." *Stanford Social Innovation Review*, June 21, 2017. https://ssir.org/articles/entry/the_next_wave_in_fundraising_collaboration. Jason Lee is the Chief Advocacy and Strategy Officer and General Counsel of the Association of Fundraising Professionals (AFP).

8. See Nonprofit Finance Fund for tools, research, and resources on debt financing. http://nonprofitfinancefund.org/nonprofit-finance-101.

9. See https://www.cdfifund.gov/Pages/default.aspx.

10. "Pay for Success/Social Impact Bond Initiative." http://www.nonprofitfinancefund.org/pay-for-success.

11. See http://www.payforsuccess.org/resources/new-york-becomes-first-state-launch-social-impact-bond.

12. See https://charityvillage.com/Content.aspx?topic=Investing_in_the_nonprofit_sector_The_Social_Impact_Bond_makes_its_Canadian_debut#.VqWFkZorLIU.

13. See https://www.missioninvestors.org/system/files/tools/ximize-your-philanthropic-capital-a-guide-to-program-related-investments-lucia-benabentos-justin-storms-carlos-teuscher-and-jon-van-loo-linklaters-llp.pdf.pdf.

14. *"Strategies to Maximize Your Philanthropic Capital—A Guide to Program-Related Investment,"* 11. A TrustLaw publication by the Thomson Reuters Foundation for Mission Investors Exchange, April 2012.

15. For more on PRIs and their impact see, *"Doing Good with Foundation Assets: An Updated Look at Program-Related Investments,"* developed by the Foundation Center, 2010. http://foundationcenter.org/gainknowledge/research/pdf/pri_directory_excerpt.pdf Published by on

16. Smart Growth America. "Locus Opportunity Zones National Ranking Report." December 11, 2018. https://smartgrowthamerica.org/resources/locus-opportunity-zones-national-ranking-report/?download=yes&key=45731661; Barlow, George, and John Sciarretti. "Pairing NMTCs with Opportunity Zone Incentives." *Novogradac Journal of Tax Credits* 9.4. December 18, 2018. https://www.novoco.com/periodicals/articles/pairing-nmtcs-opportunity-zone-incentives.

7 Finding a Home
Site Selection for Nonprofit Centers

Securing a site is when a project moves from planning and feasibility to reality. Seeing a building and imagining the activity there breathes life into the project. This chapter discusses the site selection process in more detail, outlining the key considerations of site selection and reviewing the kinds of opportunities available to nonprofit center developers. "Sites" are broadly defined—they are a vacant piece of land, an existing building, a campus of buildings, a commercial condominium, or a space within another property.

WHAT'S FIRST: KEY CONSIDERATIONS FOR SITE SELECTION

Before looking for a site, it is important to establish key criteria that will guide the site selection some of which should have been established in the design feasibility phase of the project, discussed in detail in Chapter 6: The Development Process. The difference here between the feasibility and the site selection stages is that this stage is now about *implementation*, when we turn dreams and ideas into the reality of an actual project at an actual site. Organizations and their staff and board leadership can waste time pursuing projects that ultimately are a wrong fit. The site search should not be used to help refine criteria of the project; in other words, the site search is not a shopping exercise to see what feels right. Because organizational resources are at stake—time and money—it's important to have clear parameters set around the site search. This is not to say that an organization can't be nimble and respond to new opportunities, but the criteria established at the outset should be the guide.

Neighborhood

Where should the project be located? This depends on the mission of the project, the clients served, and the staff needs. Different neighborhoods might be better served by public transit options; others might be located near other agencies or funders or government players. The lead nonprofit organizations may serve specific neighborhoods or areas where their key populations live. Selecting several neighborhoods, a certain county, a key highway interchange or other locational preference will help narrow the search.

Before looking at properties, it's important to complete a space planning exercise to establish how big the property should be. This exercise involves understanding all of the activities that will take place in the project and how much space they will require. For example, if one of the goals is to provide meeting rooms for community groups, it's important to understand how large the room(s) needs to be. Market information from the needs assessment conducted as a part of the project feasibility study (discussed in Chapter 6) can inform this. The assessment should answer questions such as: What other spaces are available for community meetings? Are they generally available or mostly booked? How many people need to be accommodated in meetings? Do the meetings require a catering kitchen attached for food service? What types of meetings are community groups looking for—small meetings or larger conferences with break-out sessions? Answering these questions will guide the square footage requirement for this use. Each use of the space should follow similar thinking: Who is the space for, how many people will use it, and when and how will the space be used?

It is a best practice to establish a size range for a project, or a small, medium, or large version with core spaces and some "nice to have" spaces. This will afford more flexibility in the site search.

Type of Property

The purchase and lease discussion from Chapter 6 guides some of the central financial decisions around shared space projects. Each option has different financial requirements at specific times in the life of the project. Deciding on lease or ownership is important and contributes to driving site selection decisions. It is also important to decide on a stand-alone building or a space in an office building (whether lease or owned). Further refinement includes the requirement for a ground floor retail-like space or a warehouse or industrial space. Each type of property should match the uses that will take place in the building. Whether on-site parking is needed and how many spaces are important criteria.

Different types of buildings come with corresponding obligations. A stand-alone building might have more property management responsibilities that come with it, even in a leased situation; for example, a tenant might have to manage snow removal or other maintenance functions. On the other hand, a stand-alone building gives greater visibility to the project with the opportunity for signage. Some nonprofit centers may not want high visibility—for example, those devoted to serving victims of domestic violence—while others may seek the stand-alone building for just this purpose. It's important to figure out which type of property is the right fit for this specific project.

Special Uses

The ideal site is also determined by any special uses required for the project. For example, food pantries often need loading docks; performance spaces need high ceilings and wide, open spaces without columns; and a children's space might need access to outdoor space or specialized drop-off zones. All of these considerations will inform the site search and should be catalogued to help select sites to visit and ones to eliminate.

TACKLING THE MARKET: TRADITIONAL AND NONTRADITIONAL OPPORTUNITIES

Once these basic criteria have been established: the location, the size, and the type of property, it's time to start looking at available properties. Some projects hire real estate brokers for this effort, others work with architects, and still others work with seasoned board members who may have real estate experience. In any case, having outside expertise is helpful in evaluating sites.

Chapter 6 discussed the basic two approaches to embarking on a site search: pursuing traditional opportunities in the open market or nontraditional, "off-market" opportunities. Both are discussed in further detail in the following paragraphs.

Traditional Opportunities

The traditional approach is the standard approach: seeing sites that are advertised on the open market. Properties are advertised on general commercial property websites, on signs outside buildings or land, and on specialized commercial property websites that brokers access. If a property is represented by a real estate brokerage firm, it's important for the lessee or buyer (the shared space organization) to also be represented in the transaction. Brokers earn their commissions from the transaction, usually paid out by the landlord or seller. In general, brokers are not paid by the organization seeking the space. Once a site is selected, the parties will exchange "proposals" or "term sheets" laying out the key terms of the transaction. From there, in a lease, the terms will be agreed to and then a lease will be drafted for negotiation. In a purchase, a Purchase and Sale Agreement will be drafted. Real estate legal representation is required to guard the organizations' interests.

The advantage of pursuing a site on the open market is that, in general, the lessor or seller is motivated to make a deal and the asking price will be advertised and known. Presumably, the lessor or seller is also sophisticated in the process and the transaction can move along smoothly. The disadvantage is that nonprofits will be competing against everyone else who is pursuing these same properties; this includes for-profit businesses and firms who may have more resources. This competition can be a major obstacle in areas of high gentrification and rising rents and is much less present in more stagnant markets. The more affordable sites on the open market may not be particularly inspiring—retail strip malls, small undistinguished buildings, and floors in an office building, but they can nevertheless be designed to become appealing spaces.

Nontraditional Opportunities

Nontraditional sites open up new possibilities for nonprofit centers and can be exciting to pursue. While they take more work and are generally more complex, these sites can be the perfect fit for shared spaces; they can be cost-effective and the buildings can accommodate creative uses.

So what are the nontraditional opportunities? These projects present the chance to reimagine and reactivate abandoned or underutilized spaces. These are the decommissioned schools, military base, old theaters, and sacred buildings. Other public-sector buildings can fit the bill too: power stations, excess fire stations, former town halls, mills and factories, and other publicly-owned properties. Nonprofit centers have been created in all of these types of properties. What makes the opportunities nontraditional is that they are offered for Request for Proposal (RFP) from public-sector entities or nonprofits so they are not available on the open market. For sacred spaces, religious bodies might seek tenants or buyers. Nontraditional opportunities can also simply be private buildings or sites that fit all of the desired criteria for the project, but the property is not on the market. In these cases, building relationships with owners over time may unlock these properties.

On the downside, nontraditional properties take substantially longer to develop than market-based traditional sites. Responding to RFPs, meeting with public officials, cultivating relationships, and lining up funding for these sites is complicated and time consuming. Some projects take years. In the end, however, many of these sites prove worth it because of their uniqueness—their design, quality of construction, and rich history.

Reimagining Old Spaces: Adaptive Reuse

Repurposing existing real estate, or adaptive reuse, helps not only nonprofits, but simultaneously answers some of the problems of the aging real estate and excess infrastructure found in varying ways in both urban and low-population areas. It can further contribute to the revitalization of communities, while housing nonprofits at affordable rents.

Nonprofit centers have taken advantage of these kinds of buildings with some examples provided as follows:

- The Women's Building, San Francisco, California: originally an historic immigrant athletic club, in 1979 it became the first US women-owned community center and nonprofit hub, which also houses nine nonprofit partners serving women. See a photo of the mural on the front of this building in Chapter 4: A Profile of Nonprofit Centers (Figure 4.2).
- Fairhill Partners, Cleveland, Ohio: a former psychiatric hospital building now connects people to opportunities for lifelong learning, intergenerational relationships, and successful aging and houses twenty-five nonprofit and commercial organizations serving the aged.

FIGURE 7.1 *Bronson Centre, Ottawa, Ontario.* This photo depicts the Bronson Centre in Ottawa, founded in 1996. It houses more than forty organizations in more than 45,000 sq. ft. of the former Immaculata High School. A common adaptive reuse among nonprofit centers is former schools, sometimes decommissioned by local school districts or repurposed parochial schools, as in this case. Schools are well located and offer multiple kinds of spaces; at the same time, their larger spaces (cafeterias, libraries, and auditoriums) can be challenging to reprogram for income-generating purposes. *Photo credit: Bronson Centre.*

- Samaritan Center, Detroit, Michigan: an adapted medical hospital campus, offers a multifaceted community resource center for neighborhoods in Detroit's lower-income East Side, ranging from dialysis to employment services.
- Bronson Centre, Ottawa, Ontario: This former Immaculata High School was converted into a community hub that "has 40 permanent tenants, all of whom are non-profit service organizations"[1] Its mission is "to provide educational, emotional, physical and spiritual support aimed at empowering people to take responsibility for their own lives with renewed dignity and hope."[2] See a photo of the Bronson Center in Figure 7.1.
- Artscape Wychwood Barns, Toronto, Ontario: This former streetcar repair facility is now a community cultural hub development by Artscape Toronto. It houses arts, culture, food security, urban agriculture, environmental, and other community activities.[3] See Figure 7.2 for a photo of Wychwood Barns.

All these examples of adaptive reuse have brought desired services and cultural resources to neighborhoods and communities while also preserving important infrastructure and reanimating underutilized assets.

Preserving Historic Buildings

An aspect of adaptive reuse that presents both social and financial opportunities is the preservation and renewal of historic buildings and sites. Historic preservation fosters a connection to national, regional, or local heritage through structures that typify national and local identity, culture, and values. It also opens up possibilities for new sources of funding, both public and private.

In the US, this trend can be traced to the 1949 founding by congressional charter of the nonprofit National Trust for Historic Preservation. The Trust "protects

FIGURE 7.2 *Wychwood Barns, Toronto, Ontario.* This photo depicts the exterior of Artscape Wychwood Barns, a century-old former streetcar facility that serves as a community cultural hub. It includes spaces for twenty-six artist live/work studios, fifteen artist work studios, nine nonprofit arts and environmental organizations, and an event venue. *Photo credit: Ted Chai.*

significant places representing our diverse cultural experience by taking direct action and inspiring broad public support."[4] A parallel nonprofit organization, the National Trust for Canada, was established in 1973, and its vision is "to be recognized as an essential source of services, tools, inspiration and funding for people working to save places that matter, and to be recognized as a brand associated with great places to live, learn, work and play."[5] These organizations advocate for and advance thinking around preserving historic sites and buildings.

Nonprofit centers have capitalized on this opportunity, helping to bring new vitality and respect for heritage to their communities. The Lyceum in Hartford, Connecticut, was built in 1895 by the archdiocese serving Hartford as a community center for immigrants coming to this city, to be "a wholesome gathering place for young men"[6] After many other uses, this building, near the state capitol, is now the home of a hub for housing and homeless advocacy and community development organizations, as well as an active conference center for civic and community concerns.[7] Its notable facade remains a part of this community's history.

Military Reuse

Another application of adaptive reuse is converting military assets for civilian reuse. Seventy years of relative peace in the West, changing military objectives, and modern technologies have led to the closure of many military installations. Several nonprofit centers have been established in historic sites that were decommissioned military installations, using their closure as an opportunity to keep them in public use. They include the theme center Thoreau Center for Sustainability (now Tides Converge) in

FIGURE 7.3 *The Armory, Lansing, Michigan.* This photo depicts a great example of another kind of adaptive reuse, that of repurposing former military installations for nonprofit centers. The Armory is located in Lansing and was developed by a private developer for nonprofit organizations in 2011. Gillespie Group, the developer, also has their corporate headquarters there. Military buildings offer excellent adaptive reuse possibilities, and there are examples of nonprofit centers in them across the US. *Photo credit: Gillespie Group.*

The Presidio and the generalist site, Fort Mason Center, a large mid-century military embarkation site, both in San Francisco, as well is the Liberty Station campus in San Diego, California, a former naval training center. Liberty Center, a themed center focused on the arts, has developed several historic buildings to house nonprofits that, among other things, present exhibits and community entertainment.

Another example is the Armory in Lansing, Michigan, now a nonprofit center renovated by a local commercial developer. Tenants include the Capital Area United Way, Michigan Nonprofit Association, Michigan Association of United Ways, and Food Bank Council of Michigan, among others. The Armory was first formerly occupied by the Army National Guard and was an active training site until 2005. The building was decommissioned by the military in 2008 and remained unoccupied until November 2011.

The Armory was historically preserved and retrofitted to serve as a collaborative headquarters for several local nonprofit organizations allowing them to share facilities and services. "One of the main goals of preserving the building was to ensure that the historical features remain to 'tell a story' for all to enjoy."[8] Figure 7.3 shows the exterior façade of The Armory project.

Brownfields

Perhaps the most complicated nontraditional opportunity to pursue is a "brownfield." Brownfield sites are typically former industrial sites and can vary in terms of their level of contamination; sites include former dry cleaners, gas stations, and factories. The US Environment Protection Agency defines a brownfield as "a property, the expansion, redevelopment, or reuse of which may be complicated by the presence or potential presence of a hazardous substance, pollutant, or contaminant. It is estimated that there are more than 450,000 brownfields in the U.S."[9] With proper clean up these sites can be repurposed for new uses. There are incentives and/or grants at the national and statewide level for brownfield mitigation to help spur their clean up and redevelopment. For nonprofit centers, though complex, these sites represent meaningful opportunities and should be considered.

CONCLUSION: THE RIGHT SITE MAKES THE PROJECT

Finding the site for any project is one of the more stressful junctures in the nonprofit center development process. Yet finding the site and securing it will galvanize support for the project and bring new momentum to the entire project. Determining the criteria in advance is the most important aspect of the site search so that organizations can only pursue sites that fit their needs. If strategically planned, the site search can also be a fun process—visiting sites and imagining what the spaces could be. From old schools to abandoned buildings, to empty office space, nonprofit centers have brought life to these properties and provided new assets for their communities.

NOTES

1. See Bronson Centre. Accessed March 5, 2017. http://bronsoncentre.ca/.
2. See Bronson Centre. Accessed March 5, 2017. http://bronsoncentre.ca/.
3. See http://www.torontoartscape.org/artscape-wychwood-barns. Accessed January 29, 2018.
4. See https://nationaltrustcanada.ca/ website.
5. See National Trust for Canada. 2017. https://nationaltrustcanada.ca/.
6. See The Lyceum. www.lyceumcenter.org/about.
7. See The Lyceum. www.lyceumcenter.org/about.
8. Restore Lansing 2018. Accessed March 2018. http://restorelansing.com/Commercial-Projects/Renovations/Marshall-Street-Armory.
9. US Environmental Protection Agency. Accessed January 15, 2018. https://www.epa.gov/brownfields/overview-brownfields-program.

8 Stories from the Field

The Alliance Center
Colorado's Hub of Sustainability

John Powers and Janna Six

Alliance for Sustainable Colorado
Denver, Colorado

When spider webs unite they can tie up a lion.
—Ethiopian Proverb

WHY THE ALLIANCE FOR SUSTAINABLE COLORADO

Imagine the whole of humanity on an ecological bus barreling toward a cliff. If you're looking out the side windows, the scenery can be pleasantly distracting. But if you're looking straight ahead, you'll realize that because of the momentum, everyone on the bus is going to have to pull together to change direction if catastrophe is to be avoided. It doesn't matter if you're sitting in the front, middle, or back seats financially; we're all going wherever this bus goes.

The existential threat to all life on earth is climate change. Climate instability is an exceedingly complex problem. If we are to solve it, or even mitigate it, we need the collective expertise of people with all perspectives and skills. The challenge is to get people to work together cooperatively, for survival hangs in the balance.

In 2004, the Denver-based nonprofit Alliance for Sustainable Colorado (the Alliance) was established to blend the idealism and vision of nonprofits with the innovation and practicality found in many businesses and instill it in the policies of government to create truly effective solutions, which we must teach to our children. The cornerstone project of the Alliance is its building, the Alliance Center (the Center). The intentions of the Center are to:

- Create Colorado's physical and intellectual hub of sustainability to attract people to work together, both tenants and non-tenants.
- Facilitate synergies and enhance productivity.
- Model collaboration, civility, and mutual respect.
- Demonstrate and educate about green building design and technologies.
- Be a model for alliances in other states, headquartered in their capital cities.
- Inspire people to work together with positive purpose.
- Create hope.

The Alliance is committed to the development of policies and implementation of practices of sustainability to:

- Protect and preserve the integrity of ecological systems, that make life possible, and address the foremost threat of climate change.
- Respect the natural environment and the limits of the planet's finite resources.
- Ensure that everyone has access to adequate food, housing, healthcare, education, and jobs.
- Protect and promote the civil rights of all Coloradans.
- Assess decisions in terms of local economic benefit, environmental quality and social well-being, the triple bottom line.

The Alliance provides an unparalleled opportunity for nonprofits, businesses and elected officials to interact on a daily basis about the issues that matter to us all. None of us can go it alone, and the Alliance makes links among diverse interests and the connections we need to build a sustainable future for Colorado.
—Colorado Governor John Hickenlooper

ORIGIN OF THE ALLIANCE CENTER

In 1990, John Powers learned that the building shared by two nonprofits in Santa Fe, the New Mexico Environmental Law Center and Project Lighthawk, was being sold. The organizations were going to lose their significant benefits of being co-located. At the same time, Powers observed environmental organizations often working on very similar issues, but unaware of each other. One solution he envisioned was a building shared by many nonprofits. The attempt to establish such a building in Santa Fe didn't come to fruition.

The whole is greater than the sum of the parts.

In 1997 Powers worked with then restaurateur, now Colorado governor, John Hickenlooper, for the Colorado Environmental Coalition to move into the historic warehouse in Lower Downtown (LoDo) Denver, across the floor from Hickenlooper's Wynkoop Holdings Company headquarters. Hickenlooper co-owned the building with Joyce Meskis, owner of the Tattered Cover Bookstores. During 2003, Powers worked with Ms. Meskis to negotiate leases for eight more nonprofits to move into the building thereby collecting the nucleus of tenants for a nonprofit center. In February 2004, Ms. Meskis offered to sell the building to Powers and Janna Six to create a nonprofit center. See Figure 8.1 for a picture of the building. With guidance from a pro bono attorney, they quickly filed application papers in March to establish a 501(c)(3) public charity to own the building. China Brotsky, then executive director of the Nonprofit Centers Network (NCN), was hired to consult on the creation of a "Multi-Tenant Nonprofit Center," a term coined by the Network. To build the tenant base, over two hundred nonprofits were surveyed to identify

FIGURE 8.1 *Alliance Center, Denver, Colorado.* A photo of the front of the Alliance Center showing the historic façade, 2016. *Photo credit: Alliance for Sustainable Colorado.*

organizations with compatible sustainability missions and interest in moving in with the nine existing tenants. On June 17, the (c)(3) application was approved to create the Alliance for Sustainable Colorado, and on June 30, 2004, the Alliance closed on the purchase of the building. The vision was finally realized, and the Alliance Center was born.

Mission-Driven Building

The Alliance was incorporated with the intent to catalyze collaboration on sustainability policy, education, and outreach programs among nonprofit tenants with non-tenant partners. Tenants are selected by their missions and their potential to contribute to the collaboration in the Center. By co-locating nonprofits, the Center supports their missions by reducing their costs, providing a healthy workspace, and increasing their productivity and effectiveness by enhancing synergies, while affording donors the opportunity to support many groups at once by funding the Alliance.

FIGURE 8.2 *LEED and Energy Star Building Awards.* The Alliance Center became the second building in the world to earn two US Green Building Council LEED certifications while also earning US EPA Energy Star Leader status. *Photo credit: Alliance for Sustainable Colorado.*

In 2004–2005 the warehouse was built out with offices and meeting rooms using green design and became a demonstration and tour site of resource efficiency and high performance, allowing tenants to walk their talk. As shown in Figure 8.2, the Center became the second building in the world to earn two US Green Building Council (USGBC) LEED (Leadership in Energy and Environmental Design) certifications—Existing Buildings Gold and Commercial Interiors Silver, while also earning US EPA Energy Star Leader status.

ACHIEVEMENTS
Collaboration

Because the Center is mission driven, it provides a base for resident organizations and a core for the growing statewide sustainability network, which others can join. Collaboration within Alliance Center has led to stronger coalitions and partnerships.

Sustainability Policy Gains

Within its first few months of operation in 2004, the Center provided office and meeting space for the successful statewide citizens' ballot initiative Amendment 37, The Colorado Renewable Energy Requirement Initiative. This was the first voter-approved renewable energy portfolio standard in the US. It required that 10% of retail electricity sales from investor-owned utilities be generated from renewable sources and became the first step toward the current standard of 30% for investor-owned utilities and 20% for rural co-ops, which were raised incrementally by the legislature.

Because of the Alliance's experience and leadership with green buildings, in 2005 staff and partners created the Better Building Coalition to press the Colorado

FIGURE 8.3 *Legislative Victories Are Fostered at the Alliance Center.* Governor Ritter of Colorado, at a press event in front of the Alliance Center, signing one of the many pieces of clean energy legislation supported by the tenants and partners of the Center. *Photo credit: Alliance for Sustainable Colorado.*

legislature to set high performance standards for public buildings. Three years of work culminated in the passage of SB 07-051 Requirement for Increased Resource Efficiency for State-Assisted Buildings; see the bill being signed in Figure 8.3. The State Architect adopted LEED Gold certification as the required standard for new construction and renovations of state-funded buildings over 5,000 sq. ft.

The Alliance and its tenants and partners championed other successful legislation over the years. Some examples are:

HB 07-1146 Requirement That Certain Local Governments Adopt an Energy Efficiency Code in Connection with the Construction of Certain Buildings

SB 09-075 Operation of Low-Speed Electric Self-Propelled Vehicles on Public Rights-of-Way

HB 10-1204 Inclusion of Conservation Standards in the Plumbing Code

HB 13-1138 Benefit Corporations, and, in Connection Therewith, Making an Appropriation

HB 14-1074 Payments That a Nonprofit Owner of a Tax-Exempt Property May Receive for Reasonable Expenses Incurred without Affecting the Tax-Exempt Status of the Property.

Many other policy successes have originated in the Alliance Center. During 2009 and 2010, fifty-three bills were signed into law that were the collaborative effort of at least two Center tenants working with non-tenant partners. In 2013, Alliance Center Tenants worked to pass thirty-one pro-sustainability bills. Of these, four were the result of three or more tenants working together.

Other Collaboration Successes

Anecdotes of unusual collaborations abound. The office manager of one organization, Just Media, was also a part-time actress, so she volunteered to be featured in several YouTube videos created by ProgressNow, another tenant. The American Council of the Blind had board members with seeing-eye dogs. All tenants received sensitivity training about whether, when, and how to interact with service dogs and needs of people with disabilities. The Center for Native Ecosystems GIS team used its software and plotter to provide maps and even to print posters for numerous users inside and outside the Center. Often, tenants holding press events at the capitol have received participation and support from their peers in the Center.

Capital Improvements: Opportunities and Challenges

When the Alliance originally purchased the building, it did not have enough funds to address the aged heating and cooling systems. In 2012, the HVAC system experienced a range of increasingly frequent breakdowns that demanded its replacement. Drop ceilings blocked access to air ducts and would have to be removed. Pre-renovation offices wasted space with separate offices and halls, as shown in Figure 8.4. The Alliance had four options: (i) remove, then rebuild, the drop ceilings after all else had been completed; (ii) remove the drop ceilings to expose the higher, original wood ceilings and extend upward the existing walls; (iii) remove all existing walls and construct new, taller ones; or (iv) gut the building and effectively start over. The Alliance chose option four.

To accomplish the total renovation, tenants were relocated offsite in "swing space" from September 2013 until June 2014.

FIGURE 8.4 *Pre-Renovation Office.* An office in the Alliance Center before the 2014 renovation showing extra space unused in the room. *Photo credit: Alliance for Sustainable Colorado.*

Gensler provided the architectural services. Utilizing its Workplace Performance Index® (WPI®), Gensler measured tenant satisfaction in the existing building and captured many tenant desires in the new design. The Center was already more energy efficient than 87% of similar buildings, so operating expenses could not be compressed enough to recoup the costs of renovation. Alternatively, profitability would be improved by increasing revenue with an entirely redesigned floor plan as shown in Figure 8.5. By providing workstations and furniture, the number of occupants was doubled from 130 to 260, and the number of meeting rooms was quadrupled. All walls in the Center were deconstructed to reuse and recycle materials, and new, movable, architectural (a.k.a. demountable) glass walls were installed, which allow natural light to penetrate the interior.

The main entrance was moved from the side of the building back to its original "storefront" location on the sidewalk. The all-glass entry now welcomes people into a multipurpose, versatile event center where a concessionaire serves coffee, tea, beer, wine, and light food options backed up by a commercial kitchen available to all. A glass, retractable wall can be stacked to open an area that can hold over two hundred.

As a result of the renovation, the Center was the first building in Colorado and the fifth in the world to earn a LEED Dynamic Plaque Certification (Gold) for its real-time monitoring of energy and water use in the building. In February 2017, the Center earned LEED EBOM (Existing Buildings Operations and Maintenance), the first building in Colorado to obtain Platinum certification in any of the newest LEED v4 rating systems. The certifications further the Alliance's goal of educating visitors about energy-efficiency, low-carbon, high-performance design and technologies that focus on the productivity and comfort of tenants and attract attention to them.

FIGURE 8.5 *Post-Renovation Office.* A post-renovation office showing the doubling in occupancy due to revised floor plan with fewer private offices and glass to let in light to the interior. *Photo credit: Alliance for Sustainable Colorado.*

DC Microgrid Project

The commercial building sector consumes 40% of the energy consumed in the US. A rich opportunity to increase profitability and reduce greenhouse gas emissions is to improve the energy efficiency of existing buildings. The Alliance is pioneering an energy efficiency study with its DC Microgrid project. The first phase is converting a portion of the electrical infrastructure in the Center from alternating current (AC) to direct current (DC) and measuring the kWh savings. Energy consumption has been metered for six months to establish the baseline. Solar panels will be installed on the roof to generate 20 kWh that will be stored in batteries that feed lights, plugs, and two fan-powered heating boxes as a "test bed." The study is designed to quantify and model the value of retrofitting existing commercial buildings to lead to reduced greenhouse gas emissions.

Innovative Financing

Loans

The Alliance Center original purchase and renovation was financed by U.S. Bank with an adjustable rate loan, 2% over London Interbank Offered Rate (LIBOR), which was 1.9% at the time. Not only does LIBOR fluctuate like an EKG, it can cause arrhythmia for the borrower. August 2005, the Alliance got off the interest rate rollercoaster and converted to a conventional 5.81% fixed mortgage, twenty-five-year amortization, and ten-year maturity.

Tax-Exempt Bonds

The Alliance learned of tax-exempt borrowing available to the Alliance because the Center is owned by a nonprofit for nonprofit tenants. With the bonding authority and help of the City of Federal Heights, adjacent to the City of Denver, in March 2006 the Alliance secured a tax-exempt loan at 4.5%, twenty-five-year amortization, and ten-year term. When interest rates dropped, again with the help of the City of Federal Heights, in September 2011 the Alliance refinanced with a new tax-exempt loan through Wells Fargo Bank at 3.58%, twenty-five-year amortization, and ten-year term.

Program-Related Investment

In December 2013, the Alliance refinanced again with The Denver Foundation, which offered its first ever program-related investment through a donor advised fund at 1%, twenty-five-year amortization, and fifteen-year term. By financing an increase in the principal amount in addition to paying off the outstanding mortgage, the Alliance was able to undertake the total renovation of the Center in 2014.

Recoverable Grant

When costs for the renovation exceeded budget, in May 2014 the Denver Foundation stepped up again and awarded its first recoverable grant, which is expected, but not required to be returned to the Foundation as the Alliance is able and requires no interest payments.

Historic Tax Credits

The Alliance Center is a contributing building to the Lower Downtown (LoDo) Denver registered Historic District. As such, the Center qualifies for federal and State of Colorado Historic Tax Credits. The Alliance worked with the National Trust Community Investment Corporation (NTCIC) and East-West Bank to receive National Parks Service Tax Incentives for Preserving Historic Properties. As federal tax credits may only be awarded to tax paying entities, the ownership of the Center had to be sold to a for-profit LLC in an intricate structure of multiple LLCs required by East-West Bank, the investor that monetized the tax credits for the Alliance. The law firms of Hogan Lovells and Moye White provided invaluable pro bono legal services for these complicated transactions.

Real Property Tax Exemption

As a nonprofit-owned building for nonprofit tenants, the Center is eligible for real property tax exemption. From 2004 to 2006, the Alliance worked to qualify for real property tax exemption through the State of Colorado Department of Local Affairs, Division of Property Tax. Sale of the Center to the LLC to get federal historic tax credits would disqualify the Center from receiving real property tax exemption, which was important in the financial stability of the Center. In response, the Alliance returned to the policy arena.

To preserve real property tax exemption while obtaining the federal tax credit, the Alliance found sympathetic sponsors in the Colorado legislature to pass, in 2014, House Bill 14-1349: Concerning the Creation of an Exemption from Property Taxes for Qualifying Business Entities Controlled by Nonprofit Organizations That Are Formed for the Purpose of Qualifying for Federal Tax Credits.

KEYS TO SUCCESS OF THE ALLIANCE CENTER
Ownership Structure

The most fundamental issue in creating a nonprofit center is its ownership structure. Powers and Six chose to create a single entity "benevolent" owner, which can make quick decisions and relieves tenants of being property owners and managers, over creating a multiple entity co-op or condominium association structure. While the sale of units or shares to multiple owners would have afforded money to help purchase of the building, the mission of the Alliance would have been diluted and could have waivered due to shared ownership. With one owner, tenants can be selected for mission fit, all occupants are on equal footing, they can be obliged to follow a common set of principles, and collaboration can be fostered. With multiple owners, mission fit can be undone when unit owners decide to sell and missions of available buyers may not be congruous. The title of the building was originally held by the Alliance Center LLC, wholly owned by the Alliance for Sustainable Colorado, to benefit from the liability protection an LLC affords.

Location

The Center is eighteen blocks from the state capitol and the Denver City and County buildings, which can be reached by a free shuttle bus ride and short walk. The recently renovated Historic Union Station, the four-state multimodal bus and rail transportation center handling 100,000 passengers a day, is a block north from the Center, and the forty-mile-long Cherry Creek bike path is a block south. This location made it very desirable for the policy-oriented tenants the Center wanted and created demand even in the Center's early years when rents approached market rates.

Tenancy

The Alliance accepts applications for tenancy to choose complementary partners with shared values, who wish to collaborate for mutual success. Donors to the Alliance help hold down rents, which reduces costs for all tenants. In several instances, tenants have received contributions and grants from visitors to the Center and referrals from other tenants.

Green Building

The Alliance Center's green building certifications are core to the DNA of the Alliance for several reasons. First, the Alliance strives to provide the healthiest, safest, lowest cost, and most productive workplace for tenants and visitors. Second, green building certifications and publicity attract visitors to learn about green building design and technologies. These visitors become acquainted with the work and the potential of supporting the tenants and experience collaboration in action. Third, the Center has been the focus of study for fifteen university and college graduate and undergraduate courses and has provided experience for budding practitioners pursuing higher levels of LEED accreditation. Fourth, operating expenses are reduced through investments in energy efficiency, which help hold down rental rates.

Awards

Multiple green building certifications, awards, and articles about the Alliance and the Center draw people to the building and to the collaboration it fosters. The

Alliance has been awarded USGBC's 2006 National Leadership Award for Education by an Organization; the Governor's Office of Energy Management and Conservation "Colorado Energy Champion"; the Mayor of Denver Design Award: "It Ain't Easy Being Green"; the Wirth Chair "Pioneer of the New Energy Economy"; and the Colorado Department of Public Health and the Environment "Environmental Leader Gold Award" in each year since 2008.

Licensing vs. Leasing

The Alliance now licenses "resources" to tenants, rather than leasing square footage. A resource is a furnished workspace with a chair and small set of drawers, fiber optic Internet access and VOIP phone, use of all meeting rooms, and the event space. The key distinction with licensing is that the Alliance can move licensees to different locations to accommodate changing needs of tenants and to optimize the use of the space. Tenants are charged rent per person, rather than by the building industry norm of per square foot. Licenses range from least expensive virtual tenancy (no office but use of meeting rooms and mailing address), to hot desks (use of any of the available designated hot desk seats), to assigned desks, to assigned offices.

The Center houses over two hundred sustainability champions with forty-five nonprofits and a handful of for-profit tenant organizations. One of the Alliance Center's treasured tenants is the NCN. In 2014 NCN relocated from the Thoreau Center in San Francisco and now shares an office with the Alliance.

Workplace Citizenship

Tenants agree to a set of "cultural norms" that include using mass transit or bikes when possible to get to work. Alliance Center tenants each receive free eGo CarShare memberships to encourage use of mass transit. Encouraged practices include printing on both sides of paper on a shared high-performance printer, powering computers down at the end of the day, and taking stairs instead of the elevator. Tenants are offered membership in a Community Supported Agriculture club that delivers produce to the Center during the summer.

The Alliance Center is dog friendly—well-behaved dogs are welcome. They stimulate interaction among tenants and with visitors and contribute to fun and mo-rale. According to the executive director of the Colorado Association for Recycling, "Every day is better with a dog in it."

COMMUNITY ASSET

The Center has become a community asset for its LoDo neighborhood, the City of Denver, and State of Colorado. Every day, tenants and visitors congregate in the Hub Café for food, drinks, and conversations. A patio by the café (Figure 8.6) extends the gathering space. Monthly Lunch and Learn programs and Conscious Cocktails en-gage tenants and newcomers and build relationships. Frequent presentations, board meetings, and trainings are held in the Center. The building is the gathering place for regular meetings of groups like the Truth in Media Network, Women in Sustainable Energy, Toastmasters, and the US Green Building Council (USGBC) of Colorado.

A visitor to the Alliance Center might encounter many of the eighteen meeting rooms, which can accommodate from four to two hundred, in use for collaborative meetings to advance policy, education, research, or grassroots organizing on sustainability issues. On occasion, the Center's adjoining parking lot is taken over for public events. For example, in 2008 during the Democratic National Convention in Denver, the Alliance erected its Big Tent, and hosted 400 bloggers and 160 speakers.

FIGURE 8.6 *Open Air Patio at the Alliance Center.* An outdoor patio at the Alliance Center provides flexible space for working, connecting, and entertaining. *Photo credit: Alliance for Sustainable Colorado.*

Over three hundred meetings and events are held at the Center annually. A recent sample includes Alliance-sponsored public programs in its Economy Series: Cultivating an Economy in Service to Life, cohosting the S² Sustainability Series with The Wirth Chair in Sustainable Development at the University of Colorado Denver, and presentation of "Best for Denver" in collaboration with B Lab Colorado. Dozens of private events are held at the Center each year, providing affordable meeting space in a prime location.

Alliance staff pursue additional programs that work with partners inside and outside the building. One is the Colorado Energy Futures Study. The Alliance has assembled a high-powered advisory committee to guide an ambitious new study commissioned by the Alliance to explore the economic implications of scaling up reliance on renewable energy in Colorado. The fifty-five members include representatives from large commercial energy users, electric utilities, the clean energy industry, energy advocacy groups, elected representatives, officials with Governor Hickenlooper's office, and other key energy policy constituencies. Once armed with evidence from the study and supported by the advisory committee, the Alliance will work with partners to disseminate the results and promote energy conservation and renewable energy.

Collaboration with diverse partners will be essential to promote sustainable energy at the community level, pass key legislation and implement critical statewide policies.
—from the Colorado Energy Futures Study

TURNING VISION INTO REALITY

The Alliance for Sustainable Colorado believes in sustainability as the foundation for a future where health, happiness, equity, and prosperity can be accessible to everyone and where communities are empowered and enabled to balance their environmental, social, and economic priorities in harmony. As the statewide hub for sustainability, the Alliance will continue its efforts to support physical and programmatic collaboration, facilitating connections among leaders, issues, resources, and strategies, to create a more sustainable future.

9 Stories from the Field
A Developer's Perspective
The David Brower Center

John Clawson

Equity Community Builders
San Francisco Bay Area, California

WHAT IS THE DAVID BROWER CENTER?

One of the Bay Area's most advanced green buildings, the nonprofit David Brower Center is an inspiring home for environmental and social action, combining both offices and program facilities in a 50,000 sq. ft. space. The façade of this LEED Platinum building in shown in Figure 9.1.

FIGURE 9.1 *David Brower Center, Berkeley, California.* This photo depicts the David Brower Center from the Oxford Street View. It is a 50,000 sq. ft., mixed use, LEED Platinum, new construction building. The site is located less than one-quarter mile from local transit, public schools, the library, retail, restaurants, parks, and the University of California Berkeley campus. *Photo credit: Equity Community Builders and David Brower Center.*

Conceived as a vibrant community of like-minded individuals and organizations committed to a just and ecologically sustainable society, the Brower Center is an invaluable asset for the region and a landmark for anyone, anywhere committed to the planet and its inhabitants.

By investing in a centrally located workspace and gathering place, the Brower Center is using real estate as an enduring progressive strategy and building a destination for activism and education. Until now, there has been no physical space in the Bay Area designed to foster collaborations between like-minded environmental organizations and individuals, engage new people in environmental advocacy, and facilitate cross-sector communication and partnerships.

The David Brower Center provides a central address for the nonprofit community, a place to discover the connections between issues, build lasting relationships, and affect real, substantive change.

David Brower, the first executive director of the Sierra Club, then founder of Friends of the Earth, League of Conservation Voters, and Earth Island Institute, was a visionary. He was always ahead of the curve. In the middle of the last century, he saw the potential power of mobilized wilderness lovers, and he orchestrated America's first successful citizen campaign against a big government project—the grassroots defeat of proposed dams in Dinosaur National Monument. He followed this success with victories against dams in Grand Canyon. He was instrumental in the creation of Pt. Reyes National Seashore and Redwoods and North Cascades national parks.

From the start, Brower grasped the importance of the media in spreading the environmental ethic, and to that end he became an essayist, film-maker, and publisher. He was one of the first environmental globalists. It is obvious to many now, but he saw it then: the planet makes the ultimate ecosystem; what affects the Niger Delta or the Mississippi Delta or the Siberian steppes or General Motors affects us all. When you try to pick out anything by itself, you find it hitched to everything else in the universe.

The David Brower Center incorporates that special vision in its programs. It employs the tools Brower himself brought to the movement—leadership, inspiration, mentorship, and strong conviction about the importance of education, the media, and the cross-fertilization of groups and ideas. It seeks a permanent spot ahead of the curve. The Center:

- *Informs* the public about the environmental challenges we face and the bold actions that must be taken if ours is to remain a living planet.
- *Inspires* people to recognize their own power and responsibility to act on behalf of Earth.
- *Connects* individuals and organizations dedicated to social equity and ecological sustainability.

The Brower Center is a facility designed to inspire and nurture current generations of activists and to build a foundation for future generations. The Center provides:

- A hub for environmental education and activism; a source for new strategies in the conservation, preservation, and restoration of ecosystems-a center for planetary CPR.
- A community center where tenants, students, area residents, and activists from around the globe can gather for conferences, workshops, meals, and events.
- A place of inspiration that energizes resident organizations and engages the public with the images and stories of the environmental movement.
- A collaborative workplace for a wide range of nonprofit and progressive for-profit organizations; a place where shared resources, networks, and facilities magnify the work of both resident and nonresident groups.
- A model of green, New Urbanist design that promotes sustainable, mixed-use development; a unique co-location of eco-friendly retail stores, environmental organizations, and affordable workforce housing near public transit.
- A tangible asset that creates stability and builds equity for the progressive community.

The David Brower Center, governed by a board of directors, employs a staff that is actively engaged in the operation and management of the center, outreach to potential tenants, and fundraising to support the Brower Center's ongoing operations and program development.

PROJECT BENEFITS TO THE CITY AND THE COMMUNITY

- *Strengthen downtown retail core.* The Oxford Plaza and David Brower Center increased retail demand with new residents, office workers, conference attendees, and visitors. The project's mix of a very successful destination restaurant and retail uses have strengthened Berkeley's downtown retail district.
- *Employment benefits.* The Brower Center and its resident organizations and the project's retail/restaurant operations have brought over two hundred new employees to downtown Berkeley.
- *Workforce housing.* The housing component of the project has helped satisfy the overwhelming demand for affordable housing for Berkeley's workforce and their families—teachers, public service employees, and administrative personnel—who work in downtown Berkeley or can commute by BART.
- *Green design.* The David Brower Center was one of the first new buildings on the West Coast to receive the US Green Building Council LEED Platinum rating. The building has generated widespread media attention and drawn thousands of visitors. The Brower Center has become a model for the practical implementation of environmentally responsible design.
- *Enhancement of the Arts and Entertainment District.* The Center hosts scores of events each year bringing visitors from the Bay Area and around the country. These visitors are introduced to the lively arts and cultural scene Berkeley has

created, and add diversity to the offerings of the Arts and Entertainment district. The vitality of the district is enhanced by the wide range of programs offered at the David Brower Center.

- *Berkeley's civic image.* The David Brower Center is a permanent, prominent, and visible expression of sustainability principles, enhancing Berkeley's civic reputation as an environmental leader.
- *Resource for the nonprofit community.* By offering first class facilities for meetings, presentations, conferences, and exhibit space to the wider nonprofit community, the missions of all those groups are supported and enhanced. With the David Brower Center's support facilities, these groups can devote more of their time and money to mission critical work.
- *National model,* Creation of a center to support the nonprofit community in such a prominent location is seen as strong leadership in recognizing the critical role of the "social equity" community and the responsibility of cities to support that sector.

PROJECT DESCRIPTION

Completed in 2009, the Oxford Plaza and David Brower Center project has four primary components—the Center, retail, housing, and a below-grade public parking garage. The site is located on Oxford Street, between Allston Way and Kittredge Street in the heart of downtown Berkeley's Arts and Retail district with convenient access to local and regional (BART) transit systems.

The David Brower Center

The David Brower Center combines office, conference, gallery, and restaurant uses in a model of environmentally responsible design that achieved LEED Platinum certification. The office space is primarily targeted for nonprofit users with a focus on environmental issues. The conference facilities include a 175-seat auditorium, four flexible meeting rooms ranging in size from 400 to 1,600 sq. ft., a 1,200 sq. ft. gallery for rotating exhibits and events, and a large reception, prefunction, and lobby space.

Total Building Area	**49,500 sq. ft.**
Conference Facilities	8,500 sq. ft.
Restaurant	3,200 sq. ft.
Office Space	33,100 sq. ft.

The Brower Center is a four-story building that fronts on Allston Avenue. The primary entry to the Brower Center is on Allston and provides access to the ground floor reception, auditorium, meeting space, and gallery. A two-level lobby and grand stair provide access to second floor offices, meeting space, and an outdoor terrace. At the corner of Allston and Oxford Street, Gather, a 3,000 sq. ft. restaurant provides catering for the Brower Center conference and event spaces, creates a social center and gathering place for the project, and further demonstrates the benefits of natural and sustainable food production. The restaurant has been highly successful and helps activate the Brower Center courtyard fronting Oxford Street, providing a public space for outdoor dining, events. and exhibits on two levels.

The majority of the second floor and all of the third and fourth floors are configured as flexible office space that accommodates a range of nonprofit organizations from a 4,400 sq. ft. user to individual offices for smaller organizations. The current tenants of the Brower Center, at the time of publication, include American Rivers, Bay Area Open Space Council, Center for Ecoliteracy, Climate Earth, Earth Island Institute, Friends of the Earth, Gather Restaurant, Institute for Environmental Entrepreneurship, International Marine Mammal Project, Sacred Land Film Project, Sustainable Agriculture Education, Transportation Sustainability Research Center, and Women's Earth Alliance.

The relatively narrow sixty-five-foot width of the Brower Center building accommodates this mix of large and small tenants while optimizing the use of natural ventilation and day lighting, critical design strategies in an environmentally efficient building. See Figure 9.2 for an example. The building structure

FIGURE 9.2 *Natural Light Enhances the Space.* This photo depicts the second-floor common space, an open, airy space that takes advantage of natural ventilation and daylighting, key components of LEED buildings. It looks down over the first-floor lobby and features an exhibition about David Brower, the building's namesake. It is also right next to a shared kitchen and bathrooms. It is adjacent to a second-floor courtyard, which can be used for receptions. *Photo credit: Equity Community Builders and David Brower Center.*

is concrete and the mechanical systems capitalize on this structure to provide thermal mass to minimize heating and cooling requirements. The exterior of the building is designed to provide operable windows for natural ventilation, sun-shade screens to control heat gain, and special glass and light shelves to direct natural light into the center of the space. A sweeping steel cornice expresses the building's environmental design by combining shading on the south side and a rack for photovoltaic panels that satisfies a significant share of the facility's electrical needs.

Retail

The Oxford Street Retail, on the ground floor below the Oxford Plaza Housing, helps strengthen the shopping district between downtown and the university with active retail and commercial uses. The retail development also includes forty parking spaces, which are leased to residents of the affordable housing complex constructed above the retail.

Oxford Plaza Housing

Oxford Plaza provides ninety-seven units of affordable workforce housing for families and individuals in the heart of downtown Berkeley, located less than one-quarter mile from local transit, public schools, the library, retail, restaurants, parks, and the University of California–Berkeley campus. The affordable work-force housing includes a mix of studio, one-, two- and three-bedroom units with good natural light, ventilation, and outlooks onto the street or the central court-yard. Because it is designed to accommodate families, nearly 50% of the units are two- and three-bedroom units. The building includes space for resident services, community rooms, and a roof terrace with a tot lot, to provide a protected play area for smaller children.

The residential building is constructed of five stories of metal stud framing over a first-floor concrete podium. Energy efficient heating and lighting systems combine with rooftop solar hot water panels to create a model for energy efficient and environmentally responsible residential development. Other residential green features include no and low volatile organic compound (VOC) paints, natural linoleum, Energy Star appliances, high recycled content carpeting, and certified lumber. All of these insure the highest indoor air quality for the residents at the same time contributing to the sustainable design elements of the building.

Public Parking

A below-grade public parking garage is accessed from Kittredge Street with 103 parking spaces on one level. Figures 9.3 and 9.4 provide floor plans of the ground and second floors of the entire complex.

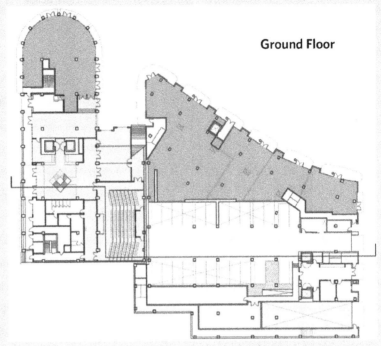

Ground Floor

FIGURE 9.3 First-Floor plan shows Brower lobby, gallery, and Gather restaurant on the left with retail/commercial above parking and housing entry on the right. *Source: Executed as WRT/Solomon E.T.C.*

Second Floor

FIGURE 9.4 Second-Floor plan shows space for Brower Center offices on the left with housing on the right. *Source: Executed as WRT/Solomon E.T.C.*

OWNERSHIP STRUCTURE AND DEVELOPMENT PROCESS

Oxford Street Development, LLC (Oxford) was formed in 2003 for the development of the Oxford Plaza and David Brower Center project. The two members of Oxford Street Development, LLC are Resources for Community Development (RCD), a Berkeley-based nonprofit housing developer and the David Brower Center, a California 501(c)3 nonprofit organization. Oxford acquired the parcel from the City of Berkley and subdivided it into four air-rights parcels for the development of the four project components—the David Brower Center, retail, housing, and public parking. Oxford sold the housing air-rights parcel to a partnership controlled by RCD for the development of the affordable housing. The affordable housing was separately financed utilizing a variety of housing funding sources. Oxford constructed the Brower Center, retail, and public parking improvements on the remaining three parcels. Upon completion of construction, Oxford sold the public parking to the City of Berkeley for $1 and leased the Brower Center to the David Brower Center and leased the retail to an entity controlled by RCD at a rent required to cover the debt service on the project financing.

Equity Community Builders (ECB), a San Francisco–based developer and project manager, was retained by Oxford Street Development to serve as the developer/development manager for the overall project. ECB worked closely with representatives from the Brower Center and RCD to:

- Negotiate a development and disposition agreement with the City of Berkley.
- Coordinate the design, approval, and permit processes.
- Develop and maintain project budgets, schedules, and operating projections.
- Structure the overall project financing for the Brower, retail, and parking components.
- Manage the construction process.
- Assist in lease negotiations with office and retail tenants.
- Serve as property manager for the Brower Center during the initial years of operations.

The development and financing of the Oxford Plaza and David Brower Center project was extremely complex and extended for over six years from initial selection and negotiations with the City through project completion. ECB combined the development expertise and capacity to manage this complex process with substantial experience working with nonprofit organizations on similar mission driven and multi-tenant projects.

Figure 9.5 illustrates the ownership structure that incorporated New Markets Tax Credit (NMTC) financing for the Brower Center, retail, and parking components of the project.

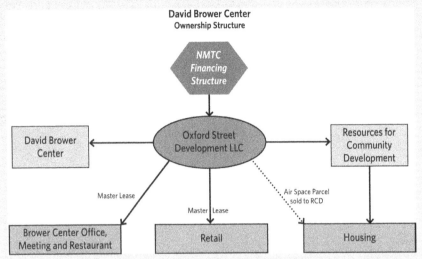

FIGURE 9.5 This graphic depicts the Ownership Structure at the David Brower Center, including the financing structure and the lease agreements with the different tenant groups—Brower Center Office, Meeting and restaurant, retail, and housing. Note that the David Brower Center is both a member of the owner, Oxford Street Development LLC, and a tenant of the space. *Source: Equity Community Builders.*

PROJECT ECONOMICS AND FINANCING
Development Budget

The total development cost for the Oxford Plaza and David Brower Center project was $78.3 million. The budget for the Brower Center, retail, and public parking components of the project is approximately $37.6 million as summarized in the sources and uses in Table 9.1.

Project Financing

Table 9.2 is a summary of the funding for the Brower Center, retail and public parking components of the Oxford Plaza and David Brower Center.

Figure 9.6 illustrates the complex financing structure for the David Brower Center, retail, and public parking components.

New Markets Tax Credit

Oxford utilized New Markets Tax Credits (NMTC) to assist in the project financing. To maximize the benefit of the NMTC, a leveraged financing structure was utilized whereby all project funds were structured as loans to a single-purpose investment fund, which in turn invested those funds into three Community Development Entities (CDEs) with an allocation of NMTCs. The Reznick Group was retained, along with ECB, to assist in the evaluation, negotiation, and appropriate structuring of the NMTC financing. These funds were structured as loans from the CDEs at a low interest rate and a long amortization period that may either be forgiven or bought out by Oxford at a nominal cost.

Table 9.1 Sources and Uses of Funds

Source: Equity Community Builders.

David Brower Center				
Summary Sources and Uses of Funds—Brower, Retail and Parking Components				3/21/2007
	Brower Center ($)	Retail ($)	Parking ($)	Total ($)
Project costs				
Share of land/public parking cost	2,012,729	1,872,573		In Brower Center and Retail
Hard costs	19,070,032	2,619,814	6,211,470	27,901,316
Hard cost contingency	1,092,783	154,081	478,844	1,725,709
Soft costs	6,811,709	1,367,097	1,978,606	10,157,412
Total development costs	28,987,254	6,013,565	8,668,921	39,784,437
Sources of funds				
Bank financing—RSF	3,200,000			3,200,000
Program related investment loans	4,000,000			4,000,000
Section 108 Loan	2,000,000	2,000,000		4,000,000
LCD/Clearinghouse Loan		1,000,000		1,000,000
New Market Tax Credits	8,185,886	1,256,656	2,630,734	12,073,276
Charitable contributions	11,439,340			11,439,340
BEDI grant		1,767,000		1,767,000
Interest income during construction	162,028	214		162,242
33% Brower capital contribution			2,012,729	In Brower Costs
36% Housing capital contribution			2,152,885	2,152,885
31% Retail capital contribution			1,872,573	Retail Costs
Total financing sources	28,987,254	6,013,565	8,668,921	39,784,437

Notes: This table shows the sources and uses of the more than $39 million in project costs for the Brower Center, Retail and Parking components. It includes the hard and soft costs and the various sources of capital to fund the project, which include debt, capital campaign, grants, New Markets Tax Credits, and capital contributions. BEDI = Brownfield Economic Development Initiative.

Table 9.2 Summary of Project Financing

Source	Amount	Component	Comment
Bank financing	$3.2 million	Brower Center	RSF Social Finance
Program-related investment loans	$4.0 million	Brower Center	Center for Ecoliteracy
Sections 108 loan	$4.0 million	Brower Center and Retail	City of Berkeley/HUD
New Market Tax Credit Equity (loan)	$12.1 million	Brower, Retail and Parking	USBCDC as investor with USBCDC, Opportunity Fund, and Clearinghouse as CDEs
BEDI grant	$1.8 million	Retail	Awarded to the project by HUD
CDE loans	$1.0 million	Retail	Opportunity Fund and Clearinghouse
Charitable contributions	$11.4 million	Brower Center	David Brower Center Capital Campaign

Notes: This table depicts the Summary of Project Financing including the varied sources, amounts, and uses for the funds. The largest amount was the New Markets Tax Credit loan of more than $12 million with its transaction structure detailed in Figure 9.6. Public and private sources were used to support this project including federal dollars from the US Department of Housing and Urban Development (HUD) and local money from the City of Berkeley. USBCDC = U.S. Bancorp Community Development Corporation. CDE = Community Development Entity. BEDI = Brownfield Economic Development Initiative.

Source: Equity Community Builders.

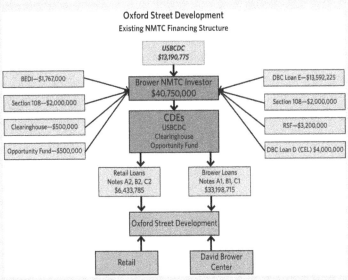

FIGURE 9.6 This chart depicts the complex New Markets Tax Credit financing structure for the David Brower Center, Retail and Parking components. The project used the New Markets Tax Credit (NMTC) tool to assist in the project financing. The NMTC financing structure was subsequently dissolved at the end of the tax credit period, and the Brower Center was refinanced with long-term debt. *Source: Equity Community Builders.*
NMTC: New Markets Tax Credits; CDE: Community Development Entity; USBCDC: U.S. Bancorp Community Development Corporation; DBC: David Brower Center; RSF: Rudolf Steiner Foundation; CEL: Center for Ecoliteracy; BEDI: Brownfields Economic Development Initiative

Brownfield Economic Development Initiative Grant

A Brownfield Economic Development Initiative (BEDI) grant of $1,767,000 was officially awarded by US Department of Housing and Urban Development (HUD) to the City of Berkeley for this project in March of 2006. These funds were structured as a loan to the investment fund with a nominal or contingent interest payment and a subordinate position to all other funds.

Section 108 Loan

The City secured a $4 million Section 108 Loan from HUD in April of 2006. These funds are secured by a pledge of the City's Community Development Block Grant funds. The Section 108 loan was structured as an interest only loan to the investment fund for the first seven years at an interest rate of approximately 1% per year. It is anticipated that this loan will be repaid at the end of the seven-year NMTC period in concert with an overall refinancing of the project.

Charitable Contributions

The David Brower Center initiated an $11 million capital campaign to fund the initial development and ongoing operations of the Brower Center. A bridge loan of approximately $6 million was provided at closing to cover the outstanding balance to be funded from the capital campaign.

Program-Related Investment Loans

David Brower Center secured a program-related investment loan of $4 million from the Center for Ecoliteracy that was provided to the investment partnership at an interest rate of 4%. These funds are subordinate to the bank and Section 108 financing.

Bank Financing

Oxford secured $3.2 million in bank financing from RSF Social Finance, which also flows through the investment fund.

Debt Service Coverage

The net operating income from operations of the Brower Center and retail components provides adequate cash flow to support the financing sources with an adequate debt service coverage and loan to value ratio. Further security is provided to the lender by the fact that the office rents are being offered at below-market rental rates.

PROJECT OPERATIONS

Oxford Street Development, LLC, master leases the Brower Center to the David Brower Center nonprofit organization and master leases the retail components of the project to RCD. The completed public parking was sold to the City for $1 in exchange for the land. The revenue generated from the operations of the Brower Center and the retail components support the master lease payments to Oxford, which are sufficient to cover the debt service on project financing. The following is a summary of the operating assumptions for the Brower Center and retail components.

David Brower Center

The David Brower Center was initially projected to generate gross income of approximately $1.4 million from rental of the office and restaurant areas and conference center operations. Operating expenses before Brower Center staff were estimated to total approximately $770,000 resulting in a net operating income of approximately $630,000. The net operating income funded the master lease payment of approximately $600,000 to Oxford Street Development to cover the debt service on the project financing. Table 9.3 summarizes some of the key components of operating income and expenses.

Table 9.3 Operating Revenue and Expense

Revenue/Expense	Income/Cost	Description
Rentable office area	31,122 sq. ft.	
Restaurant area	3,242 sq. ft.	
Conference area	6,150 sq. ft.	Includes meeting rooms, theater and gallery
Office rent	$29 per sq. ft.	Full service including utilities and janitorial expenses
Restaurant rent	$38 per sq. ft.	Triple net rent (NNN) with all expenses and taxes passed through to the tenant.
Office and restaurant income	$1,075,000	Rental income and partial reimbursement of operating expenses and taxes
Conference and meeting revenue	$320,000	Gross revenue from conference center operations including theater, gallery, and meeting room space rental
Building operating expenses	$375,000	Operating costs exclusive of conference center operations, staff and property taxes
Conference center expenses	$270,000	Direct costs, exclusive of staff, for conference center operations
Brower Center staff and overhead	$730,000	Staff and overhead costs for the Brower Center organization, conference center and property operations
Property taxes	None	The Brower Center is exempt from property taxes for that portion of the building occupied by nonprofit organizations.

Notes: This table shows the Operating Revenues and Expense for the overall project highlighting the square foot area by each use and the rent charged to each of the tenant categories (restaurant and office). Conferences and meetings generate sizable revenue for the project. The property is exempt from property taxes for the portion of the building occupied by nonprofit organizations.

Source: Equity Community Builders.

Revenues from office/restaurant rental and conference center operations cover basic building operations and master lease payments. Ongoing financial support is required to cover Brower Center staff for ongoing conference center operations as well as program, development, and related administrative activities.

This summary of revenues and expenses was based on initial operating projections. Actual income and expenses have not been confirmed but sufficient net operating income was generated during the seven-year NMTC compliance period to make the master lease payments to Oxford Street Development. In 2014, the NMTC investor exercised its right to sell its interest in the NMTC investment fund to Oxford Street Development, and the Brower Center and RCD exercised their right to purchase their respective ownership in Brower Center and retail components of the project, resulting in the effective unwind of the NMTC financing and ownership structure.

Retail

The retail component of the project includes approximately 8,080 sq. ft. of retail space and forty parking spaces that are leased to residents of the housing development. The estimated net operating income from these retail and parking uses is $259,000 (before reserves).

OWNERSHIP INFORMATION

Oxford Street Development LLC: Oxford was formed in 2003 for the development of the Oxford Plaza and David Brower Center project. The two members of Oxford are RCD, a Berkeley-based nonprofit housing developer, and the David Brower Center, a California 501(c)3 nonprofit organization.

David Brower Center: The David Brower Center is a California 501(c)3 nonprofit organization formed in 2001 to create a center and facility for like-minded organizations to focus on environmental issues.

Resources for Community Development: Founded in 1984 by concerned Berkeley community members, RCD is a nonprofit affordable housing development corporation dedicated to creating and preserving affordable housing for people with the fewest options, enriching lives and building communities.

Development Team

Developer/Development Manager—Equity Community Builders: ECB is a San Francisco–based real estate developer specializing in urban infill projects that exemplify innovative, environmentally responsible design and creative financing solutions. A majority of ECB's projects have involved the development of facilities on behalf of nonprofit organizations and have included several multi-tenant nonprofit centers such as the Thoreau Center for Sustainability (now Tides Converge) in San Francisco's Presidio National Park and the Ed Roberts Campus in Berkeley.

Architect: Solomon E.T.C.

Daylighting Design: Loisos + Ubbelohde Associates.

MEP Engineer: Rumsey Engineers.

Sustainability Consultant: Siegel & Strain Architects.

Structural Engineer: Tipping Mar + Associates.

General Contractor: Cahill Contractors, Inc.

NMTC Accounting Firm: Reznick Group.

PART 4
OWNERSHIP AND GOVERNANCE

10 Who Drives Decisions
Ownership and Governance of Nonprofit Centers

The single defining characteristic of shared nonprofit space is that it occupies real estate of some kind, which is owned or leased. As a consequence, two important topics arise: the ownership of the real estate, and its governance.[1] No matter how much the collaboration, the services, and the sharing may be extended, such sites must begin with the control of some piece of real estate, regardless if it is owned, leased, or donated. Thereafter, some governing body must decide financial and operational issues and assure that the real estate will be dedicated to its intended use.

Moreover, in our North American society, real estate has financial value. Financial resources must be expended to own or lease the real estate, to adapt and modify it if needed, and to maintain it over time. For that reason, owning real estate creates both opportunities and risks. Once occupied, there are a variety of governance models for making mission-driven decisions about the space and its uses. This chapter outlines a variety of key considerations in creating both ownership and governance structures to manage these opportunities and risks.

This discussion of ownership structures is translatable into other types of control over real estate—for example, long-term leases, master-leases, and land trust ownership—and many of the governance considerations outlined in this chapter will be relevant for those structures as well.

In what follows we will be describing ownership structures separately from governance considerations. Governance issues occur whether real estate is owned or leased. In addition, governance can provide a significant voice for partners and constituents who are not actually part of the ownership structure.

KEY CONSIDERATIONS IN OWNERSHIP STRUCTURES

There are several key issues to take into consideration in developing an ownership structure for a nonprofit center. These include the mission of the project, issues of risk, working with partners, financing considerations, and tax considerations—all of which are explored in this section.

Mission of the Project

There are a variety of ownership structures that we will outline in the following discussion, but as with other aspects of shared space, clarifying the mission and goals of a project is one of the most important variables and an essential first step for a successful structure. For example, an organization's plan may be to slowly fill its building over time as staff expands. In the meantime, it will follow a sole owner or master lessor approach and rent the extra space in the building to smaller, unrelated programs. Such an arrangement demands an ownership structure very different from a community or joint ownership approach used for an intentional collaboration by a number of organizations to provide integrated social services in a low-income community. In the first, a single organization will normally ensure its long-term control over space. In the second, a different, more complicated structure of joint ownership and governance may be necessary to protect the collaboration for the long-term.

Resources and Risk

Valuable resources like real estate require funds to own or control. With that control come both rewards and risks. Having control allows the owner/s to create exciting shared endeavors, to create value for the owning organization(s) and the community over time, as well as the ability for nonprofits to enjoy stability and legitimacy in the community. But risks abound:

- Resources spent on real estate are not available for other critical organizational needs. In particular, there is an opportunity cost to the significant outlay of time and resources necessary to acquire, manage, and maintain owned real estate that is above and beyond leased space.
- Mortgages, and other forms of debt, so often used to acquire real estate, require ongoing payments to maintain ownership, no matter the state of the economy or the financial status of the owners.
- Cash flow problems at a crucial time can result in loss of the project altogether, as well as losing the investment made to that point.
- Few spaces are acquired or leased in exactly the right configuration and condition. Additional, unanticipated money is often required to make the space usable, even if it has been donated. Ongoing funds for operating costs, repairs, and ongoing renovations are necessary to keep property desirable and efficient for occupants.
- Finally, capital campaigns create a set of expectations from donors that must be satisfied for the organization/s reputation to be maintained.

Managing these financial obligations effectively depends in large part on the effectiveness of the control structure for making critical decisions, whether it is to set rents, decide on repairs, evaluate tenant financial viability, or create budgets for acquisition, renovation, and operations. Figure 10.1 outlines the continuum of risk in a shared space project in graphic form.

Continuum of Risk

| TENANTS | TENANT COUNCIL | BOARD MEMBERS | CO-OWNERS |

Low — Responsibility, Risk, & Control — High

FIGURE 10.1 In designing an ownership structure, often it is the entities with the most financial investment (owners) or fiduciary duty (board of directors) who will need the most control to mitigate risks of the project. *Source: Nonprofit Center Network.*

Thus, very often in shared space projects, we see the organizations providing the start-up and ongoing resources, either in cash or credit, and advocating for structures that will give them the control to manage these risks. Similarly, organizations may choose leasing over purchase in nonprofit center site acquisition not only because of lack of funds but to minimize financial risk and maintain organizational flexibility.

Partners and Partnerships

A third key factor in ownership and governance structures are the partners and stakeholders involved with the building, and their constraints and opportunities.

We often see nonprofits partnering with others such as foundation funders, governmental bodies, and other operating nonprofits to create a shared space project. Key considerations in determining ownership structures include the relative financial strength of the participating organizations, alignment of their visions for the project, management compatibility, and fundraising abilities. See Box 10.1: Prerequisites for Building Strong Partnerships, for a discussion of essential criteria to use in evaluating partners and partnerships.

Successful projects have been created through partnership with government entities that can provide real estate and/or funding for a project. But government stakeholders often have more diverse needs than the nonprofits involved in the project. Agreement in advance on what control the governmental entities need in the project is crucial, as well as clarity on the expected longevity of their support and what must be needed to maintain it.

Working with the public sector on a capital project brings its own risks and rewards. Government involvement can slow down projects as the bureaucratic processes can be cumbersome and time-consuming. Nonprofit organizations may not maintain as much control and leverage when the public sector is involved.

At the same time, the public sector is unique in owning many diverse, often underutilized, public buildings—we see nonprofit centers in former county office building, schools, bus barns, utility buildings, firehouses, and the like. The governmental sector has financial resources for capital and operating expenses. Government can be an excellent partner for these reasons. As with all projects, structured agreements between the parties are key. (See Chapter 24: Partnering with Allies for an expanded discussion of this material.)

Box 10.1 Prerequisites for Building Strong Partnerships

Similar Levels of Organizational Readiness

Before embarking on a shared space project together, each partner needs to go through its own organizational readiness project to make sure its board is supportive, its financial position is strong enough to take on the project, and the project fits appropriately into its strategic plan. If partners have reached this stage independently, collectively they can move forward with the demands of the project with strength. Without this, several partners may be ready to move on to a purchase or a lease, for example, while others are still scrambling to line up internal support and the real estate opportunity may be missed.

Complementary Missions

Even if organizations may be carrying out very different activities in a shared space, it's important that the activities are complementary in terms of constituencies served, design needs, and acceptable locations. Without that, operational issues like competition for conference rooms, needs around security and conflicts between constituency needs can lead to difficult operational challenges down the road. Harmonizing financial objectives and risk tolerance is also important to do in advance.

Compatible Personalities

The boards and staff of multi-stakeholder projects will be spending a lot of time together and making hard decisions during the process. If you find yourself just not getting along with the leaders of another organization, think deeply about whether this is the right partner for the project.

The Existence of Structured Agreements

No matter how much partner organizations have worked together in the past, having written agreements is an essential ingredient in any shared space project. It's important to think through all the contingencies and potential conflicts with a supportive lawyer and decide in advance how you want to handle them, from making construction decisions to governance structure to what happens if one organization needs or wants to leave the partnership. Undoubtedly, when those conflicts arise, the people will be different and leaving them a clear roadmap of project intentions is essential. The middle of a conflict over money is always the worst time to come up with a decision-making process. For these reasons, executing an MOU or a formal partnership agreement, approved by the boards of each organization, in advance is vital.

The private and philanthropic sectors have also partnered with nonprofits to create nonprofit centers. These arrangements have included the spectrum ranging from a commercial owner providing a master lease or donating a building, to foundation loan guarantees on acquisition debt, to foundations creating and operating centers for their communities. The Nonprofit Centers Network has examples of projects led by community foundations, United Ways, family foundations, and other local funders who have a deep connection to their communities and are uniquely positioned to provide needed space for collaboration or services for their grantees.

Partnerships to create nonprofit centers almost always follow this cardinal rule: *the more partners, the more time the project will take.* The time is usually well worth it in terms of the results—more resources, enhanced collaboration, better community outcomes—but underestimating what's involved can lead to needless frustration and mistakes. The authors have observed that the more carefully agreements are worked out at the onset of a project, even if it takes more time, the more likely the project is to reach success.

Financing Considerations

A fourth key consideration in determining an ownership structure is the financing structure of the project. When banks consider making loans, they look for organizations with strong credit standing and often also a strong revenue track record, even if it is primarily successful fundraising over time. Thus, a newly formed nonprofit may have a hard time reassuring a lender of its financial stability. The banks may require loan guarantees from the strongest nonprofits in the collaboration or even from their board members. These participating nonprofits in turn may require more ownership control in the project in return for the financial risks they have assumed.

Impact of Tax Considerations on Ownership Structures

How a project is structured can make a big difference in how it is taxed. While a few important areas of taxation are mentioned here, all projects should consult a tax attorney to understand the applicability of these and other issues to their specific situation. Please note that Canadian and US tax considerations are broken out separately.

US Income Tax Considerations

In the United States, nonprofits in general are exempt from income tax on rents received from another nonprofit, a very common occurrence with nonprofit centers. However, if the property is "debt-financed property," namely, that it was acquired with debt financing, or is subject to a mortgage or other form of lien or encumbrance, then net income from that property may be subject to corporate income tax. In other words, net income from the leasing activity, after taking into account depreciation and other operating expenses, will cause the nonprofit to pay federal and sometimes state Unrelated Business Income Tax (UBIT) on the net income. It is important to understand that the tax is only on net income. Nonprofits that break even or even run deficits on their unrelated real estate operations may end up owing no tax even if the income it receives is unrelated.

The UBIT applies, however, only to "unrelated" income. Thus, if the income is related to the exempt function of the nonprofit, if its program revenue, the income will not be subject to the tax. If the leasing income is directly related to the tax-exempt mission of the nonprofit center, it is not unrelated, and the fact that the facility is debt-financed will not cause the net income to be taxable. Box office ticket revenue of nonprofit theatres is an example of this kind of program revenue. If the purpose of the organizing nonprofit is to run a nonprofit center and that's enshrined in their by-laws, rental income would generally be considered program revenue and not unrelated income. The US Internal Revenue Service (IRS) has granted exemptions to nonprofits that own and operate nonprofit centers, when the facts support a finding that the leasing activity furthers the charitable purpose of the property owner. This determination means that their rent revenue is not subject to income tax.[2]

Nonprofits in the US contemplating creating a nonprofit center should be sure in advance to consult an attorney to understand the tax implications of what is in their articles of incorporation and by-laws and whether their new venture's purposes fit within their legally defined purposes or whether the documents need to be amended.

Property Tax in the US

In the US, nonprofits are often also exempt from property tax on real estate they own. The laws are complex and vary by city, county, and state, but, in general, achieving property tax exemption for an acquired property can significantly reduce operating expenses and allow lower rents to tenants over time. But there are complexities. Some jurisdictions have been known to assert that property tax is payable on any nonprofit-owned property that is rented, even to other nonprofits. Other jurisdictions are more liberal and will allow tax-exemption for parts of a building even if other parts are occupied by for-profits. In some locations with lots of large universities and hospital, taking a property off the tax rolls can be challenging. During the site selection, the authors recommend understanding a property's tax status and any local hurdles that might prevent the property from becoming tax-exempt.

We will return to this issue in the individual structures in the following discussion, but understanding the property tax rules in your geographic area is a crucial step in planning a project.

Canadian Income Tax Considerations

In Canada,[3] tax laws governing the creation and operation of nonprofit centers are a bit more limiting and complex than in the United States. There is no provision in the tax code for tax payments on unrelated business income to charities as there is in the United States with UBIT. Rather, violation of the tax laws through operation of a disallowed "unrelated" business venture[4] can lead to revocation of charitable status. In addition, as is discussed in the following paragraphs, tax treatment of nonprofit centers is very different for registered charities as opposed to nonprofit organizations.[5] These limits are being successfully negotiated by charities and non-profit organizations across Canada, but we want to emphasize the important of consulting an attorney early and often in creating your project. (See Chapter 12: The Common Roof™ for a creative application of the basic rules and Figure 10.2 for a photo of a successful Ontario shared space.)

We're going to look separately at two different types of Canadian legal entities that could operate a shared space—registered charities and non-profit organizations.[6]

1. *Registered Charities:* Charitable organizations and public foundations can run shared space operations under two different tax provisions. Private foundations are not allowed to do any business activities what so ever.

    Umbrella Organizations: The most favorable provision for achieving charitable registration for operating a nonprofit center is under what the Canadian Revenue Agency calls umbrella organizations and title-holding organizations. This is spelled out in Canada Revenue Agency Policy Statement CPS-026 Guidelines for the registration of umbrella organizations and title-holding organizations, May 1, 2008.[7]

    Under the policy guidelines, Section A umbrella organizations are most suitable for shared space projects. Under this section, "promoting the efficiency and effectiveness of other registered charities" is an acceptable charitable activity. The Charities Directorate's position is that providing a service or assistance that directly improves the charitable programs of other registered charities, that improves the efficient administration of other charities, or that enables charities to realize economies of scale that they could not achieve on their own is "charitable." In other words, the

FIGURE 10.2 *CSI Spadina, Toronto, Ontario.* Marcus Huynh, CSI Spadina Community Animator and CSI 192 Coordinator, attends the 2017 annual celebratory Wine & Cheese held by the Center for Social Innovation in Toronto at 215 Spadina, location of one of their current six shared spaces. *Photo credit: Centre for Social Innovation and Nyo Mudzingwa from You the Best Photography.*

activity would qualify as a charitable activity of the charity; therefore, the activity is not a business activity. As such, the charity can charge reasonable fees (including rent) and accumulate reasonable surpluses through those operations.

In the Policy Statement, "providing a facility, at below-market rates, to house the operations of other registered charities" is specifically named as qualifying for charitable status as is the provision of various kinds of support and training on "operational and management issues," which happen in many nonprofit centers.

An important caveat is that at least 90% of the beneficiaries of these umbrella organizations must be registered charities and support to non-profit groups is strictly limited. This could have the impact of seriously limiting the ability of a nonprofit center to rent to Canadian non-profits (which are not charities). If the goal of the project is also to provide rental space for tenants or users that are not registered charities, the rental in general would need to be either structured as a passive rental investment of the charity, which would act as a passive landlord, or the rental must meet the criteria as a related business explained in the following text. In either case, the charity must charge fair market value rent and substantiate the reasons for providing services to non-charitable recipients among the presentation of a variety of other factors.

Also covered under this same policy statement are what are called Section C charities established to hold title to property. These charities hold title and may carry out property management and other functions for property owned by another related registered charity. This model would seem to be advantageous for organizations that for various reasons would not want the operating charity to own title to real property and therefore move ownership of the property in to a separate land holding charity. In this case an acceptable charitable purpose would be "to promote the efficiency and effectiveness of Charity ABC's charitable programs by providing and maintaining facilities for this purpose."[8]

As will be clear in reading the policy statement, Section B of the policy statement[9] creates so many restrictions for umbrella organizations in serving noncharitable entities that the section seems a stretch to be used for shared space project charitable registration.

Related Businesses: In the Canadian tax statute, there are also provisions for related businesses which are outlined in Canadian Revenue Agency Policy Statement Reference Number CPS-019 What is a related business? March 31, 2003.[10]

We must remember that carrying on an unrelated business can result in a charity losing their charitable registration.[11] Related businesses are those that are linked to a charity's purpose and could conceivably include a facility run by an organization with exclusively charitable purpose. However, the policy statement requires that the business be subordinate to the charity's primary purpose which creates difficulty in qualifying a nonprofit center for that purpose.

2. *Non-Profit Organizations:* In Canada, distinct from the US general usage of the term, non-profits are non-charitable organizations described in Paragraph 149(1) (l) of the Income Tax Act—as "organized exclusively for social welfare, civic improvement, pleasure, recreation or any other purpose except profit."[12] Similar but less regulated than US 501(c)4s, non-profit organizations can be corporations or unincorporated associations. They are generally tax-exempt, but donations are not tax-deductible as they are for registered charities.

> Non-profits in theory can run a business on a non-profit basis, but the Canadian Revenue Agency is restrictive on types of income and amounts of surplus that nonprofits can have. Whether an activity is acceptable can only be determined on a facts and circumstances basis. As in the US, earning profits just to fund not-for-profit purposes is not considered not-for-profit activity, and in Canada carrying out of prohibited (non not-for-profit) activity can result in loss of non-profit status and becoming taxable.[13]

Property Tax in Canada

The framework for property tax is set on a provincial basis.[14] For example, in Ontario, property tax is outlined in the Ontario Assessment Act. This governs property tax on both residential and commercial properties. There is also a section on exempt properties outlining certain types of property like churches or schools or properties owned by certain types of charities that can be exempted from tax. But there is no blanket exemption for property owned by charities or non-profits. And ultimately whether a property is tax-exempt is based on use of the property, not on just its ownership. Using property owned by a charity for a business use can make it not exempt.

Within this framework rates are set by municipalities. Localities may enact their own by-laws to provide benefits like rebates or lower tax rates to further policy objectives. Property tax changes may have huge impacts on shared spaces and public policy on this must be followed closely.[15] Under these regulations, sometimes charities may pay lower rates. And some locations may determine this on a facts and circumstances basis. Thus, for every project, initial planning should include analysis of the nature of the owners, the use of the project and the city and province as it affects property tax.

THE OWNERSHIP MODELS

What does all this mean for creating a nonprofit shared space? Next, we outline a series of specific ownership models that can help answer this question.

Sole Ownership or Master Leasing of Space

Many nonprofit centers use this model of sole ownership or its equivalent in master leasing. Here, one mission-driven entity owns the space, often a building or a commercial condominium unit. The entity is most often a nonprofit, but in coworking or commercial examples, the entity can be a for-profit or even a government entity.

The model also can include shared space where one organization master-leases a space directly from the owner/landlord and subleases to other organizations, both nonprofit and for-profit. The details of this model are outlined in Figure 10.3.

This model provides the most control for the owner/master-lessor as they can independently pick tenants, set rents, decide on renovation levels, and related issues. The single owner enjoys 100% of the benefit from increases in the building's value. On the other hand, this model also brings the most risk for the owner, as it is solely responsible for debt payments, building maintenance, and rent payments (in the case of master-leasing), whether or not sufficient rents come from tenants to cover their costs.

This model is often seen in "naturally occurring" nonprofit centers where a nonprofit owns a building and fills its excess space with other tenants or where landlords understand the benefits of nonprofits as tenants and fill their building with nonprofits. Over time, more proactive collaboration and shared services may develop among the tenants.

In cases of a single organization's purchase of a building, lenders for purchase or renovation will rely on the creditworthiness of the owner, although commitments from large or "anchor" tenants can bolster banks' willingness to lend.

Sole Ownership Model

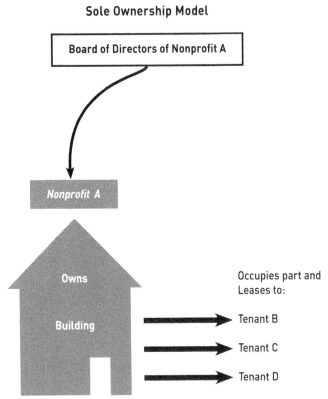

FIGURE 10.3 In this model, one organization owns or leases a space, occupies part of it, and leases the remaining space to other organizations—nonprofit, for-profit, or government.
Source: Nonprofit Centers Network, as modified by authors.

In this model, consideration in advance of tax-exemption issues is key. Most nonprofits or registered charities do not, by their by-laws, have a charitable purpose of providing stable, affordable rents to other nonprofits or charities. If the charitable purpose does not include the leasing activities, the income may be treated as unrelated business income in the US (see previous discussion on US tax considerations) and may also put the charitable status at risk in Canada. In addition, if you are contemplating for-profit tenants, it is important to understand how local tax authorities will assess property tax on those portions of the building or the building overall.

One way to address the income tax issues, especially in the US, might be by structuring the ownership through a wholly owned for-profit subsidiary or nonprofit supporting organization (or other controlled entity like a sole member LLC), which is explicitly created with the charitable purpose of creating shared space and services. This model can also protect the parent nonprofit from liabilities associated with owning and operating property, which is why this model is used by many for-profit real estate concerns. This model can also allow for creating a board of directors with expertise more relevant to operating a real estate concern than the nonprofit parent's board. Be sure to consult with legal counsel about the effect of this structure on property tax-exemption before finalizing any new structure.

Community Nonprofit Ownership

This model is more explicitly designed for collaboration among two or more nonprofit or mission-driven entities. This includes projects where community members and donors and nonprofits have come together to create nonprofit centers either by buying, building, or master-leasing space. Alternatively, this is a model for several nonprofits coming together and sharing resources and a capital campaign to create a community resource.

The concept is to create a nonprofit asset that will outlive any individual organization. Risks of ownership are centralized in a new nonprofit ownership entity, which can protect the financial resources of the stakeholders and any organizational board members. The partners work together jointly through the new entity's board of directors to finance, acquire and begin operation of the new shared space. No individual entities or people would benefit from ownership as they could with a LLC model, discussed in the following text. Figure 10.4 shows the various components of this model.

A new entity must develop a careful financing plan if enough resources cannot be raised through capital contributions. This plan often includes third-party or bank loans, which may be based on stakeholder guarantees, and the value of the building or other collateral.

The new entity will typically have a governing body that includes representatives from the stakeholder organizations and/or individuals other than the tenants. The governing body will be responsible for maintaining financial health and community support and may also have to make hard decisions about the property's future. Past

Community Nonprofit Ownership Model

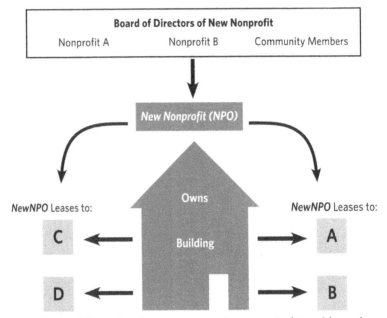

FIGURE 10.4 Designed for creating a long-term community resource. In this model several nonprofits, often with community members, come together to create a new nonprofit that will acquire space and lease it to tenants. Tenants often include the founding partners. *Source: Nonprofit Centers Network, as modified by authors.*

experience has shown that tenants on a board are often reluctant to approve rent increases, for example, even if financial sustainability demands it. This tendency can be mitigated by having tenants represented by their board members rather than staff, with the staff of the tenants being more involved in day-to-day operating decisions.

With these considerations taken into account, some wonderfully effective and collaborative centers have been created with this ownership model.

The Community Land Trust Model

Community land trusts present a second opportunity for shared ownership with an existing nonprofit entity that has a track record and experience in real estate acquisition and ownership. Land trusts are most commonly known for acquisition of natural areas and wilderness for preservation purposes. Community land trusts most often work to address affordability and equity in housing. Using a ground lease, the community land trust will acquire housing. They then sell the structure (commonly a single-family home) to low-income families while retaining ownership of the land underneath. This makes the home more affordable to individuals and allows the homeowner to build equity. As nonprofits, land trusts can also receive foundation grants and individual donations to support their purchases.

Land trusts can also bring this shared ownership structure to commercial real estate. Community land trusts often hold and operate real estate in perpetuity including nonprofit and art centers. Urban Land Conservancy, a community land trust in Denver, operates three nonprofit centers among their real estate holdings (see Chapter 25: Denver's Test Kitchen).

These land trusts can also play an interim ownership role for nonprofits wanting to buy buildings who don't have sufficient capital for a purchase. For example, the Oakland Community Land Trust in California helped four grassroots nonprofits facing displacement buy their building called the 23rd Avenue Community Building in 2017. This project also includes eight affordable apartments. This building had a long history of tenants doing grassroots activism and without a purchase would have been lost to gentrification. Given the limited capital of each of the tenant organizations, this transaction would not have been possible without the partnership with the land trust. Now these organizations have a permanent home and can build equity and ownership over time.[16] As in this example, land trusts can help organizations that are already located in a de facto nonprofit center acquire their building.[17]

Limited Liability Corporation Model

A Limited Liability Corporation (LLC)[18] is a US equity ownership structure that has worked well for cooperative ownership, including by nonprofits where each owner would like to benefit from appreciation of the property and the assets they've put into the project. This legal form is created as a business entity, which, under state or local law, has independent existence from its equity owners. One or more organizations will own what are called membership interests, which may include voting and economic rights in varying percentage interests in the entity. The right to occupy space is separate from equity ownership in the business entity. Thus, if an equity owner (member) also wants space in the property, the right to use the space is governed separately by the lease agreement. Often one or more of the owners also are tenants, paying rent for whatever amount of space they need for a given period. This structure also allows the space to be rented to other, non-owning tenants. See Figure 10.5 for a graphic illustration of this model.

One advantage of this model is that it allows for outside investors as limited members who have limited risk and control while the core organizations may retain control (and responsibility) as managing members. This was done successfully by the Ninth Street Independent Film Center in San Francisco with the contractor and philanthropist, Steve Oliver, temporarily taking back an ownership interest for the work done until his interest was bought out by the nonprofits.[19]

LLCs can obtain debt financing to acquire or maintain the property. However, it is important to understand the financial strength of each member going into the project because the organizations often will be responsible jointly for all the debt. In that case, the default of one owner may adversely affect the other organizations, either directly, if all are jointly and severally liable on the debt, or indirectly, if the LLC defaults and loses the property because one member fails to meet its obligations. Inability to make timely debt payments to cover the defaulting member

Limited Liability Corporation (LLC) Model

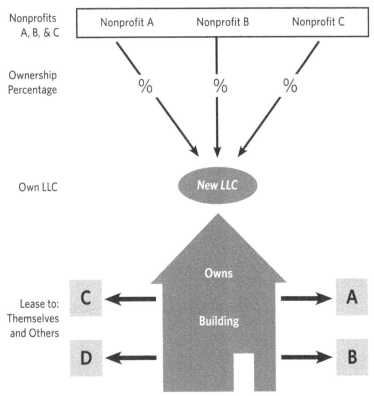

FIGURE 10.5 This is an equity ownership structure that has worked well for cooperative ownership, including by nonprofits where each owning organization would like to benefit from appreciation of the property. *Source: Nonprofit Centers Network, as modified by authors.*

can cause the loss of the whole property. Knowing your partners well before buying together is an important strategy to mitigate risk for this ownership model.

An advantage of the LLC ownership is that the value of the property will accrue to the members, and each member can benefit from an increase in the value of its share. The members of the LLC will typically determine in advance their respective rights to transfer or redeem their interests in the company. Ordinarily, the membership rights are not freely transferable, because each member typically wants to have approval rights over who is substituted as a member. Thus, it is important to decide at the time of formation whether the other members have any right to purchase before an outside purchaser, the approval rights for admission of substitute members, and how the property will be valued if a member wants to be redeemed by the LLC. These and other considerations are included in the LLC operating agreement at the time of its creation, so time spent upfront with a competent attorney thinking through future contingencies and how to deal with them is time well spent.

It's important to note that even if all the members and tenants are nonprofit organizations, the LLC may not be eligible for property tax exemption in your jurisdiction, so that is another factor to research early on. This structure is often treated differently when the LLC has only one member, as a subsidiary of a nonprofit, as previously discussed in the sole ownership model, and the LLC can get the sole member's tax status.

LLCs are often not eligible for grant support because they are not nonprofits. If a shared capital campaign is still desirable, organizations can each receive money separately while collaborating on the campaign and deciding in advance on how the money raised will be spent. Examples also exist of LLCs setting up a management entity for their project, which is a nonprofit and can accept grants for building improvements and especially for developing programs in the building while the actual ownership stays in the for-profit LLC.

Condominium Ownership

The next formal model we will discuss is that of condominium ownership. This is another model where the individual organizations expect a long-term increase in equity from their investment of resources and where combining resources with other compatible partners at the time of acquisition and throughout the ownership of the property is seen as useful.

This model works almost exactly as in the commercial sector where office condos are becoming increasingly common. This model is similar to a residential condo, where each organization owns their unit of the condo space, whether it be a floor or building or warehouse. The square footage and boundaries of their unit are legally defined in the property deed, and in many jurisdictions, documents (e.g., a Condo Declaration) are legally filed with a government entity. In some localities, condos in the same building need certain required partitions between the units. As owners of its unit, the owning organization can either occupy its unit in whole or in part or rent the unit to tenants. This model is illustrated graphically in Figure 10.6.

In addition to the separately deeded space in a condominium, there is also condominium common space, which can be everything from parking lots to roofs to boilers, lobbies, conference rooms, elevators, and hallways. Ownership of common space, and the attendant responsibility for resources to maintain it, are shared by all the condo owners based on their relative percentage of the total square footage of their units. This is a particularly appealing aspect of the condo structure, especially when there is a lot of shared common space, such as conference rooms.

Condominium ownership requires creation of a condo association, controlled by the unit owners, which operates the common space of the building and whose existence is enforced through its by-laws, deed covenants, and government documents.

In a condo situation, each owner acquires its own financing to purchase its unit, which eliminates the shared liability on debt of an LLC and maximizes independence. This separate ownership also makes it easier to get property tax exemption for your unit. However, space flexibility is much reduced since changing the common space, for example by adding a shared conference room, would require amendments to all the relevant legal documents.[20]

Office Condominium Model

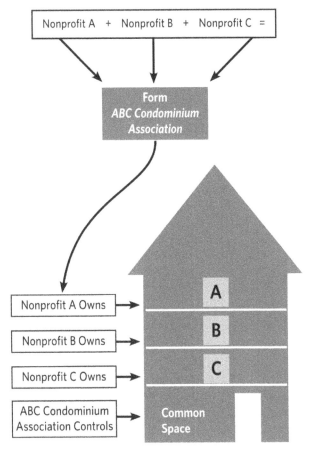

FIGURE 10.6 This is a model where each organization owns (and is required to finance if necessary) its own portion of the building while common parts of the building like lobbies and elevators are owned jointly through a condominium association. *Source: Nonprofit Centers Network, as modified by authors.*

This model is less frequent among nonprofit centers but has been used successfully. In one example, the project had both for profit and nonprofit condo owners, while the nonprofits went a step further by creating a nonprofit shared services structure among themselves.

For-Profit Ownership

The authors have observed commercial landlords adopting aspects of the nonprofit center model as they understand the benefits brought by nonprofit tenants. These benefits include social value, stable tenants, and a good-sized market in most larger cities.

But beyond welcoming nonprofit tenancy, in both the US and Canada, successful shared spaces with explicit social purposes have been created in for-profit legal structures. The previously outlined LLC structure falls in this category. Nonprofit centers created by renting a portion of a for-profit building also fall in this category, as do the growing number of hybrid business structure (sharing both social and profit purposes) including the low-profit limited liability company (LC3) in the US and the British Columbia community contribution company and the Nova Scotia community interest company in Canada. Some coworking spaces like Impact Hub San Francisco[21] are certified B corporations. B corporations, while not a distinct legal entity, are certified by the nonprofit B Lab[22] to meet rigorous standards of social and environmental performance, accountability, and transparency.[23]

In addition, real estate development companies in both Canada and the US have developed for-profit projects explicitly intended to house nonprofit and arts organizations. These types of projects obviously allow a wider range of activities, especially in Canada, and their full taxability can be somewhat offset by charitable and sponsorship contributions.

Importance of Legal Support

The choice of business structures and ownership models is wide and allows for structures customized for the specific location and mission of each project. The key considerations above will help inform the choice. But in each case, the authors have found that early and ongoing support from a creative, mission-driven attorney can help ensure the success of the model and the decision-making.

KEY GOVERNANCE FACTORS

Up to this point in this chapter, the authors have focused on ownership structures and the partnerships often involved in creating a nonprofit center or other shared space projects. But governance considerations go beyond this to include the input and involvement of all the varied stakeholders in the project. Governance structures often need to evolve over time to include these stakeholders and the larger community, and upfront planning for this will do much to ensure the long-term sustainability of the project. In addition, even when the real estate is leased and not owned, some form of governance is needed for meeting the project's goals. We thus turn to this aspect of governance for the remainder of the chapter.

Timeline

Governance typically evolves over the life cycle of the project. As a project evolves from pre-development to acquiring or leasing real estate to operating the occupied space, different structures are needed, and more people may be involved. A typical project starts with a nonelected steering committee of the organizations involved in creating the project, operating with a memorandum of understanding (MOU) which has been approved by all the boards. This often evolves into a board of directors to set building policies, rent levels, and collaboration directions if desired. Organizations leasing together create operating committees. Or in a solely owned building, this board governance may come from a board real estate committee. A project manager or a program director (if a new entity is created) is often hired, something we recommend. Our experience shows that adding the creation and operations of a shared space to a nonprofit executive's existing role leads to overload and mission drift and is not a recipe for success.

Tenant Participation in Governance

But many other stakeholders can be invested in the project, and cultivating that investment is important for project sustainability. Tenants can be involved through tenants' councils, town hall meetings, and collaborative meetings of tenant operations directors or program directors. Setting building operating policies with the collaboration of the tenants encourages smooth operations. Regular meetings of the tenants' executive directors can encourage collaborative programming and shared staffing and avoid conflicts within the organizations over use of shared facilities, especially between large and small organizations. On the other hand, when tenant input is not encouraged and solicited, legitimate tenant complaints often go unheard and needs unmet. Prospective tenants are discouraged by the existing tenants and eventually vacancies can create serious financial problems.

Although these new governance structures do not replace the responsibility and risk of financial partners, they create a context where a larger community is contributing to the success of the project. Often project funders have expectations of interorganizational collaboration or shared services, and institutionalizing tenant and partner dialogue is key in meeting those expectations.

At the same time, as reflected in Figure 10.7, even projects with a very collaborative governance structure will need to take risk into account when codifying which partners have what kinds of control. Stakeholders who are responsible for making debt payments will be more concerned to ensure the financial stability of new tenants than a tenant council focusing on programmatic collaboration or building operations.

Collaboration and Community

Another key stakeholder is the surrounding community. Given the cost of real estate, projects often locate in low-income communities where real estate is more affordable. Some projects are aimed specifically at meeting community needs through providing social services, food services, homes for community entrepreneurship, etc. But even nonprofit centers created for a sector unrelated to the neighboring community (arts, international development, etc.) still exist in a physical context. Attention to the relationship with the community can make the difference between an isolated bubble, possibly facing community hostility, or a vibrant addition to a community with meeting spaces open to all and programming that meets community needs and supports community issues. Creating cafés or art galleries open to

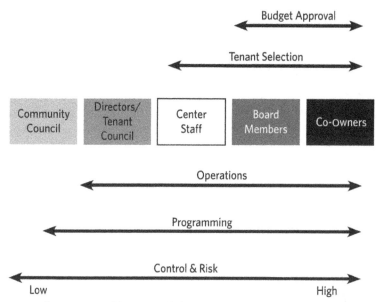

FIGURE 10.7 The most successful centers include the tenants and even the surrounding community in their governance structure. At the same time, issues of risk and control help define the governance roles of each partner. *Source: Nonprofit Centers Network.*

the public is another way to draw community into commercial buildings, even those created primarily to provide affordable space to tenants. Whatever your goals, your center will be most successful if there is a community engagement strategy from the beginning.

Community outreach and town hall meetings create vital links to the larger community even if decision-making is not involved. One best practice in some circumstances is to consult with community even before moving in or as early as the start of planning. Some of the most successful projects have been engaged in this community outreach over years. And such outreach can include marketing and public relations to the donor and government sectors to establish the value of these projects over time.

Although many centers reach self-sufficiency from earned income alone, others find the need for periodic operating or capital fundraising. The more centers reach out to the community, the more likely a successful argument for support can be made.

Governance That Sticks

A key best practice is the institutionalization of governance. Even in the early stages of a project, legally sound MOU's between the partners lay the foundation for a successful collaboration, delineating each partner's responsibilities and contributions, and creating a successful dispute resolution mechanism.

Legally binding governance structures like a board of directors also help bring in community and occupant input and avoid the problem of one donor, one community foundation, or one government agency having significant but misguided control over a project. In a similar vein, a board of directors that includes only the executive directors of the tenants of a project leads to conflicted interests that hinder effective decision-making. As mentioned earlier in this chapter, few nonprofits find it easy to increase their own rent. In a condo or leasing situation where this kind of partner representation makes sense, the governing body should include partner board members who are already being asked to see the bigger picture. And including community members on such a governing body has been seen to help long-term sustainability.

CONCLUSION

Picking the right ownership and governance structures can make or break a shared space project over time. It is crucial for all the parties involved to be as clear as possible from the beginning on their short- and long-term goals: both financial and social. Start with the mission and work from there through the previously outlined considerations.

Make sure that staff and board are aligned on these goals for the project. And make sure each organization is aligned on level of risk they are willing to take. Choose partners wisely and talk through these issues together, both staff and boards.

The beauty of shared space projects is that there is no one best answer for all. All the ownership and governance models outlined here can be adapted to meet the particular needs of your organization, your location, your partners, and your community. Across Canada and the United States, organizations just like yours are transforming physical space and building community. You just have to get started.

NOTES

1. The authors would like to thank Cynthia Rowland, an attorney in San Francisco specializing in nonprofit organizations, for her assistance with this chapter. Of course, any errors are the authors' responsibility.
2. See Internal Revenue Service Rev. Rul. 69-572, 1969-2 C.B. 119 on the subject of Tax Exempt Status for Organizations Created to Manage a Building to House Nonprofits. https://www.irs.gov/pub/irs-tege/rr69_572.pdf. For further discussion, see Wexler, R. A. "Legal Framework for Earned Income." Paper presented at the Social Enterprise Alliance, Long Beach, California, April 2007. https://www.adlercolvin.com/wp-content/uploads/2017/12/Legal-Framework-for-Earned-Income-00160444xA3536PDF.pdf.
3. The authors would like to thank Theresa L. M. Man, a solicitor with Carters Professional Corporation in Ontario, for her assistance with this section. Of course, any errors are totally the authors' responsibility.
4. The technical term in Canada is "unrelated" business in that charitable organizations and public foundations may engage in a business that is "related." Private foundations cannot engage in anny business activities, regardless of whether it is related or unrelated.

5. We use "non-profit" as opposed to the more general "nonprofit" terminology in this section to keep clear the distinction between registered charities and non-profit organizations under Canadian tax law.

6. In Canada, there are two main types of tax-exempt organizations. One category is *registered charities*, which must be established and operate exclusively for charitable purposes. Donations to them can bring tax credits to the donor. A second category is *non-profit organizations*, which are organized for a variety of social welfare purposes and are similar to IRS 501(c)(4) organizations in the United States. Although contributions to them do not bring tax credits to the giver, the nonprofit center models in this book are also very relevant to Canadian non-profits and US 501(c)(4) social welfare organizations.

7. Canada Revenue Agency Policy Statement CPS-026, "Guidelines for the Registration of Umbrella Organizations and Title HOLDING Organizations." May 1, 2008. http://www.cra-arc.gc.ca/chrts-gvng/chrts/plcy/cps/cps-026-eng.html.

8. Canada Revenue Agency Policy Statement CPS-026, "Guidelines for the Registration of Umbrella Organizations and Title Holding Organizations." May 1, 2008. http://www.cra-arc.gc.ca/chrts-gvng/chrts/plcy/cps/cps-026-eng.html.

9. Canada Revenue Agency Policy Statement CPS-026, "Guidelines for the Registration of Umbrella Organizations and Title Holding Organizations." May 1, 2008. http://www.cra-arc.gc.ca/chrts-gvng/chrts/plcy/cps/cps-026-eng.html.

10. Canadian Revenue Agency Policy Statement Reference Number CPS-019, "What Is a Related Business?" March 31, 2003. http://www.cra-arc.gc.ca/chrts-gvng/chrts/plcy/cps/cps-019-eng.html.

11. Canadian Revenue Agency Policy Statement Reference Number CPS-019, "What Is a Related Business?" March 31, 2003. http://www.cra-arc.gc.ca/chrts-gvng/chrts/plcy/cps/cps-019-eng.html.

12. Man, T. L. M. "Canada Rules: Legal Structures, Taxation, and Financing." A lecture given at the Conference of the Nonprofit Centers Network in Denver, Colorado, June 2013.

13. Another useful reference on legal structure for Canadians is the paper "Knowledge in Action 1: Corporate Structures and Regulatory Context," part of the Shared Spaces Learning Series created by NCN Canada, a project of Tides Canada and written by Roman Katsnelson and Erin McFarlane. This paper is available from Nonprofit Centers Network at http://www.nonprofitcenters.org/canadasr1/.

14. Man, T. L. M. Personal communication with China Brotsky, October 20, 2016.

15. For information on how new developments are playing out in Toronto in 2018, see https://www.thestar.com/entertainment/visualarts/analysis/2017/12/18/reprieve-seen-in-torontos-new-tax-break-for-arts-spaces.html.

16. This information from a personal conversation of China Brotsky with Saul Ettlin from the Northern California Community Loan Fund in December 2017. Also see https://www.youcaring.com/thetenantsandthecommunity-773671 for more information about this project.

17. For more on community land trusts, visit the National Community Land Trust Network's website: http://www.cltnetwork.org.

18. LLCs are a US form of ownership and do not exist in Canada. Limited liability partnerships are available to hold real estate in Canada, but the law varies from province to province. Be sure to consult an attorney if considering this option.

19. For a 2018 update, see https://www.sfchronicle.com/movies/article/San-Francisco-film-festival-groups-learn-to-live-12753115.php. Also see the Ninth Street Independent Film Center website at https://ninthstreet.org/our-building.

20. In locations like New York state, which also grant nonprofits sales tax exemption, condos with only nonprofit owners have been able to add language to the condo association

by-laws that no individual can benefit from the entity and achieved sales tax exemption for condo association costs as well as property tax exemption.

21. See http://sanfrancisco.impacthub.net/our-story/.
22. See https://www.bcorporation.net/what-are-b-corps/about-b-lab.
23. One interesting model is that of Peerspace, "an online marketplace that makes it easy to rent space for events, meetings and film shoots. It connects, small business and nonprofits who have excess space with people who need it. By creating a standardized listing and booking process, Peerspace makes it easier to discover and book. We are surfacing the world's dark space, shining a light on underutilized venues, all while creating an ecosystem of people doing creative, interesting, memorable activities. We believe that by connecting people and space, companies and individuals will be able to celebrate more often, work together more often, and create great things more often, simply because it's easier than ever to do so." From author's personal communication with Daniel Watson, January 1, 2018 and http://www.peerspace.com.

11 Stories from the Field

Building Community, Not Just Buildings
United Way Greater Toronto's Community Hubs

Lorraine Duff

United Way Greater Toronto, Toronto, Ontario

Toronto is Canada's—and the world's—most diverse metropolis, attracting thousands of newcomers each year with the promise of opportunity and prosperity. It is also the nation's economic engine, hosting major banks, businesses, government, and academic institutions.

TORONTO'S NEIGHBORHOOD WELLBEING CHALLENGE AND A CALL TO ACTION

Yet despite its wealth, Toronto is also a place of increasing disparity, especially for people living in low-income neighborhoods. In 2004, United Way Greater Toronto (United Way) and the Canadian Council on Social Development released a ground-breaking report, *Poverty by Postal Code,*[1] which uncovered large pockets of neighborhood-based poverty and related health and social challenges. It tied well-being directly to one's address and showed us that place-based disparity had taken firm root in Toronto. We know that this phenomenon has been echoed in other North American cities.

The City of Toronto and United Way established a Strong Neighborhoods Task Force which produced a report, *A Call to Action 2005*, which challenged that:

No one—no family, no child, no senior—should be disadvantaged by where they live in the city . . . no one should have to accept inadequate services or limited opportunities because of the neighborhood in which they reside. There needs to be broader recognition that community services and facilities are a vital contributor to strong, vibrant neighborhoods.

The report identified thirteen priority neighborhoods in areas outside the city core for targeted change and reinforced the need to implement neighborhood-based strategies and the concept of locally led Community Hubs.

At United Way, we understood that we would need to shift a portion of our funding approach to focus on neighborhood well-being to tackle the root causes of social and economic issues. We would need to make it easier for people to access a full range of services and supports to keep their families healthy and improve neighborhood conditions for the long term.

THE BIRTH OF OUR NEIGHBORHOODS STRATEGY

We responded by launching our Building Strong Neighborhoods Strategy to build the assets, strengths, relationships, and structures that would enable disparate neighborhoods to become places of opportunity, vitality, and well-being. We defined "strong neighborhoods" as those that are socially and economically vibrant, cohesive with strong bonds of trust and reciprocity, safe in terms of how people feel and actual measures of safety, and inclusive with a strong sense of belonging and respect for diversity and differences.

The strategy focused our efforts on three key interrelated areas: (i) helping communities to create vital spaces in their neighborhoods; (ii) supporting resident-led action; and (iii) targeting donor funding and advocating for increased funding and public policy changes.

INTRODUCING COMMUNITY HUBS

One of our responses was to develop Community Hubs, which we defined as central physical spaces in neighborhoods that provide community space, offer access to services and promote resident engagement and leadership. They were designed to be truly local in that they serve as a resource for everyone in the neighborhood, regardless of age or need; bring together local residents and service providers; offer a broad range of services and programs that respond to expressed community priorities; and leverage and build on strengths and assets. An example of how a Community Hub can influence the lives of Canadian newcomers is captured in an immigrant's words in Box 11.1.

The provincial government also announced the development of Community Health Centre satellites to facilitate access to comprehensive health services in several marginalized neighborhoods. We knew that co-locating health and social services would have even greater benefits. We leveraged this opportunity by creating a strategic partnership with the provincial government to develop five joint Community Hubs. A photograph of one of the Community Hubs in which United Way Greater Toronto has been involved is shown in Figure 11.1.

THE BUILDING BLOCKS: HOW HUBS WORK

Hubs have a number of common features which have been adapted in each neighborhood.

Box 11.1 The Hub at the Heart

The Hub at the Heart of a Community

"As a community, we are less isolated now that we have this place. A place like The Hub has been needed for a long time—it has the community at heart."

George has lived in one of Toronto's priority neighborhoods since he and his wife first emigrated from Jamaica twenty years ago. The neighborhood is home for George, but for a senior living on a fixed income, it once lacked many important services. Then one day, he noticed a new Community Hub in a local plaza.

He saw that the Hub had many offerings under one roof, like community, health, and dental services, as well as diabetes education, health promotion, and social programs for seniors. "Visit the Hub and you will feel life going on around you," says George.

As a prediabetic, George joined a diabetic workshop. He no longer needs to take two buses to see a dentist. He uses the Hub's foot care clinic, attends a weekly cooking class, coaches a youth cricket group, and plays cards with friends while his wife attends a yoga class. "Having these options at the Hub makes it easy for me to get treatment, stay healthy, and make new friends. There was no place like it in our neighborhood before."

Community Hub Guiding Principles

Hubs were founded on seven operating principles that have been locally applied:

- *Neighborhood-based and locally responsive* to reflect the needs and interests of residents and neighborhoods. Residents, service providers, and other community stakeholders are involved in the design, development, and ongoing operations.

FIGURE 11.1 *One of the Community Hubs Created by the United Way.* The Bathurst Finch Hub brings together several organizations that offer primary healthcare, counseling, and dental services, as well as employment, settlement, and legal services. The Hub is also home to Action for Neighbourhood Change (ANC), which supports residents who want to become involved and make positive changes in their neighborhood. *Photo credit: United Way Greater Toronto.*

- *Accessible and engaging diversity* of the local community. They are inclusive places where everyone can be involved and have their needs met.
- *Community involvement in decision-making* and accountable to residents where everyone is encouraged to participate in setting Hub priorities.
- *Service coordination and collaboration* across agencies to deliver a broad array of locally relevant services.
- *Community space* that is readily available to residents and grassroots groups to ignite community engagement and activities.
- *Financial sustainability* mechanisms that effectively and efficiently manage resources and secure additional revenue to support ongoing operations.
- *Evaluation* to ensure Hubs assess progress of operations as well as effectiveness and impact of building opportunities in the community.

Lead Agencies

Hubs are facilitated by lead agencies that are responsible to deliver on the Hubs' mission and mandate by working with both anchoring service partners and local residents.[2] Lead agencies need to have the capacity to operate the space, facilitate partnerships, engage residents and a broad range of stakeholders, and uphold the guiding principles. They facilitate everything from visioning to the construction and development process to the creation of partnership agreements.

During the planning phase, they are responsible for assessing local service needs, locating suitable space options, and identifying partner agencies, while involving residents throughout the process. Once established, they provide services along with anchoring service partners (see the following discussion) and other agencies that provide occasional programming. Lead agencies are responsible for managing partnerships and facilitating ongoing planning and involvement of residents, partners, and stakeholders in the Hub's evolution.

One of the Hubs decided to develop a different structure and separately incorporated with its own board of directors to govern the entire Hub. The board sets the direction and ensures all the roles of the lead agencies are implemented.

Anchoring Service Partners

Lead agencies secure other agency partners to ensure the Hub offers a broad range of service and programs that are rooted in the local community.[3] These partners play an important role in animating and sustaining the Hubs. They have dedicated office or program space at the Hub, contribute to operating costs through rent or staffing, and they may have planning, community engagement, or other responsibilities related to the management of the Hub. Ideal service partners offer programs that attract people to the Hub site, facilitate opportunities for people to meet their neighbors, and have a flexible approach to programming that is adaptive and responsive to changing community needs.

Community Space

Hubs are more than a place to attend programs; they are also welcoming community spaces for the use of local residents and occasionally agency partners. The community spaces within Hubs are designed to be flexible to accommodate a variety of groups. They range from community kitchens, computer rooms, resident lounges, open spaces, and café areas. Community groups, service partners, and other community stakeholders can use the space on a rotating basis. Guidelines for management and use of the space are developed by Hubs and the community participates in setting priorities for its use and ensuring equitable access. As shown in Figure 11.2, shared space can be used as a positive gathering place to bring residents together in creative activities.

Governance

The lead agency's board of directors holds the fiscal and legal responsibility for the Hub. However, each lead agency convenes various community committees to shape and inform the Hub's governance and strategic direction. These include agency partnership committees and resident/community advisory councils, which also help to ensure service coordination and responsiveness. One Hub has designated resident positions on its board of directors.

FIGURE 11.2 *Community Space at a Toronto Hub.* At one of the Hubs of the United Way Greater Toronto, community members come to sing together and enjoy an activity that is both creative and social. *Photo credit: United Way of Greater Toronto.*

Funding

United Way provides financial support to Hubs throughout their development:

- Phase 1: Assessing local service needs and locating spaces.
- Phase 2: Construction, visioning and collaborative design.
- Ongoing: Annual funding for operating costs and capacity support.

Constructing and operating costs range across Hubs. Community Health Centre-led Hubs are costlier to build and/or renovate because of the health service infrastructure and related building requirements. United Way provides CAN$1 million to CAN$3 million for Hub construction costs and CAN$153,000 annually, which covers a portion of shared staffing and operating costs. Lead agencies generate rent income and work to secure other sources of funding. Hub budgets have vacancy and building repair reserves that United Way has supported with one-time funding.

Donors

We have had tremendous support from individual and corporate donors who believe strongly in Community Hubs and their impact in community. We have raised close to CAN$9 million from donors for capital construction and repairs, which has leveraged over CAN$30 million from all levels of government and a major charity. We have also raised funds for a small grant program and some operating costs. But donors do much more than give money; they provide in-kind donations of furniture and computers, pro bono support for visioning and strategic planning, and funding for programs like yoga and science, technology, engineering, and math (STEM). An example of a key corporate donor to Community Hubs is described in Box 11.2.

Box 11.2 A Corporate Donor Who Led the Way

From the beginning, BMO Financial Group was an advocate of the Building Strong Neighborhoods Strategy. And, as a champion for coming together to fight poverty and its effects, BMO was an early investor in Community Hubs. Thanks to BMO's corporate investment and personal donations from senior leaders, three Community Hubs were built.

Furthermore, the staff at BMO bank branches near one Community Hub have supported and volunteered at its annual holiday dinner each year.

HUBS MAKE A DIFFERENCE

When we began our Hub journey in 2005, we believed that our efforts and investments would lead to improved conditions in neighborhoods that experienced the greatest disparities. From December 2009 to 2012, seven of eight Hubs were completed.

Although there were lots of bumps along the road, important achievements have been made in each of our key outcome areas as shown in Table 11.1, and a more personal statement of a Community Hub's impact on one community member is shown in Box 11.3.

Table 11.1 Hub Outcomes and Achievements

Outcomes	Achievements
More integrated and accessible services	More than 168,000 sq. ft. of multiservice space now hosts a wide range of services from early years' programs, to youth services and spaces, and activities for seniors, as well as counseling, settlement, employment, and community-visible locations in the neighborhoods, with five in private rental space, one in a renovated school, and one in a new build on school lands, They range from 10,000 to 77,000 sq. ft., with the majority around 20,000 sq. ft. Hubs ensure ease of access to and between over 50 anchor agency partners been used over one million times. We've also learned that residents were sometimes surprised to discover the range of services that are available at the Hub, which means that continuous outreach and promotion are important.
Increased community space	Over 27,000 sq. ft. of free, accessible and welcoming space is now available for a variety of activities. Nearly 600,000 residents have participated in activities and events organized by residents and service providers. (See Box 21.3.)
Increased resident connections	Hubs facilitate a sense of belonging and intercultural exchange where people feel safe and more open to social connections. They are places where people go for events and when there are challenges like extreme weather or safety incidences. Over the last two years, community spaces have been used over 31,000 times for events, helping people to make new connections and reduce feelings of isolation.
Increased skills in collaboration and community organizing	Hubs provide residents with multiple volunteer and training opportunities that facilitate skills development in collaboration and community organizing. These can provide a pathway to employment and economic development, along with enhanced social connections and communication and leadership skills.
Increased resident connections to decision-makers	Along with being involved in Hub governance and operations, residents are also involved in events and consultations that provide opportunities to meet and provide feedback to decision makers on municipal issues and policy decisions. Over the last two years, 2,000 residents volunteered in Hub governance or operations and 47,000 were involved in outreach, community events, and consultations.

(continued)

Table 11.1 Continued

Outcomes	Achievements
Increased public and political understanding and support for place-based approaches	Our success has garnered attention from other organizations, government and communities, We've presented out learnings to the Ontario Premier's Community Hub Framework Advisory Group and been invited to participate in subcommittees shaping implementation. Other United Ways and organizations developing Hubs have reached showcased stories of successful neighbourhood revitalization, and in a two-year period 630 neighborhood stories have appeared in various publications. Our work to influence public policy has helped to change zoning laws to allow community spaces like Hubs to be built in the main floors of high-rise apartment buildings.

Note: This table summarizes some of the benefits and impacts on low-income communities resulting from the United Way's Community Hubs program.

Source: United Way of Greater Toronto.

WHAT WE'VE LEARNED

The journey has taken longer than anticipated: we started in 2005, and the first Hub was built in 2009, followed by six more by 2012, with the final Hub still in progress. We've learned many lessons along the way, but for now we offer six highlights:

1. *Build on the Hub principles—and allow for local application.* We did not want to take a "cookie cutter" approach because Hubs needed to respond to the needs and interests of local communities. Instead, we developed principles and allowed

---

Box 11.3 A Space to Realize Dreams

"Many people in my community are newcomers and feel disconnected from their neighbors. I wanted to find a way to bring local residents together. After all, music is the universal language."

Music has always struck a chord with Christianne who, at eighteen, dreamed of starting a community choir in the neighborhood where she grew up. In Toronto, it's difficult to find free space to meet or host events. School space, for example, requires a permit that many can't afford. Christianne easily found a free space at her local Hub. She purchased a piano and sheet music with a small grant from United Way.

Before long, nearly thirty people were attending the now weekly practices. Members like Roger say they felt isolated and alone before joining the choir. "I feel like I'm really contributing to my community. People enjoy coming to our performances." What began as residents sharing a love of music has transformed into a vibrant community activity.

flexibility for lead agencies to work with partners to interpret and apply the model. While this has allowed for necessary variations, it has resulted in varying interpretations and relative weighting of the principles. Some Hubs brought partners and residents together to develop a shared vision and clarify how principles were applied. As well, lead agencies with a strong community development background and a track record of working with residents tended to be more successful in implementing the Hub model.

2. *Trusting partnerships are key—and they're complicated.* A range of partnerships were needed to make Hubs work, including residents who were actively supported to be a voice in the Hubs, agencies that understood the importance of one-stop access for everyone, and funders and donors who believed in and funded the model. However, partnerships were time consuming and challenging with many players, expectations, and cultures. Generating support and buy-in for Hubs was challenging in the early days because the costs were unknown. We couldn't calculate the costs until we knew who would opt in.

   We learned that building strong and trusting relationships was essential to being able to work together, solve problems, and sustain people who were willing to go the extra mile, even when it felt frustrating. Those people (and organizations) proved this could be done. The importance of tireless champions can't be understated.

3. *The elephant in the room: Who "owns" this Hub anyway?* We struggled at times with confusion about roles and who "owns" the Hubs and how they were branded. Some of the lead agencies saw the Hub as an extension of their own agency and not as a separate collective entity, which creates confusion with partners and with the community. Also, having United Way as the funder at the table sometimes created role confusion and power dynamics. Though lead agencies ran the Hubs, as a core funder and partner United Way could prescribe deliverables and accountability for the elements that we support. Traditional funders are stepping into nontraditional, community-building roles, and we need to keep learning how to do this well while acknowledging and managing the inherent power dynamics.

4. *Sustain core functions.* To remain viable, Hubs require sufficient, sustained funding for three interrelated functions:
   - Core operational requirements, including staff resources to provide reception, administrative, and management support and maintain regular and extended operating hours.
   - Resident involvement in Hub development/governance; and
   - Building and enhancing agencies' commitment and capacity to work collaboratively to ensure "one-stop shopping" and to respond to new and emerging community needs.

     Securing sustained funding has been challenging. Most funders support programs and time-limited projects and not the costs associated with core Hub operations, which are essential for the model to succeed. In the absence of sustained funding, lead agencies have had to rely on income from rent, which is a challenge as agencies cannot always afford the original rent nor the increases. In addition, lead agencies are required to spend a lot of time applying for grants, which are challenging to get.

5. *Investing in capital isn't straightforward.* Venturing into capital projects was new for us, and it took much longer than we originally anticipated to see results. We had a lot to learn and a lot of money to raise, and we also needed to support our community partners through the process. We were new to this work, and community agency staff and residents didn't have experience in developing spaces, so everyone was learning. It was also hard to find spaces to rent and funds to purchase and renovate buildings. As a result, organizations often needed to rent and renovate from private landlords, which was an expensive use of both donor and public funds that didn't really create a community asset. As well, public assets like schools make great Hubs, but they were being sold at market value, and they often required significant upgrades that were not affordable for most community groups. Figure 11.3 illustrates the effort to make Hubs easily accessible to local residents; the pictured Dorset Park Community Hub rents space in a shopping mall that also includes parking.

6. *It's about collaboration—moving to integration is hard.* Many funders assumed that Hubs would offer cost efficiencies. In some cases, shared elements like back office (e.g., photocopier, Internet, and phones), reception, meeting rooms, and staff spaces did offer cost savings. However, the purpose of Hubs was coordination and collaboration of services and accessible community space, not simply co-location. Though we have had some success making collaboration work, it has still been challenging.

FIGURE 11.3 *Hubs Serve as One-Stop Shops for Community Services.* The Dorset Park Community Hub is a "one-stop shop" where this neighborhood's residents can access community health programs and social service programs, as well as community space. It offers seniors' programs, child and family programs, a food bank, a newcomer center, employment services, community mental health supports for youth and families, and a computer lab accessible to the public. *Photo credit: United Way Greater Toronto.*

Every agency came in with its own organizational practices and culture, and it took time to build trust between organizations. Privacy issues made information sharing difficult, and the funding environment created competition among agencies rather than reinforcing collaboration. We learned that it takes leadership skills and mindsets to break down established silos. Our goal over the next few years is to strengthen collaboration and build new approaches to move towards integration. One of the important benefits of organizations working together is briefly summarized in the comments of an executive director of one of the organizations housed at Rexdale Community Hub, included in Box 11.4.

Box 11.4 A One-Stop Shop

"There's nothing quite like being across the hall and being able to say to a client, 'Let's go over together. There's someone we know and trust who can help.'"

The Rexdale Community Legal Clinic is a busy place that helps residents seeking assistance on tenant and income issues or expertise in family, refugee, or criminal law. "No one ever comes in with only one problem. And the difficulties they're experiencing aren't always necessarily legal, though they may result from a legal problem," says the clinic's director of legal services.

That's where the Community Hub model makes a difference: when residents' needs extend beyond the clinic's scope, help is just down the hall. The wrap-around services of the Hub's partner agencies can provide a one-stop shop for solutions to what are often multiple, interrelated issues. To resolve today's problems and prevent tomorrow's, the strong connection between the clinic and other agencies at the Hub is a relationship that can make a difficult situation that much easier.

INFLUENCING SYSTEMS CHANGE

In August 2015, after extensive consultations, the Premier's Special Advisory Committee on Community Hubs released a report, *Community Hubs in Ontario: A Strategic Framework and Action Plan*, which included the following recommendations to facilitate Community Hub development and operations in Ontario:

- Establish a provincial lead for community Hubs.
- Foster integrated service delivery.
- Develop a provincial strategy for public properties.
- Remove barriers and create incentives.
- Support integrated and long-term local planning.
- Ensure financial sustainability of community Hubs.
- Increase local capacity.
- Evaluate and monitor outcomes.

The government accepted all the recommendations and is moving forward with implementation. We are pleased that they have prioritized the creation of a Resource Network, as we know community groups need support to manage the complexities involved with developing and sustaining Hubs. We are pleased that the provincial government has taken a leadership role in recognizing Hubs as the core of strong, vibrant communities, and we will continue to support this work as it unfolds.

MOVING FORWARD

In late 2015, United Way Greater Toronto's Board of Trustees made a continued commitment to Hubs as a central aspect of our Building Strong Neighborhoods Strategy. The refined strategy supports:

- *People* referring to residents, along with social service agencies, community-based organizations, local businesses, political institutions, and other institutions (schools, hospitals, funders) within the neighbourhood. In addition to the individual entities, our definition refers to the connections and relationships each entity establishes with one another.
- *Space* that provides a welcoming outdoor and indoor environment where residents and community groups can congregate, have meaningful interactions, plan, and organize around issues that affect their lives.
- *Services* (e.g., social, arts and culture, recreation and commercial) that are delivered in neighborhoods and that contribute to residents' well-being and neighborhood livability and vibrancy.

We recently merged with our neighboring United Way York Region and are now working in an area twice as large that encompasses both urban and rural communities. We are in the process of identifying areas of need in both Toronto and York region, compiling relevant socio-demographic data and completing an inventory and mapping of community services, resources, and assets to determine potential future Hub sites.

We have learned a great deal and developed many new competencies on our Hubs journey, but we have not figured it all out. As we move into the next iteration of Community Hubs, we will continue to make improvements and build capacity. Stay tuned for the next chapter in our ongoing journey.

NOTES

1. United Way Greater Toronto & The Canadian Council on Social Development. *Poverty by Postal Code: The Geography of Neighborhood Poverty, 1981–2001.* Toronto: United Way Greater Toronto, 2004. http://www.unitedwaytyr.com/document.doc?id=59.
2. Lead agencies and related Hubs are Access Alliance Multicultural Health and Community Services (Access Point on Danforth Hub), Agincourt Community Services Association (Dorset Park Hub), Scarborough Centre for Healthy Communities (Mid Scarborough

Hub), Unison Health and Community Services (Bathurst Finch and Jane Street Hubs), and Working Women Community Centre (The Victoria Park Hub); Rexdale Community Hub has the board of directors.

3. The Hubs have over fifty anchoring service partners. Just a few examples include Rexdale Community Legal Services, Yorktown Child and Family Services, Centre for Victims of Torture, YMCA Scarborough Employment & Community Services, Toronto Public Health Dental Services, North York Community Services, and Toronto Employment and Social Services.

12 Stories from the Field

The Common Roof™
A Values-Driven Approach
to a Rural Nonprofit Center

Glen Newby

New Path Foundation, Barrie, Ontario

With few exceptions, many multi-tenant nonprofit centers are located in large urban or suburban locations where the majority of nonprofit organizations are found. Central Ontario follows this usual pattern with most organizations having a head office in one city or town location with multiple satellite office spaces dispersed elsewhere. For these nonprofits and other physically isolated organizations across the continent, challenges such as accessibility, isolation, and lack of resources and infrastructure create numerous roadblocks for trying to fulfill their missions. The Common Roof™ is a standout example of a rurally based nonprofit center that has been able to succeed in developing two centers in central Ontario (Barrie and Orillia) with more sites in the development stage.

THE BEGINNINGS OF THE COMMON ROOF™

The Common Roof™ value-driven model of a nonprofit center was conceptualized in 2005. A group of five established nonprofit human services organizations, each operating out of Barrie, Ontario, came together, concerned about needed facility space. They were the Canadian Mental Health Association Barrie Branch, Simcoe Outreach Services, New Path Youth and Family Services, Children's Treatment Center, and Catulpa Community Support Services. All five agencies provide direct client services across rural Simcoe County with a head office in Barrie. Collectively, the services of these nonprofits include child and youth mental health, addictions services, youth justice programs, child and adult developmental services, special needs services for children, violence against women services, a medical family health team, and partner assault treatment services. Each organization required better functional space and more professional work and program space. Together these five organizations decided to collaborate on a facility that could meet common needs and better serve their client populations.

The New Path Foundation facilitated the process of establishing the nonprofit center. New Path is a registered charity in Canada that is affiliated with New Path Youth and Family Services (child and youth mental health). The Foundation's initial purpose was to protect physical assets of New Path Services (various designated funds and real estate) and to conduct fundraising events that benefited New Path Services. However, the Foundation has since changed its Canada Revenue Agency designation from a community foundation to a charitable organization. Essentially, this change means that New Path Foundation can do more than just raise funds; it is now allowed to enter into various youth-focused social enterprise activities, to donate to other registered charities in Canada, and to invest in real estate that supports other registered nonprofits obtaining accommodation in its two Common Roof™ multi-tenant centers.

New Path Foundation saw the needs of the five organizations as consistent with its purpose and that the initiative was a real estate investment and opportunity to develop and manage philanthropic investment and to mobilize community support to meet the needs of children, youth, and families. It was also an ideal opportunity to invest in real estate to support other nonprofits in the community. The Foundation offered to take a leadership role and to use its various spheres of influence (political, financial, and reputational) and its social enterprise orientation to coordinate, develop, purchase, and renovate the first Barrie Common Roof™ building facility. It was a red brick, 26,000 sq. ft. space in Barrie, Ontario, that opened in 2006, and its photograph is shown in Figure 12.1.

FIGURE 12.1 *The Barrie Common Roof™ Building in Barrie, Ontario.* The Barrie building contains 26,000 sq. ft. and opened in 2006. It has five partner agencies, all established nonprofit human services organizations, that provide direct client services. They all deliver direct client services across rural Simcoe County, and they collaborate to best serve their clients. Collectively, their services include child and youth mental health, addictions services, youth justice programs, child and adult developmental services, special needs services for children, violence against women services, a medical family health team, and partner assault treatment services. Barrie's population is estimated to be over 154,000 residents by Population Canada 2018. *Photo credit: The Common Roof™.*

The Collaborative Approach of the Barrie Common Roof™

The five organizations each committed to moving forward using a collaborative approach in the development of this project. Most decisions involving site selection and design configurations were developed by joint committees from the five organizations with the help of expert consultation. Their intentional collaboration resulted in the creation of a shared vision for the Common Roof™: putting the client first in all decision-making. This commitment to clients penetrated all decision-making on the design of the building. These decisions included determining office locations; parking principles (free, with clients having closest access); interior functional flow for clients, guests, and staff; and even the color of offices and shared/common space, which depended on the age of the clients being served (children vs. adolescents vs. adults).

One example of this commitment to clients is that all offices and program space utilized by clients (counselling and therapy rooms, group meeting sites, and clinical assessment rooms) were located in spaces with windows. In contrast, board rooms and various administrative offices were all located on the interior, without windows. Agency CEOs agreed to occupy the smallest offices located on the interior since they did not see clients. During the development stage, one potential organization demanded a windowed corner office for its CEO. Although there was much discussion, in the end the collective decision was made not to accept that particular CEO and the organization. The Common Roof™ is not for everyone, and it is definitely not for organizations unable to "walk the talk" about doing what's best for their clients.

Shared Administrative Services

As the Common Roof™ design developed, it was recognized that some organizations had greater capacity and expertise in certain administrative services, while others had greater capacity in a different function. The building design sought to capitalize on the sharing of administrative functions; hence, the major administrative services from all five tenants (finance, information technology, and human resources) were located together in pods to enhance the informal integration of these functions. Over time, the five tenants began to integrate more formally, thereby increasing their effectiveness and reducing their costs. For example, one tenant's finance department formally contracted with another tenant to provide financial services, while a different tenant contracted with another for shared IT services. Now, should space become available, any new tenants who may choose to enter can receive a menu of available services so that they can share these functions at a prorated cost, based on the square footage of space they use. Tenants recognize these benefits, and they are pleased with this value-added component of their lease.

Other shared services include building reception. The receptionists are New Path Foundation employees, and the staffing costs are shared on a prorated basis among all organizations. Reception staff is trained regarding the services provided by each tenant, and they manage the direction and flow of clients to various meeting rooms. They also coordinate all room bookings. Shared services at the Common

Roof™ exemplify both the financial benefits gained by each tenant and the increased level of shared expertise and capacity building of each tenant, both formally and informally.

The Barrie Common Roof™ enterprise was a huge success, and it was fully occupied at opening in 2006 and remains so today. The Common Roof™'s success occurred even though there was very little research beforehand on the best practices to help guide the process. New Path began to track the benefits to tenant organizations including reduced costs (60% of space was shared/common), greater efficiencies (shared finance systems, IT systems, reception services, and maintenance), improved client service (one-stop shopping), and enhanced marketing and promotional opportunities from being part of a leading-edge initiative. More recently, a research group from the Ontario government included the Common Roof™ as a case study in its survey on rural social enterprise.

NEW PATH FOUNDATION'S BUSINESS MODEL

The business model at the New Path Foundation is unique. As the owner and operator, the Foundation enters into lease agreements with tenants, determined at market-value rates. These agreements state that the tenant meets strict requirements including mission alignment, financial stability, community credibility, and a commitment to the values and principles of a Common Roof™ environment.

Partner Agencies

Leases are arranged to allow for the tenant agency to become either a partner tenant or a standard tenant. Partner tenants enjoy additional rights and responsibilities. These include the partner tenant contribution of an upfront fee (CAD$100,000 for Barrie and CAD$75,000 for Orillia). This fee assists with building purchase and/or leasehold improvements. In return, Partner tenants enjoy a ten-year, fixed-rate lease except for maintenance, interest, taxes, and utilities. They also gain group decision-making authority for the location they are leasing (includes things like building hours, structural configurations, paint colors, acceptance of new tenants or not, and other building-related items).

Furthermore, partner tenants are also eligible for an Unrestricted Sustainability Grant (USG) given by the New Path Foundation. The grant is a very significant and unique benefit of being a partner tenant. The USG is granted to the partner tenant when they renew for a five-year or more lease term upon the expiration of their initial ten-year lease. The grant amount is determined by taking 60% of the partner tenant's annual base rent from the renewed lease. A grant of this amount is provided each year that the partner tenant remains in good standing at the Common Roof™. These grants are considered unrestricted in that the partner tenant may use it in any way they wish, although New Path Foundation does encourage the grant to be applied to client services.

The USG enhances the long-term sustainability of the partner tenant. New Path Foundation can conduct business in this manner because the USG's timing is projected to coincide with the discharge of mortgages and other financial commitments for the facility. The asset value of the facility has increased greatly over the ten years; the initial purchase and renovation costs for the Barrie Common Roof™ were $3.5 million, and the current value is approximately $7 million. This increased asset value is leveraged to support capital requirements of new Common Roof™ projects. As a result, in the second Common Roof™ building in Orillia, the partner fee is only 75% of the original Barrie Partner fee. Scaling opportunities of this model are excellent, and plans are underway for other Common Roof™ projects in Ontario.

Other tenants who choose to be a standard tenant (without the requirement of an initial fee) may lease for a set term of up to ten years (with potentially escalated base rent), but they do not have any of the benefits of a partner tenant. At the original site in Barrie, all tenants joined as partner tenants with a ten-year lease. At the second Common Roof™ site in Orillia, eleven of the fourteen tenants are standard tenants with lease terms of five years or less.

Tenant Collaboration

Collaboration at the Common Roof™ is intentional, and it is grounded in shared values such as mission alignment of all tenants. Collaboration is also encouraged through more formal expectations of tenants. Both Partner tenants and regular tenants must agree to participate on interagency committees that relate to health, safety, and building improvements. These committees also ensure compliance with regulatory requirements. In addition, it is understood that tenants will have representation on the social committee (organization of facility-wide activities such as "Pizza Day") and the Art Committee, which is responsible for maintaining an art gallery and art throughout the common areas.

All tenants must pay, as a part of their lease, $1 per square foot toward a building fund that is set up to provide resources to support building improvements. Only the partner tenants may approve such improvements. For example, all Common Roof™ facilities are nonsmoking and scent-free; yet, it was recognized that the culture of Aboriginal clients utilized smudging from time to time. (Smudging is a traditional cultural component of Aboriginal people whereby sweet grass is ignited in a small dish and the smoke "cleanses" individuals, helping to create open honest communication prior to meetings). This is a very important part of the Aboriginal culture and was inconsistent with the nonsmoking policy and the principle of cultural inclusiveness. The partner tenants had to maintain an inclusive facility; thus, they approved a structural redesign of a common meeting room (using the building fund account) so that Aboriginal clients could use that room since it included a dedicated exhaust system to remove all smoke present from smudging.

The Common Roof™ as a Social Enterprise and Community Catalyst

An intentional goal of the Common Roof™ projects is that each is operated as a social enterprise. Our definition of a social enterprise is a business venture that generates a surplus, does good for people and human service agencies, and is environmentally friendly. Surpluses from tenant rental income are allocated back to partner tenants through the USG. The shared services and shared space provide a one-stop shopping experience for clients within a modern, client-centered environment, in which respecting the environment is a component of all business practices.

Common Roof™ facilities intentionally create a hub for further creative social enterprise activity. One example is a cleaning service run by New Path Foundation for the Common Roof™ facilities. This service engages, employs, and provides training for disadvantaged young adults (potentially current or past clients of a tenant organization) to learn environmentally friendly office cleaning skills under supervisors that understand and accept their challenges. The further development of this business model will include marketing the cleaning services to other community-based nonprofits and potentially tapping into the business community.

Another intentional goal of Common Roof™ projects is to influence the community regarding the missions of the tenant organizations and to advocate on behalf of the clients. For example, the strength of the Barrie Common Roof™ pushed the City of Barrie to install sidewalks and handicapped bus shelters to help clients access the location. The strength and visual aesthetics of the Orillia Common Roof™ created an economic revitalization in what was a poorly maintained part of town. Local businesses began to relocate or improve current retail outlets in the neighborhood that now boasted a beautiful new and modern building. Staff working from the Common Roof™, and sometimes clients, also frequent local restaurants and shops, providing needed economic activity.

SCALABILITY OF THE COMMON ROOF™ MODEL

The success of the Common Roof™ in Barrie led to the creation of a second, 36,000 sq. ft. Common Roof™ facility in Orillia, Ontario, which opened in 2011. It was helped by a CAD$2.7 million government grant for which it successfully competed. The model remains consistent with Barrie's approach, but there is a noticeable difference in tenant make-up and physical structure. Tenants in Orillia number about fourteen and are much smaller organizations than at the Barrie facility. Many use the space as a satellite office to shorten the distance for potential clients. The agencies at Orillia Common Roof™ also provide human services but with a much greater variety. They include Alzheimer services, administration offices for a palliative care organization, a medical health unit, a foot clinic, a walk-in clinic, a community kitchen, and a Native housing support service for First Nation Metis and Inuit tribal members. Shared and common space continues to make up 60% of the leasable space. The facility is a new build and modern in design and layout. At the time of writing,

FIGURE 12.2 *The Common Roof Model was Replicated in Orillia, Ontario.* Building on the success of The Common Roof™ in Barrie, The Orillia Common Roof™ Building in Orillia opened in 2011 and has approximately twelve partner or tenant organizations. Its modern building, several stories high, contains 36,000 sq. ft. It also shares the Common Roof vision, "Building a healthy, growing community for children, youth and families for today and tomorrow." The photograph shows the shared reception area in the Orillia building. *Photo credit: New Path Foundation.*

approximately 85% was occupied. Figure 12.2 shows the shared reception area at the Orillia Common Roof™ building.

Current negotiations are currently underway in North Bay, Ontario, for a third Common Roof™ facility. Each Common Roof™ will look and feel differently, depending on the needs of the specific community. However, each will enjoy a similar business model of long-term sustainability and scalability. There are some potential elements of the Common Roof™ that can be replicated. They include the collaborative nature of tenant engagement, the "client first" focus of all decision-making, the real estate investment strategy, the solid business plan to ensure sustainability for both the tenants and the Common Roof™ facilities, and the increasing interest of major funders (such as the Ontario government) to support nonprofit multi-tenant centers as a cost-effective way to maintain quality services.

SUCCESS COMES WITH CHALLENGES

New Path has enjoyed success by having the right vision at the right time, strong leadership, and a willingness to take a measured risk. Despite these successes, there were many challenges along the way. The most significant was not ensuring that leases were fully signed and executed before conducting improvements for the tenant. This situation occurred in Orillia where the Common Roof™ was scheduled to have a large day care center (accessible to tenant agency staff as well). Construction was completed fully, including all the licensing requirements for the facility (kitchen and washroom facilities, playground yard space, etc.). By the time the lease was ready for signature and was move-in ready, the day care center had closed because a local funder had pulled out operating funds, and the organization could no longer afford to run its programs. This situation resulted in New Path Foundation having to pay CAD$150,000 to structurally repurpose the space to allow for other uses of the space.

How did this happen? A part of the governance body of New Path Foundation at the time had a dream of creating a day care space for staff members, and this dream simply did not allow for any mitigation of the potential risks involved. This large cost could have been avoided by improved risk management controls being in place and applied in each and every tenant case, regardless of how attractive a partner tenant seemed.

The early years of the Common Roof™ relied heavily on trust and relationship. As maturity and scaling occurs, a more business-like approach needs to be integrated with those initial, and essential, values that ground our work: trust, collaboration, and relationships.

PART 5
DESIGN

13 The Design Process
Creating a Working Shared Space

No discussion about shared space is complete without understanding how to design the space. The design is where the mission and vision take tangible form and come alive in architecture. As was reviewed in Chapter 6: The Development Process and Chapter 7: Finding a Home, many shared space projects reuse buildings that previously had different uses; others are in rented spaces, and still others are newly constructed. In all of these instances, smart shared space design can be incorporated into the project. This chapter reviews the best practices in shared space design. We also share common pitfalls and offer practical advice for making the space functional, beautiful and reflective of the building's purpose.

MISSION LEADS DESIGN

Nonprofits can come to a real estate project in many ways—they can inherit a building, be designated a building in a public-sector bidding process, or buy or lease a piece of real estate on the open market. In all of these cases, the design of the space is the key to making it function. The mission of the space—what its purpose is and what it is supposed to do for the people who work there and visit—should be the driving force for site selection and design decisions. At all times, these decisions, about neighborhood, amount of space, type of space, and the overall look and feel should be rooted in the building's purpose. If nonprofit center projects can maintain this mission integrity, decisions about the site and the ultimate design will be successful.

SPACE PLANNING: SETTING THE SCALE OF THE PROJECT

Like the planning for mission, vision, and then the financial feasibility, developing a "space plan" or programming study is important to ground the site section and design process. The programming study or space planning is one of the components of the overall feasibility process outlined in Chapter 6, and also discussed in Chapter 7. The study should evaluate how many people will use the space and what kinds of spaces they need. For example, there might be four proposed organizations sharing a nonprofit center. Each organization needs its own office space and cubicles. It also needs use of the conference rooms, work rooms, pantries, and the like, spaces that can be shared with other organizations. The space planning exercise is an early assessment to determine how large theses space will need to be and what spaces are duplicative. It also should articulate what spaces will require unique features such as acoustical sound proofing for confidential rooms, performance and exhibit spaces, or food uses. These specialized spaces will impact the site selection and the ultimate construction budget as specialized spaces naturally cost more to construct.

Role of an Architect

An architect, real estate consultant, or other design professional can assist with an early space planning study and the site search. However, it should be noted that an architect is just one discipline required on a complex project. The architect should not lead the site search, as discussed in Chapter 6, but can help out in assessing sites or locations along with a finance team and program staff. Additionally, any design professional should have shared space experience and certainly community facility experience to avoid common design mistakes.

After an organization completes the feasibility to address basic design questions outlined in Chapters 6 and 7, the parameters for the entire project should be set: the scale of the nonprofit center, the key uses, the preferred locational requirements, and any specialized features required. The planning exercise will yield a clear articulation of the building's functions, providing a blueprint to identify the ideal property in the marketplace.

Uses and Users

A second area of testing the design feasibility is to understand the uses and users of the eventual space. Often confused, uses and users are at the heart of good design. The uses of the building are the *functions* taking place in the building such as office and meeting uses, or delivering services. This is what happens in the building, which is different from the users of the building, defined by us as the visitors and people who frequent the building. Thinking about both how the space will be used and by whom is critical. At a basic level, some key initial questions are as follows.

Uses

- What will the space be used for? What activities will take place there? Will the building be used for many different activities?
- When will the building be used (hours and days of operation)?

Users

- Who will use the building on a daily, weekly, and monthly basis?
- What do each of these groups need to do in the building (park a car, work in a private office, attend a meeting, visit an office, receive services, eat, attend a performance)?

- Are the expected hours of operation for the building different for tenants and visitors?
- How will people move through the building?
- What level of security is needed for visitors and tenants?
- What kind of parking do visitors need?

In new construction, if there is adequate budget, the project design can meet the users' full needs in the building. In a renovation, where the basic space is already constructed, designing the new space is trickier as some of the space might be immovable such as the building envelope, walls, hallways, elevator shafts, plumbing, and stairwells. In those cases, where the building floorplan and floorplate are "as is," good design is more about determining the right flow of the space for the users, maximizing light and color, clear signage and wayfinding, and creating the right look and feel of the space to match the mission of the building. Good design for shared space can take place at any budget and in any space.

DESIGN PHASES IN SHARED SPACE PROJECTS

There are six main phases of design in real estate projects, not only for shared space projects: (i) concept design; (ii) schematic design; (iii) design development; (iv) construction documents and bidding; (v) construction; and (vi) close out. These are summarized in Figure 6.2 in Chapter 6. Concept design is just that: the broad conceptual design for a shared space. This phase usually takes place before a site is selected. For a shared space project, it might be a description of the shared space detailing plans for a common reception area, open office, and lots of conference rooms. Sometimes it might include artistic renderings based on this conceptual design, again not using an actual location. This phase is used to get stakeholders excited and to distill the core elements of the project.

The subsequent phases continue to get more and more specific: schematic design is an actual rough layout of all of the functions (uses) in an actual site, prepared by the architect or designer. This is the first floor plan the project developers (owners, developer, project manager) might see. It is not necessarily "designed" per say, just laid out in the space to make sure it all fits and all of the components are accounted for. Other deliverables in this phase may include site plans or building elevations. It is important to carefully evaluate the schematic design to ensure that it's accurate and realistic for the intended purposes of the building. (One such avoidable mistake: a direct services nonprofit center was built without a janitor's closet. This meant that there was no slop sink or place to store mops and cleaning supplies; another space had to be repurposed for this use after the building opened. While seemingly minor, this oversight was a costly mistake and could have been caught during the schematic design phase.)

Once this basic layout is agreed upon, design development starts, the phase where the details and the design become specific and the technical specifications begin to be articulated. There will be more detailed floor plans, drawings for the building systems (mechanicals, electrical, plumbing, etc.). Detailed decisions will be made in this phase—what kinds of materials and finishes will be used, how big or small each space will be, what kinds of heating and cooling systems will be used, etc. This phase is when the design is locked down to prepare a set of construction drawings to be used to put the project out to bid to contractors.

A detailed cost estimate of the capital project may be done around this phase, either after schematic design to get a sense of the order of magnitude of the project or at the design development phase, or sometimes both. A rough estimate at schematic design contributes to the overall project understanding. The estimate at the later phase will be more detailed and help inform the eventual cost that contractors will propose. The project will be bid out to contractors for them to accurately prepare a price. The construction phase is self-evident: it's when the project is under construction. During this phase, the architect and project manager ensure that the building is constructed according to the design, timeline, and budget. The lead project partners monitor progress during construction and approve changes that arise due to unforeseen conditions, design challenges, or cost increases. The close-out phase often takes place after a project is close to opening or even occupied and includes "punch list" items to complete. The punch list is created by the architect and is comprised of generally smaller items that need to be repaired or finished (paint touch-ups, installing electrical outlet plates, and sometimes larger items like systems furniture hook-ups). Monitoring of mechanical, electrical, and plumbing (MEP) systems can go well into the first year of the building's operations as the building is newly occupied with people and new uses.

GUIDING PRINCIPLES

There are design principles that should guide shared space projects as these projects are important neighbors in communities. In some respects, because nonprofit centers serve wide audiences and diverse constituencies, they have a responsibility to showcase an elevated design ethos.

Take the Long View

In Chapter 1: A New Model for Nonprofits, we discussed that nonprofit centers can help resist forces of nonprofit displacement and gentrification by providing stable, affordable space for organizations. From a design perspective, nonprofit centers should take a long view, recognizing that the mission of the organizations operating in the center is a long-term one. The social challenges that organizations confront and tackle may take generations to solve and therefore the space should reflect that. Nonprofit centers are beacons in their communities and the design should reflect this: design that is value-driven and reflects the mission. For some centers that means professional and polished; for others, it could mean bright colors and family-friendly.

Safety and Security

Safety and security needs are concerns running through any shared space. The level of security depends on the type of building, the uses of the building, and its users. For example, a one-stop center serving families and children will want to have a security plan to ensure safety for children. For the Family Justice Centers, thirteen multia-gency spaces across the US that serve victims of domestic violence, sexual assault, elder abuse, child abuse, and/or human trafficking, safety for its staff and visitors is understandably paramount. Some centers serve both victims and perpetrators, and so the design must ensure confidentiality where needed and separation of con-flicting populations so there can be total security for everyone in and around the building.

On the other hand, a shared space devoted to the capacity-building needs of nonprofits, located in an existing office building and welcoming invited guests might not need as elaborate a security plan or design as the Family Justice Center example. In these cases, and in other instances where the public visits the space, the security design might mean that public rooms and spaces need to be separated from staff spaces (easily designed with keycard access) so that staff can securely work alongside any public meetings. These more open spaces might want to maintain transparency and accessibility which must be balanced with safety concerns.

Green Building

Some nonprofit centers have been leaders in developing environmentally sustain-able buildings. Obvious examples are those that are themselves housing environ-mental organizations, for example, the Alliance Center in Denver, Colorado, or the Cleveland Environmental Center in Ohio, the first commercial green building ret-rofit in Ohio.[1].In both cases, they have taken historic buildings and retrofitted them to conserve energy and minimize water and waste.

Other nonprofit centers have also made efforts to be more sustainable. Some have applied for and received some level of Leadership in Energy and Environmental Design (LEED) certification, the most widely used green building rating system and administered by the US Green Building Council or the Canada Green Building Council. Examples include Tides Converge New York (formerly the Thoreau Center New York) in New York City, The Center for Healthy Communities in Los Angeles, and the Boulder Jewish Commons in Boulder, Colorado.

In this same vein, a number of nonprofit centers have reduced their building's pollution and been certified by the energy-saving Energy Star Building Program administered by the US Environmental Protection Agency. An example of an Energy Star rated building is the Community Service Building in Wilmington, Delaware, which houses over seventy nonprofit tenants[2] and also has an extensive recycling program.[3]

Other nonprofit centers have embraced green building practices without pursuing a formal rating. This path toward sustainability is less costly than pursuing the ratings but may not be as visible to the wider community. Some of these practices include motion-sensitive lighting fixtures (see The Center for Philanthropy, The Northwest Health Foundation Portland, Oregon) or geothermal heating, nonvolatile organic compound (VOC) paints and adhesives, and recycled content floor coverings (North Penn Community Health Center, Colmar, Pennsylvania). Low-flow toilets and sinks, window glazing to minimize heat retention, solar panels, and other green building practices can also be incorporated. TSNE MissionWorks in Boston, for example, has committed to an extensive recycling program including recycling, composting, and e-waste diversion.[4]

These steps taken by nonprofit centers contribute to the health, well-being, and sustainability of their communities, and they benefit the employees, volunteers, and visitors in these buildings. Employee morale has been shown to be higher in buildings with green features (see Chapter 5: Making the Case). Any new nonprofit center project should explore the sustainability factors at the outset to determine the appetite and budget for green building. Planning for green construction or LEED certification in advance reduces the construction cost of these measures. As is widely noted, the added expense for green building is reduced every year as materials and technology become more readily accessible. In addition, many these green building practices, while costly up front, will create ongoing operational savings as they pay for themselves over time. Green building should be considered a best practice in the field.

Universal Design

Nonprofit centers serve a wide range of populations, clients, and constituents. Each of these populations, whether it is seniors, people with disabilities, or others have unique design requirements for space. Universal Design is the approach that incorporates the specialized needs and requirements of different users in a building to ensure comfort, accessibility, and ease of use. Any nonprofit center that seeks to serve a specialized population should engage with a design team with experience working with that population to customize their universal design (e.g., incorporating talking elevators in a building serving people with visual disabilities or ramps and curb cuts for people using wheelchairs and baby carriages).

In the typology of nonprofit centers, Universal Design falls under the rubric of the "Building as a Workplace" as depicted in Figure 1.1, in the first chapter. Universal Design is one of the ways that nonprofit centers elevate the work space for its inhabitants.

[Universal Design] creates products, systems, and environments to be as usable as possible by as many people as possible regardless of age, ability or situation. Other terms for Universal Design used around the world include Design for All, Inclusive Design, and Barrier-Free Design. Universal Design terminology and meanings differ from one country to another and often reflect each nation's societal values. Cultural differences influence how the movement has been adopted in different countries. However, the common goal of social inclusion transcends national laws, policies, and practices.[5]

The Ed Roberts Campus in Berkeley, California, is a notable example of a universal design space, depicted in Figure 13.1. Chapter 14: Universal Design: Creating the Ed Roberts Campus, offers more detail on its universal design. This center features[6]:

- A helical ramp winds upward to the second floor, permitting easy access and safe evacuation.
- Accessible elevators, automatic doors, and wide corridors create easy circulation.
- Restrooms accommodate all ability levels and include private rooms for assisted individuals.
- Specially designed signage and way-finding devices guide people who are blind or have low vision.
- Hands-free sensors and timers control lighting, acoustical, and security systems.

FIGURE 13.1 *Ed Roberts Campus, Berkeley, California.* The 80,000 sq. ft. Ed Roberts Campus features universal design including this helical ramp permitting easy access and safe evacuation. *Photo credit: Leddy Maytum Stacey Architects.*

Finally, in keeping with social advances, gender neutral bathrooms are increasingly designed into shared spaces (see Asian Arts Initiative, Philadelphia, Pennsylvania).

Placemaking and Art

Another design principle for nonprofit centers is placemaking and the use of art. The Project for Public Spaces has outlined,

As both an overarching idea and a hands-on approach for improving a neighborhood, city, or region, Placemaking inspires people to collectively reimagine and reinvent public spaces as the heart of every community. Strengthening the connection between people and the places they share, Placemaking refers to a collaborative process by which we can shape our public realm in order to maximize shared value. More than just promoting better urban design, Placemaking facilitates creative patterns of use, paying particular attention to the physical, cultural, and social identities that define a place and support its ongoing evolution.[7]

Placemaking in the nonprofit center context refers to the notion that nonprofit centers can become hubs in their communities, attracting varying populations and visitors. Art also plays a major role in this placemaking function, whether or not the shared space is exclusively arts-focused or incorporating arts elements. While not all nonprofit centers are open to the public or want to be widely accessible, many do, and art is instrumental in attracting new audiences. It also improves the working environment for resident organizations. Art exhibits, temporary installations, and other cultural events are strategies to bring communities to nonprofit centers. Requiring curation and staff attention, these projects can be done efficiently and without a lot of expense.

From the design perspective, placemaking strategies can include providing attractive outdoor spaces for informal gatherings, interior spaces for gathering (at a coffee bar, bookstore, or library). Fundamentally, placemaking centers on participatory processes, and for the nonprofit center, this means engaging with communities and end users of the space to make the center more inviting and usable. Figure 13.2 depicts a placemaking event at Liberty Station in San Diego.

DESIGN CONSIDERATIONS BY NONPROFIT CENTER TYPOGRAPHY

Each nonprofit center type, first outlined in Chapter 1 in the Beyond Buildings section, has different design considerations, which are briefly summarized here.

Generalist

Generalist Centers, by definition, serve broad audiences, and their design is characterized by meeting the different needs of various types of uses and users.

FIGURE 13.2 *ARTS DISTRICT Liberty Station, San Diego, California.* Nonprofit centers often serve broad audiences including tenants, people served by those organizations and the public. Placemaking is an important function for nonprofit centers, creating activities and events to attract people to the place. Good design fosters opportunities for placemaking, depicted here. The ARTS DISTRICT is made up of forty-five buildings on one hundred acres. The NTC Foundation oversees twenty-six of those, in which there are eighty-three artists, galleries, museums, dance groups, cafes, nonprofit offices, and creative work space for commercial businesses. *Photo credit: Liberty Center*

These considerations include the type of work the tenant does (administrative or client-serving); the space needs of the organizations for their employees, volunteers, and equipment; the ages of populations using the building; and any needs for easy access, including parking or bus access by the public. If meeting rooms are accessible to the public, they should have separate entrances and be able to be closed off from staff and office spaces, especially for evening use. Some centers "democratize natural light," allowing corridors and cubicle areas access to the most light for the most people, as in the Common Roof spaces in Ontario described in Chapter 12: The Common Roof™: A Values-Driven Approach to a Rural Nonprofit Center. Others pursue flexible design that allows for easy reconfiguration. The Carroll Nonprofit Center in Westminster, Maryland, a project of Anverse, Inc., for example, built its space with flexibility in mind: offices can be easily reconfigured without the costly expense of redoing the heating and cooling (HVAC) duct work.[8]

Service Centers

Design considerations for direct service centers are more specialized and include accommodations for heavy traffic, proximity to public transportation, accessibility for children, and other specialized populations, and buildings, rooms, and technological systems designed to guard clients' confidentiality. Circulation of different populations is important to address as well. For example, "intake" rooms near a reception area or a children's play area near where parents might receive services are critical considerations. Further, as previously mentioned, spaces that serve various populations must be carefully designed to keep populations in conflict safe and separated. Other shared resources in these centers may include shared reception and compatible shared databases that allow clients to be seen by different agencies without having to go through intake again or designed with shared reception areas.

Theme Centers

Design considerations for Theme Centers should reflect the purpose of the building whether it is sustainability, arts, education, peace, women, etc. For example, sustainability buildings, as discussed in the Green Building section should employ green features; many of these buildings display and explain the green attributes in the building. The Z Place at Evie Dennis Campus in metro Denver, for example, is an education-themed family childhood and support center with the nonprofits sharing space on a school campus. The inviting and bright space also includes meeting space and a community bank for young people to open bank accounts. Figure 13.3 depicts the exterior of Z Place.

FIGURE 13.3 *Exterior of Z Place, Denver, Colorado.* Z Place on the Evie Dennis Campus in Denver is a comprehensive, community-based early childhood and family support center and network on a public school campus. This Theme Center houses an early learning center, family support services, and a bank serving young people, among other partners. *Photo credit: Z Place.*

Flexible Space Centers

These nonprofit centers are designed to be more flexible. Coworking and incubator spaces generally house individuals and small organizations and companies. Hallmarks of these spaces are the open floor plans, which can include long work tables for intermittent use, along with private offices for rent. Some more traditional nonprofit centers have developed coworking spaces within the larger space to better meet the needs of smaller organizations. Design elements emphasize connectivity, interaction, and access to light. The HiVE space, for example, in Vancouver, British Columbia, provides phone booths for private phone calls, lockers for storage, bike hooks for commuters, and large commercial-sized refrigerators to accommodate lots of users. The space has a common reception lounge area and, like many of these types of spaces, buzzes with energy and activity.

Maker-spaces are a subset of coworking spaces, with a goal of sharing equipment to make things whether it's art, metalworks, furniture, or digitally printed objects. Design for maker-spaces emphasizes large open spaces to accommodate heavy equipment. These spaces might also need reinforced floors for the equipment, special venting for fumes, and sound attenuation for noisy machinery.

SPECIAL DESIGN CONSIDERATIONS
Overall Look and Feel: Color, Warmth, and Character

Whichever type of nonprofit center being developed, the overall look and feel of space is critical. Attention to lighting, paint color, and access to natural light is important to consider and should be designed around the users of the building. Service centers, for example, should have scaled spaces to make children and families feel welcome and be warm and inviting places for people to visit. Likewise, Thoreau Center for Sustainability (now Tides Converge) in San Francisco is a welcoming space filled with natural light, a café space for casual interaction and connection, and wide hallways for ease of circulation and mixing.

Soliciting feedback from end users about how they want the building to feel is an important part of early planning. And while not all desired design elements can be incorporated, it is still important to listen to end users about how they want the building or space to function.

Common Spaces

One of the biggest tasks facing the design of shared spaces is determining the layout for the common spaces—the conference rooms, meetings room, pantries, reception areas, resource spaces, and other gathering spots. There is no firm ratio of offices to meeting spaces; instead, each nonprofit center is different depending on the purpose of the building. However, a common complaint among nonprofit centers is that there are never enough conference rooms and flexible spaces for meetings, and certainly not enough storage space. As part of the feasibility exercise, it is a worthwhile exercise to "map" potential conference room use, including sizes, types, and frequency of meetings and technology requirements. Understanding the demand for the space will help inform an intelligent design solution for the conference rooms. Rooms of all sizes are important to build into the plan—small rooms for meetings of two to four people, medium-sized spaces for meetings of eight to ten people, and larger spaces for board meetings and trainings. Box 13.1 highlights some of the important design advice for design of common spaces.

> **Box 13.1 Design Tips for Common Spaces: Flexibility in Common Spaces Is a Winning Strategy!**
>
> ♣ Build conference rooms with flexible or folding walls so spaces can increase or decrease in size.
>
> ♣ Outfit meeting rooms with lightweight movable furniture on wheels for different meeting configurations.
>
> ♣ Create ample storage in conference rooms to store equipment and furniture when not in use.
>
> ♣ Supply adequate power to conference rooms to equip them for high-quality audiovisual technology including conference calls and video conferencing.
>
> ♣ Link common spaces to kitchen/pantry to facilitate catering functions.
>
> ♣ Provide comfortable furniture in unexpected places in the building to foster spontaneous interactions.
>
> ♣ Design common spaces with access to natural light to help foster productivity and happiness among workers.

Visual and Performing Arts Spaces

Arts spaces are unique among nonprofit centers. These are generally considered Theme Centers, but from a design perspective, they have additional requirements. Arts centers are visual or performing arts spaces and can encompass office, rehearsal, exhibit, and performance spaces. Some are even live-work spaces. There are shared space arts centers throughout North America representing all different types of spaces; some examples: Spaces at 520 (office and rehearsal space in an office building in New York City for off-off-Broadway theater groups); 18th Street Arts Center in Santa Monica, California (gallery and work spaces for artists); the Arts Factory in Vancouver, Canada, profiled in Chapter 26: A Strategic Use of Municipal Assets: The Arts Factory; and PS 109 in New York City, a live-work project of the Minneapolis nonprofit developer, Artspace.

Arts spaces have unique design needs such as high ceilings, wide column spacing, movable walls, extra power for stage lights, raked seating, natural lighting for visual arts, suspended floors for dance, venting for chemicals produced by visual artists, and slop sinks for cleaning. Arts spaces are also uniquely positioned to share common resources such as box office, rehearsal, performance, and exhibition spaces. These are all relatively costly and specialized spaces to build and sharing them among several organizations helps amortize the costs among multiple parties.

There is institutional support for developing arts spaces, in both Canada and the US. Two groups stand out as examples of arts-focused developers who understand the unique design elements in the arts: Artspace provides consulting and development on live-work spaces and more in the US, and Artscape, the Toronto-based "urban development organization that makes space for creativity and transforms communities. Artscape leverages the power of the arts to support artists and catalyze community transformation through a proactive practice known as creative placemaking," operating in both Ontario and British Columbia.[9]

Access: Public Transit, Parking, and Biking

Many nonprofit centers often stumble over planning for parking, especially centers located outside of dense urban cores that are served by reliable public transit. For centers that serve a public function, and that are not served by good transit, having adequate and safe parking is fundamental. Many nonprofit centers do not consider parking requirements or underplan for parking to the detriment of the center. Still others may not have parking available as part of the site and might have to provide parking offsite or provide no parking at all. In either case, wayfinding, signage, and even a walking safety escort service might be necessary. Regardless of the parking requirements, it never seems to be enough, and nonprofit centers continue to grapple with this issue.

Additionally, some centers have parking requirements for specialized vehicles or must accommodate buses, charters, or vans to serve specific populations. Some centers do enjoy access to public transit, and, where lacking, centers have been able to meet with local municipal officials to reroute bus routes to increase access. Finally, nonprofit centers can provide bike racks (or even provide space for local bike-share efforts) to match growing efforts around creating bike-friendlier places.

Signage and Wayfinding

Signage both inside and outside the building is also important and should not be neglected during design and budget planning. Sensible and clear wayfinding signs make a nonprofit center more accessible and attractive. Exterior signage identifies the building and helps visitors navigate. Signage overall helps establish the building's "brand" and should be a core element of the overall design.

Service Spaces: Pantries, Kitchens, and Loading

Like conference rooms and parking, kitchens are problem areas at nonprofit centers but are also hubs of activity and potential interaction. How many kitchens and pantries are necessary, and who cleans and maintains them? Does the kitchen need to accommodate tables for informal gatherings? These questions are the daily nuisances and joys facing nonprofit center managers across North America. Kitchens and break rooms should be designed for easy accessibility and a variety of users. Some of these spaces have roll-up windows that attach to conference rooms for easy catering access; others have industrial-sized refrigerators and/or dishwashers. Others have community bulletin boards for posting events and notices. Some offer free drinks and snacks to encourage interaction and connectivity.

Still others feature commercial kitchens used to teach cooking classes or to generate rental revenue. The Wellness Center in East Los Angeles, for example, offers nutrition classes in healthy cooking to further its mission "to inspire and empower residents and patients to take control of their own health and wellbeing by providing culturally sensitive wellness and prevention services and resources that enable prevention, address the root cause of disease and improve health outcomes."[10] Other neighborhood-oriented facilities include industrial kitchens as part of encouraging new social enterprises among neighborhood residents.

Loading docks are also important for some nonprofit centers. It is important to understand if the loading dock will need to accommodate hand truck deliveries or large-scale deliveries of palettes or other large items. The loading dock may need to house large dumpsters or garbage and recycling functions. Nonprofit centers that feature food pantries and arts spaces, for example, have heavy loading requirements that should be considered during site selection and the design of the space.

CONTEXTUAL DESIGN AND RESILIENCY

All the design elements for shared spaces discussed in this chapter are important, but they largely deal with the actual building and what goes on inside. It is also important for nonprofit centers to be socially rooted in their neighborhoods and surrounding communities. To achieve this, as part of the planning phases, nonprofit center leaders can convene local stakeholders and communities to share plans for the building and solicit ideas on its design and programming. Nonprofit centers should endeavor to be excellent neighbors—reflecting the communities they are in, amplifying a neighborhood's assets and serving as a focal point for local stakeholders. A design charrette—a participatory, collaborative planning exercise—is a useful process to solicit needs and desires of communities served by the nonprofit center, including its design, and is an important step to create local buy-in.

Climate change is clearly a dominant macro consideration that any real estate project needs to consider. Cities and towns are addressing the threats of climate change by becoming more resilient, a concept referring to strategies to adapt to climate change through policy change and even design solutions.

Nonprofit centers, like other real estate projects, can tap into local efforts to confront climate change and can be effective agents of change in this arena. Siting the building in a previously developed site as opposed to a greenfield, designing energy efficient spaces, fostering biking and transit access, and employing energy saving operating strategies are tangible ways that nonprofit centers can contribute to the resiliency movement. Participating in local policy task forces and other planning and legislative efforts can also inject nonprofit voices into the local strategy.

MOVING THE DESIGN FORWARD

Designing the nonprofit center can be fun, challenging, and inspiring. Good design comes in many forms and budgets. There are six best practices summarized here to advance the design process for any shared space project under consideration.

1. Complete a design assessment as part of the overall feasibility plan to determine that the project pursues the right site at the right location and scale and reflects the purpose of the project.

2. Design a space to meet the needs of both the functions of the building and varied users of the space.

3. Assemble the right team to create the design and hire people with expertise in the features needed for the particular nonprofit center project and who support the mission.

4. If the building is an adaptive reuse project, ensure the design team understands the structural and other condition(s) of the building, and any deferred maintenance issues.

5. The team should understand how to tackle the design of an historic building for a new use, and the capital budget should have ample contingencies to cover unforeseen conditions.

6. Remember to design not just what is inside the building but also what surrounds the site—the building's relationship to the local neighborhood and community, transportation, and outdoor spaces.

CONCLUSION

The design is the most visible aspect of a nonprofit center project. Done well, it has the potential to elevate the project and bring new visibility to its inhabitants and the work that they do. While many projects inherit the site or building for their project, there are still many ways and avenues to inject good design principles into the space that mesh with, and reflect, the mission of the project.

NOTES

1. For more on the Cleveland Environmental Center, see http://virtuallygreen.com/vtbs/vtbs_app_with_chat/index.php?tourid=1. Accessed April 18, 2018.

2. Community Service Building. "About Us." 2009. Accessed November 26, 2017. http://www.csbcorp.org/pages/aboutUs.html.

3. Community Service Building. 2009. Accessed November 26, 2017. http://www.csbcorp.org/pages/recycling.html.

4. Email correspondence with the author and TNSE Missionworks property manager, January 8, 2018.

5. See http://www.universaldesign.com/what-is-ud/. Accessed April 18, 2018.

6. Ed Roberts Campus. "Universal Design Welcomes Everyone." Accessed March 14, 2017. https://www.edrobertscampus.org/design/.

7. See https://www.pps.org/reference/what_is_placemaking/.

8. China Brotsky's personal conversation with Marty Sonenshine, Executive Director of Anverse, Inc., 2016.

9. Toronto-based Artscape is a nonprofit urban development organization that makes space for creativity and transforms communities. Artscape leverages the power of the arts to support artists and catalyze community transformation through a proactive practice known as creative placemaking. Its approach involves clustering creative people together in real estate projects that are designed to generate positive cultural,

economic, social, and environmental bottom lines. Artscape's growing portfolio of unique cultural facilities includes community cultural hubs, multipurpose creative spaces and artist live/work projects. See www.artspace.org/ and www.torontoartscape.org. Email correspondence by authors with Lori Ann Girvan, Artscape COO, February 2018.

10. See http://www.thewellnesscenterla.org/ourmission. Accessed April 18, 2018.

14 Stories from the Field

Universal Design
Creating the Ed Roberts Campus

William Leddy

Leddy Maytum Stacy Architects
San Francisco Bay Area, California

Born in 1939, Ed Roberts was one of the key figures in the independent living and disability rights movement. Polio contracted at age fourteen left him mostly paralyzed from the neck down, but although he rode a wheelchair and had to sleep under an iron lung, he fought to gain access to the same educational opportunities as all his peers. He was the first student with severe disabilities to attend the University of California, Berkeley, and he founded the university's Physically Disabled Students Program. He went on to become a director of the Center for Independent Living, a nonprofit organization that supports people with disabilities in leading independent lives. Later, he served as the first California State Director of Rehabilitation to have a disability and was cofounder and president of the World Institute on Disability. In 1984, Ed was named a MacArthur Foundation Fellow in recognition of his pioneering work.

After Ed died in 1995, disability community leaders decided to honor his work by establishing a center that would support collaboration among disability rights organizations and increase opportunities for people with disabilities. Seven agencies formed a consortium, called the Ed Roberts Campus (ERC), and began hunting for a site to create a headquarters building they could share with each other. In 1998, they selected a parking lot at the Ashby Bay Area Rapid Transit (BART) station in south Berkeley. The ERC negotiated with the city of Berkeley to acquire air rights and the BART district to acquire the land, and the consortium reached out to a Bay Area developer, Equity Community Builders, to serve as project manager and development manager.

The next challenge was to create a facility that would be a model of universal design—an environment that would be as easy and intuitive as possible for individuals of all abilities to navigate and use. At the same time, the ERC community wanted the building to help revitalize the neighborhood, enhance access to public

FIGURE 14.1 *Exterior of the Ed Roberts Campus.* The Ed Roberts Campus is built on the former parking lot at the Ashby Bay Area Rapid Transit (BART) station in south Berkeley. The seven agencies of the consortium wanted to create a facility that would be a model of universal design. They also wanted the building to help revitalize the neighborhood, enhance access to public transportation, and celebrate diversity while welcoming everyone with an environment that didn't have an institutional feel. *Photo credit: Leddy Maytum Stacey Architects.*

transportation, and celebrate diversity while welcoming everyone with an environment that didn't have an institutional feel (see Figure 14.1).

DESIGNING THE CAMPUS COLLABORATIVELY

To achieve these goals, Leddy Maytum Stacy Architects (LMS[A]) designed the 85,000 sq. ft. facility in close collaboration with the tenant organizations. We worked with the ERC board to create a design committee with representatives from each of the consortium's original partners—the Bay Area Outreach and Recreation Program, the Center for Accessible Technology, the Center for Independent Living, the Computer Technologies Program, the Disability Rights Education and Defense Fund, Through the Looking Glass, and the World Institute on Disability, as well as representatives of people with various ability levels.

The ERC community has an extremely sophisticated awareness of universal design, both as individuals who navigate their environments every day and as nonprofit organizations that have been national and international leaders of the Disability Rights and Independent Living Movements for decades. So the design team benefited enormously from the collective knowledge and expertise of the broader ERC community, as well as various experts from across the nation.

Two members of the ERC board of directors led the effort throughout the project—Dmitri Belser, executive director of the Center for Accessible Technology, and Susan Henderson, executive director of the Disability Rights Education and Defense Fund. Jan Garrett, executive director of the Center for Independent Living at the time, was chair of the ERC board of directors in the early days of design and was a key participant. Her insights and enthusiasm helped to galvanize community support. The ERC's community coordinator, Caleb Dardick, was another key person during design and outreach. In addition to regularly scheduled project meetings with the design committee, we held a series of larger ERC community design workshops—lively, well-attended sessions where we presented design options and received important input. An extensive public process involved neighbors, local merchants, and the historic preservation community as well.

APPLYING UNIVERSAL DESIGN PRINCIPLES AT A CIVIC SCALE

During the design phases, we became aware of two particular aspects of applying universal design at a civic scale. First was what Belser dubbed "dueling disabilities"— the idea that what one group might find beneficial; another group might see as an impediment. For example, highly textured pavement is often used to assist with way-finding for people with sight disabilities. However, people riding wheelchairs are sometimes sensitive to the vibrations these textures create. We worked hard to identify these areas of potential conflict and resolve them through design.

For example, Chris Downey, an expert in the design of environments for people with vision impairment, assisted the team in calibrating contrasting pavement textures that were perceptible without becoming a barrier to wheelchair riders. Floor finishes are minimally patterned, and fire alarm strobes are low frequency, to meet the needs of those with photosensitive epilepsy. Occupants and visitors of the ERC have a wide range of requirements that need to be accounted for in restroom design, so the hands-free restroom suites, including family restrooms, have specialized lifts and meet a wide range of abilities.

The second aspect was the realization that universal design is really anything *but* "universal." Every individual is, of course, unique, with a particular set of needs and preferences. In designing spaces that welcome everyone, it's impossible to satisfy every individual's personal preferences, but it's essential to address the pressing needs of everyone to the greatest extent possible.

Jan Garrett was one inspiration in this regard. She's an accomplished attorney and administrator who happens to have no arms or legs. During design, our team came to see her as a kind of "avatar" for the diverse users of the building, helping to make universal design both personal and practical. We came to believe that one of our most important jobs was to design an environment that would allow Jan to arrive at the ERC after hours, get to her office, and do her work, all without any assistance. Whenever we were faced with a design problem, we always asked ourselves, "How do we solve this for Jan?"

Design Goals Made Real

Two design goals were key. First, to seamlessly integrate universal design strategies within attractive, welcoming spaces, and, second, to emphasize the use of off-the-shelf components to prove that advanced universal design is achievable for everyone. The consortium wanted the ERC to be a case study of affordable, replicable best practices, built at the cost of a typical Class B office building in the San Francisco Bay Area.

Within this context, the ERC community contributed several universal design innovations in collaboration with the design team. Long-range card readers allow people in wheelchairs to approach and open locked doors hands-free. Low-tech wayfinding strategies rely on contrasting floor and wall colors and light textures to meet the needs of everyone. Entrances, circulation routes, and overall building organization are laid out to make wayfinding easy. Acoustical landmarks, including a fountain in the atrium space, further help with orientation for people with vision impairment. At the same time, we fine-tuned the building's acoustics to be sensitive to those with hearing disabilities. The corridors are seven feet wide to provide plenty of room for wheelchair riders. Hands-free building controls include automatic doors and occupancy-sensor-controlled light fixtures.

At the request of our client, our design process itself evolved to meet the needs of everyone. We printed floor plans on a Braille printer provided by one of the ERC partners and built tactile models to help communicate with people with vision impairment. During design meetings, we learned to verbally describe our ideas more fully in collaboration with an interpreter for the deaf and hard of hearing.

We selected finishes with high durability and low maintenance requirements. Advanced digital and communications technologies meet the needs of users with a wide range of abilities. A public elevator connects to the BART station below street level. To be easy for wheelchair riders to control and use, all elevators are designed with foot paddle controls for hands-free operation, and they can accommodate a high number of riders.

To connect the first and second floors, in addition to making a typical American with Disabilities Act (ADA)–compliant ramp, we wanted to create a work of public art that would symbolize universal design principles. We created a two-story helical ramp in the lobby at the heart of the building, beneath a skylit rotunda. Clearly visible from the street through the glazed entry façade, the ramp functions as both a dramatic sculpture expressing the ideal of access for all and as a practical solution to circulation, inviting everyone, regardless of their ability level, to the second floor. Fifty-six feet in diameter, the helical ramp has become widely recognized as one of the most innovative applications of universal design in the project. Several wheelchair-using occupants have expressed their relief to be working in a building where they feel safe—capable of exiting on their own in an emergency.

A public exhibition space occupies the center of the ramp. Beyond the ramp at the center of the building, an enclosed courtyard brings in natural daylight and serves as a community gathering space for all the tenant organizations as shown in Figure 14.2.

FIGURE 14.2 *Courtyard.* The enclosed courtyard in the Ed Roberts Campus brings in natural daylight and serves as an informal community gathering space for all the tenant organizations. While not a LEED rated building, the project was constructed with sustainable design principles including access to natural light, materials and ventilation. *Photo credit: Leddy Maytum Stacey Architects*

The exterior of the building creates an embracing, semicircular plaza facing Adeline Street, welcoming everyone while also providing drop-off and entry to the ERC building and connecting to buses, taxis, BART, and bicycle parking. The plaza is generously sized to accommodate public gatherings. The building form itself responds to the low-scale and fine-grained texture of the residential neighborhoods to the south and east; ipe wood screens help the facility blend in with nearby wood shingle houses.

SUSTAINABLE DESIGN STRATEGIES

Creating a building with a high level of sustainable (green) design strategies was also important to the consortium. To make the most of a limited budget, the consortium elected not to pursue certification under the US Green Building Council's Leadership in Energy and Environmental Design (LEED) Green Building Rating System. However, the building is equivalent to a LEED Gold facility. Located at a major public transportation node, it offers direct access to the BART station below. The ipe wood screens on the exterior are sustainably harvested and provide shading. Extensive daylighting minimizes the need for artificial lighting, and energy-efficient mechanical systems and lighting further reduce heating and cooling costs. Building materials include recycled, sustainably harvested, and renewable materials.

The project was designed to meet rigorous LEED standards for indoor air quality (the construction phase predated the Living Future Institute's Living Building Challenge and its Red List of worst-in-class building materials). Natural ventilation, use of nontoxic materials, and the filtration of outside air all help improve air quality inside the building. People with severe chemical sensitivities were nonetheless very concerned that the building provide the healthiest possible environment for them. To address this concern, the ERC commissioned third-party air quality testing at various locations within the building after final completion and furniture installation. The test results, which were posted on the ERC's website, proved that the air quality in the building is among the healthiest in the region.

Project Funding

Project cost was carefully managed and succeeded in meeting the budget of a typical Class B office building in the San Francisco Bay Area. However, financing the project was still a daunting task, requiring a creative blend of many disparate funding programs. These included city, state, and federal grants; private foundation grants; and loans from both private and public institutions. Funding for the interior buildout and furnishings was obtained through the federal New Markets Tax Credit program by using a unique, creative structure ("Targeted Populations") that required reliance on the ERC's commitment to providing employment opportunities for low-income people.

A MODEL FOR UNIVERSAL DESIGN

The building opened in 2010, providing a home not only to the ERC partners but also to several other tenants working in support of people with disabilities, such as the Ala Costa Centers, the Alameda Alliance for Health, the California Department of Rehabilitation, the California Telephone Access Program, the Lighthouse for the Blind, and Toolworks. The facility also includes exhibition space, community meeting rooms, a childcare center for children with disabilities, a fitness center, offices, vocational training facilities, and a café. A below-subgrade garage provides parking for staff and visitors and connects to the BART station.

The feedback for the project has been overwhelmingly positive, and the building has become an international example of universal design applied at a civic scale. The tenant organizations report an increase in productive collaboration among them, and despite a long public approvals process, neighbors have come to appreciate the added vitality the project contributes to their community. The central atrium space has been used for a wide variety of public events we never anticipated, including dance performances, art exhibitions, operas, weddings, and community gatherings of all kinds.

The responses we've heard from visitors to the building have been gratifying too. Some time ago, during a meeting in the second-floor conference room, one of the participants arrived a little late. He was riding a motorized wheelchair, with limited use of his hands and arms, and he seemed a little emotional. When his colleagues asked him what was wrong, he replied that he had arrived by BART and taken the elevator up from the station. On the way, he realized it was the first time in his life that he had entered a building in such a way without needing any assistance.

This was deeply moving to hear. We look forward to a time when universal design becomes universal in application—a time when this kind of experience is so common in buildings that no one remarks on it.

PART 6
OPERATIONS

15 Facilities that Facilitate
Nonprofit Center Operations

Saul Ettlin and Kim Sarnecki

Nonprofit center building operations are a combination of traditional property management and a blend of programs, amenities, and services that strengthen organizations, build community, and foster collaboration. The goal is that the building operates in service of its occupants' social purpose missions. Traditional property management seeks to maximize financial returns on behalf of its owner through cost containment, risk mitigation, and maximizing rents. Well-run nonprofit centers, in turn, work to deliver both solid building operations as well as offer a program set that supports their tenants. They achieve this by adding some mix of below market rate rents, community building efforts, opportunities for collaboration, and/or service offerings on top of the basics of property management. This means that nonprofit center operations are likely to be more diverse and layered in their operations than their for-profit counterparts.

For those looking to build their general property management knowledge and skills, there is a wide range of resources available to learn about the common elements of operating and maintaining commercial real estate. There are numerous books written on the topic and many ways to get training. Building Owners and Managers Association (BOMA) and the International Facilities Management Association (IFMA) offer webinars, trainings, and conferences. Public universities and community colleges also offer courses, certificates, and degrees in commercial real estate and property management.[1]

Given the readily available resources on the topic of property management, this chapter touches only briefly on the six main areas that are core to operating multitenant commercial projects. The balance of the chapter focuses on areas where nonprofit center operations are distinctly different from or in addition to traditional commercial real estate. The chapter will first cover revenue. Revenue, while important to most centers, isn't always the primary financial objective. We will then touch on green operations, now more common in commercial real estate. Nonprofit centers have had a deep and long commitment to sustainable building operations. With an understanding of revenue and centers' green efforts, we will go on to staffing, community, and culture. The staffing structure of nonprofit centers is where we see some of the strongest differences from commercial real estate, and community and culture are what truly sets nonprofit centers apart in their ongoing operations. We conclude by touching on where commercial real estate is headed. Shifts in the way we work are already impacting how we use the office. These changes may bring nonprofit centers and general commercial real estate management closer together. We touch on subjects also covered in other chapters to give the subject of building operations sufficient context to implement the ideas presented in this chapter.

GENERAL BUILDING OPERATIONS

While nonprofit center operations are likely to be more complex than those of traditional office facilities, the basics of property management still apply. Six key areas, discussed in the following text, are consistent regardless of the type of property under management (for nonprofit centers, these areas have different solutions based on the ownership model).

Leasing and Rent Collection

This includes refreshing spaces after a tenant moves out, advertising and showing vacant spaces, negotiating rates and agreements, renewing leases with current tenants, and accommodating their changing space needs. It also includes invoicing tenant rent and other receivables and managing delinquencies. In sum, making every effort to keep the building fully occupied and keeping track of the revenue. Most of these functions can be completed in-house; in some cases, renewals of space and negotiating rents and agreements, especially in larger buildings, are handled by a broker hired by the ownership.

Managing Tenant Improvements

Tenant improvements (TIs) are modifications to a space to meet the needs of the tenant. TIs are negotiated during the leasing or renewal process and are often paid for by the building owner through financial allowances. The building owner, or their representative, sometimes manages these construction projects, and sometimes the tenant manages them.

Daily Maintenance

From keeping restroom, common areas, and offices clean to maintaining the overall safety and security of the building to managing the comfort of the tenants in terms of heat and noise, the daily maintenance of the facility is the backbone of property management. This includes monitoring all the building's systems (heat, cooling, electricity, elevators, water, etc.). This function is completed generally by an in-house maintenance staff or a third-party property manager.

Ongoing Tenant Relations

Good building operators make concerted efforts to stay in regular contact with their tenants, so they can have an ear to the ground on what is happening in their building. A well-run building with regular tenant communication leads to happy tenants and better tenant retention. The function of tenant relations management is generally completed by a tenant coordinator or some other staff person.

Capital Improvements

Over time, it will be necessary to make investments into the property. From replacing or upgrading heating and cooling systems to replacing the roof or adding additional square footage, property owners need to plan for regular significant upkeep of the property and should maintain a capital reserve to undertake these construction activities. A best practice is to work with an outside property manager or consultant to develop a long-term asset management or capital investment plan for your real estate. This plan details repairs and revenue needed to be set aside for them as reserves over a five- to ten-year horizon.

Vendor Management

Property management is often about managing a series of vendors including janitorial, window washing, carpet cleaning, security, engineering, plumbing, painting, heating/cooling, electrical, and general construction. Getting bids, negotiating contracts, securing maintenance contracts, and maintaining clear communication with vendors is a time-consuming and critically important part of commercial real estate management.

RENTS AND REVENUES

The financial objectives of nonprofit centers vary widely. Some centers don't want or need to be at market rate rents (e.g., when a building is donated). Other centers are comprised of organizations banding together to reduce their occupancy costs. Still others develop spaces specifically to drive revenue for their organization while providing support to others in the sector. These varying financial motivations for nonprofit center operators mean that we see everything from space that is donated to full market rate rents. Each revenue model comes with its own considerations.

According to a 2015 survey conducted by the Nonprofit Centers Network, 74% of centers offer their tenants below market rate rents.[2] Whether at 50%, 80%, or some other target compared to market, these centers seek to support social mission organizations by helping them reduce their occupancy costs so that important, limited resources can go toward delivering program and meeting mission. Offering below market rate rents dovetails with the notion of stabilized rents. While the center may have a set target against market rate, the operator may choose not to chase the market, but rather to keep rents steady with modest but consistent increases at lease renewal (like a continuing 3% annual escalator). The advantageous financing tools available to nonprofits (no property taxes and tax exemptions on revenue, low-interest debt, and philanthropic contributions) help these centers pass on savings to their tenants. For more on these financing tools, see Chapter 6, The Development Process.

Free space is sometimes offered by foundations, governments, or others that own a building larger than they need for their intended uses. See Chapter 24: Partnering with Allies. These spaces are not always entirely free with owners often passing on direct operating expenses (electricity, janitorial, etc.) and/or common area maintenance charges (proportionate charges for common spaces). Rents are sometimes forgiven as a grant, and sometimes there are performance metrics attached with the nonprofit's tenancy as is the case at the Deschutes Children's Foundation in Bend, Oregon. We also see free space given for a specific period of time (like three to five years) to help accelerate the start-up of new organizations.

Less common are centers that charge full market rate rents. When a nonprofit center is at market rate it is often because they are leasing space and then releasing the space to other nonprofit tenants. This model can be advantageous as it eliminates many of the previously outlined property management challenges (because the landlord takes care of them) allowing center staff to focus on building community and fostering collaboration. Being in a market rate nonprofit center can still be advantageous to nonprofit subtenants as they often are able to be in higher quality space than they might otherwise have access to, connect to services and amenities they may not be able to afford on their own, and participate in a peer learning community.

Beyond rent revenue, centers also bring in resources through various other means. The revenue from these offerings are often used to help reduce cost for the tenants or sometimes sold to tenants if the owner/master leaseholder cannot afford to absorb the costs. Next, we explore some of the most common alternative revenue sources in centers.

Coworking

Offering a coworking option in a facility is growing in popularity with both non-profit and traditional real estate. Coworking is generally a limited membership model; members pay month-to-month on a license instead of a lease and with no long-term commitment. Members may not have an assigned desk and may not be in the office a full forty hours a week. Coworking is often a good option for tenants who don't need a full-time office and are looking for greater flexibility (like short-term projects or seasonal changes in the number of staff). Coworking is also ideal for start-up nonprofits looking to minimize fixed expenses in the beginning of operations and for consultants who don't need more than a desk or a single office but do need conference rooms and reception. In high-demand markets, coworking can yield revenue per square foot that exceeds that of traditional leases. Many coworking spaces rent offices and dedicated desks as well as simple usage plans so coworking models work well in a nonprofit center. Smaller organizations can graduate over time to offices and then office suites, creating a pipeline of tenants. Managing

FIGURE 15.1 *Tides Converge Coworking Space (formerly Thoreau Center for Sustainability), San Francisco, California.* Tides space offerings at their 150,000 sq. ft. adaptive reuse facility in twelve former military buildings in the Presidio National Park includes coworking. Pictured here is the Tide Pool—the central hub of their coworking program. *Photo credit: Saul Ettlin.*

coworking space can be more complicated and is often higher touch than traditional leasing but also has the potential for higher levels of interaction and collaboration between members. Figure 15.1 shows the Tides Pool, a coworking space in the Tides Converge space in San Francisco.

Event Rentals

Some nonprofit centers have conference and event facilities available for their tenants. These centers may also rent out spaces to outside community groups, businesses, and individuals for everything from board meetings, trainings, retreats, and fundraisers. We even see centers that host weddings. For some centers, event rentals can be a significant revenue stream, but we also see centers where they give conference room space away as a community benefit. Either way, managing event rental space is time-consuming and brings its own operational challenges that are very different from general leasing.

Selling Back-Office Services

All included or a la carte? Centers vary widely in their back-office service offerings, generally referred to as shared services. Some centers offer shared services as a menu of choices for tenants to selectively pick and choose from. These can include phone service, postage, copies, Internet access, and conference room usage. Others offer them as a bundle that can be a separate charge paid by the tenant or included in rent, which can be attractive to potential tenants. They can be priced to just pass along the costs to the tenants or are sometimes marked up to cover administrative costs or to make a little revenue for the center. Some centers move beyond just the operational services to offer shared services such as back-office accounting, joint marketing services, or IT services. See Chapter 21: Deepening the Model for more information.

Parking

A few centers have parking facilities for which they can charge. This can be a robust source of revenue that can help offset rents. For instance, the Community Service Building in Wilmington, Delaware, owns a parking structure where they rent out parking stalls to downtown workers.[3] The revenue generated from the parking garage is used to keep office rent down for their nonprofit tenants.

Grant Funding

Most often, grant funding for centers comes in the form of programmatic support. Whether it is to build deeper connections between tenants, foster new types of collaboration, or support shared services programs, grant dollars often go to a specific purpose. Rarely do we see general operating support go to nonprofit centers. For those that do receive general operating grants, they should continue to strive for a financial structure that works without those dollars as funder's interests change over time. The most successful centers operate without needing to raise ongoing philanthropic support.

At the same time, some centers have developed community fundraising programs with memberships, annual galas, barbecues, and the like to encourage both a stable stream of individual donations and to grow their base of community support for future capital campaigns.

In the end, all potential revenue sources should be considered when building the operating budget of a center. The budget must ensure that there is adequate revenue to cover ongoing operations and capital costs, staff the center appropriately, and offer robust tenant programs. A sound budget that includes reserves will ensure that a given center will be able to weather changes in the market, tenant vacancies, and unexpected expenses, as well as meet planned capital expenditures.

GREEN PRACTICES

According to the US Energy Information Administration, approximately 20% of US energy is consumed by commercial real estate, making office spaces a prime target for continued conservation efforts.[4] Having both positive impacts on the planet and the bottom line, efforts to reduce the energy footprint of office buildings are by no means unique to nonprofit centers. Nonprofit centers, however, often go beyond efficient lighting and climate control strategies and employ other efforts around recycling, sharing resources, and promoting alternative transportation. Additionally, some nonprofit centers employ leases with green provisions to ensure sustainable practices are used consistently in tenant spaces.

Resource Conservation

Leadership in Energy and Environmental Design (LEED), Energy Star, and other rating systems give guidance around achieving sustainability in building construction and operations. We see a variety of goals in nonprofit centers with many looking to achieve efficiencies in their energy consumption. Some buildings, like the Bullitt Center in Seattle, Washington, strive to be zero footprint buildings and are on the cutting edge of green building design (see Figure 15.2). As outlined in Chapter 8: The Alliance Center: Colorado's Hub of Sustainability, The Alliance Center in Denver, Colorado, was an early green nonprofit center specifically designed as a demonstration project for green renovations. For most buildings, it comes down to deploying efficient lighting, maintaining HVAC systems (when possible upgrading to more efficient units) and water conservation efforts. We also see the use of solar panels and buildings purchasing sustainable energy sources (wind, solar) from their local utility in efforts to "green" their supply of energy.

FIGURE 15.2 *Bullitt Center, Seattle, Washington.* Developed by the Bullitt Foundation, the Center is said to be "the greenest commercial building in the world." The building features, among other things, waste water reclamation, solar panels, sustainable materials for construction, and advanced monitoring that "automatically adjust passive and active systems to keep the building comfortable and efficient." *Photo credit: nic lehoux photographie architecturale | architectural photography.*

Individual Actions

How people behave at work is as important as how the building operates in efforts to tread more lightly on the planet. Because nonprofit centers develop and sustain active communities, they are able to foster other green practices through shared commitments, regular communications, trainings, and orientations. This can include anything from composting lunch leftovers to helping tenant staff look for alternative transportation to work. Some centers have the luxury of robust offerings from their municipality that include "no-sort" recycling and composting. In other places, nonprofit centers take the lead instituting their own in-house composting and recycling efforts. The Centre for Social Innovation in Toronto has even had a worm farm to breakdown kitchen scraps. Beyond recycling and composting, some centers have staff who work with tenants to adjust computer settings to minimize energy use. Others host office supply swaps that allow tenants to bring excess furniture and equipment to be claimed by other tenants. Still others offer a bike share and carpooling programs to get people out of their cars. While some of these practices can seem to be working on the margins, when scaled, for instance, to a 150,000 sq. ft. property with hundreds of employees, or to multiple centers across the country, they create collective positive impacts for the environment.

Green Leases

One way to solidify sustainable practices at a center is the use of green leases. These leases outline specific commitments by both the building owner and the tenant to operate their organizations in as green a manner as possible. This can include everything from mandating the use of nontoxic cleaning chemicals, and low volatile organic compounds (VOC) paints and glues in improvement projects to purchasing recycled office supplies. Centers might also include special monitoring of energy usage, including submetering, and air quality. When using green leases, management staff should be ready to have a list of vendors and resources available for tenants, so they can easily comply with the mandates set forth in the agreement.

With a combination of using the latest technologies to achieve the greatest energy efficiency, promoting tenant behaviors that reduce energy consumption and minimizing material going into the waste stream, many nonprofit centers are doing their part to make the work place a greener and healthier place for all while often seeing operational savings and higher staff morale along the way.

STAFFING AND THIRD-PARTY MANAGEMENT

Because of the priorities of running great real estate, building community and delivering program to both the tenants and broader community, nonprofit centers often deploy more staff than what we see in traditional commercial real estate operations. That said, nonprofit center staffing varies widely. The number of positions and types of roles a center will have is primarily driven by the size of the project (total number square feet, number of buildings or floors), the density of the project (number of people on a square footage basis), and the complexity of the program being offered (more intensive collaboration vs. more independent spaces). For instance, a 10,000 sq. ft. space made up of ten to fifteen small organizations might be able to get by with 1½ staff people or less. A large 200,000 sq. ft. property with eight hundred employees might have four or five people overseeing the center and delivering programs. Additionally, the staffing structure is impacted by whether or not the property is owned versus if the space is leased. Next, we will explore some of the staff roles at centers and review in-house versus third-party property management.

A 2015 Nonprofit Centers Network report indicates that the average staff size for centers is two people, and the report reveals four thematic roles.[5] The two most common positions are Center Director and Facilities Manager. In larger or more complex facilities, these positions can be complemented by an Event Manager and a position that, depending on the facility, lands somewhere on a scale between receptionist and program manager. These positions can be subdivided into more specialized jobs in larger projects or rolled up into a "jack-of-all-trades" position in smaller facilities.

Center Director

The Center Director (sometimes called Center Manager or Property Manager) provides oversight for the facility and, where applicable, manages the project's team. The Center Director will generally be responsible for leasing the facility and all financial matters regarding the property including rent collection, bill pay, and budgeting. This position is also responsible for maintaining excellent tenant relations and communicating facility-related news and updates to the community. In larger, owned facilities, the Center Director will ensure there is a long-term plan to maintain the facility and its systems as well as oversight on the negotiation of vendor contracts. No matter the size, the Center Director has oversight on the successful execution of program goals like collaboration efforts or shared services.

Facilities Manager

Working hand in hand with the Center Director is the Facilities Manager (sometimes called a Facilities Coordinator). This position's duties can vary greatly. When a more entry-level role, it can be focused on tenant needs, basic space improvements (hanging art, painting, basic maintenance), conference room management, and light audiovisual and IT work. At one moment, this person can be setting up a projector and a sound system in a conference room and, in the next moment, be making sure there is connectivity to printers and copiers and providing basic desktop support to tenants. In facilities that bulk purchase telecommunications, this role will often be responsible for managing the phone system. They may also be responsible for meeting room setups and maintaining kitchens in common areas during the day. We see this position more frequently in coworking-like spaces and in facilities with a conference center. At more complex or larger facilities, this position is focused on building systems, intermediate electrical, plumbing, and minor construction projects, and often vendor relations.

Event Manager

Most often found in centers with conference rooms or event space available for rent to the general public, the Event Manager oversees these spaces. The kinds of events hosted in these spaces can run the gamut from board meetings to trainings to conferences to fundraising events and, as mentioned, even weddings. The Event Manager coordinates dates, executes agreements, collects payments, verifies any insurance and license requirements (especially important when alcohol is being served), and ensures the space is set up and that equipment is deployed. In the small number of centers that offer catering, the Event Manager may also work with the renter to select a menu. Beyond event space rental logistics, this role may also manage public events offered by the center like lecture series, book readings, and art show openings, although that work is more often managed by a Community Animator. Figure 15.3 shows a shared space in the Centre for Social Innovation in Toronto.

Community Animator

Depending on the center's mission, supporting the Center Director in activating and connecting the tenant community is a role many centers call Community Animator (sometimes also called Receptionist or Community Catalyzer). This role may have front-desk responsibilities, monitoring the comings and goings of the tenants and guests in the shared space, and more often is the key connector in building relationships between tenants, developing and delivering tenant programs and guiding tenants toward higher levels of collaboration. The Community Animator may also be responsible for public programming like a speaker series or art gallery curation. This role is often the glue that binds the place and ensures that the community norms are upheld and that the center is a fun and fulfilling place to work. When there is no Event Manager role, the Animator often is also the event and meeting space manager.

FIGURE 15.3 *Centre for Social Innovation Toronto, Ontario.* This is one of several conference rooms available to members of the coworking space as well as the public at the CSI building at 192 Spadina in Toronto. *Photo credit: Centre for Social Innovation.*

Building Engineer

Outside of these four key roles in center operations, larger facilities that are owned will likely require a Building Engineer. This position is responsible for maintaining building systems like heating, cooling, plumbing, electrical, and life safety. The Engineer adjusts systems, replaces filters, light bulbs and lighting ballasts, clears minor clogs, and handles an assortment of other day-to-day building mainte-nance activities. As a general rule, major systems failures will be handled by outside vendors. The Building Engineer will often be responsible for overseeing a capital improvement plan (tracking systems' useful life and anticipating replacement dates) and working with vendors (from bidding to project execution) on projects. The Building Engineer may also execute a host of small projects including painting and construction. This role is often part of an outsourced property management team.

A key decision a project will need to make is if it is going to outsource some or all of these property management functions to a vendor. A given nonprofit center may decide it wants to focus on the interaction between tenants (collaboration, com-munity, shared services) leaving leasing and facilities management to a commercial property manager or the center may decide it has its own approach to real estate op-eration and decide it's best positioned to take on the property management function. Nonprofit centers use both in-house and outsourced models and something in be-tween. The Thoreau Center (now Tides Converge) in San Francisco uses an outside vendor for all of its leasing and property management and then adds one in-house position dedicated to catalyzing community among tenants. TSNE MissionWorks in Boston has all property management functions in-house, only using vendors for specialized work. Interestingly, the Alliance Center in Denver uses a hybrid model with an outside vendor for all building systems management and reserving all tenant-facing work (leases, community building, etc.) to in-house staff.

There is no right answer to the question of which model is best. Organizations that have other primary missions might find outside property management an advantage to keep building issues from distracting from other day-to-day work. Centers that exist for the sole purpose of operating the building might find in-house property management makes the most sense. Ultimately this, and all the staffing decisions, will need to be evaluated in the business plan and pro forma outlined in Chapter 6: The Development Process, to see what kind of staff structure the revenue model can support.

COMMUNITY AND CULTURE

Most centers' missions go beyond that of just providing space. While their core mission may be to offer quality, affordable stable space and to reduce costs through shared services, many nonprofit centers also look to build deeper connections between their tenants by fostering a robust community and distinct culture. Complementing the goal of having a strong community is the desire to see tenant organizations build trust with one another in an effort to smooth the way to greater levels of coordination and collaboration. This element of center operations is where we see some of the greatest divergence from that of traditional commercial real estate. Developing a center's culture and community starts as early as space design and tenant selection, moving through orientation and into programmatic offerings that support and encourage interaction and engagement between tenants.

Space Design

In general, space design questions are answered in the development phase or are dictated by a building's existing layout, but it's worth noting that design decisions can either encourage or be a barrier to creating a robust community. Not surprisingly, we find that centers where tenants can see each other tend to see community grow more organically as supposed to those where organizations' offices are completely separate. This is also true for centers that have other natural or designed gathering points like a café, outdoor areas, art gallery, lounge, or coworking hubs. When centers don't have these offerings and there's a desire to see more interaction, creating these spaces becomes an operational task. It is important to continually rethink space and consider new possibilities for usage over time. By watching tenant interactions and patterns of use, center staff may be able to reimagine and create new collaborative space in underutilized areas.[6]

Tenant Selection

Space design can foster community, but it's the people who make it. While not all nonprofit centers are intentional in who they select as tenants (or may not have the luxury to do so due to revenue or other market demands), most have some kind of screen for tenant selection. For centers with a specific theme (like environment or performing arts), tenant selection can be easier as it is focused on the issue area and mission of the organization. For instance, the Posner Center in Denver shown in Figure 15.4 is focused on international development and their mission is "to build a community of innovators who grow lasting solutions to global poverty."[7] This focus on one broad theme not only sets a clear standard for who can become a tenant, the tenants' shared mission also greases the wheels of community. Tides' Thoreau Center for Sustainability (now Tides Converge) in San Francisco is open to all nonprofits and social enterprises that are aligned with Tides' broad mission to accelerate the pace of social change toward a more just, sustainable and equitable world. However, to determine fit, Tides relies on an application that asks prospective tenants not only about their mission and program but also about what they want to get from and give to the community, preferring those that show a commitment to engaging with other tenants. Regardless of the method, building strong community means going beyond just the organizations' ability to pay rent and engaging them more deeply around their interest in being at the center—including their interest in being part of a learning community and evaluating how they will participate in that community.

FIGURE 15.4 *Posner Center, Denver, Colorado.* Housed in an 1867 building, Posner Center is an example of a Theme Center with tenants all having missions related to international development. Colleagues from World Affairs Challenge meet in the Posner Center's small tenant zone, also named "the Corral," in homage to the building's origins as a horse barn for the local trolley system and later a warehouse. Today, it's a vibrant community hub providing space for offices and hosting a wide range of convenings, lectures, and trainings. *Photo credit: Image by Shotzr Photographer, Evan Semon.*

Tenant Onboarding

Once an organization moves into the center, the newly arrived staff will need to be acculturated. The two most common ways we see this is through use of community charters and by center staff giving regular orientation tours. Community charters specifically outline center norms and are either signed by leadership or by all staff. Charters are also sometimes posted in common areas. Orientation tours, most often led by the Community Animator, outline all of the services and amenities offered by the center, and also go into the center's norms and opportunities to engage with other tenants. Even though these are most often offered when an organization first moves in, orientation tours should be regularly available since most tenants undergo staff turnover over time.

GROWING AND SUSTAINING CENTER COMMUNITY

Growing and sustaining center community is a purposeful activity that uses a range of tools. It can take the form of a gentle nudge or a more scripted program. At the most basic level, centers use visuals to promote community and culture. Pictures of all staff in the building, lists of center norms, or even posting all community events are products of a place's unique culture. Most center staff are knowledgeable about what their tenants are focused on and can connect organizations working on similar projects or facing similar challenges—in essence playing a kind of matchmaking role. After encouraging organizations to learn more about one another comes keeping tenants updated about what each other is doing. This is generally done either through a tenant listserv (where they can send out updates or request help/advice) or through electronic newsletters that highlight center happenings as well as what's going on with tenants.

Beyond these more passive means is active tenant programming including:

- Fun/social activities like a center-wide potluck or happy hour. We've seen other fun activities like "Race Through Our Space," a center scavenger hunt and "Tenant Olympics" with games and prizes. Still other activities seen at centers include: art gallery openings, holiday bazaars, and tenant craft fairs.
- Tenant-centric programming helps tenants get to know one another. These include offerings like "Take Ten" (a short presentation given by one tenant on their work), open houses inviting all tenants to tour each other's' space, and tenant speed dating where tenants give very brief pitches on their work to each other speed dating style.
- Informative programming like brown bag lunches on specific issues, lecture series with outside speakers, or policy briefings.
- Capacity-building efforts to build the skills of tenant staff. This can include peer learning (like tenant staff who work in communications meeting quarterly or monthly meeting of executive directors) or more formal trainings given by content experts on anything from fundraising to board management and more.

While some community and culture develops naturally, the Community Animator or Center Director coordinates much of it. Their work doesn't happen in a vacuum and many centers with strong programs also have some kind of Tenant or Community Council. This council will generally give input on the types of programs to offer and may even help deliver that program. Community Councils can also help with resolving tenant conflict and are sometimes involved in tenant selection. These councils can be an enormous asset to a center, but some find it challenging to get tenants to commit the time needed. (For more discussion on stakeholder involvement see Chapter 10: Who Drives Decisions.)

Most of center life can be energizing and rewarding, but sharing space does not come without its challenges. The three most common challenges include kitchens, noise, and conference room availability. Maintaining a clean and easy-to-use shared kitchen is a constant battle and one with no silver bullet to solve—except to just pay someone to keep it clean. Noise, especially in open plan spaces, can be challenging. Most often this is resolved with specific, separate areas for focused work and those dedicated for more interaction or socializing. The challenge with conference room use comes from either people squatting without a room reservation and using the room as offices or meetings running over and conflicting with other people's scheduled use. None of these problems are going away and just come with the territory. However, by setting clear expectations and with good communication, these conflicts can be minimized.

Investment in community and culture by nonprofit centers varies widely, but it is this investment that makes nonprofit centers special. Robust tenant community with great programming can help organizations become more capable of meeting their mission. It also builds trust between organizations that can pave the way to deeper levels of coordination and collaboration, and that can help organizations become more efficient and effective as they work to scale their impact.

PUBLIC PROGRAMMING

Nonprofit centers often serve as de facto community centers with programs delivered both by tenants and the center itself. As discussed earlier in this chapter, programming takes on many forms including lecture series, book readings, performances, wellness fairs, and more. Some centers also play host to the visual arts with rotating exhibits or permanent installations hung in either specific gallery space or utilizing common areas. Human service centers have high public traffic as the community comes in to receive services. Arts facilities may have extended hours to meet the needs of their performing arts tenants. Public use of the nonprofit center adds important vitality to the facility. What could be a sterile place is brought to life by its wide range of users and constant activity.

The operational consideration for public programming is twofold. First, the center must decide how it will staff the facility to accommodate extended hours. A center that is open 9 to 5, Monday through Friday, is going to have very different staffing considerations than one that is open seven days a week and until 10 at night. The second consideration is security. A facility that is predominantly an administrative office with few guests can reduce their security costs through a key card system. More open facilities have to do a deeper dive into whether they can get by with a straightforward front desk person, or if they have to institute stronger measures by having a guard in addition to reception staff. Of course, a lot of this has to do with where the center is located, community norms, and possibly the population the center is serving (In New York, a front desk guard is the norm while in San Francisco you may not see one). This, like so many of the items we have discussed, ultimately comes down to creating a set of services that meets the needs of the tenants and their constituency while staying cognizant of the financial performance of the facility. An open courtyard that facilitates community programming is shown at The California Endowment building in Los Angeles, California, in Figure 15.5.[8]

CONCLUSION: THE FUTURE OF WORK AND ITS IMPACT ON THE OFFICE

As nonprofit centers are evolving, so too is the way we work and the design of the office. Millennials want to work differently than the generations before them. There is a strong interest in collaboration, particularly when it comes to knowledge work. Technology means we may not need to be in the office Monday through Friday from

FIGURE 15.5 *The Center for Healthy Communities at The California Endowment, Los Angeles, California.* Located in downtown Los Angeles, The California Endowment has created a spectacular new-construction building built around a welcoming courtyard. The lower floors feature a conference facility that is widely used by community groups. Organizations devoted to healthcare are located on the upper floors. *Photo credit: Reproduced with permission of The California Endowment.*

9 to 5. A shift to contract work is changing individual's relationship to organizations. All this means that the office of tomorrow, and how we use it, will be different than what we see today.

The rise of the open space office plan and its coworking counterpart are telltale signs that the shift is already underway. Like nonprofit centers, these spaces drive new ways of sharing that rely on a solid community to be successful. Indeed, part of what coworking space is selling is community.

Some prognosticate that the office of the future may be more of a service and social hub where workers come to connect with colleagues, catch up on news, and get support and services around their work. These potential shifts, and the ones that we've already seen, mean that nonprofit centers will need to be ready to adapt their operations for the needs of the not-too-distant-future workers. Given nonprofit centers historic work around building community, fostering collaboration, and providing shared services and amenities, they are primed for the future.

NOTES

1. Building Owners and Managers Association. http://www.boma.org/. International Facilities Management Association. https://www.ifma.org/.
2. Nonprofit Centers Network Staff. Author interview, July 2016.
3. Bilton, Jerry, Executive Director at Community Service Building Corporation. Author interview, July 2016.
4. "Energy consumption Estimates by Sector." U.S. Energy Information Administration, https://www.eia.gov/consumption/.

5. Nonprofit Centers Network. *State of the Shared Space Sector Survey 2015: Changing How Nonprofits Work*. Denver: Nonprofit Centers Network, 2015.

6. Tides' Thoreau Center (now Tides Converge) in San Francisco is a large multi-building campus. Its café serves as a natural gathering point. However, staff there identified the need for additional space for tenants to linger and for a landing spot outside of café operating hours. Tides was able to repurpose its reception area into a coworking-like lounge giving tenants a new space to work away from their office and around each other. This has created new opportunities for chance interactions and interorganizational sharing.

7. See http://posnercenter.org/about/mission-and-vision/.

8. Hagy, J. "Profile—The California Endowment's Center for Health Communities." New York Law School Rooftops Project. Fall 2012. https://digitalcommons.nyls.edu/cgi/viewcontent.cgi?article=1009&context=rooftops_project.

16 Stories from the Field
Creating Social Innovation Through Shared Space, Social Bonds, and Community Animation

Centre for Social Innovation
Toronto, Ontario

The Centre for Social Innovation (CSI) is a social enterprise with a mission to catalyze social innovation in Toronto, the province, and around the world. As a coworking space, community, and launchpad for people who are changing the world, CSI provides both structured and informal support to projects that benefit people and the planet. There are currently four coworking locations in Toronto and one in New York City.

HISTORY

In so many ways, the story of CSI is still unfolding, but let us try to tell you how we got here.

In May 2003, while attending the Social Innovators Summit in Toronto, Margie Zeidler heard from participants (especially younger ones that were struggling to establish new projects) that they felt isolated. Often working out of their homes, they found it difficult to connect with others doing work in social innovation. Nine years earlier she had transformed "401 Richmond," a 200,000 sq. ft. factory building, into a thriving community focused on the arts but including a diverse group of tenants: for-profits, nonprofits, makers, designers, studio artists, etc.

During that same period, Margie attended a Nonprofit Centers Network conference on nonprofit centers in New York. For the first time, she was exposed to the multitude and variety of existing centers in the US (nonexistent in Canada at that time). The conference was hugely inspiring and had a profound influence on the thinking behind the creation of CSI, providing both ideas and examples.

At the time, Margie was completing the renovations on a new project up the street: the Robertson Building at 215 Spadina Avenue. There were 5,000 sq. ft. of unoccupied space in the 100,000 sq. ft. former factory. Margie decided and announced (on the second day of the Summit) that she would use that space to create this space for social innovators, which she had heard was missing in the city.

Margie was joined in this effort by the facilitator of the Social Innovators Summit—Mary Rowe (then President of Ideas That Matter). As luck would have it, former 401 Richmond tenant Tonya Surman heard what Margie was up to and asked if she could help. Tonya was the perfect partner as she had been building online communities and multi-sector collaborations and had also been exploring this idea of shared spaces. The prospect of working together seemed like a perfect fit.

Many, many people lent a hand, gave advice, and encouraged the project. Two, in particular, played an important role in the creation of CSI: Pat Tobin, who was with the Department of Canadian Heritage at the time and had commissioned a study earlier that year called The New Workplace Commons to examine how 401 Richmond provided a model for economic development), and Eric Meerkamper, a partner at DECODE at the time.

This group (Margie, Tonya, Eric, and Mary) incorporated as a nonprofit organization (CSI). Urbanspace, Margie's company, financed the project in its entirety during the first year of operation—paying the buildout costs to create the space and the part-time salaries of its newly appointed executive director, Tonya Surman, and a receptionist. Tonya donated the balance of her time for the start-up of the project. It took four years until CSI was self-sufficient and able to fully pay Tonya. The early days weren't easy. In fact, Tonya contributed her other consulting revenues, balanced multiple projects, and secured early support from funders to bridge the gap to get this social enterprise off the ground.

This group of civic innovators was visionary but pragmatic, trying to tackle challenges faced by many in the social mission sector. They asked themselves some core questions: How can we improve access to office facilities? How can we lower the cost of administration and let organizations focus on their mission? How can we share? How can we tear down the silos that keep organizations apart? And, how can we best catalyze social change?

CSI Spadina opened its doors to fourteen founding tenants in June 2004. The model worked. The members were happy, the broader community was drawn to the space, and the small staff team now had the room to begin supporting new projects. Early after opening, CSI began experimenting with "virtual tenancy"—a collaborative work idea that would ultimately be referred to as "coworking." When the opportunity to assume more space (14,000 sq. ft. on the fourth floor at 215 Spadina) arose in late 2006, again Urbanspace stepped up to secure and renovate the space for CSI. This time, Urbanspace's support came in the form of assuming direct costs and an interest-free loan. This was matched by the Canadian Alternative Investment Cooperative, and CSI got its first social finance investment. In the two and a half years since opening its doors, CSI had quadrupled its square footage and grown its membership twelvefold!

FIGURE 16.1 *CSI Spadina.* The first Centre for Social Innovation (CSI) at 215 Spadina in Toronto already embodied the theories of space, social and soft animation that underlie CSI's practice. *Photo credit: Centre for Social Innovation and Nyo Mudzingwa from You the Best Photography.*

By the end of 2007, CSI would become home to over 175 social mission groups in sectors including arts, environment, social justice, and education. For them—and for CSI—sharing space together meant more than simply being officemates. It meant sharing ideas, strategies, and experience. It meant collaborating, learning, growing, and becoming resilient in ways never imagined in isolation. Its creation is celebrated annually at a wine and cheese event held on the rooftop garden at 215 Spadina and shown in Figure 16.1.

In 2010, CSI took a giant leap forward by purchasing a beautiful brick and beam building, now called CSI Annex. The financing was fueled by our own innovation in social finance, the Community Bond (see following discussion). Two million dollars was raised in community investments to help bring the vision to life. With the support of its incredible network, CSI purchased, renovated, and filled a 36,000 sq. ft. building with more than four hundred world-changing social entrepreneurs.

EXPANSION USING COMMUNITY BONDS

As previously mentioned, in 2010 CSI was looking to buy a building to accommodate our growing waiting list. By then, CSI had built a strong reputation in the community and had cultivated deep networks over six years of operation. But CSI had no assets to leverage and practically no money: only $50,000 in accumulated surplus. The building that CSI wanted would cost $6.8 million to purchase and renovate. The gulf was enormous.

The first thing the CSI leadership team did was secure a loan guarantee from the City of Toronto that enabled CSI to get a mortgage for 75% of the projected value of the building after renovations. This agreement was a large improvement over the

65% of the purchase price, originally offered by the banks. However, $2 million was still needed to realize the project, and there was no clear strategy for how we would raise that amount in such a short time.

So, CSI leveraged the only asset it had—its community. The result of this work is the Community Bond, an innovation in social finance. This financial tool allowed CSI to offer a Registered Retirement Saving Plan–eligible investment opportunity to our network of supporters. In a four-month flurry of activity, CSI raised $1.4 million (and eventually the full $2 million), inked the deal on its newest property, and prepared to welcome over three hundred new organizations to CSI's second shared space project.

In September 2012, CSI opened another site. Artscape[1] had approached us to be part of an exciting project in Regent Park, Canada's largest social housing complex, which is currently undergoing Canada's largest revitalization initiative. CSI's leadership wanted to know what it would mean to take our model into a community in transition—a community comprised primarily of newcomers from around the world who speak eighty-five different languages. We decided to rent 10,000 sq. ft. space in the now-called "Daniel's Spectrum." Since opening, the team has begun to discover the many ways in which CSI and Regent Park's residents can collaborate and co-create. Besides even more potlucks and events that intentionally invite the community into the space, Box 16.1 describes another collaborative effort that emerged at Regent Park CSI.

Then in 2014 came our new site in New York City. CSI was approached by a passionate (and persistent) entrepreneur. He was determined to make a connection between CSI and RXR Realty, one of the leading forward-thinking realty companies in New York City and the broader tri-state area. CSI would be the perfect complement to the growing tenant community of creators and innovators at the recently purchased Starrett-Lehigh building in New York's Chelsea neighborhood. It has been three years since the New York location was opened, and it has already been named by some blog sites as the best coworking space in New York City. The space is beautiful, functional, and buzzing with activity. Members are hard at work, making an impact, collaborating, and launching incredible new initiatives. One example is Drive Change, a social enterprise which emerged at CSI New York City. It uses work

---

Box 16.1 From a Community Report-Back by CSI

In response to the worldwide migrant crisis and the conflict in Syria, The Canadian Arab Institute (CAI) based out of CSI Regent Park, ramped up its citizen engagement efforts with a five-month voter education and motivation campaign, which emphasized youth engagement and multiculturalism. CAI also co-founded Lifeline Syria, which recruits, trains and assists sponsor groups welcoming Syrian refugees in Toronto. For its part, CSI hosted a peer circle to connect and support the many members of the community working on resettling Syrian refugees. In times of increasing divisive rhetoric, working together is an imperative act of defiance.

Box 16.2 Drive Change NYC

New York is one of two states that automatically arrests and tries kids as young as 16 as adults. Drive Change was founded because when young people leave jail/prison with felonies rather than juvenile adjudications they face immense barriers to employment/educational options. . . . Drive Change uses the food truck workplace to run a year-long Fellowship to broaden access for young people (ages 17–25) returning home from adult jail/prison so they can obtain preferential employment and educational opportunities. . . . The Fellowship includes:

♣ Paid, quality employment experience.

♣ Transferable skills curriculum that generates industry credentials.

♣ Empowerment through community/advocacy work and leadership development.

---

at a food truck to teach work/life skills to youth returning home from adult jail/prison. Box 16.2 has a description of the program from their website.[2]

In 2014, CSI marked another new milestone; it bought a 64,000 sq. ft. building at 192 Spadina Avenue. It is the second building that CSI owns and is its fourth location in Toronto. It is conveniently located across the street from CSI Spadina near Queen St. West and Spadina, and it is a beautiful brick and beam building. Buying a building meant several things for CSI: more space, protection for CSI and for its members from the rising cost of rent, bigger offices to accommodate larger organizations, and, when the mortgage is eventually paid off in 2035, a surplus to reinvest in social innovation.

Now with five sites to operate, CSI is currently investing in its technology infrastructure to be able to reach and support more social entrepreneurs across Canada and globally. It is also continually creating new partnerships to develop innovative programs that catalyze social innovation.

CSI'S THEORY OF CHANGE

CSI is often asked how social innovation occurs. Its experience has shown that there is no single or simple answer. Social change is the result of a tremendously complex mix of ingredients. Environmental conditions, social conditions, and individual actors collide to spark world-changing ideas. There is an underlying magic to social innovation that precludes any simple recipe for success.

Making It Simple: The CSI Pyramid

Our Theory of Change is most succinctly communicated through the image in Figure 16.2.

We begin at the bottom of the pyramid, focusing on the creation of the physical space. We do this carefully, designing a space that is functional, whimsical, inviting and energizing.

FIGURE 16.2 This figure illustrates CSI's Theory of Change. Designing creative space and carefully curating a community becomes the basis for social innovation's emergence. *Source: Centre for Social Innovation.*

The next layer is community. What begins as a group of people looking for a place to work becomes a community through conscious and careful curating and programming.

These layers form the basis for innovation—the serendipity that happens when the right people, the right values, and the right environment are mixed together; when there is a setting up of the right conditions *for social innovation's emergence.*

The results are unpredictable. And often astonishing.

WHAT CSI HAS LEARNED ABOUT SOCIAL INNOVATION

What CSI has learned to do is create the spaces that best foster social innovation. The staff's observations find that these are the spaces that provide people with exposure to new ideas, connections with incredible people, and systems and structures to help turn the seeds of an idea into an achievable plan. CSI has been working hard to create these conditions in its home base in Toronto, and experiences there have led the staff to a few important conclusions.

Diversity

First, social innovation occurs most frequently in environments that are diverse. Innovation rarely occurs within homogenous or staid structures. It happens at the peripheries, where differing approaches bump up against each other and stimulate new ways of thinking. The diversity of our system leads to new opportunities and robust and flexible responses to common challenges. For CSI, this means doing away with the silos that keep sectors and structures apart. CSI often refers to the "social mission sector"—an umbrella term that includes all the individuals and organizations whose primary mission is to produce some benefit for people or planet.

The CSI community reflects this diversity. Its social mission members include nonprofits, charities, for-profits, entrepreneurs, and activists working in areas from health and education to the arts and environment. Change is not created by doing the same things that have always been done. By introducing diversity there is the provocation of discovery.

The Right Physical Environment

Second, social innovation needs a conducive physical environment. Social innovators need actual spaces to spark, develop, and apply their ideas. Without access to resources and support structures, even the best ideas have trouble taking flight. As a space-based organization, CSI is finding ways to create and curate spaces that foster social innovation as shown in Figure 16.3.

When "bearing down" on the task at hand, social innovators need a functional work environment with reliable office infrastructure. But all work and no play makes Jill a dull girl! CSI recognizes the critical importance of unstructured social space. There is far more serendipity around the kitchen table than the boardroom table. By balancing these characteristics, CSI creates a dynamic that stimulates new ideas to germinate and blossom.

Community Animation

Finally, CSI has developed the concept of community animation to promote social innovation. In addition to the physical space and a diverse mix of people, it is the interventions and learning opportunities created by staff that help make connections

FIGURE 16.3 *Kitchen, CSI New York City.* This picture of the kitchen at CSI New York City shows the mix of whimsy and functionality that exemplify CSI design. *Photo credit: Centre for Social Innovation*

and stimulate new thoughts and ways of doing. CSI brings innovators together with capacity-building workshops, informal social mixers, network, and more. It fosters individual and collective growth, and it creates an environment that produces original action.

Its key is to adopt a light touch. CSI does not offer programs with an expectation of uniform engagement by community members. Opportunities are offered so that individuals can "find their own level"; social innovators can dip in and dip out of the community in a way they find comfortable and natural. And when a new idea begins to surface, that same gentle touch helps it to grow. This is the team's role within the centre: to animate the ideas that have developed in the spaces it has created and to nurture a participatory culture where all members feel welcome to bring their ideas and to leave their fingerprints.

Defining Community Animation

In the early years, the CSI team struggled to find ways to explain what specifically community animation is and looks like. Since then, the team has been able to describe it in a more concrete way and evolved our community animation practice.

We like to describe community animation as the glue that holds our shared workspace together and the air that breathes vitality into the lives of everyone who moves through it. Animation is what turns our shared workspace into a community space, inspiring and connecting members while sparking new ideas and demonstrating the unique value of working together. The purpose behind animation at CSI is to create the conditions for social innovation to emerge.

Our goal of community animation is to create a physical, social, and psychological environment characterized as follows:

1. Facilitates the work of individual members and helps them discover their potential.
2. Solves problems and drives customer service.
3. Contributes to a sense of community.
4. Exudes warmth, inclusiveness, and hospitality for a diverse membership.
5. Maximizes opportunities for idea development, exchange, and collaboration.
6. Creates the conditions for social innovation's emergence.

These activities require dedicated attention and ongoing creativity to serve the emerging needs of our community while constantly pushing the envelope of what is possible. The staff's role is to model the culture they hope to see (in both their individual actions and in the organizational practices they adopt), and to empower every CSI member to be a community animator in their own way.

The Practice of Community Animation

The staff has experimented a lot over the years and has come to break down the practice of community animation into four main pillars: space animation, social animation, online animation, and soft animation. It has been found that none is more important than the others: they work in concert and to varying degrees for different purposes and for different members. And the staff are often called community animators exactly because their roles are to implement these pillars.

Space Animation

Physical animation refers to the artifacts or interventions that appear in the physical space as a means to foster connectivity and spark collaboration. Ways in which we do this include:

1. Strategic placement of our coffee machines to encourage interaction.
2. Using our chalkboards to communicate news and information.
3. Installing comfy couches and big tables for meals as in Figure 16.4.
4. Creating maps showing where members sit.
5. Creating notice boards, job postings, and events listings.

Social Animation

Social animation refers to those activities that allow people to get to know each other on a personal level. The staff try to do a formal event every quarter, and a number of informal events throughout the year. Some of the things tried include:

1. Salad Club, everyone brings an ingredient or takes turn making salads.
2. Waffle breakfasts.

FIGURE 16.4 *CSI Annex, Toronto, Ontario.* The seating area for the café at CSI Annex provides a comfortable place for eating and talking. *Photo credit: Centre for Social Innovation.*

3. Bagel bonding (can you tell we like food?).
4. Themed meetings of everyone doing the same issue or sector.
5. Six Degrees of Social Innovation Socials.
6. Lunch and Learns.
7. Community Marketplace.
8. Holiday parties (featuring the "Cookies and Cocktails" smackdown!).

Online Animation

Online animation refers to activities that happen in the online or virtual space. Members are not always onsite, and they are not always available. Creating and growing a technical infrastructure allows staff to accommodate members so they can engage on their own schedules and at their own locations. This includes but is not limited to:

1. Communicating via our email listservs.
2. Fostering connections and conversations on the member intranet.
3. Member profiles on external and internal web.
4. Sharing CSI's and members' news on social media channels.
5. Promoting events to internal/external audience.

Soft Animation

Soft animation refers to activities that happen organically and everyday but are nonetheless of crucial importance. This includes but is not limited to:

1. Smiling.
2. Greeting someone when they enter our space.
3. Being present.
4. Helping a member or another staff member with a task.
5. Making eye contact.

Unleashed Energy!

At CSI, there is an amazing team of creative and dedicated staff. But we know that this incredible staff can't possibly keep up with a community of over 2,000 individual members. CSI's goal, therefore, is not to anticipate and serve every possible activity but to create the conditions for members to offer their own ideas to the community—that is, to provide them the conditions for self-organization. This is a cornerstone of community animation.

LAST WORDS

The members of the CSI community are the best indicator of the activities and programs that should be happening in the space. The staff tries to give them the tools and supports they need to let their ideas come to life. We invite them to share their ideas, their knowledge, and their experiences with others. The staff team lets members organize themselves in the various CSI facilities and tries to make it easy for them to do things on their own. This participation has been found to create a sense of ownership among members, and it helps them to model possibilities for one another.

CSI's leadership is also really excited about the replication potential of the Community Bond work we did. Not only for ourselves (CSI bought another building in 2014 using Community Bonds) but for other nonprofits and charities. In the quest for funding, nonprofits have historically depended on those with deep pockets: government departments, foundations, corporate sponsors, and individual philanthropists. This approach has sustained the sector for generations, but it limits the contribution of "regular citizens" to modest donations. What we were really excited about regarding the Community Bond concept, was that people of average means could be transformed from occasional donors or volunteers into citizen investors.

CSI's staff learned so much through this process (the learning curve was huge!) that it had to capture the learnings and support the replication for others by writing the book *The Community Bond*[3] about our experience. CSI is truly excited that we have been able to support other nonprofits who are purchasing buildings for shared spaces.

NOTES

1. Toronto-based Artscape is a nonprofit urban development organization that makes space for creativity and transforms communities through placemaking. Accessed April 8, 2018. http://www.artscape.ca/.
2. Drive Change. "Mission." https://www.drivechangenyc.org/mission/.
3. Centre for Social Innovation. *The Community Bond—An Innovation in Social Finance.* 2017. Available from CSI. Accessed 21 March 2017. https://communitybonds.ca/shop/the-guide/. It is primarily applicable to Canadian projects.

17 *Stories from the Field*

From Grants to Earned Income
Changing the Financial Profile at NEW Center

Yodit Mesfin-Johnson

Nonprofit Enterprise at Work, Inc.
Ann Arbor, Michigan

A key challenge for nonprofit centers is financial sustainability. They often rely on charitable donations and foundation grants to supplement tenant rents. Yet, even with tremendous staff effort, donations and foundation grants are often uncertain, and foundation priorities are changing. Thus, a center's sustainability can be made more certain by further diversifying funding streams to include earned income and by being especially innovative in obtaining philanthropic support. This case illustrates how a nonprofit center, Nonprofit Enterprise at Work, Inc. (NEW), has evolved to rely on such sources to help insure its sustainability and enhance its financial profile.

NEW CENTER: A SHORT PROFILE

Often called by its initials, NEW was created in 1993 to own and manage the newly built NEW Center, an 11,000 sq. ft. multi-tenant nonprofit center situated in Ann Arbor, Michigan, overlooking the Huron River. It was initiated by The McKinley Foundation, its Founder and President, Ronald Weiser, his wife Eileen Weiser, and a diverse group of community members who were eager to replace an unsightly junkyard with an attractive and valuable community resource at the northern entrance to Ann Arbor, as shown in Figure 17.1.

NEW Center houses primarily nonprofit administrative offices. For most of the time since it opened, the NEW Center has operated at full capacity. It is currently home to twenty-two nonprofit tenants that serve various constituencies. They currently consist of four start-ups, four arts and cultural, twelve social service, and two environmental agencies.

FIGURE 17.1 *NEW Center, Ann Arbor, Michigan.* The NEW Center provides shared space for over twenty nonprofits from various fields. NEW, Inc., an acronym for Nonprofit Enterprise at Work, also provides management support, consultation, and training services to nonprofits in southeastern Michigan. The architect designed this building to resemble an historical train station, invoking the actual train tracks that still run beside it. *Photo credit: Courtesy of NEW, Inc.*

In addition to providing office space at or slightly below local market rate, the NEW Center offers tenants other shared amenities: a shared workroom with various office machines, access to meeting rooms and a kitchenette, and an opportunity to collaborate among themselves. Most recently, an informal group of nonprofit leaders (some tenants) are meeting to discuss advocacy and policy likely to impact the non-profit sector. Its meetings rooms are also used by many local nonprofits; an example of NEW Center's flexible conference room space that both NEW and its tenants use and that NEW also rents to other non-tenant 501(c)(3) nonprofits is shown in Figure 17.2.

Along with space and amenities, NEW Center also has offered educational and supportive services to its tenants and nonprofits in southeastern Michigan. Each year, more than 25,000 people visit the NEW Center, and since 2003, thousands have attended its workshops. Workshops and consultations have included organizational development, board development, fund development, nonprofit start-up, strategic planning, evaluation, leadership, diversity training, and more.

NEW has also recruited and trained scores of new board members and matched them with nonprofits seeking new trustees; its former "Board Connect" program, launched in 2000, was supported through grant money. From its inception to its sunset in 2014, this program trained over 3,000 community members in nonprofit govern-ance and matched and placed nearly 200 of those individuals on nonprofits' boards.

NEW has also responded to the evolving technological needs of nonprofits. It started by developing websites and databases for a small group of nonprofits in the 1990s; today, NEW's computer and IT program, npSERV, provides full infor-mation technology services to eighty-three agencies with 1,500 workstations across

FIGURE 17.2 *Flexible Conference Room at the NEW Center.* This double-sized conference room was designed to accommodate groups of various sizes and configurations. It can be divided into two rooms with the portable wall (in center), while not diminishing the light and river view for both sides. Four configurations of meeting spaces are also available to any non-tenant 501(c)(3) nonprofits in four-hour blocks for a fee. *Photo credit: Courtesy of NEW, Inc.*

southeastern Michigan. It was developed in response to a grossly lacking IT infrastructure among nonprofits and provides IT support that many nonprofits need.

While building nonprofits' capacities initially involved a small population of local organizations, eventually NEW grew to become the pre-eminent leader of nonprofit capacity-building work in southeastern Michigan, including Detroit. During this time, NEW has developed deeper capacity-building expertise, more acute and longer-lasting engagements with nonprofits, and, most important, a greater impact on the larger community through the strengthening of those nonprofit organizations.

Financial support for all these services was based on an evolving set of business models that needed to adjust according to the ups and downs of the larger economy and philanthropic giving. These models are discussed in the following paragraphs.

THE INITIAL BUSINESS MODEL: THE LAUNCH OF SERVICES WITH GRANT SUBSIDIES

For the better part of its first decade of operations, NEW covered facility expenses and a 10% reserve fund through the earned income from the rental of office space. The first twenty nonprofit tenants of NEW Center found immediate benefit in lower overhead costs and on-site cooperation with other nonprofits.

In 1994, the Managing for Nonprofit Excellence Workshop series was launched. It marked the genesis of programs and services that NEW offered to the greater nonprofit community in years to come. At that time, the workshops were free, and the costs associated with running them were underwritten by donations of cash and time by skilled volunteers from local corporate donors.

That same year, NEW launched the Nonprofit Consulting Consortium, with funding from the W. K. Kellogg Foundation. The consortium was designed to match highly skilled volunteer professionals with nonprofit organizations to assist them in such core management areas as board development, marketing, organizational assessment, and strategic planning.

In 2000, the Board Connect Program helped to increase board volunteerism within area nonprofits. Its popularity created such demand that NEW also began to offer on-site board governance training to the boards of other area nonprofits. NEW developed and delivered its own board governance curriculum in on-site training modules to boards at a time and place convenient for them. Initially, NEW leveraged grant dollars to subsidize the costs of staff delivering widely requested training; more than 45% of requests at that time were coming from across Michigan and outside of Washtenaw County, NEW's home base.

THE NEW EARNED-REVENUE MODEL

In 2003–2004, NEW's board began evaluating the long-term sustainability of the organization. The relatively stable economic environment in the 1990s had catalyzed NEW's programs, but to maintain stability and prepare for growth, it investigated our ability to scale up our programs and become less reliant on contributions. So, after nearly a decade of stable operation of the building and the Center's modest program offerings, *long-term* financial sustainability of NEW's programs became a key goal of our service delivery system.

At that time, fees for service comprised roughly 33% of our annual revenue, and almost every program at NEW endeavored to cover some of its own expenses, but it was not enough earned revenue to support long-term sustainability.

Clients' Fees for Services

The introduction of new products and services contributed to our earned revenue, and it was through the on-site board training sessions that NEW introduced its fee-for-service model in 2004. Nonprofit organizations now paid a fee for on-site trainings. However, we recognized that for many nonprofits—especially small nonprofits, those in low-income neighborhoods and those providing services to people of color—these costs represented the outside limit that they could afford to pay. By continuing our relationship with key funders and donors, we were able to ensure that those organizations were not excluded. By keeping fees low enough to involve many nonprofit executives—many of whom became "repeat customers"—the reputation of NEW's programming grew, attracting more new participants to take advantage of its growing capacity-building services.

The new program offerings also proved scalable, netting more revenue to aid NEW's bottom line. NEW's continued financial growth hinged on its ability to continue to diversify its program's funding streams and to expand its service area.[1] By including environmental scans and interviews in neighboring communities in our planning sessions, we discovered that NEW did not have much market reach outside of its home county. We began to realize that the whole of southeastern Michigan is home to nearly 25,000 nonprofit organizations in several other counties, with a plethora in or near Detroit.

Moreover, we also had a number of colleagues leading nonprofits in Detroit who were interested in bringing our capacity-building services to their organizations; at that time, Detroit had fewer capacity-building resources available to its nonprofit community when compared to Ann Arbor. NEW's entry into Detroit started small, with limited offerings of workshops and on-site trainings to nonprofits, mostly on an on-demand basis.

Expanding the Client Base

In 2006, as a result of consultation with the Nonprofit Centers Network (see Chapter 29: It Takes a Network to Build a Field), we gained the skills and expertise to open a satellite office in downtown Detroit, inside of Hannan House, another multi-tenant nonprofit facility. Thereafter, while NEW remained headquartered in Ann Arbor, it added several staff to its Detroit satellite office to expand its programs' reach.

Back-Office Services

By this time, our computer support program, WebConnect, had begun piloting a "Service Network" to provide shared back-office services for nonprofits. The first service focused on IT support. As of spring 2008, NEW had emerged out of the "pilot" phase and into the growth phase. We revised our business plan to include a more aggressive revenue growth plan for the next three fiscal years.

The major variables in this aggressive plan were new tiered fees, and the related growth rate that would need to be sustained to achieve our targets. The WebConnect program was retired, and npServ emerged as our comprehensive IT support program. The program's mission was to provide shared back-office service solutions to nonprofits to enhance their operations, reduce overhead, and ultimately to allow a stronger focus on their core missions. The goal of npServ's technology service would be a high-value, community-oriented solution to the typical technology woes that afflict nonprofits in southeastern Michigan.

The solutions that NEW offered were based on an innovative technology foundation that used the Linux thin client system architecture, open source and Web-hosted application software, and a centralized data center. NEW's board decided that in order to sustain this innovative approach, it would leverage a portion of our reserves to grow this business.

In npServ's business model, clients pay a fixed support rate based on a per-workstation/per-month fee structure, which allows for predictable technology costs. Thus, the costs of IT support for an organization were based on their staff's growth.

The IT support is available to clients as needed, and clients are encouraged to call if they need help, without the concern of a fee each time they call.

Like for many other nonprofits, 2007 and 2008 brought increased external pressures on NEW. This plan had the goal of achieving break-even financial status by the 2010–2011 fiscal year—a goal that was not met due to the global financial crisis that impacted nonprofits so strongly. Yet the success of our IT service continued to grow in the years to come. The recurring revenue that npServ earned was based on achieving new economies of scale, thereby making the program more competitive.

In 2017, npServ offered typical system and application needs, as well as shared administrative solutions for common nonprofit back-office functions (e.g., accounting and fundraising administration). Our clients benefit from improved system performance and the repurposing of older PCs. We have added additional services including remote automatic backup, groupware functions, and shared files, as well as home or remote office access. npServ now provides IT support to eighty-three nonprofits throughout southeastern Michigan, which together have nearly 2,000 workstations and servers under NEW's care.

Private–Nonprofit Partnership

NEW also strives to remain nimble and responsive to challenges and opportunities that are surfacing within the nonprofit sector. For example, compelling data shows a leadership crisis in the nonprofit sector, and that a leadership deficit will occur within its workforce once the baby boomers retire in the coming years.[2] (Some are staying in their leadership roles longer than originally expected.) Yet, emerging candidates face barriers to enter these leadership positions; they lack the requisite experience, leadership techniques, and tools to run the nonprofit sector.

In 2014, in response to this thinning pipeline of leaders in the sector, NEW piloted a new leadership fellowship program called Leadership DELI. It is a first of its kind, private–nonprofit partnership for NEW. The private partner is ZingTrain, the award-winning training arm of Zingerman's, a successful Ann Arbor social enterprise in the food industry, known for its progressive employee practices and its high and consistent level of customer service. The founding nonprofit partners are the Ann Arbor Area Community Foundation and NEW, and in subsequent years, the Community Foundation of Southeastern Michigan also joined on as a funding partner.

The plan was to take the private sector expertise of ZingTrain and adapt it to the nonprofit sector. We set out to co-create and implement a dynamic curriculum that captures Zingerman's valuable knowledge and experience in the for-profit sector in a manner that is directed to a nonprofit audience. Our intention was that this collaboration would start to produce a talent pipeline of skilled individuals to fill the upcoming leadership void in the southeast Michigan nonprofit sector.

The fellowship took place over seven months in 2015, and it included thirty mature and emerging executives from fifteen nonprofit organizations. Its goals included: enhance the skills and knowledge of key stakeholders in the nonprofit sector in Michigan; offer a space for leaders to reflect and innovate in their field, based on their experiences and lessons learned; create a successful partnership between nonprofit and private entities; and produce a network of nonprofit professionals in Washtenaw County who will impact the sector by strengthening its leadership and organizational capacity to ensure sustainability.

This program ran again in 2016, and a third cohort is in session at the time of this writing. Future cohorts are planned throughout southeast Michigan, and the program is on track to earn a small profit.

New Contractual Relationships

The board programming NEW previously offered was well used and recognized in the community, but the transactional nature of the engagements with boards meant that we had no guarantees of revenue for the program year after year.

Although NEW has become a regional and national model for excellence in the area of capacity-building services, we believe that there are emerging trends that hold great potential for further strengthening the nonprofit community in southeastern Michigan while also enhancing NEW's bottom line. For example, many nonprofits are frustrated by their inability to pay for the training and assistance they need to thoroughly integrate NEW's expertise into their operations.

To overcome this barrier, NEW is deepening its relationship with key funding partners to help structure how they make capacity-building investments. In addition to our traditional relationships with them, NEW now earns fees for managing capacity-building projects on a contractual basis with foundations and others that want to strengthen nonprofits they engage with. These projects involve an in-depth assessment of the organizations, followed by the provision of carefully coordinated services that are specifically tailored with each organization and based on their prioritized needs identified during the assessment process.

While NEW's current service model strengthens the local nonprofit community, it is imperative that we also continually explore fresh approaches to building management capacity in the local nonprofit sector. Such comprehensive development of nonprofit organizations, when balanced with elements of the current earned income model, could revolutionize the way in which NEW serves southeastern Michigan.

Other Steps Taken to Balance the Budget

In addition to its earned revenues strategies, NEW has also explored other approaches to balancing its budget and creating stability in the organization.

Longer-Term Philanthropic Commitments

Initial funding for our inaugural training sessions came from the Ford Motor Company Fund, and later the Ann Arbor Area Community Foundation and the W. K. Kellogg Foundation were instrumental in starting NEW's programs. But to reduce the need for continual foundation fundraising to cover NEW's actual costs, NEW's board implemented a new "Partnership Program" in 2003.

NEW approached several well-regarded and community-minded corporate institutions, ones that had a vital and sympathetic interest in the success of the nonprofit community. They were asked to fund a significant portion of NEW's annual operating gap by giving multi-year funding commitments. These longer-term contributions from NEW's partners supported many of the capacity-building programs and services that NEW provided (and presently continue to do so).

Staffing

NEW has also undertaken steps to make the staff more efficient. In 2012, NEW hired a CFO staff member who helped restructure our staff assignments to streamline our internal functions and better utilize our staff resources.

Efficiencies and Improvements at NEW Center

In 2015, we also made important renovations to the NEW Center building and procured funding to make it a more energy-efficient building and a more attractive office and meeting space. These investments have attracted a new wave of tenants who share suites. In addition, over 25,000 people each year use our meeting room space, where we earn modest fees from non-tenant nonprofits.

Another efficiency move that NEW is considering is in environmental upgrades. NEW can save about $10,000 a year by converting T12 fluorescent bulbs to LED lighting. Installing an energy-efficient building management system to regulate mechanical and electrical equipment would save an additional $2,000 per month.

CONCLUSION

Over the years, NEW has encountered funding challenges due to changes in the economy and the supportive nature of our mission. For example, we do not do broadscale fundraising at the individual level, since it would compete with the very nonprofits NEW serves. Thus, we are limited in our solicitations of individual donors, apart from our board. So, NEW primarily raises funds from foundations and corporations. While NEW has always earned revenue through rent and service fees, over the past six years, we have focused more intentionally on a primarily earned revenue business model that has reduced our reliance on contributions. Through increased partnerships, development of several innovative programs, and increased focus on increasing our impact to the nonprofits we serve, we have succeeded in increasing the streams of earned income.

Since 2007, we have increased earned revenues from 29% of total revenue to 76% of total revenue, while maintaining a pricing structure that makes NEW's services accessible to nonprofits of all sizes and budgets. We anticipate that earned revenue will continue to increase and have projected reaching the 80% milestone by 2020.

Revenue growth in our IT program has been the primary driver of our overall earned revenue growth; our npServ IT program now contributes more than 50% of our growing annual earned revenue budget. The program is projected to double in earned revenue from approximately $425,000 in 2016 to over $850,000 by 2020.

We manage the growth of our programs by continuously reviewing our pricing for both new and existing clients in our IT and consulting programs, as well as in our rents at the NEW Center. (Today we hover slightly below market rates for commercial real estate in Ann Arbor). At NEW, besides a sustainable financial return, we are also consistently striving to meet the other essential aspect of our work—contributing to a more effective and efficient nonprofit sector. Our ability to generate earned revenue is catalyzed by (but not totally contingent on) the support of our funding partners.

Whereas NEW's building was once our source of profit, we are increasingly reliant on our service programs and consulting to fund our growth.

In sum, NEW's financial profile has evolved over the last twenty-four years, and we expect that it will continue through our diverse earned revenue program offerings. We continue to explore and uncover new opportunities for innovation through impact and creativity that we develop with our clients and stakeholders. An example is the recent expansion of our organizational development consultancy to include topics and training related to diversity, inclusion, and equity. We will especially serve smaller nonprofits, nonprofits serving communities of color, and areas of economic disadvantage so they too have access to these services and can thrive.

Recognizing the incredible pressures that impact our clients each day, we are devoted to strong programs, stable operations, sound fiscal management, and prudent oversight of our building assets, so that we can be at the ready for our clients. We believe that our commitment to this stellar service delivery mode, without a doubt, will help us to achieve our goal of a fully sustainable business model by 2020.

NOTES

1. Given the building's limitations, there were no plans to expand NEW's building and generate more income through additional rentals.
2. See, for example, Landles-Cobb, L., Kramer, K. and Smith Milway, K. "The Non-Profit Leadership Deficit." *Stanford Social Innovation Review*. October 22, 2015. https://ssir.org/articles/entry/the_nonprofit_leadership_development_deficit.

PART 7
COLLABORATION

18 Creating Collaboration in Nonprofit Centers

The shared space model emphasizes affordable, quality real estate as a central goal, but it can also achieve other impacts. Among the most exciting aspects of shared space is the opportunity for collaboration among organizations within nonprofit centers. Collaboration comes in many forms, and nonprofit centers are fertile places for collaboration to be nurtured and cultivated. See Figure 18.1.

This chapter provides an overview of the collaboration field with an emphasis on how it pertains to shared space. It also offers some examples of collaboration and cites some of the literature shaping the topic area. To start, it is instructive to look back on Figure 1.5, Overview of Nonprofit Shared Space, to orient where the collaboration concepts in this chapter fall. "Building as a Program" is the area that distinguishes shared space projects and where collaboration and other strategies to deepen the model are found. We have devoted an entire chapter to advanced approached to nonprofit centers (see Chapter 21: Deepening the Shared Space Model). Among these advanced approaches is embedding collaboration strategies into the fabric of the nonprofit center. Other strategies include replication and shared services.

While some nonprofit centers integrate collaboration from the start, many need to build trust and a culture among the tenant organizations or other partners before embarking on it. For this reason, collaboration can be seen as another one of the "advanced" approaches. It deserves a special call-out here because it is so central to the purpose of nonprofit centers: using real estate to bring organizations together to tackle an issue or social problem together. Collaboration is a natural outgrowth of that ethos.

COLLABORATION AS A FIELD

Collaboration has been a buzzword in the nonprofit sector for decades, as funders seek to collaborate on funding initiatives and as well as encourage grantees to collaborate on programs. Both government and foundations have adopted a "two or more heads are better than one" approach to funding many types of services. In this way, nonprofits are encouraged to collaborate and bring their respective resources to bear on complex, contemporary problems:

Collaboration has become so central to public management that in many cases, partnerships are a prerequisite for funding, premised on the belief that the synergy from multiple agencies outweighs the costs involved with coordination and culture clash.[1]

FIGURE 18.1 *Posner Center for International Development, Denver, Colorado.* This photo depicts the chalkboard at the Posner Center. The tenant organizations at this Theme Center, as well as members outside the space, all work on international development issues and have developed collaboration on programs and other initiatives. *Photo credit: Shotzr Photographer, Evan Semon.*

Although it is a wide-ranging concept, collaboration emerged as a bedrock approach in the nonprofit sphere for several reasons. Nonprofits historically have been siloed into different issue areas and functions, but they now realize that they could amplify their missions and be more effective if they worked with like-minded organizations to address complex problems. More practically, nonprofits understand that there are diminishing resources to go around and collaborating with other organizations is a way to maximize resources to achieve their goals (or missions). Grantmakers for Effective Organizations (GEO) is one of the leading organizations promoting both aspects of collaboration, helping funders to collaborate and supporting grantee collaborations.[2] The Lodestar Foundation also stands out as a funder that focuses exclusively on collaboration and mergers. Now in its fourteenth year, its signature national Collaboration Prize "shines a spotlight on nonprofit organizations that choose to permanently collaborate in response to challenges or opportunities in order to maximize the impact of their work."[3]

The collaboration methodology dovetails with another current in the nonprofit sector—that of Collective Impact (see FSG's Collective Impact Forum for more on this trend).[4] Collective Impact is an organizing principle around collective action to tackle major problems and is outside of the purview of this book. At its core, however, Collective Impact is premised on five conditions of collective success articulated by John Kania and Mark Kramer: common agenda, shared measurement system, mutually reinforcing activities, continuous communication, and backbone support organizations.[5] It is also about cross-sectoral approaches to problems, bringing nonprofits, business, and government together. All of this thinking from the collaboration field and the Collective Impact sphere influences the broader collaboration strategies at nonprofit centers.

Collaboration in Shared Space

In nonprofit shared spaces, collaboration is a strategy to achieve greater efficiency and better outcomes by building on organizations being proximate to one another. In fact, increasing collaboration between tenants is often one of the central goals participants give when embarking on a nonprofit center project.

The Nonprofit Centers Network (NCN) defines collaboration broadly as "two or more tenants that work together, informally or formally, toward a common, mutually beneficial goal."[6] In its 2011 study, NCN found that collaboration among organizations works. Figure 18.2 shows the self-reported increase in organizational efficiency and effectiveness seen by nonprofit center tenant organizations involved in collaboration. In a subsequent and deeper exploration of collaboration and to test some of these findings, NCN worked with self-selected organizations for over a year in an intensive practicum on collaboration practices in shared spaces. This work is summarized in Chapter 19: The Collaboration Project: A Virtual Learning Lab.

Before collaboration in shared space can begin, we can think of a hierarchy of needs, shown in Figure 18.3, and adapted by the NCN from Maslow's 1943 landmark theory. The pyramid shows the progression of needs toward an end goal of collaboration, with meeting the basic needs of tenants, moving up the pyramid through safety, productivity, and trust-building, both in the space and among the tenant organizations. All of these needs must be adequately met before organizations can successfully collaborate for social impact.

Collaboration takes place on a continuum of engagement, from low to high as shown in Figure 18.4.[7] As defined by the participants in NCN's Collaboration Lab (see Chapter 19), on the low end, we see collaboration in *Networking and Shared Culture,* which are informal interactions among organizations such as in shared eating spaces or at social events. Further right on the continuum, organizations collaborate more intensively through *Coordination and Communication,* including, for example, cross-referrals and/or monthly executive director lunches. Finally, collaboration toward *Collective Impact and Risk Sharing* is the most intensive type of collaboration, focusing on shared goals, fundraising, staffing, and programming.

Establish Trust

At the heart of a good collaboration, and for it to be lasting, is trust. Trust is the pillar on which collaboration is built. Many nonprofits go into nonprofit center projects with ambitious collaboration goals. Yet, when organizations haven't lived together and worked toward the same goals, mutual trust simply isn't there. The building of this trust and coordination between the parties takes time for effective collaboration to ensue. The usual group development process is classically described as "forming, storming, norming, and performing."[8] By having the time to go through

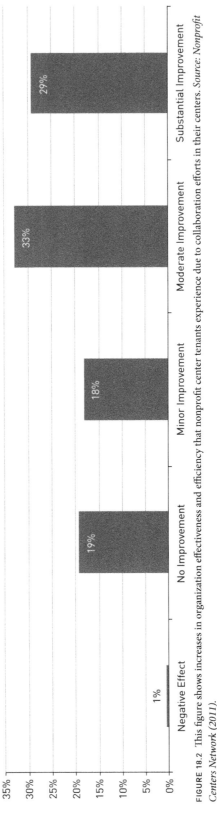

FIGURE 18.2 This figure shows increases in organization effectiveness and efficiency that nonprofit center tenants experience due to collaboration efforts in their centers. *Source: Nonprofit Centers Network (2011).*

Hierarchy of Needs in Shared Space

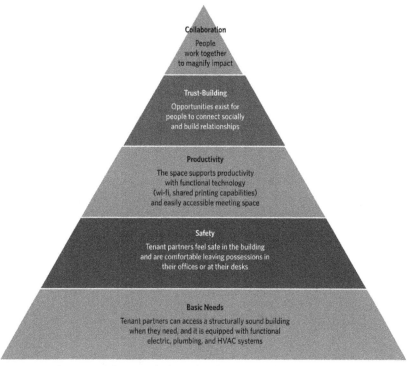

FIGURE 18.3 This pyramid illustrates the hierarchy of needs for organizations in nonprofit centers. All of the tenant needs must be met before meaningful collaboration activities can be successfully carried out. *Source: Nonprofit Centers Network.*

Level of Engagement
Tenant Continuum of Collaboration

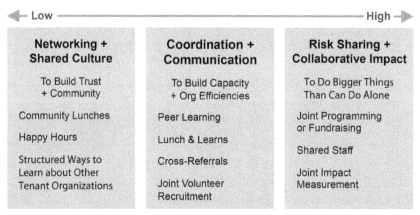

FIGURE 18.4 This figure shows the spectrum of collaboration in shared spaces and the level of engagement from low to high. *Source: Nonprofit Centers Network, as adapted by Saul Ettlin.*

this process, the participants can face challenges, tackle problems, find solutions, plan work, and deliver results. For nonprofit centers, intentionality is critical; organizations must want to collaborate, commit to collaborate, and then be facilitated to collaborate. Initially, collaborations between one to three organizations are easier to initiate than getting everyone in a center involved. Collaborations often arise as organizations meet each other in social or professional development activities like brown bag lunches and happy hours, stemming from the *networking and shared culture* end of the continuum.

A good example of nonprofit center collaboration is at the Carroll Nonprofit Center, developed by the Anverse Foundation in Westminster, Maryland. The Center's purpose is to "provide an innovative, professional and collaborative work environment at below-market rent for nonprofit organizations that focus primarily on childhood development, education, arts and the promotion of general social welfare."[9] As a first step toward developing common goals, and fostering the collaboration, the nonprofit center staff "mapped" tenant relationships in an effort to see how the tenant organizations were working together. Figure 18.5 shows this map of relationships, highlighting the entire Center's connectivity.

From there, they were able to understand natural connections and overlap between the organizations. The Center has a section on its website called "Our Goals and Commitments"[10] with four areas including collaboration:

- *Stability:* Affordable, rent free office space, to rid nonprofits of overhead cost so they may allocate more money to their programs and impact individuals and local communities of Carroll County, Maryland.
- *Resources:* Shared infrastructure of conference rooms and a resource library where any nonprofit in Carroll County can utilize the foundation directory online grant research database. We have break rooms, shared Internet, and buying power through numbers.
- *A collaborative environment:* With no duplication of services, agencies can simply walk down the hall to find out what others are doing and work together on projects or capital campaigns. They can also learn about and respond to community issues that affect us all.
- *Exposure:* Greater community visibility brings more support to the various missions of its tenant organizations.

There are other ways to complete this type of stakeholder or network-mapping including methodologies to create maps of relationships that describe the type of relationship organizations have, whether they are reciprocal, transactional, programmatic, etc. This mapping is a good initial exercise to complete to begin to understand how organizations relate to one another, how they are already working together, and what gaps exist. These maps can form the foundation of new collaborative priorities.

Larger successful collaborations often stem from community charters or contracts that incoming tenant organizations sign concurrently with their lease. These documents, usually a nonbinding amendment to the lease, obligate organizations to participate in the community however participation is defined. In some

Web of Collaboration

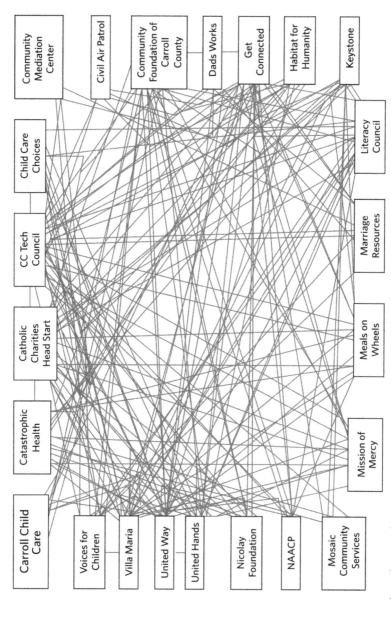

FIGURE 18.5 This figure shows the network mapping that the Carroll Nonprofit Center completed to understand the relationships between its tenant organizations as it worked to increase collaboration. *Source: Marty Sonenshine, Executive Director, Anverse, Inc.*

cases, the community charters ask organizations to participate in a tightly defined collaboration. The Jerry Forbes Centre in Edmonton, Alberta, a themed center set to open and focusing on volunteerism, has developed a Collaboration Charter that details its mission, vision, and values and then outlines the obligations of both the landlord and the tenant. The charter starts with this preamble:

This charter serves to set the tone for working together and ensure each tenant of the Jerry Forbes Centre Foundation (JFCF), and the Centre's staff and Board all recognize the value of collaboration as a way to create efficiencies and further the success of each of the charitable tenants, and Edmonton's charitable community, and those receiving its services, as a whole.[11]

For the collaboration to succeed, the participants in the collaboration often need financial support for the professional time required to develop a productive working partnership that can attain its goals. This process sometimes takes more time than expected, since each organization comes with its own particular culture, norms, and approaches to the problem. Organizations must buy in, either donating their time or actual financial resources. In some cases, funders support nonprofit collaborations to promote success.

The participants must also have—or receive consulting help with—the necessary group facilitation skills to make the collaborative process work. Successful collaborations often rest on the shoulders of a dedicated staff person. Where possible, nonprofit centers can hire community coordinators or animators to galvanize the collaboration and propel it along. Where no dedicated staff or resources are found, collaborations can peter out due to a lack of momentum and loss of focus.

Several *Stories from the Field* illustrate different and successful collaborations, including Chapter 8: The Alliance Center (organizations dedicated to legislative initiates around environmental policies) and Chapter 16: The Centre for Social Innovation (a nonprofit center that pioneered the community animator position to facilitate tenant-generated collaborative initiatives), as well as Chapter 20: The National Youth Transition Center (a collaborative of organizations both resident in the center building and outside the center). These stories, along with findings in Chapter 19: The Collaboration Project, share more best practices for collaboration in shared spaces.

BARRIERS TO COLLABORATION

In 2016, NCN, along with key partners including CultureWorks of Philadelphia, convened a day-long session on collaboration and resource sharing. The summary report cites some common psychological challenges associated with resource sharing including the example of "present bias," which values current and imminent issues and challenges rather than those in the unforeseen future and "identity" issues, which can translate to organizations feeling like they don't need help.[12] The report goes on to articulate steps to encourage nonprofits to share resources.

An academic literature review also highlights challenges to resource sharing and collaboration, findings that are common sense to nonprofit practitioners. Among many, barriers include[13]:

- Organizations are encouraged to work with organizations with whom they compete, which creates inherent organizational risk.
- By collaborating, organizations are working in different ways than how they normally work (while this could also be a benefit, in this case, its meaning here is that an organization is working outside its core competency).
- Collaborating creates an inevitable loss of organizational autonomy.
- There can be difficulty with communication and lack of accountability among collaborating organizations.

WHY ORGANIZATIONS COLLABORATE

Despite these barriers, nonprofit centers are prime laboratories for collaboration, which often arises organically (see Figure 18.6). Nonprofit centers can provide the venue and the physical space, as well as other resources including staff time and facilitation expertise and even financial resources, to encourage ongoing collaboration. Forcing collaboration can backfire as these efforts can be seen as coercive and may be damaging to individual organizations. In our best examples, nonprofit center collaborations derive from tenants and with support from the center operators,

FIGURE 18.6 *CultureWorks Greater Philadelphia, Philadelphia, Pennsylvania.* This photo depicts collaboration underway in the vibrant space at CultureWorks, a nonprofit center devoted to cultural organizations and offering both space and shared resources. CultureWorks team members Rashanda Freeman (left) and Crystal González (right) confer at the common table. *Photo credit: Courtesy of CultureWorks Commons Management, 2018.*

funders, and other stakeholders in a "bottom–up" approach. Ultimately, collaboration in shared space is about using limited resources—expertise, time, and money—to extend the mission of individual organizations and magnify impact.

NOTES

1. Graddy, E. and Chen, B. "Influences on the Size and Scope of Networks for Social Science Delivery." Journal *of Public Administration Research and Theory,* 16:533–52, 2006. O'Regan, K. and Oster, S. "Does Government Funding Alter Nonprofit Governance?" *Journal of Policy Analysis and Management,* 21: 359–379, 2000. Ostrower, F. "The Reality Underneath the Buzz of Partnerships: The Potentials and Pitfalls of Partnering." *Stanford Social Innovation Review* 3:34–41, 2005.

2. See GEO Funders. http://www.geofunders.org/.

3. The Lodestar Foundation, Collaboration Prize. Accessed January 29, 2018. http://www.thecollaborationprize.org/.

4. "The What, the Why, and the How of Building Capacity for Collective Impact. Accessed April 13, 2018. https://collectiveimpactforum.org/tags/capacity-building.

5. Kania, J. and Kramer, M. "Collective Impact." *Stanford Social Innovation Review.* Winter 2011. Accessed January 27, 2018. https://ssir.org/articles/entry/collective_impact).

6. Jakubowski, L. "8 Steps to Outcomes-Oriented Collaboration." Nonprofit Centers Network. Accessed April 13, 2018. http://nonprofithub.org/featured/8-steps-outcomes-oriented-collaboration/ Nonprofit Centers Network.

7. Nonprofit Centers Network. 2016 training materials provided to authors and adapted by Saul Ettlin.

8. Tuckman, B. W. "Developmental Sequence in Small Groups." *Psychological Bulletin,* 63(6), 384–399, 1965.

9. Carroll Nonprofit Center. "Proving Your Impact." Presentation to the Building Opportunities Conference, Nonprofit Centers Network, May 2011, Marty Sonenshine, Executive Director, Anverse, Inc.

10. See www.carrollnonprofitcenter.org/goals. March 25, 2018.

11. Jerry Forbes Centre for Community Spirit, Collaboration Charter, sourced through the Nonprofit Centers Network "Ask-NCN" listserv. 2016.

12. "Streamlining Social Good: Overcoming Barriers to Nonprofit Resource Sharing." Presented by the Nonprofit Centers Network and CultureWorks, Greater Philadelphia, September 2016, 3.

13. Proulx, K. E., Hager, M. A. and Klein, K. C. "Models of Collaboration between Nonprofit Organizations." *International Journal of Productivity and Performance Management,* 63(6), 746–765, 2014.

19 *Stories from the Field*

The Collaboration Project
A Virtual Learning Lab

Lara Jakubowski and Katie F. Edwards
Nonprofit Centers Network

There are many internal and external pressures for nonprofits to collaborate. Collaboration can lead to the greater fulfillment of mission, enhance efficiency, increase clientele, and strengthen outcomes and impact. Externally, there is considerable pressure from public and private funders to demonstrate programmatic collaboration.

Given the proximity of nonprofits in shared spaces, there is often more immediate opportunity to collaborate, especially when the nonprofits share common concerns or serve similar constituents. In establishing the recent Collaboration Project, the Nonprofit Centers Network (NCN) sought to help managers of nonprofit centers to better understand and implement collaboration in their buildings and communities.[1]

ABOUT THE NONPROFIT CENTERS NETWORK

NCN is the premier learning community for nonprofit resource sharing. We share best practices around mission-driven shared space and shared services. NCN is a network of members throughout Canada and the US. Nonprofit resource sharing makes nonprofits more effective and more efficient in achieving their goals. NCN makes it easier for nonprofits to create, maintain, and replicate shared space centers and shared service entities through trainings, conferences, online resources (tools and templates), networking, and consulting. We are based in Denver, Colorado, the home to the largest concentration of nonprofit shared space centers in the US.

GENESIS OF THE COLLABORATION PROJECT

NCN began the Collaboration Project in response to requests from network members who wanted more in-depth resources about collaboration in shared space, namely, how to define, plan for, measure, and evaluate collaboration.

Most resources on creating collaboration focus in a single-issue area, where multiple partners come together around one shared goal, such as increasing reading scores or making cities more walkable. In shared spaces, the potential for collaboration is more dynamic. Tenants/members may work together in one configuration on one issue area (e.g., developing a joint volunteer program), but others work together in a different configuration (with some overlap) on another collaboration (such as a joint fundraising project or an outreach program). The potential for many different constellations of collaborations is enormous.

A recent survey found 95% of nonprofit centers state that collaboration is part of the reason they exist; however, many nonprofit center managers are unsatisfied with the results they are seeing in their buildings.[2]

NCN wanted to provide a forum so that shared space operators could develop practice standards to address the complexity of collaboration in shared space. Center operators specifically told us they wanted to demonstrate the impact of their center through high-quality, location-based collaboration among their tenants and building communities.

Formation and Methodology

The Collaboration Project consisted of a virtual peer learning community designed to establish practice standards for collaboration in shared space centers. This nine-month process sought to define, measure, and evaluate non-profit collaboration using a rapid learning process based on individual and group exercises. Centers would develop prototypes, small-scale experiments that could be documented and replicated in other centers or taken to greater scale. Participants from centers included center managers or directors as well as staff responsible for center programs.

Projects were selected through an application process to ensure that cohort members were similar in terms of their ability to be active participants in the project. After some attrition, twenty organizations participated in the project. The cohort was diverse geographically, with representation from throughout the US and Canada, as shown on Figure 19.1.

The centers were representative of NCN membership: about one-third were one-stop community Direct Service Centers, one-third focused on a common Theme, and one-third were multi-sector centers (also referred to in this book as Generalist Centers), consistent with NCN's overall understanding of the field. (See Chapter 1: A New Model for Nonprofits for more on the typology of centers.)

Participants in the Collaboration Project

Barrie, Ontario, Canada	Midland, Texas, US
Boston, Massachusetts, US	New Orleans, Louisiana, US
Bend, Oregon, US	Philadelphia, Pennsylvania, US
Calgary, Alberta, Canada	Redmond, Washington, US
Chicago, Illinois, US	Rockville, Maryland, US
Denver, Colorado, US	San Francisco, California, US
Detroit, Michigan, US	San Juan, Puerto Rico, US
Encinitas, California, US	San Rafael, California, US
Hartford, Connecticut, US	Saskatoon, Saskatchewan, Canada
Jacksonville, Florida, US	Toronto, Ontario, Canada
Louisville, Kentucky, US	Toronto, Ontario, Canada
Loveland, Colorado, US	Toronto, Ontario, Canada

FIGURE 19.1 *Map of Collaboration Project Participants.* This figure shows the location of the nonprofit centers participating in the Collaboration Project across the US and Canada. *Photo credit: Nonprofit Centers Network.*

There were eight video conference calls between September 2015 and June 2016. Cohort members completed homework assignments between calls, and as a final exercise they reviewed another organization's homework assignments and provided feedback, either in writing or by phone.

Defining the Problem

Throughout the Collaboration Project, definitions proved to be a challenge. To identify the problem(s) that the Collaboration Project endeavored to solve, one of the first tasks for the cohort was to identify the gap between what they expected in terms of collaboration in their center and what collaboration was actually happening (the instances of collaboration that they could observe). Articulating the gap helped to crystalize the purpose of the work described in this chapter.

For building operators, the expectation gaps were expressed as follows:

- "Lack of engagement; apathy among tenants around collaboration."
- "Tenants like the idea of collaboration but don't make unilateral efforts to engage."
- "Want collaboration to be 'organic' rather than imposed by the center operator."
- "Want to see tenants carrying out large-scale program collaboration (joining forces on a campaign that encompasses both of their organizations' missions)."
- "Want to be able to track collaborations, collect data, and demonstrate impact."
- "Difficult to be 'landlord––rule enforcer' and at the same time be seen as a neutral facilitator of collaboration."
- "Original agreements with tenants around collaboration may have been formalized, but over time proved unrealistic or were never implemented."

In addition, center operators interviewed tenants/members[3] to find out why they were or were not participating in collaborative activities with other tenants. Those tenants/members who were identified as not meeting the Center operator's expectations around participation in collaboration reported the following:

- "We are too busy to collaborate."
- "Our goals are to reduce costs, not collaborate."
- "We are collaborating—we just had coffee with another tenant."
- "We are here part-time and not always on the days identified for an activity."
- "We have been waiting for opportunities to collaborate to be created. It is why we joined the Center."

The common themes among the issues raised were the lack of clarity for both the operators of shared spaces as well as for the tenants/members. Both sides identified confusion over the definition of collaboration and expectations for how goals should be met. Setting correct expectations was identified early on as one of the key components for building collaboration.

What Does "Collaboration" Mean?

The cohort developed two best practices early on that proved foundational to the rest of this endeavor. First, the group agreed upon a definition of collaboration. And, second, the group found a way to categorize centers that are in similar stages of catalyzing collaboration.

The first accomplishment of the Collaboration Project cohort was a definition of collaboration, which built upon academic literature. Cohort members applied the academic findings to their own real-world situations and settled on the following definition of collaboration in the shared space context: *Two or more tenants that work together, informally or formally, toward a common, mutually beneficial goal.* At the same time, the cohort members recognized that the definition did not reflect the full range of ways collaboration is exhibited in shared space. The group devised a scale for different levels of engagement, each of which could be called collaboration. It was important to delineate the various levels of collaboration to assist practitioners in understanding and better communicating their expectations around collaboration.

Networking. A "low" level of engagement. An example would be a low-risk, low-behavioral change interaction like meeting for coffee, or meeting someone at a happy hour or gallery opening. This level of collaboration is more centered on building relationships and creating a positive culture in a center.

Coordination/Cooperation. A "medium" level of engagement. This would involve some modest behavioral changes. It would be less focused on social interactions but rather involve the coordination of program activities (such as offering joint volunteer recruitment programs or facilitating an executive director roundtable) or cooperation (such as cross-referrals).

Collective impact and risk sharing.[4] A "high" level of engagement. This is deep collaboration that requires not only more formal decision-making structures but also strives to have meaningful impact. The cohort defined this category as an effort that achieves the following:

- It has a system or plan to measure outcomes.
- It shares risks and rewards among the partners.
- Each partner strives to enhance the other partner's capacity.
- It has a positive impact on the community.

It is important to look for *behavioral change* when evaluating collaborative efforts: What are we doing differently/better together that we wouldn't otherwise do alone? How do these behavioral changes result in better outcomes for the community?[5]

Working Groups

We found the cohort broke down into three sequential stages with regard to collaboration in their centers: relationship building, dot connecting, and impact tracking. See Box 19.1 and Box 19.2 for some examples from the participants:

- *Relationship Building*—working on building connections and trust among tenants.
- *Dot Connecting*—working on deepening connections among tenants and finding alignment.
- *Impact Tracking*—working on evaluating existing higher-order engagement among tenants.

Box 19.1 Impact Tracker

The key questions I want to answer in my prototype are: description of the types of collaborations that are taking place, an understanding of the benefit to the organization, and an understanding of the benefit to the community.

> **Box 19.2 Relationship Builder Prototype**
>
> *We will send out an online survey to all tenants. The survey will gauge how well the tenants know each other as well as give them an opportunity to list any talents/ skills that would be useful in a collaborative project. After the survey is completed, tenants will be invited to attend a building-wide brainstorming session that will give them the opportunity to learn more about each other, how their missions/goals intersect, and develop possible collaboration ideas. After this event, the same survey that was sent out before the event will be sent out again to gauge the success of the event.*

Our assumption was that centers in similar stages would benefit from a more focused conversation. We found it helpful to group the cohort members by these stages to focus on building tools and approaches that were tailored to their situation. The groupings allowed centers to interact with peers while developing their own prototype collaboration effort to allow for accelerated learning. See examples of prototypes in these stages are at the end of this case study.

PROTOTYPE CREATION AND RESULTS

Fifteen cohort members created a prototype in their centers. The goal was to rapidly implement a small-scale experiment that could be documented and replicated in other centers or taken to scale. See the end of this case study for more details on three prototypes. The approaches that cohort members took for their prototypes fell into three types of strategies as shown in Figure 19.2.

Individual

The center director and/or staff interviewed individuals directly who work in the center to gather information on their organization and their personal needs and goals. This information enabled very precise asset mapping to connect organizations and individuals who might collaborate. See the Thoreau Center prototype at end of chapter for an example of asset mapping.

Group

The center director/staff held some type of event or program that brought together all tenants/members with a single focus. They included:

- *Collaboration kick-off events*—An extended meeting to build relationships among staff from different organizations, mutually determine expectations around collaboration and how it is defined, and map out the needs of the end users (clients) of the facility and how collaboration could better meet their needs.

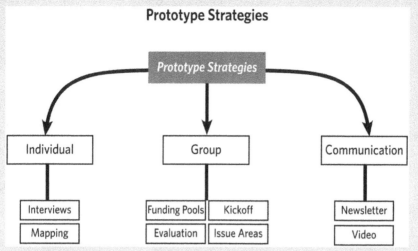

FIGURE 19.2 In the Collaboration Project the participants developed prototypes—small-scale experiments on collaboration that could be documented and replicated in other centers or taken to greater scale. The strategies tried fell into three categories, those aimed at individuals and single organizations, those aimed at groups of tenants, and those focused on communication in their centers. *Source: Nonprofit Centers Network.*

- *Evaluation*—One center engaged its members in an evaluation project to measure the impact of collaboration on their collective work. By involving everyone in the center, they strengthened their culture while producing an impact report that everyone contributed to.
- *Issue areas*—Several centers focused their prototypes on creating a training series for executive directors and other staff to attend. The goal was to provide enrichment on issue areas to engage staff and build collaboration on areas including professional development, organizational development education, HR management, etc.
- *Funding pools*—Several centers developed or augmented funding pools to incentivize collaboration. These provided small grants to collaborations being carried on by tenants. The grants provided financial support for the work involved in developing collaboration. Recipients were also to report on what worked/didn't work as well as to offer insight into (i) better understanding what types of collaboration are desirable; (ii) what they learned on how to better articulate what funders are looking for; and (iii) how to develop systems to measure results attributable to the collaboration.

Communication

Two prototypes used different approaches around communication. One developed a newsletter to be distributed to all tenants/members to increase awareness of each organization's activities. The other developed a video that documented a collaboration among partners who hadn't traditionally worked together.

Results

The prototypes succeeded in rapidly testing a wide variety of experiments on how to build collaboration in shared spaces. The cohort members were able to borrow tools that others had developed and apply them in their own centers.

The greatest outcome of the prototypes was a better understanding of which tools may be appropriate at which times. The cohort also realized that most of the prototypes they developed involved a substantial time commitment of staff and tenants/members. They identified ways to streamline the processes or the sequences to achieve time savings.

Behavioral Changes

Cohort participants were asked how their behavior changed because of developing their prototype. Some of their comments are summarized as follows:

- "I have been releasing more responsibility to tenants to drive initiatives. I have been facilitating and coaching as opportunities arise."
- "I have found that I need to be more mindful to include collaboration in our discussions and allow others to take the lead on initiatives that are of interest to them."
- "I find that I am a bit more relaxed and less impatient with the concept of collaboration. . . . It does not only rest with me but with everyone who is a part of our shared space."
- "I am trying to be more intentional about how we incentivize and track collaboration."

PRACTICE STANDARDS AND LESSONS LEARNED

The goal of the Collaboration Project was to develop practice standards for building collaboration in shared space. The collective lessons learned by the cohort yielded the following best practices.

   Intent: Know what you want to accomplish as a shared space operator. Why
      is it important to you that your tenants/members collaborate? Is there an
      imperative from your board or your funders? How do you want to evaluate
      your work?
   *Communication: Clearly communicate your expectations with your tenants/
      members.* Not just once, but continuously. Get buy-in and work together
      to define what you mean by collaboration (you can use our definition as a
      starting point). Build a common culture when onboarding individual staff
      members and organizations and use collaboration as a filter when selecting
      partners/tenants/members and others for your space.
   Resources: Make sure you have the resources you need to achieve your goals.
      Fostering collaboration is time-intensive. There is a need for a champion,

but also a recognition of their role as a catalyst; set up your tenants/members for success so they can assume a dominant role in leading the collaboration. Apply your resources appropriately for your collaboration level—group events in the early stages and more individualized approaches when your center is more mature.

Diffusion: Use a variety of channels to build a culture of collaboration. Change doesn't happen overnight. Hold a variety of events, at different times. Do in-person activities as well as passive communications like bulletin boards and email newsletters, to reach everyone by their preferred channel. Talk to tenants/members. Your job as a shared space operator is to foster relationships. Find out why certain organizations or individuals aren't participating in programs and consider altering your approach.

Motivation: Build on self-interest because everyone is busy. Curate meaningful connections in your center by knowing the individuals and organizations in the space and what their motivations and goals are. Find out what agencies need from shared action. Support nascent collaborations with tools to move forward such as short written agreements or conflict resolution policies, for example.

Reinforcement: Model the collaboration you desire. Think about the decision-making structure your center embodies—do you share governance in an authentic way? Even the terminology "tenants" or "members" implies different power structures.

Goals: If you want to be able to track the impact of collaboration, work with your tenants/members to set clear, measurable goals. Do a baseline survey, support them with regular check-ins and follow up with a final survey.

STEPS FOR REPLICATION

Based on the fifteen prototypes, the cohort was able to generate a great deal of practical tools and advice for others wanting to build collaboration. These recommendations are intended to serve as a road map for those wishing to replicate (or improve upon) the approaches used in the Collaboration Project.

1. *Set expectations—know your intent:* The first step the cohort identified was to create concrete expectations. As one cohort member stated: "Lack of expectations and direction can make participants nervous to invest time and resources."

2. *Meet tenants where they are*: For collaboration to flourish, the cohort learned the importance of understanding the building community in which you are working. In some cases, the center operators had misperceptions of tenant actions, goals, and motivations. Also, center operators need to acknowledge the rationales for engaging in collaborations and recognize that meaningful collaborations are more often motivated by self-interest rather than altruism.

3. *Fine-tune your approach to collaboration*: Centers serious about cultivating collaboration among their tenants should create collaboration plans that detail what their goals are, what level of collaboration they seek among their tenants/members, how they plan to achieve the goals, and who is accountable for success. Also, this provides a platform for measurement of the types of collaboration they desire and the outcomes that result.

Those replicating the Collaboration Project could use individual, group, or communication strategies or create their own approach. Cohort members were acutely attuned to the "people" responsible for collaboration in shared space. They suggested that job descriptions for community engagement managers or community animators should clarify whether the role requires facilitation of collaborative projects between tenants or facilitation of a collaborative culture that encourages tenants to enter into collaboration amongst themselves. They also reflected that center operators may not allocate sufficient time to be invested in this work but instead add property management responsibilities that make it difficult to do either job well. Collaboration plans should match the resources that are available on an ongoing basis.

4. *Succession strategy*: The cohort noted that another key to success in the long term is to have a succession strategy that anticipates leadership will be passed down.

CONCLUSION

The Collaboration Project originated as a peer-learning community devoted to developing practice standards around nonprofit collaboration in shared space. It was started to respond to members of NCN who were concerned that they had few resources around defining, measuring or evaluating nonprofit collaboration.

As a cohort of shared space operators, the group shared their experiences, mistakes, and successes and jointly worked to advance our knowledge of how to build impactful collaborations among nonprofits. The group developed many tools and approaches that can be replicated in shared spaces and in the wider nonprofit community. See Box 19.3.

Shared spaces are laboratories for collaboration. By modeling best practices, nonprofit shared space centers can become weavers and facilitators of greater community impact by fostering collaborative environments and nurturing deeper

---

Box 19.3 Reflections from a Project Participant

As a mature shared space center, I see benefits to both sides: collaboration facilitated by Centre staff and natural collaboration amongst tenants. When Collaboration is driven (not just expected to happen naturally) the result is better, longer, and less expensive. My advice for new centers would be that collaboration does not have to be either/or, but that it can be both.

programmatic collaborations. We hope this report lays the groundwork for many successful nonprofit collaborations in the future.

For more information on the Collaboration Project, the complete write-up is available at http://www.nonprofitcenters.org/cproject.

PROTOTYPE EXAMPLES
Thoreau Center—Dot Connector

Tides' Thoreau Center (now Tides Converge) houses seventy-five nonprofits and social enterprises, including art galleries and a café, in a decommissioned military hospital in San Francisco's Presidio National Park. The challenge facing the Tides Thoreau Center when it joined the Collaboration Project was that although it had been operational for twenty years, tenants were not meaningfully collaborating. This was due in part to the sprawling nature of the campus, as well as a dormant community charter that had not been enforced or updated in many years.

Tides Thoreau Center's prototype focused on an individualized approach to build a thorough understanding of all tenants/staff as a foundation for deeper collaboration. The process involved Tides' staff interviewing as many of the seventy-five tenants' staff as possible with a standard set of questions. After collecting information on both what community members loved and disliked about being on the campus, as well as what resources they'd be willing to share with other tenants (ranging from leading lunchtime walks to providing professional trainings on graphic facilitation), Tides created a physical asset map. The map made it easy to connect organizations and to launch shared programming.

This prototype has also led to a notable shift from Tides being the only organizer of campus programming to now having tenants leading many of the engagements. Over time, Tides expects deeper collaborations to grow.

The Hive—Impact Tracker

The Hive, a Leichtag Foundation Initiative, is committed to a vibrant Jewish life, advancing self-sufficiency, and stimulating social entrepreneurship in coastal North San Diego County and Jerusalem. The Hive was formed to provide space for organizations to collaborate and to link their work to the Coastal Roots Farm, also located on the site secured by the Foundation. Figure 19.3 shows some of the communal workspace at the Hive.

The Hive's prototype was designed to capture both quantitative and qualitative data about the collaborations that occur through a micro-grant program. Tenant organizations are eligible for up to $1,500 per year of funding for collaborative programming.

The Hive was interested in the types of collaborations that were taking place, an understanding of the benefit to the tenant organizations and an understanding of the benefit to the center community. The Hive's goal was to promote more effective partnerships by developing measures of success. They set a goal of seeing six "High Level—Collective Impact" collaborations through the prototype.

FIGURE 19.3 *The Hive, a Leichtag Foundation Initiative.* The Hive, shown here, is a coworking hub with event, meeting, and workspace in Encinitas, California. *Photo credit: Leichtag Foundation.*

The Hive has used the Collaboration Project prototype to isolate the components of successful collaborations. It helped them clarify their goals around collaboration and be better able to communicate their expectations. In turn, the recipients of the micro-grants were able to develop collaborations that matched the goals better and that used the funds more effectively. The Hive's use of funds through its micro-grant program to incentivize collaboration offers a quick study of how organizations can refine their goals around collaboration.

Jessie Ball duPont Center—Relationship Builder

The Jessie Ball duPont Center (JBdC) joined the Collaboration Project as one of the newest centers in the learning lab. It's fourteen tenants had just recently moved in to their 120,000 sq. ft. building in downtown Jacksonville, Florida. JBdC could put what they learned in the Collaboration Project to use immediately to build a new community-oriented culture. They began at the low end of the spectrum of collaboration, seeking to build relationships among staff of the various tenants. Figure 19.4 shows the entrance to the JBdC.

JBdC first surveyed all employees who worked in the building on how well they knew each other and what skills or talents they would be willing to contribute to collaborations within the center. JBdC staff and volunteers from the tenants then planned a gathering with activities aimed at relationship building and catalyzing collaboration. Activities included a scavenger hunt, discussion breakouts based on people's interests, and an activity for occupants to learn about each other's organizations.

The results of the prototype events were the formation of two committees within the center: Health and Music/Art. Each committee now works on specific goals and the JBdC staff supports them with logistical support.

FIGURE 19.4 *Jessie Ball duPont Center, Jacksonville, Florida.* This is the lobby of the recently constructed Jessie Ball duPont Center (JBdC) in Jacksonville. *Photo credit: Jesse Ball duPont Center.*

NOTES

1. This project was made possible through a grant from the National Youth Transitions Center (NYTC), a Washington, DC, nonprofit center. (See Chapter 20: Because the Future Needs Everyone, on the NYTC).
2. Nonprofit Centers Network. *State of the Shared Space Sector Survey 2015: Changing How Nonprofits Work.* Denver: Nonprofit Centers Network, 2015.
3. The Collaboration Project used several different terms for common elements in shared space projects based on the differing terminology of the participant centers. Occupants of a center are called variously *tenants, members,* and *partners. Center or building operators* refers to entities who run nonprofit shared spaces.
4. This was a participant-defined term and defined as described in the text.
5. As an example of collective impact, at the Posner Center in Denver, Colorado, their International Collaboration Fund funded an effort by four tenants/members to develop a common curriculum to teach business, entrepreneurship, and leadership skills to young women. The product was easily tailored to the unique needs of each project area in Kenya, Uganda, and Tanzania. http://posnercenter.org/resources/icf-2014-2015-edge-of-seven-into-your-hands-africa-global-livingston-institute-africaid-2/). Posner Center. *ICF 2014–2015: Edge of Seven, into Your Hands Africa, Global Livingston Institute, & AfricAid.* Accessed March 18, 2017. http://posnercenter.org/resources/icf-2014-2015-edge-of-seven-into-your-hands-africa-global-livingston-institute-africaid-2/.

20 Stories from the Field

Because the Future Needs Everyone
National Youth Transitions Center

Jessie MacKinnon and Danielle Cameron

National Youth Transitions Center
Washington, DC

NOTE FROM THE AUTHORS

This chapter was written several years ago, at the beginning of the writing of this book. It describes a detailed model of collaboration among policy, program, and service providers that was implemented in a nonprofit center. This model brings about greater collaboration among different co-located organizations that serve youth transitioning to adulthood, secondary education, and/or into the job market. Through new ties among tenant organizations and more familiarity with other community service providers, this model promotes more informed and sensitive services for transitioning youth who also have various complex medical conditions.

This collaborative effort was established and funded by The HSC Foundation, a nonprofit foundation dedicated to improving access to services for individuals facing social and healthcare barriers due to disability, chronic illness, or other circumstances. The HSC Foundation operated and funded the initial, collaborative program to create a stronger network to serve these youth in transition who encounter gaps in services and support as they grow older. The Foundation's goal for the collaboration, as it evolved, was for it to become a self-sustaining entity. Currently, the collaborative program is not staffed by the Foundation, though many tenants and community partners continue to meet. As the collaboration finds its own footing, the Foundation looks forward to seeing it flourish in the near future.

INTRODUCTION AND FRAMEWORK

Youth and young veterans with disabilities confront severe obstacles as they transition from adolescence to adulthood, military to civilian life, and school to work. The National Youth Transitions Center (NYTC) provides a single location in Washington, DC, for modeling cross-systems collaboration and improving transitions services. The NYTC exists as an innovative "collaborative community" and provides opportunities for nonprofits serving young people with disabilities to build capacity, create new partnerships, and benefit from the NYTC's national agenda. This national agenda includes policy and advocacy efforts, innovative research, and cross-sector collaborations that stimulate new thinking and learning across the country.

The Youth Transitions Collaborative (Collaborative) is the focal point of the NYTC community. This membership group, facilitated by The HSC Foundation, is comprised of regional and national organizations with a commitment to or interest in serving young people with disabilities. All NYTC tenants are members of the Collaborative. However, the Collaborative extends beyond the physical center. In addition to the eighteen tenants, over forty non-tenant members broaden the reach of the NYTC mission by utilizing the building for their trainings, meetings, film screenings, receptions, and other convening activities.

While the Collaborative had a virtual existence prior to opening the NYTC, a physical hub increased and strengthened collective efforts and partnerships. The NYTC grounds The HSC Foundation's efforts to build capacity among nonprofit organizations serving the disability community and to create a cohesive community among these organizations.

The seven-story building in Washington, DC, that was created in 2011 by The HSC Foundation houses multiple tenants who have a successful track record of making a difference in the lives of young people with disabilities (see Figure 20.1).

FIGURE 20.1 *National Youth Transitions Center, Washington, DC.* This photo shows one of the many shared conference rooms in the building, as well as a thumbnail of the building exterior. *Photo credit: The HSC Health Care System.*

CULTURE AND PHILOSOPHY

The NYTC's philosophy helps to ensure all Collaborative members are operating under the same assumptions and with the same expectations. This "learning community" philosophy is the glue that connects each individual program, unites the building into one community, and ensures that collaboration is a consistent, integral priority.

Identifying a Culture

The NYTC worked with Collaborative members to define an organizational philosophy and principle values. The relationships and atmosphere that have developed among Collaborative members is a product of these philosophical ideals and shared values that together represent the NYTC culture.

Philosophy

The NYTC is a community of individuals and organizations that share the goal of empowering young people with disabilities to create a self-directed path to adulthood and independence and to fully participate in their communities. Each member of the Collaborative commits to this philosophy by signing the Community Charter:

We, Youth Transitions Collaborative members, embrace our role as vital contributors in the collaborative community, which ultimately seeks to empower youth and young veterans with disabilities to create a self-directed path to adulthood and employment. We believe in a shared philosophy and know this community of organizations is stronger together.

Guided by their common mission, community members commit to open dialogue, the provision of responsive services, continual growth, shared outcomes, and creating or enhancing partnerships that result in effective solutions benefitting youth with disabilities.

Creating the Culture

Facilitating the development of an organizational culture occurs on several different levels, including in the design of physical space, in programmatic and administrative planning, in the managerial style of the "landlord" and its staff, in day-to-day communications, and in opportunities for side-by-side learning and collaboration. The NYTC culture is reflected in the openness of its physical space, the values adopted by Collaborative members, and the beliefs on which the community was founded.

YOUTH TRANSITIONS COLLABORATIVE

The Youth Transitions Collaborative (the Collaborative) is the focal point of the NYTC's collaborative community. This membership group, facilitated by The HSC

Foundation, is comprised of regional and national organizations with a commitment to serving young people with disabilities.

Membership

The Collaborative is a powerful community of more than forty-five organizations that share a common mission: to empower young people with disabilities as they enter adulthood and the world of work. Collaborative members also share the belief that these young people have the ability to succeed, if only they are given the opportunity.

Most Collaborative members have a history of sustained commitment to young people with disabilities and a clear track record of success. Others have demonstrated an interest in serving this community and in participating in the collective effort. As effective as the Collaborative members have been individually, they realize that they can multiply their impact by sharing expertise and resources with like-minded organizations.

The ultimate result for Collaborative members is that they learn together, build together, and succeed together. And in doing so, they bring greater awareness to the shared cause and help change attitudes about people with disabilities. *The future needs everyone*, and the Collaborative is helping to make that truth a reality.

Information Sharing and Collaborative Projects

The NYTC is a community of nonprofits that is mission-driven, meaning that although these organizations may provide different services, they share a broader mission. With the NYTC as the physical hub, there is an opportunity for these organizations to share outcomes, break down silos, and leverage each other's work. Furthermore, all use of public space, and all events, trainings, and services provided in the Center contribute to achieving the broader mission. To facilitate this process, the NYTC utilizes an information dissemination process for all outcomes, information, and lessons learned so Collaborative members will continually be informed. As a result, projects between members that address emergent issues, expand current offerings, or address gaps in services develop organically. Each year, The HSC Foundation releases Requests for Proposals (RFPs) for grant opportunities—exclusive to Collaborative members—to address issues identified by the membership.

Governance

The HSC Foundation established two advising bodies to oversee activity of the Collaborative and the Center. The Leadership Council was established as an executive-style group providing high-level oversight and commentary. The Program Advisory Committee was created to ensure all stakeholders had a voice in the activities and services of the Center.

Leadership Council

The Collaborative is guided by a Leadership Council, made up of senior executives in Collaborative member organizations. The purpose of this Council is to provide a cadre of senior executives who can guide policies and procedures and act as advocates and spokespeople for the NYTC, as well as provide sustainability of the organizational culture.

This high-level group is responsible for specific tasks such as reviewing the results of evaluation, inviting experts to present best practices related to transitions, and bringing policy makers to the NYTC to inform them of youth transition issues.

Program Advisory Committee

The Program Advisory Committee brings together a diverse group of stakeholders, including youth, and obtains from them insightful, programmatic recommendations for the NYTC and its ongoing activities. The Program Advisory Committee ensures that Collaborative members, youth and young veterans with disabilities, families, and community members have a strong voice in determining the NYTC's direction.

Capacity Building

While there are some capacity-building opportunities inherent to membership in the Collaborative, it was important that The HSC Foundation offer clear capacity-building opportunities to Collaborative members. The organizations participating in the Collaborative gave a great deal of time and energy to the process of developing and implementing this concept. Therefore, the Foundation believes capacity-building opportunities are what keep these organizations continually engaged. Specifically, it offers:

- *Joint fund development:* The HSC Foundation provides staff support to organizations interested in partnering on programs and seeking grant funding. This staff person facilitates conversations between members, identifies funding opportunities, and supports the submission process.
- *Free meeting/event space:* The NYTC offers several meeting spaces free-of-charge to Collaborative members. These meeting and training spaces provide new opportunities for organizations to host networking functions, trainings, and education sessions that further the mission of the Collaborative.
- *Networking opportunities and trainings:* The Collaborative regularly hosts networking events, meetings and trainings that bring together the membership for meet-and-greets, learning opportunities and more. These events provide capacity building through network development and, depending on the meeting topic, skill building.

Development of Collaborative Products

Within the Collaborative are three working groups, facilitated by a staff member and powered by a small group of Collaborative members. These working groups drive the development of specific "Collaborative-branded" products that can be released to the larger community for purposes of education, marketing, and more.

All of these resources are offered free of charge to Collaborative members. In addition, The HSC Foundation has developed Collaborative strategic alliances with the National Council on Disability, US Department of Education's Office of Special Education and Rehabilitative Services, and US Department of Labor's Office of Disability Employment Policy. These alliances give credibility to the Collaborative and provide members with access to federal technical assistance and communication with critical decision makers.

Evaluation

The HSC Foundation seeks to measure the outcomes of the collaborative community created within the NYTC. Through the encouragement of peer-to-peer learning and capacity-building efforts, the NYTC stimulates desired outcomes. These outcomes take the form of new partnerships, expanded capacity of Collaborative members, expanded service provisions due to the availability of accessible space, and new or additional financial support for Collaborative members.

The HSC Foundation worked with a university doctoral student to analyze its social networking regarding sharing information and resources, joint projects, and referrals. The analysis concluded that organizational size and location were not significant factors in the ability to network, and membership in the Collaborative leveled the playing field for smaller organizations with fewer resources. Additionally, it showed that the network created by the Collaborative was not dependent on one or two organizations to maintain the connections; if any organization dropped out, the integrity of the network would remain intact.

REPLICATION

The NYTC was born from an initiative developed by The HSC Foundation—a foundation dedicated to improving access to services for individuals facing social and healthcare barriers due to disability or chronic illness. The HSC Foundation realized the critical importance of timely intervention for transitioning youth with disabilities, and as a result, developed the NYTC in a newly renovated, fully accessible 30,000 sq. ft. building in 2011.

After over five years of operation, the Center continues to expand its services to the Collaborative, which currently includes more than forty-five organizations. There is great opportunity for replication of the collaborative model and application to other communities and areas of service.

Social investment funds will always be limited and thus, investors and philanthropists are continually interested in supporting programs that have the best chance at achieving efficient and effective success. When successful programs rise to the forefront, it is natural to attempt to replicate the achievements in other settings.

After reflecting on the experience of conceptualizing the Collaborative, executing the effort and observing the outcomes, The HSC Foundation identified three elements essential to the model and critical for replication.

- *Dedicated management*: The HSC Foundation provides ongoing staff support for this collaborative model. Staff members provide the backbone of the effort: coordinating common agendas, facilitating meetings, establishing timelines, ensuring follow-up and participation by the membership, and driving the progress. It is up to all Collaborative members to provide the content, the expertise, and the insight of these efforts, but without dedicated staff to manage the process, the effort would not be as successful.
- *The feedback loop:* Ongoing communications with Collaborative members help to ensure the Collaborative's relevance in the sector and, therefore, ensure continued participation by the members. With this two-way street of communication, The HSC Foundation staff members managing the Collaborative can make sure activities stay relevant to the stakeholder communities and address issues that are at the forefront of the sector.
- *Investment in the membership:* In addition to managing the Collaborative, The HSC Foundation is also a grant maker in the disability field. This facet of its work provides for real investment in the membership and in the creative solutions identified by the membership. Even if a grant-making entity is not leading the collaborative effort, it is critical to identify opportunities for investment in both individual members and collective concepts that can be brought to fruition.

CONCLUSION

In the last few years, the nonprofit sector has seen a shift toward the concept of *collective impact,* when organizations from different sectors work together to solve a specific social problem by using a common agenda, aligning their efforts, and measuring their success. The NYTC and the Collaborative are supporting their member organizations to move in this direction. By engaging a variety of both public and private organizations in sectors ranging from education to social service to business networking, the Collaborative is creating a strong foundation for future collective impact work that improves transitions for youth with disabilities. Beyond that, it is a model for other nonprofit organizations to embrace, to make their own, and to take to the next level.

PART 8
SHARED SERVICES AND REPLICATION

21 Deepening the Shared Space Model

Advanced Nonprofit Center Approaches

Much of this book is devoted to defining the shared space model and sharing best practices and strategies for developing *new* nonprofit center projects. While new projects are vital and breathe life into the shared space field and communities where they operate, there are many successful centers already in operation, some of which are detailed in the *Stories from the Field*. But, what makes a project successful? Success in a shared space project has several dimensions but a baseline benchmark is that the project achieves financial sustainability. Once projects get to this cruising altitude—they are meeting their expenses, cash flow is stabilized, the building operates smoothly and is fully occupied—some projects might want to consider *deepening the model* and exploring advanced approaches. It should be noted that the strategies outlined in this chapter are sometimes embraced at the outset of projects; for others, these approaches can be added in as projects mature. For this reason, we have highlighted them here in this chapter as advanced approaches that stable centers can embrace.

As we have described in this book, there are ways to enhance the shared space model, that is, to go beyond an affordable real estate approach to achieve other goals. It is instructive to again look to Figure 1.5, Overview of Nonprofit Shared Space, to orient where the concepts in this chapter fall. These goals to deepen the model comprise the "Building as a Program." While the goal to provide more affordable rent is important, other goals may include meeting a social outcome (such as serving as a one-stop service center for a specific population or facilitating organizations working on similar issues), or the center could influence a wider sphere beyond its walls (e.g., organizations within and outside the center collaborate on shared goals, or a center advocates on specific community or policy issues).

This section outlines four different approaches to deepening the model to help centers achieve these enhanced outcomes. One set of approaches looks inward to the existing ecosystem of tenants within the building. The other approach looks outward to the wider community of organizations and constituents served.

- *Internal:* Deepen the model by focusing on the interaction of existing tenants and services offered to them.

- Facilitate intentional *collaboration* among tenants to achieve a collective outcome.
- Beyond just space, offer *shared services* to tenants and other community organizations to reduce expenses and create efficiencies.
- *External:* Deepen the model by bringing the model outside the four walls to new audiences and communities.
  - Engage with the *public sector* to create a localized, systemic response to a specific community need.
  - *Replicate the model* to a second site to bring a working model to a new community.

SHARED SERVICES

The first approach to deepening the model is in the area of collaboration, discussed in Chapter 18: Creating Collaboration in Nonprofit Centers. Collaboration is one way in which stable nonprofit centers amplify their missions; collaboration often comes out of years of sharing space and patience in developing relationships and trust among tenants. It should be viewed as one of the approaches that advanced nonprofit centers employ to better meet the mission of the shared space. Chapter 18 and Chapter 19: The Collaboration Project both delve substantively into collaboration concepts, methodologies, and outcomes.

Shared services are a second area that nonprofit centers can cultivate to deepen the model. "Shared services," also known as "shared resources," is a term widely used within the nonprofit sector to capture a range of sharing among organizations. The Nonprofit Centers Network, in its Shared Services Guide defines shared services as the following: "Physical resources, staff, and programs which are governed and allocated across traditional organizational boundaries." It goes on to explain: "Multiple organizations, or multiple programs within a larger organization, establish shared services to collaboratively and more efficiently make use of physical spaces, equipment, staff, and program resources. We define shared services broadly as the collaborative use of resources across traditional organizational boundaries."[1]

In practical terms, we generally define shared services for nonprofit centers as *shared physical resources* including spaces (meeting rooms, conference spaces, lobbies, pantries, copy rooms, intake rooms and resource centers and even art and performance spaces, and shared infrastructure (phone and Internet service, accounting software, etc.); *shared staffing* (administrative/reception, facilities, accounting, information technology, human resources, marketing, and even program staff); and *shared programming* (client intake, shared legislative campaigns). This third area around shared programming overlaps with the collaboration discussion previously reviewed. The shared physical resources are most often sought after as a complement to the shared space offerings in nonprofit centers.

The benefits of shared services are that tenants' operating costs can be reduced and their capacity increased. Establishing trust among organizations and determining the right business model are critical to rolling out a successful shared service.

For example, a center that wants to provide IT services to its tenant organizations will need to understand who is already providing those services, if bundling them for the entire center can save on expenses and if efficiencies are found in working with a single vendor. The center will then need to determine who will provide the service, coordinate the roll out, and manage the vendor contract.

Getting Started on Shared Services

The Nonprofit Centers Network publication previously referenced is a guide to developing shared services which lays out a process for developing a coherent set of services for a nonprofit center. These questions should be answered before new shared services are developed. This process involves the following analysis:

- *Mission fit:* Do the scope and goals of the shared services support the mission and programs of the nonprofit center operator?
- *Organizational resources:* Does the nonprofit center have space, equipment, staff, time, money, and other resources available?
- *Knowledge:* Does the nonprofit center have the knowledge to develop and operate the proposed shared services? Does the nonprofit center have or can acquire the expertise needed to provide high-quality services to other organizations in this proposed service field?
- *Market demand:* Have participating organizations recognized a need for the proposed shared services?
- *Competitive advantage:* Does the nonprofit center have a competitive advantage over other providers in price, service delivery, timeliness, availability, and quality?

Benefits of Shared Services

The Nonprofit Centers Network and others have articulated the benefits of shared services.[2]

Purchasing Power

By purchasing services collectively, organizations can take advantage of economies of scale. Organizations build their purchasing power by lowering per unit prices and generating savings typically available only to large institutions. Employing the previous IT example, by joining forces within the nonprofit center, the organizations are likely able to negotiate a more attractive rate than if they secured those IT services for their individual organizations.

Efficiency

Through shared services, organizations decrease the expense of redundant services and increase investment in program-related activities to fulfill their missions.

Shared services can also standardize processes across organizations for faster service. In the IT example, this would mean working with one vendor as opposed to multiple vendors serving all of the organizations in the center across varied technology platforms.

Higher Quality Services

Shared services allow nonprofit organizations to access specialized expertise, improved services, and new technologies that could otherwise be unaffordable or unavailable. Many small organizations cannot afford dedicated HR staff but by sharing HR services or staff, they can have the expertise at a lower cost.

Employee Retention

Shared services can offer the opportunity for both skilled technical staff and program staff to focus on their core competencies, creating higher job satisfaction. By using shared and highly trained specialists, organizations can realize better quality control and reduce their overall risk. In looking at the IT example again, this would also mean that untrained staff do not have to provide IT services as part of their job and that there are dedicated resources for this service.

Stability and Investment

When mission-based nonprofit organizations create shared services programs, they are creating long-term systems to keep the associated resources, expertise, and financial exchange in the nonprofit sector. Shared services can also provide built-in backup, reducing the risk of losing institutional knowledge and practice when an individual staff person leaves, and creating overlapping service teams.[3] Box 21.1 highlights the example of shared services at Community Service Partners in Chicago.

A variation on the shared space model is in the planning stage in Rochester, New York. Inspired by a nonprofit center aimed at increasing administrative efficiency in nearby Mankato, New York, nonprofits in Rochester are working on the idea of creating a co-op with shared HR and IT services and staff. With five nonprofits taking the lead and over seventy participating, another part of their vision is a shared building with both space for tenants and a home for the co-op services to increase nonprofit visibility in the community.[4]

Shared service arrangements require careful planning and feasibility studies, and one study has found that the nonprofits that were the most viable market for shared services were those with annual budgets between $1 million and $5 million.[5] "While organizations with smaller budgets often need back-office support, they do not typically have enough funds to pay for shared services. Large organizations over $5,000,000 typically have enough resources and service demand to hire their own operations staff."[6] Shared services are most appropriate, therefore, for mid-sized nonprofits.

> **Box 21.1 Community Service Partners**
>
> Community Service Partners (CSP) was founded in 2009 to unify the business functions of several South Chicago nonprofit organizations that share a common mission of supporting the health and livelihoods of individuals with developmental disabilities. Each of the partner organizations had a computer server, but no one to maintain it. Frequent breakdowns were costly and time-consuming.
>
> To tackle this problem, partners adopted a dedicated private cloud-based system through which client records would be available to all relevant staff at the agencies all the time. After migrating to this system, CSP reduced their physical server footprint from seventeen to five—eliminating much of the infrastructure sprawled across their facilities.
>
> Additional shared services are offered to this collaborative: bulk purchasing (office supplies, janitorial supplies, insurance, etc.); document management solutions; employee benefits; human services management system collaborative, a comprehensive client case management system that can be customized to interface with state billing systems; IT services; software development; and training.
>
> *Source: https://www.communityservicepartners.org/*

Finally, it should be noted that while shared services can often be advantageous for organizations to pursue, the services might not necessarily be less expensive for those served than conventional services. Rather, the overall improvement in the *quality* of services provided makes the expenditure worthwhile. To attract participating organizations, no matter the sharing aspect, shared services need to be of high quality and a good value for organizations.

EXTERNAL APPROACHES TO DEEPENING THE MODEL

Working with external stakeholders can also deepen the shared space model. The two strategies outlined in the following paragraphs require sophisticated operations, financial acumen, a solid business model, and political capital.

Engage with the Public Sector

While we have devoted an entire chapter to the role of allies, including the government, in nonprofit centers (Chapter 24: Partnering with Allies), here the discussion of the public sector is about developing a meaningful partner to work alongside the nonprofit center in service of advancing outcomes. In this case, the external stakeholder is the public sector and the advanced approach revolves around forging a relationship to sustain the nonprofit center over the long term.

Perhaps the best example of a localized, coherent place-based strategy is Denver Shared Spaces (see also Chapter 25: Denver's Test Kitchen). This strategy grew out of the leadership of the Denver Office of Strategic Partnerships, the Urban Land Conservancy, a local nonprofit developer, and local philanthropists in Denver. Since its inception in 2009, Denver now boasts more than twenty-two nonprofit centers encompassing every type of center—theme-based centers, arts centers, human service one-stops, capacity-building nonprofit centers, and coworking spaces. Denver Shared Spaces offered facilitation, training, and consultation to new and established shared spaces, helping to promote the model locally and share best practices. This model is described in detail in Chapter 25.[7]

One of the outcomes of the number of nonprofit centers in the Denver metro area is that the ecosystem of funders, consultants, and board members is well educated on the benefits of shared space. This concentration of centers results in a shorthand understanding of the model by funders and others, which helps maintain funding and viability. Another driver of success was that Denver's mayor issued an executive order in 2012 (Executive Order 138) to establish a policy that all city agencies support co-location strategies for nonprofit organizations. Another distinctive element of the Denver model was the important role played by a local nonprofit, Urban Land Conservancy, in acquiring and managing many of the shared spaces and providing centralized real estate services to the individual shared space partnerships.

Other communities have come to Denver to learn the shared space model and there are related versions of the model in other places across North America, notably in Vancouver, Canada, with the Social Purpose Real Estate Collaborative (SPRE), a public–private collaborative to support mission-minded real estate (for more on SPRE, see Chapter 29: It Takes a Network).

Elements of the Denver Shared Spaces model are transferrable to other communities, but the mix of both public and private champions is fundamental to the success of the model. Without a project lead and clear direction for the effort and money to sustain it the cohesive strategy could flounder. The elements for success are as follows:

1. Nonprofit center or other nonprofit organization to lead the strategy.
2. Local government agency enlightened to the benefits of shared space and willing to provide infrastructure support to the sector.
3. Funding entity to seed early capacity building and ramping up of strategy.
4. Clear goals for a place-based strategy whether it's expanding the number of local centers, helping existing centers grow their capacity, or other goals.

Replicate the Center

The final approach to deepen the model is to replicate it, opening a second or third site. While many nonprofit centers are rooted in a specific community or neighborhood, some nonprofit centers serve functions that can be replicated in a new place. The advantage of replication is that operating systems are already established, and the ownership model is set. Leases, operating policies. and other facility management systems are in place and can be transferred to a new site. Further, the mistakes in the first center can often be corrected in the new project to improve the model.

A good example of this replication strategy is the Common Roof™ nonprofit centers led by the New Path Foundation in Ontario. This strategy is laid out in Chapter 12: The Common Roof™. Today, New Path operates two nonprofit centers to promote children and family mental health, the second of which, shown in Figure 21.1, was built following the same model but serving a new neighboring community. The Sobrato Nonprofit Centers is another example of a replication strategy employed by a family foundation and detailed in Chapter 27: Rent Support in a Volatile Market. This foundation operates three centers in Silicon Valley in northern California, all operating at 100% capacity. See Figure 21.2 for a map of the Sobrato Nonprofit Centers in the Silicon Valley. Finally, Chapter 16 details the replication strategy of the Centre for Social Innovation (CSI) in Toronto, a successful coworking space serving social innovators first started in 2003. In 2012, CSI replicated the model in New York City and the organization now operates five spaces in two countries.

FIGURE 21.1 *Orillia Common Roof™, Orillia, Ontario.* The Orillia Common Roof™ is the second nonprofit center of the New Path Foundation in Ontario. Opened in 2011, it is 37,000 sq. ft. and houses fourteen partner and tenant agencies. The project has helped revitalize the neighborhood, spurring new businesses and other economic activity. The building features striking red cladding, which helps it stand out in the neighborhood. *Photo credit: Common Roof™.*

Like the public-sector engagement strategy, replication requires a sophisticated lead organization and significant resources. Replication should only be considered under the following circumstances:

1. There is sufficient market demand in the new community for the nonprofit center, and the new center will not cannibalize the tenants or other resources of the first center.

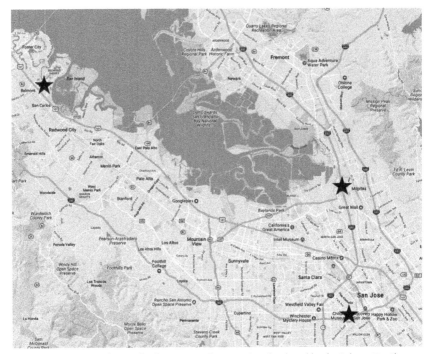

FIGURE 21.2 This map depicts the three nonprofit center sites developed by the Sobrato Family Foundation in the Silicon Valley in California. On its website, the foundation has used mapping tools to create an "impact map," which includes all of its grantees, including cash grantees and office space recipients. The grantees tend to be clustered around the three sites, highlighting the importance of the nonprofit center in the micro-ecosystem of a community of nonprofits. *Source: Sobrato Family Foundation.*

2. The lead organization has the financial and staff resources to open and maintain a second site without compromising service delivery, quality management;
3. The new project will not unduly risk the operations of the first site;
4. The new site is aligned with the overall mission and long-term vision of the original nonprofit center.

Where a lead organization is not in a position to start a new center on its own, it is possible for that organization to effectively "franchise" their model, providing consulting services on how to start up a new nonprofit center in a new community. While this is not a widely employed strategy, it is an excellent way for organizations to build on the success of others in the field; in fact, CSI has employed a similar strategy by offering consulting services in response to overwhelming demand to replicate its success. Offering tours of a successful center or offering time to shadow key staff are other ways to share best practices with other centers under development. Some of these offerings could be provided for a fee to generate additional revenue.

Replication is an excellent way to promulgate the nonprofit center model without starting whole cloth each time, and it should be considered by organizations looking to extend their reach and attain enhanced outcomes for new communities.

CONCLUSION: PUSH THE ENVELOPE

The *Stories from the Field* highlights several nonprofit centers that have employed strategies to deepen their model through collaboration, shared services, engaging with the public sector, and replication. In some cases, nonprofit centers employ multiple strategies, for example, expanding their shared services offerings and engaging with the public sector. These strategies are not mutually exclusive, and none is more important than the other. Some incorporate these strategies at the outset of a project's life cycle, particularly the shared services or collaboration approaches. Thinking about these goals early on in a project is certainly possible, but more often they represent an advanced approach to the nonprofit center, and we encourage operators to focus on the fundamentals of the nonprofit center model at first: meeting the mission, recruiting successful tenants, and paying operating expenses.

The approaches outlined here represent a menu of options for advancing the nonprofit center model and can be considered logical next steps for nonprofit centers that are looking to expand their footprints and maximize impact.

NOTES

1. Nonprofit Centers Network. *Shared Services: A Guide to Collaborative Solutions for Nonprofits*. San Francisco: Nonprofit Centers Network, 2011.
2. Rinne, A. "The Sharing Economy, Through a Broader Lens." *Stanford Social Innovation Review*. February 4, 2015. https://ssir.org/articles/entry/the_sharing_economy_through_a_broader_lens; Matan, R. "Shared Services in the Nonprofit Sector." 2008. https://www.sobel-cpa.com/sites/default/files/whitepaper.reservefunds.rm.sg.pdf; and Yoshida, V. "Why Nonprofits Should Explore Shared Administrative Services" [Blog post]. *CausePlanet*. 2006. https://www.causeplanet.org/blog/guest-articles-and-posts/why-nonprofits-should-explore-shared-administrative-services/.
3. Edwards, K. "5 Benefits of Shared Services for Nonprofits." July 11, 2016. https://www.nonprofitcenters.org/5-benefits-shared-services-nonprofits/.
4. Dubb, S. "Rochester Nonprofits Explore Forming Common Services Cooperative." January 18, 2018. https://nonprofitquarterly.org/2018/01/18/rochester-nonprofits-explore-forming-common-services-cooperative/.
5. Nonprofit Centers Network. *Shared Services: A Guide to Collaborative Solutions for Nonprofits*. San Francisco: Nonprofit Centers Network, 2011, 5.
6. Nonprofit Centers Network. *Shared Services: A Guide to Collaborative Solutions for Nonprofits*. San Francisco: Nonprofit Centers Network, 2011.
7. In January 2017, Urban Land Conservancy and Denver Office of Strategic Partnerships selected Radian, Inc., a nonprofit design center providing services to community-based initiatives to manage the Denver Shared Spaces program. Radian has expanded the program beyond nonprofits to include a focus on combatting displacement of local businesses and social enterprises.

22 *Stories from the Field*
Fiscal Sponsorship and Shared Space
A Natural Fit

Jonathan Spack

NonProfit Center, Boston, Massachusetts

In the late 1990s, TSNE MissionWorks (TSNE), formerly Third Sector New England, was an established and growing Boston-based nonprofit with a social justice mission. It was best known at the time as a fiscal sponsor—a nonprofit umbrella for unincorporated, mission-congruent groups. But TSNE faced a two-pronged challenge triggered by the so-called dot-com bubble. Space costs in Boston were skyrocketing, putting pressure on TSNE's budget; they were also depleting the resources—and even threatening the viability of—many of the smaller groups under its umbrella. After explaining the practice of fiscal sponsorship, this case study tells the story of how TSNE's decision to develop a multitenant nonprofit center (named the NonProfit Center [NPC]) as a solution to its space/cost dilemma had a salutary effect not only on the entire nonprofit community in Boston but also on its own fiscal sponsorship practice.

AN INTRODUCTION TO FISCAL SPONSORSHIP

Fiscal sponsorship[1] is a widely practiced, critically important, but largely invisible component of the national nonprofit infrastructure. There are a handful of organizations around the country where fiscal sponsorship is a core service, professionally staffed and delivered. Many of these groups came together in the early 2000s to form the National Network of Fiscal Sponsors, whose mission is to share information and best practices and to educate the nonprofit and philanthropic communities. Often, though, fiscal sponsorship is done on a small scale, a one-off or "on the side" offering by larger nonprofits and community foundations, and is typically managed by staff whose primary responsibilities lie elsewhere.

Model A or Comprehensive Fiscal Sponsorship

Despite its pervasiveness, fiscal sponsorship's intricacies are often misunderstood, even by some who collaborate with fiscal sponsors regularly. A striking example of this confusion was reported by Professor Jeffrey Prottas of Brandeis University, commissioned by TSNE in 2014 to look at how foundations view fiscal sponsorship.[2] Prottas was told by one foundation that it had a formal, published policy prohibiting the use of fiscal sponsors. Nevertheless, this foundation worked extensively with the primary fiscal sponsor in its area and, indeed, had funded a number of projects with that organization. When questioned about this, foundation staff reiterated their policy but asserted that "X" was "not really" a fiscal sponsor.

Frequently, foundation staff and others familiar with fiscal sponsorship conflate the two primary flavors of the practice (described in the following text), not realizing that they differ quite dramatically in terms of both legal structure and operations. In the full-service, or comprehensive model, the fiscal sponsor—a 501(c)(3) public charity—is the legal parent of the sponsored project, which is treated as a direct program of the sponsor. (In Gregory L. Colvin's seminal book, *Fiscal Sponsorship—6 Ways to Do It Right*, this arrangement is called Model A).[3] Project staff are employees of the sponsor and receive the same benefits as all other staff, and all back-office services—such as accounting, HR/personnel, contracting, insurance, and audit— are part of the sponsorship package, which is memorialized in a memorandum of understanding between the sponsor and the leadership of the sponsored project. Model A is found in Figure 22.1.

Financial activity of sponsored projects is reported in the sponsor's audit, and the sponsor is legally accountable for all project activity. Projects nevertheless retain control over their strategic direction, hiring and firing (with the sponsor's oversight for legal compliance purposes), and external relations and are responsible for their own fundraising. Either party is free to terminate the relationship if it has run its course or is not working out as hoped. Sponsors generally do not cover project budget shortfalls.

The benefits of this arrangement are many:

- Although all sponsors have minimum dollar criteria for accepting a project, the barriers to entry are quite low compared to creating a new 501(c)(3) organization, and fiscal sponsorship allows innovative ideas and approaches to be tested or expanded quickly and efficiently. There are also low barriers to exit if the idea peters out; thus, there is no need to unwind an incorporated nonprofit with all that entails.
- The credibility of an established fiscal sponsor is often a factor in enabling projects to obtain funding. Sponsors with robust internal systems and a track record with foundations and government agencies provide a level of comfort to funders that a small, stand-alone organization does not. Those that can bundle capacity-building supports like coaching, consulting, or leadership development with their sponsorship offer an even more appealing option to funders.

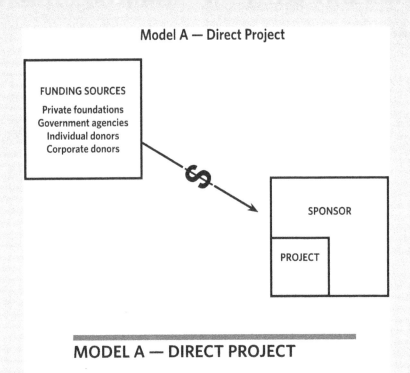

Model A — Direct Project

MODEL A — DIRECT PROJECT

Model A Direct Project Fiscal Sponsorship

FIGURE 22.1 In the full-service, or comprehensive Model A, the fiscal sponsor—a 501(c)(3) public charity—is the legal parent of the sponsored project, which is treated as a direct program of the sponsor. *Source: Gregory Colvin.* Fiscal Sponsorship: 6 Ways to Do It Right *(2nd ed.). San Francisco: Study Center Press, 2005. Used with author's permission.*

- Entrepreneurial leaders are freed up to spend more of their time building their programs and raising the funds needed rather than being bogged down with administrative tasks.
- Similar to shared space, fiscal sponsorship creates opportunities for capacity building, peer learning, and collaboration not available to individual nonprofits. Some sponsors convene their projects periodically to share best practices and funding opportunities, provide policy and regulatory updates and build relationships. TSNE also offers its project staff scholarships to its Better Nonprofit Management training series, held at TSNE's NPC, as well as fee-based access to its pool of consultants and coaches.

Model C or Preapproved Grant Fiscal Sponsorship

In the other common type of fiscal sponsorship, the sponsor has a more limited role. In that arrangement, sometimes called a "pre-approved grant relationship" (Colvin's Model C; see Figure 22.2), the sponsor serves an important role between the funder, typically a foundation, and the group selected to receive the funds. The funder makes a grant to the sponsor, which has already chosen or "pre-approved" a suitable recipient to conduct the project. (The foundation does not "earmark" the grant for the underlying grantee; it is the sponsor that has discretion and control over the selection of the recipient.) The sponsor then regrants or contracts with the ultimate recipient, a separate legal entity, for the full amount of the funding, less an administrative fee. Typically, foundations use this mechanism when the ultimate grantee is not a 501(c)(3) organization, because most foundations will make grants only to public charities whereas fiscal sponsors usually do not operate with the same restrictions. It is very common in the arts, making it easier for foundations to support the projects of individual artists. Or a foundation may use it to support the early work of a group that has not yet received its federal tax exemption.

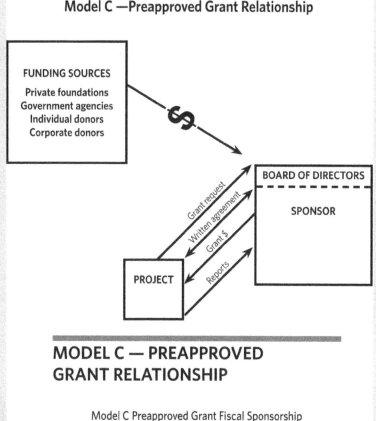

FIGURE 22.2 Model C, preapproved grant fiscal sponsorship, is useful in a situation when the ultimate grantee is not a 501(c)(3) organization. *Source: Gregory Colvin.* Fiscal Sponsorship: 6 Ways to Do It Right *(2nd ed.). San Francisco: Study Center Press, 2005. Used with author's permission.*

The sponsor has financial oversight and reporting responsibilities but does not employ project staff or provide accounting, contract management, or other back-office services. Those functions are the responsibility of the organization receiving the funds. This kind of limited fiscal sponsorship is usually defined by two separate agreements, one between the funder and the sponsor and one between the sponsor and the group that will be doing the work. These documents must be crafted carefully to assure compliance with US Internal Revenue Service regulations.

Legally and operationally, these two fiscal sponsorship models are very different. But because they are both labeled as fiscal sponsorship, they are often misunderstood by funders and others in the nonprofit community. One example of this misunderstanding is the common use of the term "fiscal agent" to describe fiscal sponsorship. In an agency relationship, the agent is required to follow the directions of the principal. But in Model A comprehensive fiscal sponsorship, the opposite is true: the sponsor is the primary legal entity; sponsored projects are required to follow the sponsor's policies and procedures. Most sponsored projects have advisory boards to guide their development and help with fundraising, but technically only the sponsor's board of directors has legal authority over fiscally sponsored projects. And even in Model C, the relationship is not one of agency: rather, the sponsor has chosen the grantee or contract recipient.

FROM FISCAL SPONSORSHIP TO SPACE SHARING: TSNE'S NONPROFIT CENTER

So, faced with rapidly rising space costs for its own operations and its sponsored projects, none of which were co-located with TSNE, the organization's leadership began to think seriously about acquiring a building of its own, large enough for itself and perhaps one or two sponsored projects. Fortuitously, other nonprofits around the country were thinking the same thing, and in early 2001 TSNE's executive director learned of the first-ever convening for multitenant nonprofit centers and those interested in developing them, presented by what was to become the Nonprofit Centers Network (NCN) in San Francisco. (For more on this NCN history, see Chapter 29: It Takes a Network to Build a Field.) He and a colleague attended the conference and returned to Boston inspired and energized. They quickly assembled a team including an attorney, a nonprofit real estate developer, an architect, and a broker, among others, and began to look for property.

They also advocated for the project with TSNE's board and staff. It was an ambitious undertaking especially for an organization with no prior real estate development experience. Fortunately, TSNE was in a strong financial position, having a reliable revenue stream and substantial liquid assets accumulated over its forty-five years of operation. It hoped to acquire a property without needing to raise outside funds. Board members were enthusiastic supporters almost immediately, as were most staff, but there was resistance from some who worried that their programs might have to compete with this new enterprise for internal support.

Early on, a primary question was around the size and scope of the project. Given TSNE's lack of experience, at first the goal was a building of 15,000 to 20,000 sq. ft., a modest size that seemed manageable financially and operationally. But, as time went on, the scope gradually increased, and eventually, with the gentle but persistent urging of the real estate developer on the team, who explained the economies of scale associated with a larger building, it became a far more ambitious—and scary—project. The team began looking at buildings in the 100,000 sq. ft. range.

At the end of 2003, TSNE acquired a seven-story 110,000 sq. ft. historic building in downtown Boston, adjacent to the city's financial district and to all its major public transit lines. The down payment for the property came from TSNE's own coffers; the balance was financed with tax-exempt bonds. Initially the team's idea was for a building exclusively for TSNE and some of its sponsored groups, but as the scope of the project grew, that was no longer feasible: TSNE didn't have enough Boston-based sponsored projects to fill a 110,000 sq. ft. building, so tenancy was broadened out. Figure 22.3 shows this notable downtown building.

FIGURE 22.3 *NonProfit Center, Boston, Massachusetts.* This exterior view of TSNE MissionWorks' NonProfit Center in downtown Boston clearly identifies the building as being devoted to nonprofit organizations. *Photo credit: TSNE MissionWorks.*

About the Building

The mission of NPC, crafted soon after that watershed 2001 NCN San Francisco conference, had three elements:

1. To provide stable, affordable, high quality space for nonprofits.
2. To foster collaboration among tenants and with the larger community.
3. To raise the visibility of nonprofits in Boston working for social change.

Tenancy was (and still is) available only to nonprofits engaged in social change at some level. At first, out of necessity, rental rates were at market levels. But as time has gone on, rates at the NPC have increased far more slowly than commercial rates in the hot Boston market; current rents are much more affordable than the market in keeping with the first element of the Center's mission.

FIGURE 22.4 *Building Community at TSNE MissionWorks NonProfit Center.* NonProfit Center Operations Specialist Eliot Melo shares information with, and answers questions from, members of the building's tenant organizations. *Photo credit: TSNE MissionWorks.*

There are now forty-three tenants in the Center, about half in shared (coworking) space, which represents approximately 15% of the rentable space in the building. The building has been full for several years, and there is very little turnover. Tenants are very happy to be in such a welcoming environment. See Figure 22.4. One organization that recently moved into a shared space suite after visiting two nearby coworking spaces operated by for-profit companies said,

We are very much interested in the NonProfit Center—in fact our second visit made it feel even more like the right kind of vibe and space for us—so much interesting work going on at every level, community-focused and utterly professional!

From the start, there have always been a handful of fiscally sponsored projects as tenants, typically four to six groups. This arrangement cuts down on paperwork, administrative time, and legal costs because as the parent entity TSNE is essentially renting space to itself in those cases. Fiscally sponsored tenants pay the same rate as others in the building but don't have to worry about getting out of a lease if their needs change. There are other advantages as well:

- Convenience. With the fiscal sponsor and project under the same roof, administrative transactions and issues are easy to connect on.
- Free or deeply discounted use of conference spaces. All NPC tenants have access to the various meeting spaces in the building, most at no cost.
- TSNE provides scholarships to tenants and fiscal sponsorship projects (whether or not they are in the building) to enable them to attend trainings at the NPC free of charge.

- Sharing both a home and administrative functions strengthens the relationships between TSNE's central office staff and the projects in the NPC.
- TSNE's ability to offer attractive, affordable space in a supportive environment and a desirable downtown location, as part of a fiscal sponsorship package, has been a key factor in some groups' decisions to join TSNE as a sponsored project.

Success of the NonProfit Center

By any measure, TSNE MissionWorks development of the NPC has been highly successful. All three elements of the mission have been well-covered:

1. *Stable, affordable rent in high quality space*: As of late 2016, rental rates are approximately 15% to 20% below market. The building nevertheless produces a healthy positive cash flow to support other TSNE programs, which include consulting, succession planning, training, leadership programming, and grant making. Meeting and event space is rented to outside nonprofits at well below market rates, which brings more people into the building and thereby contributes to the other two parts of the mission.
2. *Fostering collaboration:* Although there have been only a few formal collaborations between tenants, the NPC regularly hosts personal development and networking events open to any nonprofit and the community at large. In addition, TSNE's Better Nonprofit Management workshop series and other programs sponsored by partners bring many hundreds of nonprofit staff and leaders into the building every year. The NPC has nearly 10,000 sq. ft. of rentable meeting and event space. These spaces, which include a new 3,200 sq. ft. conference center, are in high demand by outside groups for board meetings, convenings, workshops, and even an occasional fundraising event. TSNE rents office and meeting space only to 501(c)(3) nonprofits, a requirement of its tax-exempt bond financing.
3. *Raising visibility:* It took only a short time after the opening of the NPC in 2004 for its tagline, "Boston's home for progressive social change," to become a reality. The mix of tenants, workshops, and events has made the NPC a hub of nonprofit activity in the city.

Throughout its existence, the NPC and TSNE have continued to be active participants in NCN, sharing what they've learned and learning from other centers and practitioners. In 2013, TSNE even became the Model A comprehensive fiscal sponsor for NCN.

Fiscal sponsorship and multi-tenant nonprofit centers go together naturally. Both are fundamentally about shared services and shared resources, building community capacity to serve constituents and raising the visibility and credibility of the nonprofit sector. Both also require financial resources, a long-term commitment, and a sound business plan to be successful. Besides TSNE, Tides in San Francisco and CultureWorks in Philadelphia, both discussed elsewhere in this book, have successfully combined shared space with fiscal sponsorship in developing their array of services to constituents. We hope that others will follow suit.

NOTES

1. The National Network of Fiscal Sponsors has explained: "Fiscal sponsorship generally entails a nonprofit organization (the "fiscal sponsor") agreeing to provide administrative services and oversight to, and assume some or all of the legal and financial responsibility for, the activities of groups or individuals engaged in work that relates to the fiscal sponsor's mission. Fiscal sponsorship has evolved as an effective and efficient mode of starting new nonprofits, seeding social movements, and delivering public services." National Network of Fiscal Sponsors. "About Fiscal Sponsorship." Accessed March 19, 2017. http://www.fiscalsponsors.org/ pages/about-fiscal-sponsorship.

2. Prottas, J. *How Foundations View Fiscal Sponsorship*. Unpublished paper, Third Section New England, 2015.

3. Colvin, G. L. *Fiscal Sponsorship—6 Ways to Do It Right*. 2nd ed. San Francisco: Study Center Press, 2005, 14–20.

23

Stories from the Field

The Power of Shared Services to Enhance Cultural Flourishing

The Cultureworks Management Commons

Thaddeus Squire

CultureWorks, Philadelphia, Pennsylvania

CultureWorks Greater Philadelphia (http://www.cultureworksphila.org), founded in 2010, is the country's first nonprofit arts and culture *management commons*, which is our term for the shared services model we have built for the arts, heritage, and creative community. Under our mission "to provide arts, heritage, and creative practitioners equitable access to the resources they need to flourish," we offer a flexible and affordable array of integrated services, focusing on human capital, systems, policies, best practices, and a shared nonprofit umbrella. Our purpose is to build and share all of the essential supporting infrastructure that individual cultural practitioners and nonprofit organizations or creative enterprises need for their programs, work, or services to succeed. These include staff to manage finance, compliance, human resources, legal, fundraising, marketing, and data, in addition to flexible and interim staffing, office and meeting space, advisory services, basic insurances, and nonprofit status itself. Figure 23.1 illustrates some coworking space available to projects at CultureWorks Greater Philadelphia.

DEFINING THE PROBLEM

CultureWorks was created in response to the growing lack of *cultural equity* in our country. We define cultural equity as unmitigated access to the resources necessary for cultural practice of any kind or size to flourish. These assets include money, best practices, human capital, facilities, technology, peer networks, and others.

FIGURE 23.1 *Coworking at CultureWorks Greater Philadelphia.* Depicted here is a shared workspace at CultureWorks Greater Philadelphia, where members can come to work. They also receive access to expert consulting on the "business side" of their work and extra hands to help them get things done. *Photo credit: CultureWorks Commons Management.*

Of the roughly 110,000 nonprofit arts and culture organizations operating nation-wide, 70,000 operate with annual budgets below $25,000.[1] In Greater Philadelphia, 78% of all cultural organizations operate with budgets of less than $1 million, ac-cording to the Greater Philadelphia Cultural Alliance.[2] And this does not count the growing numbers of individual artists working increasingly on a project-to-project basis outside of traditional nonprofit structures, for which we have no ready data on population or economics. Indeed, we perceive a generational shift away from traditional nonprofit corporate structures, enough so that the legally "unorganized" phase of new charitable projects is no longer just a transitional state, but rather a *permanent* state of operations for many cultural entrepreneurs.

Most of the cultural entrepreneurs who come to us, in particular those of the post–baby boomer and millennial generations, are not interested in forming and managing an independent nonprofit. They see legal and governance structures as constraining of an increasingly fluid and interdisciplinary creative environment. They would prefer to remain permanently "informal" and utilize our management commons as the way to access the essential charitable and business infrastruc-ture they need to do their work. This suggests that we may be seeing the dawn of a "fourth sector" (adding to the public, private, and charitable sectors), which we at CultureWorks have begun to call the "Informal Sector."

The clear majority of cultural organizations and individual practices are small to mid-size and are not scalable by design. The motives behind cultural practice are inherently endogenous in origin; it is about satisfying an individual itch to create or preserve, which we would argue is a deep-seated human need and an es-sential element of a whole, happy life. As a result, cultural enterprises have a "right size," as determined by the nature of the specific creative or preservation pursuit, the ambitions of leadership, the size of the market for the work, and other forces.

The business of arts and culture does not aspire to scale up to solve quantifiable exogenous social problems, such as hunger or homelessness, which often set the standard of scale for our peers in health and human services. The preponderance of deliberately small organizational scale is at once a strength—it is where we get diversity of tradition and expression, room to experiment and take risks, and cultural and geographic reach into communities. But it is also a weakness. The small budget scale of many cultural practices prohibits them from accessing the comprehensive management systems they need to truly flourish. Many address this challenge by cobbling these resources together: making staff wear too many hats, working to maintain committed volunteers, and, where possible, engaging contracted services. These solutions have more drawbacks than benefits: they are often hard to sustain, prone to instability, and too expensive, not to mention frequently lacking in essential efficiency and integration.

As a result, smaller organizations and individual practitioners increasingly struggle to access the financial and other resources necessary to *flourish at any scale*. Multiple studies in recent years point to a long-standing trend: big organizations are getting richer, while smaller organizations are getting poorer, which is reflective of the growing socio-economic divide in the United States. For example, in a 2016 article in *The Atlantic* on the state of public funding for the arts in America, Andy Hurwitz spoke with the researcher and arts advocate Holly Sidford. In 2011, she had prepared an oft-cited report for the National Committee for Responsive Philanthropy:[3]

Per Sidford's report,

55 percent of arts focused contributed income in 2009 (gifts and grants) in the US went to the two percent of arts organizations with budgets over $5 million. "It's only gotten worse, actually" [per Sidford]. Statistics from the NCCS [National Center for Charitable Statistics] indicate that in 2012, one percent of arts organizations—those with budgets over $10 million—received close to 50 percent of all contributed funding for the arts. "Not only do the big institutions continue to get the bulk of the revenue," says Sidford, "but their portion of the total is going up."[4]

The origins of cultural *inequity* are complex. As demonstrated from the previously cited statistics, philanthropy cultures favor larger, more mature nonprofit organizations and are often not compatible with the needs and behaviors of individual cultural producers operating outside of traditional nonprofit structures. Our field equates small budgets with less value and less impact, which can have a negative effect on philanthropic leverage, both individual and institutional. Our field also too often assumes that growth—as defined by bigger budgets and more programs—is the goal of *all* cultural nonprofits. This is not the case.

At CultureWorks, we call this drive to more staff, money, and programs "vertical" growth, a motivation more relevant in the health and human services fields where the scale of solutions needs to meet the scale of exigent problems. In my experience, the field, in particular the policy and consulting community, does not yet embrace as equally valid an alternative definition for arts and culture: "horizontal" growth, or the evolution of creative expression and experimentation over time, at any scale.

Adding to the challenges faced by smaller cultural practices, institutional funders for arts and culture have been moving away from unrestricted, "responsive" funding models toward restricted project grants. In response, cultural organizations must focus on earned program revenues and individual giving for core financial support. Recent research by TDC, Inc. on capitalization for cultural organizations in Philadelphia has demonstrated that it is far more expensive to raise an individual dollar than an institutional dollar. Moreover, the costs *increase* as budget sizes decrease, adding to the challenges of small-scale cultural practices.[5]

Barriers related to cultural heritage, education, and socio-economic status also leave a large population of creatives and preservationists without the social and professional networks, financial capital, and management acumen to see their visions flourish. In many cases, this is because the very approach to managing and getting work done is different from those assumed by Western corporate and nonprofit systems.

In our experience, the strength of cultural work itself can be predicated on different ways of managing and organizing than those considered "best practices." In such cases, the answer is not to force a different management culture upon the practice—that might threaten the integrity of the work. Rather we need *a platform for translating management cultures.* CultureWorks' management commons can function in this way. Utilizing our shared services, a project can manage according to its own cultural tradition while ensuring that US nonprofit operating standards are maintained. This process of management translation helps the project leverage resources offered by mainstream systems (such as institutional funding) that the project may otherwise be challenged to access.

For example, certain practices, such as areas of jazz performance, and ethnic immigrant groups engaged in cultural production prefer, or are compelled, to operate through informal, cash-based economies. This can lead to challenges in tax reporting and general compliance and, ultimately, in their ability to garner support from institutional sources and be recognized as part of the nonprofit cultural ecology. Our work with such communities has allowed some aspects of these informal economies to remain intact, while allowing the work itself to benefit from the resources offered by being a "legitimized" participant in the cultural economy.

RESOURCE SHARING AND ACHIEVING GREATER CULTURAL EQUITY

We believe that resource sharing is the solution to meeting these various challenges and to achieving *radical equity*—universal access for *everyone* to the resources they need to make or preserve cultural memory. Our *management commons* model for CultureWorks is based on Common Pool Resource (CPR) economics, the study of how we build and maintain resources that are hard to contain: water, oil, natural lands, etc. We feel that the charitable sector, as a proxy to government, is also a kind of commons, as it governs shared assets held in public trust. Why not extend this idea beyond money and natural resources to other resources? In the commons model, the *resource* is scalable, even if the work of *individual participants* is not. Following this thinking, CultureWorks is not an incubator or accelerator—grow, get out, and be independent—it is a "forever" solution for smaller-scale cultural practices to sustain their work and, ultimately, to flourish.

While much of the focus in the national conversation about equity concerns the distribution of institutional funding and individual philanthropy, we propose to broaden the discourse to embrace other approaches to achieving greater cultural equity: namely, providing *direct, affordable, and sustainable access* to the critical *infrastructure* that cultural organizations need to thrive. This disrupts a preponderant, three-step capacity-building approach characteristic of independent nonprofits: get funding, buy infrastructure, sustain or grow programs. In the arts and culture community, it is the rare instance that independent nonprofits—in particular, those operating below $1 million in budget—can "bootstrap" staff or other critical capacity investments just based on normal revenues and cash flow. In most cases, a front-end capital investment or subsidy is needed in the form of philanthropy or debt to add staff or other operational capacities. The assumption is that the investment should ultimately lead to increased revenues, sufficient to sustain the added expense by the time the subsidy runs out.

However, considering the problem of equity in our field, many marginalized organizations and communities don't even have the relationships with individual and institutional philanthropy that could provide such capital. For those that do have these relationships, this approach to capacity building—secure funds, buy capacity, run like crazy to build revenues to support the new costs—frequently fails. In some cases, such failure is owing to substantial time lags in the award process, in particular in the case of institutional funding; by the time you get the funding to address the need, the problem has grown bigger or changed. And there are other opportunities for potential failure in this cycle: a bad hire, unforeseen operating setbacks, financial assumptions that turn out to be unrealistic, and so forth.

CultureWorks' management commons model offers a different approach to building capacity that mitigates many of the barriers and risks previously outlined; it thereby offers more equitable access to capacity building resources. The first step of getting a financial subsidy to buy resources is not necessary. CultureWorks already has the human capital, systems, and other infrastructure built and at hand. New members join and pay for their share through a percentage of actual revenues generated, so a project can plug into our resources with little to no money up front. It is our job to secure capital to grow the resources we share with our membership—a far more efficient process than each of our members doing that by themselves. In this respect, we're proposing a very different model of capacity building itself, one of a collective effort, not one organization at a time. Furthermore, we are taking fixed costs and turning them into variable costs, which helps reduce financial and other risks. And we are fixing the rate of variability (through our fixed cost allocation of 12% of all revenues for each project), thereby ensuring that the investment in capacity is always proportionate to the size of the project.

OUR THEORY OF CHANGE

Based on the previous framing of the problem and proposed solution, we have defined a three-part theory of change: (i) resource sharing lowers barriers to access, which (ii) increases equity and (iii) supports greater human flourishing. Again, we define cultural equity as the unmitigated distribution of and access to the resources necessary for cultural practice of any size or nature to flourish. We believe that sharing these resources both makes them more sustainable and scalable and lowers barriers to access (cost, sourcing, contracting, managing, integrating, etc.), and it also allows for collective risk mitigation (there is safety in numbers). This resource sharing, in turn, increases cultural equity, per the previous definition. The ultimate aim is affecting more human well-being and flourishing, individually and collectively. CultureWorks' theory of change is illustrated in Figure 23.2.

BUILDING THE SOLUTION
The Genesis Story

From the beginning, our vision has been that the US becomes home to the most flourishing cultural and creative community in the world. Essential to this vision is the idea that *independence of vision* does not necessitate *independence of infrastructure*. We imagine a possible future in which the nearly 100,000 (and growing) existing arts and culture organizations operating with budgets less than $1 million (to start) *and* the currently innumerable activities of the Informal Sector flourish

01 02 03

SHARING
Reduces costs and barriersto accessing resources.

EQUITY
Is the result with more people finding support for their work.

FLOURISHING
Is our ultimate goal: creative practice in service of a whole life.

FIGURE 23.2 This is a graphic rendering of the Theory of Change that guides CultureWorks provision of shared services (and shared workspace) to its members, namely, organizations and individuals practicing in the field of cultural arts and heritage preservation. *Source: CultureWorks Commons Management.*

through shared management provided by local commons—a CultureWorks accessible to every region or city.

Following almost a year of research and modeling, we settled on "Model A" comprehensive fiscal sponsorship as our legal and operating structure for this consolidation, and we launched our new program in Fall, 2013. More common in the health and human services fields, Model A fiscal sponsorship is the most encompassing form of fiscal sponsorship, in which *all* the activities of a project or organization are brought under *one* nonprofit and managed in common. For more information on Model A, see Chapter 22: Fiscal Sponsorship and Shared Space.

To our knowledge, CultureWorks is the first arts and culture-focused organization to offer Model A. This form of fiscal sponsorship is an efficient way in which to share the staff, systems, policies, and practices of basic "back-office" functions: finance, human resources, legal, and insurances. It is notable that the field of fiscal sponsorship is expanding its narrative from one of a starter kit for becoming an independent nonprofit (or a work-around for temporary projects) to one in which the legal structure of fiscal sponsorship becomes an efficient way to share human capital, policies, management systems, and charitable status on a more permanent basis. Fiscal sponsorship provides an efficient "operating system" for resource sharing.

In structuring our Model A program, we decided on a two-entity formation governed by one board of directors. CultureWorks is a 501(c)(3) corporation, which is the sole trustee of a 501(c)(3) trust, CultureTrust Greater Philadelphia. The corporation (CultureWorks) holds all of the shared management staff, space costs, intellectual property, and other key assets shared by our member projects and organizations—it is the management company. The trust (CultureTrust) acts like a holding company for all the actual program activity of our member projects and organizations. This arrangement affords the benefits of segregated risk, greater financial transparency (since shared operating resources are kept separate from the individual program units), and more flexibility in managing human resources and legal matters.

In fall 2016, with support from the John S. and James L. Knight Foundation, we embarked on the research and program design for our final set of shared resources: a comprehensive institutional advancement support program. This program will offer our members access to staff and other resources that support individual and institutional fundraising, marketing, branding and design, data management, revenue strategy, and more. We hope to implement this program in 2018.

Our business model is a cooperative one, in which *revenue allocations* (or "shares") from the activities of our member projects support the resources they share through our management commons. Consequently, the revenue profile of the CultureWorks entity is almost entirely earned, whereas the CultureTrust entity exhibits a more diversified earned and contributed revenue profile that is typical of nonprofit cultural production. Each project is managed as a fully restricted subaccount and subtrust, each with its own earned and contributed revenue profile. As of this writing, CultureWorks Greater Philadelphia (including its subsidiary, CultureTrust) has built a core membership of more than 220, which is supported by eight full-time staff. The annual operating throughput of CultureTrust is roughly $3.5 million, with the annual aggregated revenues of CultureWorks totaling about $770,000.

We have used philanthropic subsidy only as capital to design and launch new program assets. In all cases, we intentionally design program assets to be sustained and brought to scale through the allocation of member revenues. We have built the Philadelphia office with only $260,000 in total philanthropic capital, (not counting the capital described in the following text that has supported our national expansion). We have essentially realized a "charitable return" of more than double the generous investment of our Philadelphia funders to date: venture philanthropists David and Dianne Elderkin, the Wyncote Foundation, and the John S. and James L. Knight Foundation.

Going to Scale: The Local and National Commons

To realize our vision of access on a national scale, we are taking a franchise approach; we build a network of locally formed, managed, and governed nonprofits that replicate the model and resources of CultureWorks' management commons. Each local "office" (our term for the two local entities with common governance) supports an individual and organizational membership for that city or region. In winter of 2015, we received an overture from two philanthropists in Houston, Brad Bucher and Marc Melcher, who were interested in bringing our model to their city, having been introduced to it by former executive director of the Philadelphia Cultural Fund, June O'Neill. A year and half later, following extensive discernment, planning, community engagement, and expansion readiness work, we were ready to take the first steps toward realizing a national vision. With support from the Houston Endowment, The Anchorage Foundation of Texas, and Mr. Bucher, as well as the interest of close to fifty prospective founding members, we anticipate having CultureWorks Greater Houston open in 2018.

The interest and support of the Houston community enabled us to take the leap from our Philadelphia experiment to a commons network on the CultureWorks model. Since 2010, we have gone through multiple iterations of program and delivery structures. During our readiness work, we discovered that the engine behind our commons approach and a key differentiator from other models, is our development of a co-fiduciary and co-management relationship with each of our members. We are in business with our members, literally. This requires a deliberate approach to trust and relationship building. Up to the point of considering expansion we had followed the typical "supermarket" approach to provisioning services followed by most service organizations: you could grab resources in whatever order and amount you desired. As we stepped back and examined what had worked and not worked, a more directed path approach came into view. This is now the basic architecture of our "local commons," in which the resources we have developed through the Philadelphia experiment are now organized according to "tracks."

The resources of "CultureWorks Greater Anywhere" are offered through a membership approach, built around sequential and additive tracks of resources. Basic membership is month to month, currently at $40 per month, and starts with Track 1. Members can add resource tracks as they desire and can customize the levels and extent of support within each track. (There are only individual memberships; a project or organization designates one person to be the principal member, who then makes their project or company a de facto "project member.")

Track 1 offers access to shared workspace, expert consulting, and extra hands to get things done. Our coworking space includes transient (or "hot") desks, dedicated desks, and, in the future, dedicated offices. For this basic membership, each practice or organization receives one 360-degree assessment session with our team. We learn about their work and current needs; then we make recommendations about next steps and describe how we can help through a custom report—a guide for their use of our commons. Thereafter, members can add (for incremental cost) more time or access to our shared management space and meeting areas, as well as discounted hourly services, workshops (which can include presentations like the one on "Creating a Project Budget" shown in Figure 23.3), intensives, and staff support from our team and affiliate network. The affiliates are outside professionals who contribute blocks of discounted professional time to our "service bank," which CultureWorks staff then deploys to our members, providing scoping, matchmaking, and project management support. This is the lightest touch relationship for the lowest cost and greatest flexibility. We get to know new members and help them

FIGURE 23.3 *Member Education at CultureWorks.* CultureWorks team member Jamaine Smith (left) and member Brittany Campese (right) lead a budget workshop for members. *Photo credit: CultureWorks Commons Management.*

get ready to access Track 2, if relevant to their needs. In Philadelphia, we have 220 members in this track.

For example, a theatre company joins Track 1 and its managing director, and a few part-time staff have their desks and base of operations located out of our space. Through their 360 assessment, we learn that they have some compliance and grant reporting to catch up on, and they are looking to research and model some new education programs. They buy some affiliate consulting time to accomplish these tasks and get ready for Track 2.

Track 2 provides access to a fixed bundle of general administrative resources: shared nonprofit umbrella, financial management, compliance, human resources management, legal tools, donor stewardship, basic insurance (directors and officers/general liability), and more. This is delivered through our comprehensive "Model A" fiscal sponsorship structure, in which all of the activities (revenues and expenses) of the project or organization are brought under one charitable umbrella (CultureTrust) and managed together through restricted subtrust. This arrangement creates a true co-management and co-fiduciary relationship with each "project," our term for both unorganized projects and organizations operating under Track 2. The project maintains autonomy with regard to its public identity, mission, work, and programs, and we ensure basic management, best practices, and fiduciary oversight. As of this writing, a monthly allocation of 12% of all revenues covers the costs of the previously listed resources.

Track 2 is perfect for streamlining the operations of smaller scale organizations— a more cost-effective solution than mergers or partnerships, as well as operating one-off or limited-term projects. It is designed to support unorganized projects that are not interested in seeking independent charitable status as well as existing organizations that wish to streamline their back-office operations. In Philadelphia, we currently have 101 (of the 220) members in this track.

Once our theatre company in the previous example has met the readiness criteria for Track 2, we can add those services to its membership, by bringing its operations under CultureTrust. Its board and original nonprofit (if there is one) remains intact. The board shifts its *fiduciary* function to the board of CultureWorks but retains the advisory and leadership functions of any board. The entity, if the theatre company board desires, can also remain intact but dormant, in the event that the theatre wishes to leave our commons and resume operations independently. Under CultureTrust, the theatre receives all of its financial management, HR, legal, compliance, and insurance resources.

Track 3 will hold our institutional advancement resources, currently under development. It will offer access to staff and resources to support fundraising, marketing, data management, revenue strategy, and more. There are two elements to Track 3. The first is *The CultureWorks Challenge Fund*, a giving circle that will raise money on an annual basis to match project annual revenues, prospectively at rates between 5% and 20% of income. This is not a grant program, but a shared general operating support subsidy, available to eligible members operating under Track 2.

The second element is our *Advancement Team Support*, which provides customized, full-service advancement support from our team and technology resources: individual and institutional giving, brand and program development, data management and analysis, and audience development. We foresee bundles of these services being available for between 5% and 20% of revenues for eligible members operating in Track 2. In regard to our theatre company used in previous example, since its business model is mostly driven by ticket sales and an annual giving program, if this theatre company desires and if it meets our readiness criteria, then it can opt into the *Challenge Fund* and can add services from the *Advancement Team*, such as marketing, individual giving, and data management support.

The National Commons (Our Supporting Organization)

To support this expansion, and with support from The Andrew W. Mellon Foundation, we have formed CultureWorks Commons Management (CCM), a national, nonprofit, Type I supporting organization to be the licensor (via a charter agreement) of our core intellectual property (name, systems, polices, and practices), as well as the source of a variety of shared resources and supporting services. These services include support for new office development, technical assistance, leadership coaching, planning services, innovation transfer, and other support for local offices.

Expansion affords us the development of three kinds of "capital":

1. *Innovation capital:* the increased capacity to innovate, develop, and refine programs through a new program idea or improvement, which may come from any member project or office. CCM will be responsible for developing, disseminating, and sometimes investing financial capital in such ideas.
2. *Social capital:* the increased capacity for building awareness for—and subscription to—resource sharing in the cultural community. Our biggest challenge to realizing our vision is getting people comfortable with resource sharing and, in particular, convincing existing organizations to join our commons and bring their operations under our umbrella. We view these challenges as primarily social and behavioral. There is a need to change social norms and assumptions about how charitable work is done. At present, social norms and best practices around institutional independence are a barrier, but, once changed, *new* norms around sharing can be powerful forces for continued change. Thus, we have started to expand our work from *building the machine* (our commons structure and services) to *building a community of mind and a movement.* If more people in multiple markets identify the CultureWorks name with the positive results of resource sharing, we think more people and organizations will be inclined toward resource sharing.
3. *Financial capital:* through multimarket impact and philanthropic access we hope to develop shared capital resources for our commons. The goal is to develop a Capital Support Fund for both our CultureWorks offices *and* the member projects and organizations supported by each local office. Lack of capital resources for all

kinds of needs—bridging funds, organizational change, innovation/new program development, growth, organizational recovery, etc.—is significantly lacking in the nonprofit community, and, in particular, among arts and culture practitioners and small organizations. The Fund is meant to operate separately from our local Track 3 institutional advancement support resources, as previously described.

CCM's National Resource Commons' Core Assets

Through our charter relationship, CCM will provide our local offices and their respective members with services and support from our *national resource commons:*

- *The Flourishing Index.* The goal of our theory of change is human flourishing, a term taken from the field of Positive Psychology, which studies the many dimensions of human well-being and happiness.[6] Therefore, we propose to design, develop, and prototype a new health and impact assessment tool, aimed at measuring the relationship between cultural practice, participation, and human flourishing. We posit that the ultimate purpose of arts and culture work is such flourishing and that the work created is a wonderful artifact of achieving that end. This index is envisioned to serve several purposes: (i) it becomes the fundamental tool for CultureWorks to measure its impact on its member projects over time; (ii) it is a day-to-day management tool for members to look at what is motivating their work; and (iii) it is the means through which we make the case for our collective impact as individual commons and a growing network.

  The Flourishing Index, as it is envisioned, promises two significant disruptions in our prevailing impact and health metrics for arts and heritage. First, it shifts the focus from *organizational metrics* to *individual metrics.* If we are to embrace the full spectrum of cultural activity, from individuals and the Informal Sector to organizations, the common denominator must be the *individual.* From a metric standpoint, organizations and projects are merely aggregates of individuals. Second, it expands the definition of health and impact from its current focus on *money and institutions* (economic impact) to the much broader embrace of *human well-being and social value* (flourishing).

  This second disruption is perhaps the most exciting, as it promises to redefine the very *value* of culture along human flourishing lines, as opposed to money; the latter is contributing to policy that inadvertently supports the growing economic divide in arts and culture. Those who have money count, and those who do not have money are not counted. In the world of the Flourishing Index, an individual artist could have a higher overall flourishing factor (value) than an entire symphony orchestra, for example. In the economic impact paradigm, this could never be the case.

- *Capital Support Fund.* This fund is envisioned as a new approach to addressing the great capitalization crisis in the cultural community (and nonprofit sector in general). The Fund will provide various kinds of capital (such as for cash flow management, growth, innovation, new program development purposes) to the CultureWorks offices *and*—most critically—to the individual projects and organizations they support. For example, if a project in Track 2 needs a bridge loan against a grant or donor pledge, we could provide the bridge funding internally. A member organization that runs an established annual festival could receive a seasonal loan to assist with cash flow in the offseason. If the Houston office has a great idea for a program improvement that would benefit the whole network, CCM could choose to invest immediately in that innovation and disseminate it to the other offices.

In sum, by centralizing capitalization within CCM, in the manner of a mutual insurance fund, we can leverage the funding capacity of multiple philanthropic markets and the collective value of the network membership to capitalize hundreds of organizations and informal projects through one fund. We posit this approach will be far more efficient and feasible than trying to generate discrete capital reserves on an individual organization basis.

Finally, CCM's Capital Support Fund is an essential part of ensuring greater security and stability for the network overall. Since we are proposing that our local commons are "forever" homes for cultural projects and organizations, we need to ensure their financial stability in the long term. Capital reserves are an essential resource for both attracting new members and assuring them of the resilience and stability of our management commons.

- *Equity Praxis Initiative.* CCM is working on a project, currently titled Equity Praxis Initiative (EPI), which integrates a training program and its curricula, a mutual support network, and an ongoing event series, that promises to advance substantially both conversation and action around diversity, equity, and inclusion in the arts. The planning and language framing for this program are being developed in close collaboration with Crystal González, Consulting Director for CultureWorks Greater Philadelphia. This program will draw on a wide range of thinking and practices, from anti-oppression and trauma-informed work to critical race theory. EPI is essential to our mission as a management commons and to our theory of change that maintains that sharing supportive resources makes creative practice more accessible for all. Participation in EPI will be mandated for our boards and staffs, and it will be made available to our broader local office membership.

  EPI will include one to two trainings per quarter, and it will connect participants to a network of mutual support "cohorts." The series will begin with two to three core sessions on foundational theories and practices, including diversity, equity and inclusion. Subsequent workshops will be tracked for either cultural workers or arts support workers. Our mutual support cohorts will be organized by affinity and open to all participants. These will include closed groups for marginalized communities (e.g., black, people of color, immigrant, disabled, neuro-divergent), as well as open groups for participants struggling with individual and organizational challenges (e.g., creating antiracist spaces, physical and cognitive accessibility, community engagement). Beyond the classroom, these groups will facilitate collaborative learning and the ongoing emotional and social support that is necessary for transformation.

- *Enterprise technology.* Lastly, CCM will build and maintain a comprehensive, integrated enterprise technology platform for use by the staff of our offices *and* our members. We have already developed and are using a custom transaction management portal for our Track 2 work. We now wish to integrate third-party and some custom software to provide "master dashboard"–level support for financial, legal, and customer relations; organizational management, as well as project and campaign management; and access to members across offices.

Having this enterprise solution owned and hosted by CCM has three major benefits. First, after its initial development, the platform will require full-time administration and ongoing development. Hiring a technology position and any relevant outside contractors under CCM and sharing this capacity with the offices will be far more efficient than assuming that each office will hire that function. Second, any upgrades or repairs to the system will be easily implementable system-wide, as opposed to the need for individual upgrades for each office.

Third, and most significant, being able to *aggregate and analyze data at a multimarket scale* will have significant ramifications for policy research and, most important, operational insights for our local commons. Even though the transactional, financial, and customer data for each member project under each office will be segregated, having all of the data live in one relational database allows for greater utility. These transactional data permit analyses heretofore unavailable to the field, such as sources and streams analyses of donor/funder behavior and others. Most notably, our Track 2 program is gathering and reporting the first comprehensive data set (financial and transactional) for the Informal Sector, a vital part of the cultural community about which we know very little. To illustrate, Figure 23.4 shows

FIGURE 23.4 *Office at CultureWorks Greater Philadelphia.* While the great majority of members at CultureWorks Greater Philadelphia come from the arts, heritage, and creative communities, there are also some members who are practitioners providing such services as consulting and law. Pictured here is Mark Comerata, CPA, owner of MCA Accounting and Consulting. His organization is a member that also provides a wide range of consulting services for other members, as well as other nonprofits and for-profits. *Photo credit: CultureWorks Commons Management and Mark Comerata.*

a current computer user at CultureWorks Greater Philadelphia who has access to these informative reports.

MANAGEMENT SERVICES ORGANIZATIONS AS PROVISIONERS OF SHARED SERVICES

CultureWorks is among a growing number of Management Services Organizations (MSOs) nationwide serving a variety of charitable fields, from arts and culture to health and human services. In the development of our approach, we have borrowed heavily from the health and human services fields; we are indebted to the national community of nonprofit centers and their umbrella alliance, the Nonprofit Centers Network for helping us navigate this territory. Our peer charitable fields outside arts and culture, in our view, have led the way since the 1950s in conceiving and building large-scale shared services and co-location models. These innovations include such practices as fiscal sponsorship (in particular, Model A fiscal sponsorship), co-location solutions, co-employment models where two or more organizations share employees, integrated advisory and consulting services, strategic approaches to resource pooling and regranting, and other practices.

Arts and culture have lagged significantly in adapting and embracing shared infrastructure—CultureWorks is one of about six MSO-type organizations in the US dedicated to arts and culture and the only one that embraces *both* the fine and performing arts fields and those of history, heritage, and the humanities. Peers in the cultural arena who offer elements of MSO-type services are ArtsPool in New York City, Shunpike in Seattle, Springboard for the Arts in St. Paul, and Intersection for the Arts in San Francisco. More technology and Web-based models include New York Foundation for the Arts and Fractured Atlas (both based in New York City). We consider the closest cognates to CultureWorks, however, to be located in the health and human services fields: goodcity in Chicago, Mission Edge in San Diego, and TSNE MissionWorks in Boston, to name a few.

We have been asked whether our model could be applied to other nonprofit fields. We think this is possible, but in scaling commons models such as CultureWorks to other markets, field specialization is important. While the nonprofit sector shares tax-exempt status, that's about all it shares. Business, program, and risk management models vary widely, especially across fields. For example, healthcare, education, and arts and culture all have different business models and risk management needs. If an enterprise is providing *one service*, such as bookkeeping, legal, accounting, or management consulting, it's reasonable to generalize (horizontally integrate) that service into multiple fields within the sector and even across sectors. Most professional services providers have both nonprofit and for-profit practices and provide support to a wide variety of fields in each sector.

If an organization's mission is to *share comprehensive back-end infrastructure*, specializing (through vertical integration) within a particular sector *and* field becomes paramount and essential, in our view, to providing maximum efficiency in program delivery, risk management, and business sustainability. Either the mission of an MSO focuses on *one service* delivered to *multiple fields* or it joins *many services* delivered to a *single field*. In the case of fiscal sponsorship, field specialization is even more critical, as the sponsoring organization is legally assuming a great deal of the liability for the sponsored projects' activities. Understanding the intricacies of the program that you are sponsoring is critical. For example, it is a very different business managing a drug rehabilitation clinic versus a theatre. And much of the value delivered in the fiscal sponsorship relationship pertains to being able to leverage and share deep subject matter and field knowledge.

CHALLENGES

In developing our model, we continue to wrestle with two principle challenges.

Resistance to Resource Sharing

The culture of the charitable sector, particularly in US arts and culture, is not predisposed to share resources. Many of these barriers are psychologically and socially constructed, as previously noted. For example, arts and culture (thankfully) do not have a uniform, objective metrics of success, in contrast to such metrics as reduction of homelessness or number of patients cured in the health and human services. In the absence of these indicators, the arts and culture community reaches for proxies, many based on our equation of a certain kind of independence with success and self-worth: "If my budget is getting bigger, my work must have value." Or, "If I have my own ____, I'm successful." There is a belief that one's independence of vision requires independence of infrastructure. While this can be true, it is *not necessarily* true. In this context, resource sharing is often seen as an indicator of reduced value and legitimacy, or even failure. Our CultureWorks model and others like it are proof that creatives and preservationists can celebrate and nurture independence of vision while sharing everything else behind that vision.

Outdated Policy and Practice Assumptions

The field largely still assumes that capacity building means getting bigger ("vertical growth" in our previous definition). While this may be true for some fields of work, and certainly some cultural nonprofits, it's not the case for most cultural practice. Contributing to this focus on vertical growth is the primacy of the independent charitable form. We have built the charitable sector in the image of the private sector, privileging a sense of independent formation. As mentioned earlier, philanthropy is still strongly geared toward the formation of independent nonprofits and favors growth or scale as measured by conventional metrics, such as budget size, number of services, etc. It is time that we start to look at how to encourage capacity growth and scale for the *field as a whole*, rather than the growth and scale of individual *organizations*.

Most pernicious perhaps is our history of cultural funding policy that is based on a supply-and-demand, "industrial" production market model. This analysis has consistently led us to conclude that cultural products (production supply) outstrip audiences (consumer demand), and therefore the arts and culture field is overbuilt, and the herd needs to be thinned. This view is the result of a primary market analysis, which predominates the arts and culture policy field: it contends that the known market is finite and saturated, and producers of arts and culture are competing in this tight market.[7]

I feel the primary market approach is the wrong analytic framework. Artists and cultural producers, in reality, are in the business of new product development every day they go to work. Regardless of whether interpreting canonical works or making new works, each expression is fresh to the market. Artists *make* the market for their work. New product development operates in an inchoate market, where the market is developed as products are created—think Apple computers, not applesauce.

If you apply a primary market frame to an inchoate market, you will find that there is more supply than demand at any given moment—demand *always* lags supply. Instead of interpreting this finding for arts and culture as an inherent (and positive) trait of an inchoate market, policy makers have read it as a negative attribute of an oversaturated primary market. This negative interpretation—that supply is greater than demand and therefore supply needs to be stemmed and demand enhanced—has led to decades of cultural policy predicated on scarcity and economic Darwinism. I would argue this policy approach is doing more damage than good to our cultural ecosystem. In the process of market-making, more is more. "Churn" is good (not everyone will stick around), but we should be encouraging *more* cultural production, collectively supported, not less cultural production, independently supported.

CONCLUSION

We need to ask different a question. Instead of the Darwinian question, "Who should we allow to exist?" we should ask, "How can we get better infrastructure under more projects and organizations and allow for greater proliferation of cultural practice?" The latter is the question we ask every day at CultureWorks. Our model is predicated on encouraging plenty, pushing back every day on the notion that we live in a world dedicated to sorting, thinning, and intense competition for scarce resources.

Many of the challenges we face in resource sharing are predicated on a scarcity model, that the market is precious and finite in the face of endless creative supply. In creating the charitable sector in the image of the private sector, we have valued independence, scale, and market competition over diversity, proliferation, and the value of sharing. The CultureWorks model and its commons approach asserts a different vision: that the infinitely expanding horizon of human expression can be met with an infinite horizon of supporting resources. The proliferation of management commons is essential to this vision of plenty, in which the human impulse to make and preserve may truly flourish and, with it, the well-being of our communities and society as a whole.

NOTES

1. Horwitz, A. "Who Should Pay for the Arts in America?" *The Atlantic*. January 31, 2016. Accessed September 11, 2017. https://www.theatlantic.com/entertainment/archive/2016/01/the-state-of-public-funding-for-the-arts-in-america/424056/.

2. Greater Philadelphia Cultural Alliance. Portfolio 2014. Philadelphia: Greater Philadelphia Cultural Alliance, no. 15. Accessed September 11, 2017. https://www.philaculture.org/sites/ default/files/2014_portfolio_spreads_0.pdf.

3. See Sidford. H. "Fusing Arts, Culture and Social Change: High Impact Strategies for Philanthropy." National Committee for Responsive Philanthropy. 2011. Accessed March 29, 2018. http://heliconcollab.net/wp-content/uploads/2013/ 04/Fusing-Arts_Culture_and_Social_Change1.pdf.

4. In Horwitz, A. "Who Should Pay for the Arts in America?" *The Atlantic*. January 31, 2016. Accessed September 11, 2017. https://www.theatlantic.com/entertainment/archive/2016/01/the-state-of-public-funding-for-the-arts-in-america/424056/.

5. Nelson, S. and Koo, J. with Crump, A. and Woolworth, N. *Capitalization, Scale, and Investment: Does Growth Equal Gain? A Study of Philadelphia's Arts and Culture Sector, 2007 to 2011*. Boston: TDC, 2014, 28–35. Accessed November 20, 2017. http://www.tdcorp.org/wp-content/uploads/2015/02/TDC-Does-Growth-Equal-Gain-FINAL.pdf.

6. See, for instance, Seligman. M. E. P. *Flourish: A Visionary New Understanding of Happiness and Well-Being*. New York: Free Press/Simon & Schuster, 2011.

7. See McCarthy, K., Heneghan Ondaatje, E. and Novak, J. L. *Arts and Culture in the Metropolis: Strategies for Sustainability*. Pittsburgh, PA: RAND, 2007, 61–63.

PART 9
GOVERNMENT, PHILANTHROPY, AND SOCIAL ENTERPRISE

24 Partnering with Allies

Government, Philanthropy, Social Enterprise, and Community Development

Any collaboration needs partners, and the growth of the nonprofit centers field has been fueled in many places by the support and funding of the government and philanthropic sectors. When embarking on the creation of a center, a careful review of the potential roles of local or national partners in these fields is crucial. These roles often extend beyond funding and financing.

In addition, there are other areas in the nonprofit and for-profit sectors that have great potential as allies and supporters in the creation of nonprofit centers. The emergence of the social enterprise movement, both in the United States and Canada, is discussed in this context. As we describe, many nonprofit centers are archetypal social enterprises, and their inclusion in this growing movement can strengthen both parties.

The more established community development field is another area for intersection with the nonprofit center field. The inclusion of the nonprofit center model in planning strategies for communities has been underutilized and could strengthen that work in many locations.

THE IMPORTANT ROLE OF THE PUBLIC SECTOR AT ANY STAGE OF A PROJECT

An excellent source of funding and support for a project is government. The public sector can also be an imaginative and creative partner for shared space projects beyond just providing funding. Across North America, shared space projects employ the resources of government, from cities and counties to provinces and states and even federal governments. The roles that the public sector can play are varied and include:

- *Providing buildings:* Including schools, utility sites, public housing, cultural facilities and other decommissioned spaces such as hospitals, libraries, etc.
- *Convening groups:* To serve as a neutral convener of potential project partners.
- *Providing seed money:* To support feasibility assessment and other predevelopment costs.

- *Providing grants and financing*: For capital and operating expenses, sometimes as part of specific initiatives (food uses, social services, etc.).
- *Providing loan guarantees.*
- *Serving as a matchmaker with real estate developers*: Deploying incentives (zoning bonuses, tax breaks) for new development projects to incorporate community facilities and nonprofit centers, in particular.
- *Supporting government policies to create a welcoming environment for nonprofit centers.*

Examples of the Public Role in Creating Nonprofit Centers

Perhaps the most comprehensive support for nonprofit centers has occurred in Denver, Colorado. As profiled in Chapter 25: Denver's Test Kitchen, nonprofits, the City of Denver, and local philanthropies collaborated on many of the previously listed roles. The public sector at all levels can be a supportive partner to shared spaces. An important Canadian example is profiled in Chapter 26: A Strategic Use of Municipal Assets.

The Kukui Children's Foundation was founded in 2004 to create a children's service center in Honolulu, Hawaii. The Harry and Jeanette Weinberg Kukui Center, which opened in 2009, has nine tenant organizations that serve abused and vulnerable children and their families. One of their programs is shown in Figure 24.1. In addition to Community Development Block Grant funding from the City and County of Honolulu to purchase the building, the project received considerable federal and private support to fund the renovations.[1]

FIGURE 24.1 *A Youth Program in Action at the Harry and Jeanette Weinberg Kukui Center, Honolulu, Hawaii.* Hale Kipa's Independent Living Program is one of the Kukui Center programs. This picture shows a youth-organized activity to share Hawaiian traditions and culture through a traditional fishing expedition. *Photo credit: Harry and Jeanette Weinberg Kukui Center.*

Local and provincial governments have provided important educational and financial resources for the field. The City of Edmonton created the "Edmonton Non-Profit Shared Space Feasibility Toolkit: A Resource for Non-profit Co-Location Initiatives in Edmonton" with funding provided by the Government of Alberta. Although done several years ago. the Toolkit helpfully covers Canadian ownership structures, shared services creation, financial feasibility, and a variety of other important aspects of creating nonprofit centers. It also profiles local centers in Edmonton.[2]

One of the most significant initiatives has been by the Province of Ontario to support the development of community hubs in local communities, essentially one-stop shops for the provision of integrated direct services. See Chapter 11: Building Community, Not Just Buildings for a more detailed account of Hub development in Ontario. In 2015, the former premier of Ontario appointed a special advisor and a Framework Advisory Group which came up with twenty-seven recommendations on how to support Community Hub development. In the period since then, significant progress has been made on the recommendations including streamlining the transfer of usable province surplus property like schools for use as Hubs, increasing the flexibility of program funding, supporting integrated service delivery and the creation in 2017 of a Community Hubs Resource Network "to support stakeholders across the province at all stages of community hub development."[3]

Local governments have also created nonprofit centers.[4]. Often a city or government entity will help in the coordinating and mission alignment part of bringing groups together. Then they will incubate the effort as a separate nonprofit is created to manage or own it. Alternatively, the government entity will be the landlord but will take a hands-off approach to what is happening within the nonprofit center.

The San Diego Family Justice Center was started and run by the District Attorney's office of San Diego. It provides a variety of co-located services to domestic violence survivors in a single building.[5] Pioneered by San Diego, there are now over eighty family justice centers across the US and Canada following this model, and they are usually run and funded by city and county governments.[6]

Another example is The Link, in Georgina, Ontario. The Link was started in a former school by the Town of Georgina to provide a "collaborative, community learning space" under one roof.[7]

Government offices can also be tenants of nonprofit centers, supporting it by paying rent and collaborating with direct service providers. The Under One Roof Human Service Center in Thousand Oaks, California, opened in 1988 after a group of concerned citizens, frustrated in the early 1980s by reduced funding for community-based social service agencies, hit on an idea to help keep these small organizations afloat.[8]

The fair market rents paid by government agencies, along with fundraising by Community Conscience, the nonprofit owner and operator of the center, meet the cost of operating the building.[9] This center has about thirteen nonprofit social services agencies that operate rent free at the 22,000 sq. ft., building, providing them approximately $250,000 per year that they can then use to deliver services in the Conejo Maria Valley area. In addition to such nonprofit groups as the Conejo Free Clinic, Hospice of the Conejo, Senior Concerns, and Conejo Youth Employment

Services, the County of Ventura Human Services Agency is located within the complex.[10]

The authors applaud these leadership efforts and recommend the early and on-going engagement of the public sector in shared space projects as a tool to advance the local nonprofit sector.

Other Considerations in Government Partnerships

Of course, the public sector is not always a welcome actor in shared projects. On the risk side, a sudden government policy shift can leave a subsidized project in desperate financial straits. Moreover, government is regarded as slow in capital projects: funding can take a long time to reach the project, and transfer of prom-ised public properties can also have a long-time horizon. Some projects elect to be autonomous from government involvement for these reasons. On balance, public-sector resources offer much to shared space facility projects and should be explored thoroughly.

ROLE OF FOUNDATIONS IN CREATING SHARED SPACE

Foundations, especially in the United States (and, to a lesser extent, in Canada) have played an important role in creating nonprofit centers and building the field. At the time of the 2011 Nonprofit Centers Network (NCN) survey, foundations had created approximately 20% of self-identified nonprofit centers.[11] They've done so in a variety of creative ways, using many of the methods in the philanthropic toolkit. The authors' hope here is to provide interested foundations with an overview of the contributions by foundations to the nonprofit center field.[12]

Why this interest in bricks and mortar real estate as the new century tips us fur-ther into the digital age? Primarily because real estate projects can lead to increased fulfillment and enhancement of a foundation's charitable mission. Real estate projects create a concrete difference in communities, all flowing from the face-to-face collaboration and improved direct services these centers engender.

The authors have already discussed the destructive impact on the nonprofit sector of rising rents and gentrification. Well-spent resources on creating nonprofit centers can replace multiple scattershot requests for capital and rent funding. They can help ease nonprofit displacement while enhancing the programs and long-term stability of participating nonprofits. (See Chapter 27: Rent Support in a Volatile Market.) This more efficient use of foundation resources can also leverage addi-tional charitable and private sector resources to bring sorely needed capital to the nonprofit sector.

A foundation's involvement with nonprofit centers can bring increased visi-bility and interaction with grantees, colleagues, and the community, especially when the foundations are themselves co-located in the centers. As foundations expand their grantee support to include convenings, hosting, and technical assistance, foundation-run nonprofit and conference centers have proven to be great locations for this work.

Centers have been created by family foundations, community foundations, corporate foundations, and health conversion foundations, both small and very large, and have filled all the categories in our typology from Theme to Direct Service to Coworking and Generalist. In this process they have created economic, community, and environmental benefits for varied and crucial stakeholders.

What Does Foundation Involvement Look Like?

Foundations have used a variety of ownership structures, financing options, and community involvement strategies in developing centers. Their strategies are shaped by the impact they want, the partners involved, and their own mission and vision. One such example follows.

One Gift Serves Many

Collaboration to create the Community Service Building (CSB) in Wilmington, Delaware, began in the early 1990s in the offices of some of Delaware's major givers. The Longwood Foundation and DuPont Company's Corporate Contributions Office met in response to a growing demand for capital campaign grants. As they saw it, they faced "the challenge that there was a constant flood of applicants for facility related capital projects and that not all the needs could be met immediately by the current method of funding."[13]

When a DuPont office building was being vacated, the funders thought it more efficient to have the nonprofits co-located and just have one building's maintenance to worry about. In addition, the refurbishment of this office building and the construction of a modern parking structure that serves and helps support its rent both contributed to the further renewal of Wilmington's downtown area. The project was fully funded without debt by sixteen corporations, seven foundations, and the State of Delaware. Today the CSB provides affordable rent to over seventy-five tenants (including the Longwood Foundation)[14] from a broad range of nonprofit organizations. See the photo of its twentieth anniversary celebration shown in Figure 24.2. Its mission remains "to improve the quality of life for current and future generations of the State of Delaware by providing an innovative, professional, and collaborative work environment at below market rent for the administrative offices of charitable nonprofit organizations of various sizes and purposes."[15]

Foundations Creating Centers

Several *Stories from the Field* highlight foundation-created centers. In other examples, The Philanthropy Hub at The Alaska Community Foundation provides co-location for a variety of philanthropic organizations.[16] The HealthSpark Foundation created—and is located in—the Community Partners Center, the first nonprofit center in Pennsylvania. Since its creation in 2008, HealthSpark continues

FIGURE 24.2 *Twentieth Anniversary Celebration at the Community Service Building, Wilmington, Delaware.* The CEO of the Community Services Building (CSB), Jerry Bilton, speaks at the twentieth anniversary celebration of the CSB, which houses over seventy-five Delaware nonprofits in a successful Generalist Center. Tenant names are shown on the wall behind the speaker. *Photo credit: Moonloop Photography, Joe Del Tufo.*

to provide affordable space and state-of-the-art meeting space in the Center, along with its significant grants program for Pennsylvania nonprofits.[17]

Akin to grants, shared space is sometimes offered by foundations, governments, or others that own a building larger than they need for their intended uses. One significant example is the Center for Healthy Communities created by The California Endowment in downtown Los Angeles. The Center includes a high-quality conference center available to grantees—needed nonprofit infrastructure the Center offers at its other California offices as well.

Foundations are sometimes able to offer free or low-cost space because they can fund building costs from their operating budgets. They often give their additional space to their grantees or to groups who work on issues related to the foundation's mission or interest areas. Sometimes we see foundations giving space focused on local nonprofits as in Chapter 27 on the Sobrato Family Foundation. These spaces are not always entirely free with owners often passing on direct operating expenses (electricity, janitorial, etc.) and/or common area maintenance charges (proportionate charges for common spaces).

Capital and Operating Grants

The most common form of foundation support is grant money, but even here there is variety. Seed grants can provide the funds for the business plan or feasibility study to get a project off the ground. Capital grants for purchase or for tenant improvements can be combined in innovative ways with bank financing and tax credits to reduce the cost to create a project and allow for affordable rents, even in a rising market. Bridge loans can sustain a project while it collects on capital campaign pledges. Operating grants can help sustain a nonprofit center over time and through periods of vacancies. The authors strongly suggest that projects aim for self-sufficiency through earned income; however, grants to support the move toward self-sufficiency can bring great benefit. (As an example, see Chapter 17: From Grants to Earned Income.)

Loans and Investments: Program-Related and Impact Investing

Foundations are increasingly moving into the loan-making field.[18] Many foundation loans and investments are made as program-related investments (PRIs); PRIs are mission-related disbursements that qualify as charitable expenditures by the foundation and are explained more fully in Chapter 6: The Development Process. Sometimes these take the form of loan guarantees, which help nonprofits with weak or unproven credit histories but a strong track record of grant income to access bank financing.

Other PRIs come in the form of direct loans to a nonprofit or for-profit entity or even as an investment in a business enterprise. PRIs can also be used to fund a foundation's headquarters, which may be shared with other tenants. PRIs can be large or small depending on the foundation size, but some of the largest nonprofit center projects in the US have used this vehicle as shown in the cases of the Hutton Parker Foundation in Santa Barbara, California, and the Meadows Foundation in Dallas, Texas.

The Hutton Parker Foundation (Hutton Parker) has for many years defined mission success as building the capacity, sustainability, and stability of local area nonprofits so they can provide the programs and services most needed by the community. One of its primary methods has been purchasing and developing real estate properties and converting them to nonprofit centers, which provide long-term leases with reduced and stable rents to the nonprofits they house. They also aim for the "added benefit of interaction and communication of the nonprofits with their peers, creating a sense of community and synergy."[19]

Hutton Parker opened its first building in 1998 and today operates sixteen centers in Santa Barbara and surrounding communities, housing over seventy-five nonprofits as well as providing community meeting space.[20] The Foundation has converted office buildings, an old Coca Cola bottling plant, and even a school to nonprofit tenancy. It make its investment in the centers as PRIs out of their endowment, earning a modest return, which allows it to continue to grow the endowment. It also carries out a regular grant-making program, giving over $4 million a year, and offer PRI loans to individual nonprofits.[21]

One of the largest nonprofit center initiatives by a foundation has been the Wilson Historic District developed by the Meadows Foundation in Dallas, Texas, using a similar model to Hutton Parker. The dual purpose was to undertake adaptive reuse of historic homes and structures in the city and to create a neighborhood of nonprofit agencies housed in rent-free office space in a "collaborative philanthropic community."[22] Today, the twenty-two acres of the Wilson Historic District are home to more than thirty-five Texas-focused nonprofits, and it includes both turn-of-the-century Victorian houses and new buildings in matching styles. The District also includes The Meadows Conference Center for the use of coalitions and nonprofit organizations.

The Wilson Historic District is unique not only for its architecture, boasting the largest collection of late nineteenth-century houses in Dallas [see Figure 24.3 for an example], but also in its current use as a model incubator project for local non-profit organizations.[23]

While most PRIs are made at below market rates, many foundations are also evolving to adopt the practice of mission or impact investing. These mission-related investments are designed to generate both a social and a financial return for the foundation's endowment rather than being funds being invested with rate of return as the primary investment criteria. A good example of this is the Meyer Memorial Trust, one of Oregon's largest foundations. As a place-based foundation, it has increasingly moved away from its worldwide investments to mission-related investing in the Pacific Northwest.[24] The subsequent section on social enterprise discusses in more detail the potential for nonprofit center creation in the mission-investing field.

FIGURE 24.3 *Wilson House, Wilson Historic District, Dallas, Texas.* Henrietta and Fredrick Wilson developed the Wilson Block in 1899, which included their Queen Anne family home, shown here, and six rental homes. The Meadows Foundation acquired the block in 1981 and refurbished the homes to their original designs after the area had fallen in disrepair. The foundation originally located its headquarters in the Wilson house and now provides rent-free office space to nonprofits there and in a number of other properties. *Photo credit: Mike Morgan Photography.*

Supporting intermediaries is another way that foundations can extend their reach and leverage and amplify their grant dollars.

For foundations focusing on a specific geographic area, loans, and grants to local community loan funds can provide important support for community facilities. These institutions, along with the Community Development Corporations (CDCs), described in the following text, have provided crucial technical assistance, real estate expertise, and loans to projects under development.

Foundation grants have been important in supporting the growth of the Nonprofit Centers Network (NCN) and NCN Canada, intermediaries supporting the development of shared space and services and other community real estate (see Chapter 29: It Takes a Network).

An innovative new nonprofit organization is modeled on the community land trust example discussed in Chapter 10: Who Drives Decisions. The Kenneth Rainin Foundation and other private- and public-sector funders seeded the creation of the Community Arts Stabilization Trust (CAST). CAST purchases space for use by non-profit arts and culture organizations facing potential displacement from rising real estate prices in the San Francisco Bay Area. As of the end of 2017, this intermediary owned and operated two buildings while their tenants worked to purchase them over time.[25] One of them is shown in Figure 24.4.

SOCIAL ENTERPRISE AND NONPROFIT CENTERS

Over the last twenty years, social enterprise has been a growing trend in the non-profit, philanthropic, and for-profit sectors. By social enterprise, we refer to both (i) earned income generating activities of nonprofits and (ii) triple bottom line for-profit enterprises combining profit, social, and environmental good, at times in hybrid structures like B Corporations. While nonprofit centers see themselves as naturally aligned with social enterprise, many social enterprise investors and practitioners have not seen nonprofit real estate and shared space as a relevant category of social enterprise. One clear exception is RSF Social Finance, which has provided financing to some of the projects mentioned in this book and whose integrated capital approach profiled in the *Stanford Social Innovation Review* is a model well-suited for nonprofit centers.[26]

In many ways, the nonprofit center is the classic social enterprise. Its goal is social—to provide quality and affordable workspace to nonprofits and social entrepreneurs doing essential work in communities. It provides an ongoing revenue stream (rents) that can support operations and debt. At the same time, it can only succeed as an enterprise if operated on strong business and real estate principles, with attention paid to capitalization, budgets, operations, and other management challenges. The most successful nonprofit centers have achieved financial self-sufficiency; they do not rely on ongoing philanthropic subsidies, except at times for capital renovations.

FIGURE 24.4 *Luggage Store Gallery, San Francisco, California.* The Community Arts Stabilization Trust (CAST) in San Francisco purchased this building for use by the Luggage Store Gallery, a visual arts nonprofit, facing displacement from rising real estate costs. CAST is leasing the building at below market rent, while the nonprofit raises the funding to purchase the building over time. *Photo credit: Kegan Marling.*

If social enterprise funders and investors can begin to make this connection, they could truly leverage the potential of this new infrastructure strategy and bring new resources to the nonprofit centers field. Direct service hubs that provide one-stop social services, arts centers, and shared advocacy buildings could join investment portfolios with nonprofit-run bakeries, urban farms, thrift stores and catering companies that hire populations with barriers to employment. Blended coworking social enterprises like the Impact Hubs[27] and the HiVE[28] in Vancouver are modeling this by including workhorse nonprofits providing critical services in neighborhoods as a core constituency. See Chapter 16: Creating Social Innovation through Shared Space, Social Bonds, and Community Animation on the Center for Social Innovation for another example.

As the social enterprise sector begins to give more focus to low-income communities in North America, solutions to individual community members' needs for education, employment, and housing would be strengthened by parallel attention to the nonprofits struggling with operational and infrastructure needs— including real estate needs. It is vitally important both nationally and internationally and merits the attention of investors, donors, and business school graduates alike.

COMMUNITY DEVELOPMENT AND NONPROFIT CENTERS

The US community development sector has focused historically on low-income housing, workforce development, job creation, and small business services. Now it is expanding its focus to encompass education, health, fresh food access, and transit-oriented development.[29] All these strategies envision a central role for nonprofit agencies in making deep community changes. Thus, the community development sector would seem to be an ideal partner to extend the concepts of nonprofit centers and social purpose real estate.

As the community development field matures, its leaders encourage inclusion of recreation centers and early learning centers in planning while continuing to en-courage local commercial investments and supporting individual wealth creation, all important in transforming a community.[30] In the US, national intermediaries like Local Initiatives Support Corporation (LISC), Living Cities, Enterprise Community Partners, and the Low Income Investment Fund are playing an important role in helping local community development organizations and their local loan fund part-ners to work successfully. But adequate provision to affordably house the nonprofits who nourish community growth and development and provide the programming for those centers is often not part of their plans. The incorporation of shared offices and facilities for nonprofit organizations has rarely made it into the strategies of na-tional organizations or the large national foundations that fund them.

There are, however, several local models of integrating nonprofit centers into urban planning and especially community development. One such project is Daniels Spectrum in Toronto created by Artscape and shown in Figure 24.5.[31]

Other examples include the work of the Northern California Community Loan Fund and the East Bay Asian Local Development Corporation in the San Francisco Bay Area, which incorporate nonprofit centers in their loan, consulting, and devel-opment portfolios.[32] This has proven an effective strategy not just for community development but for combatting nonprofit displacement caused by gentrification. Cities like Toronto and the work of Artscape and the other examples discussed earlier in the chapter are good models of cities recognizing the economic and so-cial benefits of nonprofit centers. An expansion of the use of nonprofit centers as a useful planning strategy to contribute to community development could have sim-ilar impacts in other cities.

FIGURE 24.5 *Daniel Spectrum, Toronto, Ontario.* Daniels Spectrum is a community cultural hub with a mix of arts spaces in the Regent Park neighbourhood in Toronto, Ontario. It is a joint venture between Artscape, Toronto Community Housing, The Daniels Corporation, and the Regent Park Community. It is part of the larger revitalization of the neighbourhood that began in the mid-2000s, which has included the construction of affordable ownership homes by Toronto Community Housing. *Photo credit: Garrison McArthur Photography.*

CONCLUSION

The shared space field benefits greatly from financial resources and technical assistance, particularly from government and philanthropy and, to a lesser degree, from the social enterprise and community development fields. There are exemplary examples in each of these sectors for support of shared spaces and these efforts should be applauded. Yet, to grow shared space into a meaningful, replicable, widely accepted infrastructure strategy, these allied fields need to embrace the model more fully and understand its benefits. At the same time, the shared space field must continue its efforts to intersect more intentionally with these allied fields, working to fold the shared space strategy into the already well-established models and operational systems of these other fields. If the shared space model could be more wholly embraced by these allied sectors, the potential for addressing the critical space challenges facing nonprofits could be ameliorated in a large-scale, systemic way. We look forward to that moment.

NOTES

1. Kukui Center. "About the Kukui Center." Accessed December 17, 2017. http://www.kukuicenter.org/about-the-kukui-center/.
2. The City of Edmonton Community Services. "Edmonton Non-Profit Shared Space Feasibility Toolkit: A Resource for Non-profit Co-Location Initiatives in Edmonton." https://d10k7k7mywg42z.cloudfront.net/assets/506b66dfdabe9d103a015735/nonprofitsharedspacetoolkit.pdf.

3. Queen's Printer for Ontario. "Two-Year Progress Report on Community hubs in Ontario." © Queen's Printer for Ontario, 2012–2018. https://www.ontario.ca/page/two-year-progress-report-community-hubs-ontario-strategic-framework-and-action-plan. See also the original "Strategic Framework and Action Plan," © Queen's Printer for Ontario, 2012–2018. https://www.ontario.ca/page/community-hubs-ontario-strategic-framework-and-action-plan; "One-Year Progress Update on Community Hubs in Ontario, © Queen's Printer for Ontario, 2012–2018. https://www.ontario.ca/page/one-year-progress-update-community-hubs-ontario-strategic-framework-and-action-plan.

4. Thanks to Katie Edwards, Executive Director of the Nonprofit Centers Network for the information in this section. China Brotsky, personal conversation with Katie Edwards, January 2, 2018.

5. See https://www.sandiego.gov/sandiegofamilyjusticecenter. Accessed January 6, 2018. © City of San Diego, 2002–2018.

6. See https://www.familyjusticecenter.org/about-us/. Accessed January 6, 2018. © Family Justice Center Alliance, 2018.

7. See https://www.georgina.ca/discover-georgina/arts-and-culture/link. Accessed January 6, 2018. © Town of Georgina, 2015.

8. Community Conscience. "About Us" 2016. Accessed April 1, 2018. http://www.communityconscience.org/about-us/.

9. Community Conscience. "About Us." 2016. Accessed April 1, 2018. http://www.communityconscience.org/about-us/.

10. Community Conscience. "Community Conscience Agencies." 2016. Accessed April 1, 2018. http://www.communityconscience.org/agencies/.

11. Nonprofit Centers Network. *Measuring Collaboration: The Benefits and Impacts of Nonprofit Centers (Executive Summary).* San Francisco: Nonprofit Centers Network, 2011.

12. Although this report is a little outdated, some detail on early adopters of these foundation initiatives can be found in Nonprofit Centers Network and Tides Shared Spaces. *Planting a Seed: Foundations Build Communities with Shared Nonprofit Workspace.* http://www.nonprofitcenters.org/?s=Planting+a+Seed%3A.

13. Community Service Building Corporation. "About Us." Accessed December 26, 2018. http://www.csbcorp.org/index.html.

14. Community Service Building Corporation. "About Us." Accessed December, 2018. https://www.csbcorp.org/our-history.

15. Community Service Building Corporation. "Our Mission." Accessed December 26, 2018. https://www.csbcorp.org/our-mission. The CSB is 172,000 sq. ft., twelve stories, with seventy-seven tenants, and has a 473-space garage for free tenant parking. The amounts tenants save on parking is almost as much as their rent costs. The CSB has two for-profit tenants (a bank and a restaurant) that fund a sizable capital reserve. Information from China Brotsky's personal communication with Jerry Bilton, retired CEO of CSB on March 31, 2018. For more information see also Abraham, T. "5 Notable Nonprofits Working Out of Wilmington's Community Service Building." Technical.ly. January 23, 2018. https://technical.ly/delaware/2015/09/10/5-notable-nonprofits-working-wilmingtons-community-service-building/; "Debt-Free, Fully Occupied Community Service Building Marks 20th Anniversary." *Delaware Business Now.* April 5, 2017. https://delawarebusinessnow.com/2017/04/debt-free-full-occupied-community-service-building-marks-20th-anniversary/.

16. See https://alaskacf.org/about/philanthropy-hub/. Accessed December 2017. © The Alaska Community Foundation.

17. See https://www.communitypartnerscenter.org/ourstory. Accessed January 26, 2018.

18. The Mission Investors Exchange, a clearinghouse for impact investors, can provide comprehensive information for funders on both program-related and impact investing. Accessed December 20, 2017. https://missioninvestors.org/resources/building-place-based-impact-investing-ecosystem and https://missioninvestors.org/. © Mission Investors Exchange, 2017. The Foundation Center website also provides access to other free resources for foundations on PRIs. Accessed December 20, 2017. http://philanthropynewsdigest.org/news/foundations-launch-program-related-investments-resource?_ga=2.246988932.1625736573.1513820704-1311794802.1513820704. © The Foundation Center, 2017.

19. See http://huttonfoundation.org/under-one-roof/, 2015. Accessed December 20, 2017.

20. Personal correspondence of China Brotsky with Pamela Lewis, COO of the Hutton Parker Foundation, January 2, 2018.

21. See http://huttonfoundation.org/our-history/. 2015. "Our History." Accessed December 20, 2017. The authors suggest reading *The $100 Million Secret*, a book on the Hutton Parker strategy written by its CEO Tom Parker and available from the foundation.

22. "Wilson Historic District." Accessed January 27, 2018. https://www.mfi.org/WHD.html. © The Meadows Foundation, Inc., 2018.

23. "Wilson Block Historic District." Accessed January 27, 2018. http://www.preservationdallas.org/who-we-are/visit-us/wilson-block/. © Preservation Dallas, 2018.

24. See https://mmt.org/news/icymi-investing-place-based-impact. Accessed December 21, 2017. © Meyer Memorial Trust, 2015–2017.

25. China Brotsky's personal correspondence with Moy Eng, Executive Director of CAST on January 24, 2018. See also this 2018 newspaper article on CAST at https://www.sfchronicle.com/movies/article/This-CAST-of-characters-helps-keep-SF-arts-groups-12753123.php.

26. Shaffer, D. "Integrated Capital for Social Enterprises." Accessed January 6, 2018. https://ssir.org/articles/entry/integrated_capital_for_social_enterprises. © Stanford University, 2018. Shaffer is president and CEO of RSF Social Finance. See also information on RSF Social Finance's program to bring diverse voices to the integrated capital approach and to develop "powerful strategies to leverage capital as a tool for long-term change" and "to support enterprises that are solving complex social and environmental problems." Accessed January 6, 2018. http://rsfsocialfinance.org/2017/08/31/inaugural-cohort-integrated-capital-fellows/. © RSF Social Finance, 2017.

27. See www.impacthub.net. Accessed December 13, 2017.

28. See www.hivevancouver.com. Accessed December 13, 2017.

29. Andrews, N. O. and Erickson, D. J., eds. *Investing in What Works for America's Communities*. San Francisco: Federal Reserve Bank of San Francisco & Low Income Investment Fund, 2012; in particular, see the contribution by Paul Grogan, "The Future of Community Development," 189.

30. Franklin, S. F and Edwards, D. "It Takes a Neighborhood: Purpose Built Communities and Neighborhood Transformation." In *Investing in What Works for America's Communities*. Edited by N. O. Andrews and D. J. Erickson. San Francisco: Federal Reserve Bank of San Francisco & Low Income Investment Fund, 2012, 177.

31. Artscape is a nonprofit urban development organization that makes space for creativity and transforms communities, especially through a proactive practice known as creative placemaking. http://www.torontoartscape.ca. See, in particular, their projects Daniels

Spectrum, Artscape Youngplace and Artscape Wychwood Barns for their relationship to community economic development.

32. Northern California Community Loan Fund is a local CDC (http://www.ncclf.org) that works in multiple counties in the greater San Francisco Bay Area. East Bay Asian Local Development Corporation (http://www.ebaldc.org) is a nonprofit community development organization.

25 *Stories from the Field*

Denver's Test Kitchen
Creating A Recipe To Nurture and Coordinate A Region's Shared Spaces

Megan Devenport

Denver Shared Spaces, Denver, Colorado

Effective shared spaces create a sense of place, extend the reach of organizations housed within them, and accelerate positive outcomes for local communities. As such, shared space models have the potential to be a key tool for achieving municipal goals of economic and community growth. The problem is that it takes a lot of time, energy, and expertise to get just one shared space center off the ground and running smoothly, let alone coordinate between disparate centers and across sectors. The opportunity to leverage shared space approaches as part of a regional development strategy is generally missed in the absence of a champion for this kind of coordination and without a mechanism to provide broad-based support across centers.

Yet, through a unique, multi-sector partnership, the City and County of Denver seeded the first broad-based municipal movement to integrate shared spaces as a community and economic development strategy and coordinate the growing local shared space movement. The resulting public–private partnership is Denver Shared Spaces, whose mission is to cultivate and support a regional ecosystem of thriving shared space centers that enhance the community. The collaboration was established in 2009 by a partnership representing nonprofit, foundation, and City agency interests. Since its founding, the program has grown to include staff and volunteer expertise from all sectors. The result is a dynamic approach to connect the dots between municipal policy, urban planning, real estate development, and vital nonprofit services and amenities. Figure 25.1 shows the interior of the Posner Center, one of the nonprofit centers whose creation was supported by Denver Shared Spaces.

Building on early work, challenges, and successes, Denver Shared Spaces now provides consulting services, professional development programs, and policy

FIGURE 25.1 *Posner Center for International Development in Denver, Colorado.* The Posner Center houses organizations, both nonprofit and for-profit, with an expertise and focus around international development and who work in over one hundred countries. Skylights create a light-filled space in the building interior; the actual workspace is an important driver of happiness and productivity. *Photo credit: Image by Shotzr Photographer, Evan Semon.*

advocacy. By connecting nonprofits and community-minded businesses with vital real estate expertise and consultation, Denver Shared Spaces fosters collaboration, maximizes financial resources, and simplifies complex real estate logistics within and between shared space centers. Locally driven professional development programs serve to network the many types of shared spaces located in the region as well as help inform the broader national dialogue through Denver Shared Spaces' partnership with the Nonprofit Centers Network (NCN).

The third component of Denver Shared Spaces' approach is to influence policy at the municipal and state levels to create an enabling environment for shared spaces to thrive. Since its founding, Denver Shared Spaces has directly supported more than twenty-five shared space centers and anchor development partners, and the program has grown to include partners from multiple City agencies, local foundations, commercial real estate and development groups, and nonprofits.

This chapter explores how such an innovative collaboration took shape, the necessary ingredients for its success, and its impact on economic and community development in Metro Denver. Throughout this exploration, we keep an eye toward how the Denver story can be distilled and applied to other municipal contexts and collaborative settings.

INGREDIENT #1: CONNECT TO A NATIONAL MOVEMENT AND BUILD ON LOCAL EFFORT

Innovations—solutions and ideas that seem to be brand new—have often been quietly taking shape for years before they gain acknowledgement and become widely adopted. This is the case with the concept of "shared space" in Metro Denver. The current state of affairs—the highest concentration of shared space facilities in the country and a growing ecosystem of support—is the result of both independent and collective efforts over many years. The creation of Denver Shared Spaces came about in July of 2009 only after nearly a decade of pieces being put into place nationally and locally.

National Context

Nonprofits have long operated under the implicit assumption that collaboration makes us stronger. Analogies abound—clasped hands, web of life, woven tapestry, humming hive. No matter how much a cliché, we have a sense that it is better, safer, stronger, and more productive to work in community with others. Almost all nonprofits espouse this idea and have long relied on each other to accomplish programmatic or policy goals. Similarly, nonprofits have long co-located as a way to economize on limited resources, improve service delivery or access, and carve out space to get the job done. In Denver, the concept of intentional co-location began to crystalize in the 1990s, with a focus on making space sharing more formal and intentional and, ultimately, a tool for increased effectiveness through collaboration. Specifically, nonprofits began to explore how these types of space solutions could increase the effectiveness of their programming toward achieving their mission.

The increasing awareness and capacity support at a national level was a key ingredient in setting the stage for Denver Shared Spaces' formation. National organizations like NCN contributed to the development of the multi-sector collaboration in Denver. NCN was born out of a small convening of nonprofit center operators in the San Francisco Bay Area in the early 2000s and grew from an informal network into a dynamic, peer-led membership association and capacity-building organization. NCN is now an established platform for best practices around mission-driven shared space and shared services, facilitating a peer-sourced network of members throughout North America (see http://www.nonprofitcenters.org).

Early on in the Denver exploration of the shared space movement, the connection to NCN was invaluable. Even before the program was conceived, local leadership participated in trainings and conferences hosted by NCN, and NCN consulted on the creation of one of Denver's first shared spaces, the Alliance Center. These experiences informed the budding strategy among the three founding partners of Denver Shared Spaces—the nonprofit Urban Land Conservancy (ULC), the city's Denver Office of Strategic Partnerships (DOSP), and the Piton Foundation. Through this connection, the founding partners were exposed to the diversity of thinking and experimentation around shared space approaches. In addition to providing access to information, NCN took steps early on to add credibility to the growing Denver partnership by providing a national stage on which to share the collaboration's progress. Shortly after Denver Shared Spaces officially launched, NCN invited the founding team to present a webinar to its national membership. Titled "Making the Case for Nonprofit Centers: Approaches to and Importance of Government Partnerships," this experience contributed to Denver Shared Spaces' local credibility while also adding to the national dialogue.

The NCN connection facilitated further access to other national players in the shared space arena. In May 2010, Denver Shared Spaces hosted the Denver Funders Forum, which featured China Brotsky with the Tides Foundation and Pamela Lewis with the Hutton Foundation. The Forum provided a group of twenty-two funders with guidance on how foundations can engage in shared space efforts. This format was particularly helpful, given that the presenters represented national foundations and therefore provided a peer perspective for local funders. The first full year of Denver Shared Spaces' launch culminated with an important opportunity to present the opening keynote address at the first Social Purpose Real Estate Conference in Vancouver, British Columbia, in December 2010.

Through these opportunities to convene and present, Denver Shared Spaces contributed to the growing national dialogue while, perhaps more importantly, gaining access to vital information and relationships. By joining the national membership network and engaging at that level, Denver's champions were better equipped to pursue their local strategy. Exposure to the NCN network and others working in this space also reinforced that few cities were pursuing a coordinated approach to using shared space models as part of a robust community development strategy.

Local Movement

As the 1990s drew to a close, the Denver region was experiencing significant growth in both economy and population. It was in this context that intentional government and nonprofit space sharing began to take root. As shown in Figure 25.2, in the decade prior to Denver Shared Spaces' founding, three key shared space centers developed independently of each other—the Richard T. Castro Human Services Building, the Alliance Center, and the Phillips Center, a multi-service center (now known as the Tramway Nonprofit Center. While not all self-identified as "shared spaces" at the start, each modeled different ways in which intentional space-sharing could enhance impact and efficiency for the organizations housed inside. These examples provided a starting place for the broader shared space conversation in the city.

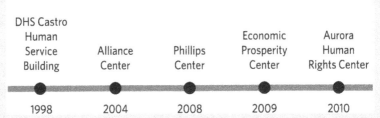

FIGURE 25.2 This figure shows a timeline of the development of shared spaces in the Denver metro region beginning with the Human Service Building in 1998. *Source: Megan Devenport.*

In 1998, the City and County of Denver opened the Richard T. Castro Human Services Building. The facility is approximately 307,000 sq. ft. and houses over eight hundred employees. Primarily occupied by the City and County of Denver's Department of Human Services (DHS), the mission of the facility is to provide space to streamline and improve services for people in need. DHS provides benefits and services to one in three Denver residents, making this central location a highly visible, high-traffic facility. At the Castro, residents can access assistance programs including food, cash and medical benefits, child care, child support, and general assistance.

While the majority of the services available in the building are provided by City programs, the Castro also houses nonprofit-provided services like financial counseling, childcare, and employment training. Early in the planning process for the facility, the City intentionally opened the vendor selection process to qualified nonprofits. As a result, DHS hired a nonprofit culinary training program called Work Options for Women to run the employee cafeteria and an additional nonprofit partner to provide on-site childcare. This early public–private partnership proved successful, with both vendors winning the contract again when reissued for competitive bids. The co-location allows for improved access to services and enhanced quality through higher levels of coordination between City employees and nonprofit providers. While it took years for DHS to recognize this building as a "shared space center," its existence reflects an early example of municipal leadership taking action vis-à-vis the concept of shared space.

The Alliance Center, operated by the Alliance for Sustainable Colorado, was developed in 2004 inside a renovated 41,000 sq. ft., six-story warehouse building originally constructed in 1908. The Alliance for Sustainable Colorado purchased the building with the intent to create a showcase and educational outreach center promoting environmental sustainability and the reuse of historic structures to achieve sustainable cities. This building continues to provide a home for over forty nonprofits focused on sustainability. Large anchors in the building include Conservation Colorado, along with smaller organizations like the Colorado chapters of Sierra Club and Trout Unlimited.

The Alliance Center was significant to Denver Shared Spaces' formation in several ways. This space was one of the first self-identified multi-tenant nonprofit centers in Denver. Leadership clearly communicated the mission-driven nature of the building and attracted publicity as a thematic shared space. Locally, the Alliance Center was a highly visible example of the growing shared space movement. In addition, the Alliance Center was an early member of NCN. The connection to the NCN membership supported getting Denver "on the map" and increasing national attention on the innovative, collaborative work in the City. (See Chapter 8: The Alliance Center for a portrait of this project.)

The third early example of shared space was developed at the Phillips Center, now the Tramway Nonprofit Center. In 2008, the Urban Land Conservancy (ULC) acquired and redeveloped this 115-year old, 95,000 sq. ft. former Denver Tramway Company maintenance facility. Located in northeast Denver, the building provides a stable, affordable location for over fifteen nonprofit organizations. The Tramway Nonprofit Center is an example of adaptive reuse of an historic building in the heart of a low-income neighborhood. While it had long been home to a variety of community-based nonprofits, deferred maintenance and an undercapitalized owner put the long-term viability of the structure at risk. Its purchase by the ULC brought increased capital investment in improving the space as well as increased ability to fully lease the available space to nonprofits in a more intentional fashion. The ULC committed to maintaining lease rates at a third or more below market rates to ensure a long-term location for nonprofits in the Cole neighborhood. The neighborhood location was important as it brought services closer to residents that needed them and stabilized an entire block within an otherwise residential area that could have become blighted.

This project was important in the genesis of Denver Shared Spaces because it created an opening for the ULC to deepen its commitment to preserving commercial affordability for nonprofits. The building also provided a platform for increased partnership between the ULC and the Denver Office of Strategic Partnerships (DOSP) due to the intersection with DOSP's nonprofit energy efficiency programs, which were leveraged to improve the space. The Piton Foundation was also drawn into the conversation as the building became home to several programs and services focused on children, a key funding area for the foundation. In this way, the Tramway Nonprofit Center acted as a catalyst to cement relationships, secure commitment, and build buy-in from the core founding organizations and individuals to move the Denver Shared Spaces project forward.

INGREDIENT #2: ENSURE YOU HAVE THE RIGHT ORGANIZATIONS *AND* THE RIGHT PEOPLE

Denver Shared Spaces was founded as a volunteer-driven collaborative—with no dedicated staff and a limited budget. As such, its start-up phase relied heavily on the organizational infrastructure of the three founding partners—the DOSP, the ULC, and the Piton Foundation.

The driving force for the initial strategy was the DOSP. DOSP was created in 2004 by then-Mayor John Hickenlooper as a resource to connect the nonprofit sector with City government. While the programs provided by DOSP have evolved over the past decade, the agency still holds the core belief that by working collectively, the public and nonprofit sectors can be more efficient and effective in strengthening Denver's communities. The Office engaged in the shared space conversation as a result of its dual focus on nonprofit efficiency and effective cross-sector collaboration. Shared space became a clear avenue through which the Office could address goals in both these areas. DOSP provided Denver Shared Spaces with strategic connections into City government, a bird's-eye view of the local nonprofit sector, and significant cross-sector collaboration capacity. In addition to these knowledge-based and interpersonal resources, DOSP also contributed the funding to underwrite the program's early work.

The second founding partner was the ULC, highlighted in the previous section as the owner/operator of the Tramway Nonprofit Center. The ULC is a nonprofit organization founded in 2003 to invest in real estate for the long-term benefit of Metro Denver communities. The ULC intervenes in the real estate market in two primary ways. The first is by responding to opportunities that would otherwise be lost to the market or that the market may be unable to address. Additionally, the ULC acquires, develops, and preserves community assets in urban areas to address a variety of community needs, such as schools, affordable housing, and office space for nonprofits. The ULC's real estate expertise was key to the early work of the program. Given that the ULC's staff team had specialized expertise in real estate financing, acquisition, and development, their participation informed the research efforts that helped lay the groundwork for Denver Shared Spaces. The ULC also allocated skilled staff to manage the development of the early strategic framework and outreach tools, such as the Denver Shared Spaces website.

The final partner was the Piton Foundation, founded nearly forty years ago to invest in efforts that improve the lives of low-income children across Colorado. Since its founding partnership with Denver Shared Spaces, the Piton Foundation has evolved to become Gary Community Investments. This new company includes the Piton Foundation as its operating foundation arm as well as an impact investment side of the house to leverage a full spectrum of financial tools to help address the issues facing Colorado's low-income children and their families. The Piton Foundation allocated staff time and expertise early on in the development of Denver Shared Spaces because the foundation recognized the critical connection between nonprofit success and stable nonprofit operations.

Additionally, the Piton Foundation sought to amplify nonprofits' impact by supporting effective collaborations within the sector. Denver Shared Spaces was viewed as a potential resource for the nonprofit sector to improve the stability of real estate solutions as well as the quality and impact of collaborative efforts. While it was important to have early stakeholder input from the philanthropic community, the direct relationship between Denver Shared Spaces and the Piton Foundation waned after the first year of the program.

As with any new endeavor, it was not just the organizational affiliations of each of the founding members that set Denver Shared Spaces up for success. While those were important, it was just as critical that the founding team had the right people from those organizations committed to the effort. The three founding members, as representatives of their organization, brought complementary skills, expertise, and resources to the table, and formed the core governance structure. These founding steering committee members had an effective balance of vision and implementation, advocacy and data analysis, and content knowledge and professional networks. In addition, they all had trusting working relationships that predated the Denver Shared Spaces effort. In reflecting on the foundation of the Denver Shared Spaces collaboration, it is clear that both the right organizations and the right individuals were critical for success.

INGREDIENT #3: KNOW YOUR STUFF—RESEARCH BUILDS CREDIBILITY AND GUIDES STRATEGY

In addition to having the right founding partners early on in the process, Denver Shared Spaces also relied on a strong research basis to guide program development and inform the goals of the fledgling collaborative. Table 25.1 outlines the research publications reviewed by the founding steering committee as the program took shape.

Upon review, the committee recognized a gap in knowledge of two critical elements. While local- and state-level research did explore facility costs, renovation planning, and nonprofit economic outcomes, there was neither systematic investigation of the commercial real estate market's appetite to better meet nonprofit facility needs nor of the capacity of nonprofit leaders to manage real estate issues.

After a thorough review of the relevant studies, and in light of the dramatic, negative changes to the economy wrought by the recession of 2008, Denver Shared Spaces launched an in-depth exploration into the connection between facility needs and opportunities, as wells as opportunities for collaboration. Culminating in the publication of a community report, *An Investment Worth Making*, Denver Shared Spaces solicited feedback from hundreds of nonprofits and dozens of real estate

Table 25.1 Local Research Informs Denver Shared Spaces Framework

Date	Research Publication	Led By
2002	Nonprofit Facilities in Denver/Boulder: A Market Assessment	Funded by Daniels Fund and Rose Community Foundation
2004	Facility Expansion/Renovation: Planning for Capital Projects and Campaigns	Funded by Gates Family Foundation
2008	Survey of Arts Organizations and Creative Business	Funded by the Metro Denver Scientific and Cultural Facilities District
2008	Return on Investment: The Economic impact of the Nonprofit Sector in Colorado	Funded by the Colorado Nonprofit Association

Note: Local funders have supported critical field research, providing needed resources to document the successes and impact of shared spaces in Denver.

Source: Megan Devenport.

professionals to better understand nonprofit real estate needs, interest in shared space, and market realities. The resulting report drew several key conclusions from the research. The findings indicated:

- Momentum for expansion of intentional shared space opportunities in the Denver community.
- Strong need for capacity support for convening and vetting new shared space partnerships.
- Lack of necessary real estate expertise within nonprofits.
- Lack of partnership development skills among both real estate professionals and nonprofit professionals.

This research investigation allowed the new program to test interest in space sharing within the nonprofit sector and gather information about perceived gaps in knowledge and capacity on the topic. Further, the study provided a forum to engage the commercial real estate profession to better understand the market landscape in Denver post recession. As a result, Denver Shared Spaces identified an early strategy for supporting existing shared spaces and creating a local coordinated movement.

INGREDIENT #4: CLEAR DIRECTION AND STRATEGY ENGAGES EARLY ADOPTERS AND BUILDS MOMENTUM

Beyond the three founding members, Denver Shared Spaces expanded its steering committee in the first year to include additional key stakeholders. Much like building a working board for a start-up nonprofit, Denver Shared Spaces' early steering committee focused on recruiting for interest-aligned people whose volunteer participation in Denver Shared Spaces governance and program work would also be beneficial to their own personal or professional interests. Recruitment was completed simultaneously with the *Investment Worth Making* research, allowing new members an immediate, concrete project in which to engage. The result was a committee of 8 people representing all sectors—public, nonprofit, and for-profit.

With an expanded set of volunteers around the table, Denver Shared Spaces moved on to strategy development. Based on the findings outlined in the research report, the expanded steering committee developed an ambitious five-year plan, which included the following goals:

- Actively create five multi-tenant nonprofit centers by 2015.
- Develop general resources to help support nonprofits in creating shared space.
- Streamline city and community resources to realize strategic efficiencies around investment in nonprofit facilities.
- Create a formal network of Denver-based multi-tenant nonprofit centers.

Developing these values and goals were critical to give shape and direction to the project, as well as providing the expanded volunteer governance structure with direct opportunities to contribute. These served to build the base of support and momentum for the program.

INGREDIENT #5: TAKE TIME TO LEARN FROM BOTH SUCCESS AND FAILURE

Using the four goals set out in the first work plan, the Denver Shared Spaces steering committee developed the first formal programs. Perhaps most ambitious, the goal to actively create five new shared spaces in five years required significant planning and seed investment. The group opted for an approach that provided funding for consulting support to two competitively selected groups of nonprofits. The groups, or "cohorts" as described by Denver Shared Spaces, participated in a facilitated feasibility process to assess the opportunity to create two new shared space centers. Through a Request for Proposal process, two groups, comprised of self-selected partners, were chosen and matched with consulting teams. The first phase of the consulting grant began in July 2010. One cohort was comprised of nonprofits serving youth and families—referred to creatively as the Family Services Cohort. This cohort completed the first phase of planning and recognized the partnership was not feasible and would not lead to a new shared space. The cohort disbanded and pursued real estate solutions independently. The second group, comprised of five nonprofit capacity builders, did successfully advance through the consulting process to open the Colorado Collaborative for Nonprofits in November 2013.

In addition to the Family Services Cohort, Denver Shared Spaces invested time, expertise, and funding resources into other early projects that did not take shape as planned. Much like the successful projects undertaken early on, these challenges and false-starts contributed valuable lessons for fine-tuning the new program's approach. These early "lessons learned" shaped the values and approach of the program work, informing assessment and partnership readiness tools still in use today. The central importance of trusting relationships runs throughout Denver Shared Spaces' work. Get the relationships right and many other components of a partnership or project fall into place. Beyond that, early projects highlighted the importance of clear communication to address power dynamics, define expectations, and clarify roles.

GROWTH AND IMPACT

Building on the early project approaches, Denver Shared Spaces has expanded to include professional development support, fee-for-service consulting with real estate developers and landlords, and policy advocacy to make it easier to develop and manage effective shared spaces in the region. Since 2009, Denver Shared Spaces has provided consulting services, directly or through grant making, to over twenty-five clients. These include groups of nonprofits, real estate professionals, and government entities. These services resulted in new or improved operations for eighteen shared space facilities, representing more than 250 organizations and 1,500 employees. Supported shared space facilities include:

- Posner Center for International Development, dedicated to alleviating global poverty shown in Figure 25.3.
- edXchange, a shared space collaborative of education advocacy organizations.
- Z Place, a shared space within a broader Denver Public Schools shared campus housing a broad range of "cradle-to-career" services.
- Daniels Veterans Service Center, a wrap-around service center owned and managed by the Volunteers of America–Colorado Branch.

FIGURE 25.3 *Introducing New Organizations at the Posner Center.* Regular block parties introduce the Posner Center community to new organizations or existing organizations launching new efforts to create awareness and identify opportunities for collaboration. The Posner Center aims to break down organizational isolation with a mission to convene, connect, and catalyze the international development community, both tenants and off-site members, to collaborate for greater impact. *Photo credit: Image by Shotzr Photography, Evan Semon.*

In addition, Denver Shared Spaces has worked to cultivate a local community of practice, providing targeted support to managers of shared spaces, who meet monthly in a professionally facilitated peer-learning structure. These efforts have both contributed to and benefited from the growing profile of coworking and other shared space concepts in the commercial real estate market.

Denver Shared Spaces has also influenced the local policy landscape through direct advocacy and research. In 2012, the collaboration successfully advocated for the first municipal policy in the US prioritizing shared space models as a community development strategy for City agencies in Denver. (See a copy of the text of

Executive Order 138: Coordination of Shared Space and Nonprofit Facilities Support, by Michael B. Hancock, the Mayor of Denver, 2012, as an appendix to this chapter.) This framework has since provided avenues for Denver Shared Spaces and partners to work toward building additional structures, funding mechanisms, and policy interventions to address barriers faced in developing new intentional shared spaces.

Throughout this growth and evolution, Denver Shared Spaces has continued to receive primary funding from its founding partners DOSP and ULC to support one full-time staff person. Over the past two years, this staffing structure has allowed the program to begin generating revenue through consulting and technical assistance services as well as develop a formal business plan for this "social enterprise." The goal is to diversify the financial model and reduce reliance on DOSP and ULC, expand the services and programs provided to the community, and establish a more robust internal infrastructure that will sustain the program into the future. In sum, the "creation story" of Denver Shared Spaces is not one of creating a new shared space center but rather of cooking up a voluntary, capacity-building structure within the region. Denver Shared Spaces' recipe highlights many of the patterns and lessons learned that are common to most collaborative efforts and shared by many emerging nonprofit centers. This also illustrates that, by combining the proper "ingredients," a major metropolitan area can prioritize and support shared space models as one piece of its broader economic and community development strategy.

DENVER SHARED SPACES IS NOW COMMUNITY SPACES (BY MEGAN YONKE, RADIAN|PLACEMATTERS)

Since 2009, Denver Shared Spaces has served a programmatic mission of connecting real estate and social impact under the fiscal sponsorship of the ULC, with significant support from the DOSP. This work was primarily focused on expanding opportunities for nonprofit organizations to share space to reduce operational costs and to maximize collaborative impact. As detailed in the preceding chapter, these efforts were successful in cultivating nonprofit centers throughout the Denver Metro Region.

In January 2017, Denver Shared Spaces took a step in a new and exciting direction. Seeing that displacement pressures throughout the Denver Metro Area were affecting low-income residents, small businesses, and nonprofit organizations, Denver Shared Spaces identified an opportunity to focus on expanding social-purpose real estate opportunities to combat this displacement. This new direction not only includes but also expands focus beyond core local nonprofit partners to include anchor local businesses and social enterprises. To achieve these ends, Denver Shared Spaces transitioned from being a distinct program under the ULC to serving as a key offering called Community Spaces under Radian|Placematters Inc. Radian|Placematters, Inc. is a nonprofit community design center that provides urban design and architectural services to community-based initiatives, focused on creating healthy and sustainable communities in underserved areas. The combined Radian|Placematters team believes that social-purpose real estate can battle residential displacement by building the capacity of existing neighborhoods, providing crucial services to existing residents, and sustaining/creating spaces for diverse residents to gather.

Denver is growing at a rapid rate, and new developments are generally not incorporating uses that benefit existing residents of surrounding communities. Real estate developers often have a challenging time identifying community-serving organizations with feasible business models to incorporate into their projects. One of the key ways to achieve financial sustainability and affordability is through the development of shared space business models. The Radian|Placematters Community Spaces offering targets community-serving shared space uses such as fresh food (markets and incubators), early childhood education, makerspace, commissary and commercial kitchens, office and retail spaces for social enterprises, industrial warehouse and storage space, and nonprofit office space. Radian|Placematters seeks to understand and structure business models for these types of community-serving shared spaces and develop partnerships to deliver on these uses in both new and existing developments.

Radian|Placematters secures funding and fee-for-service projects associated with Community Spaces, based on subject matter expertise, consulting on design and feasibility, matchmaking, space creation, and activation on the previously mentioned community-serving spaces in the Denver Metro Area. Activation in this context means creating a vibrant community in a particular space. Subject matter expertise includes surveying, relationship building, and partner ecosystem mapping. Where operational capacity gaps exist, Radian|Placematters will consider serving as a master tenant in partnership with real estate developers to offer community services. In implementing these projects, Radian|Placematters advances the mission of combating displacement while being financially sustainable. Radian|Placematters believes that development of feasible business models and key partnerships are critical to developing the community space to keep residents of diverse communities in Denver. More information about Radian|Placematters is available at https://www.radianinc.org.

EXECUTIVE ORDER 138

Executive Order 138 was the first municipal policy in the US prioritizing shared space models as a community development strategy. We have included the full text here from the Denver Office of Strategic Partnerships as a potential guide to other localities. The actual Executive Order was signed by the Mayor of Denver and nine of his department heads including General Services, Public Works, Environmental Health, Finance and Community Planning and Development.

Executive Order No. 138

TO: All Agencies Under the Mayor
FROM: Michael B. Hancock, Mayor
DATE: August 15, 2012
SUBJECT: Coordination of Shared Space and Nonprofit Facilities Support

PURPOSE: This Executive Order establishes a policy of the City and County of Denver for coordination of City agencies with the Denver Shared Space Project and encourages agencies to support co-location for organizations with a public purpose, particularly nonprofit organizations, as a specific consideration in their work.

1.0 **Applicable Authority**: The applicable authority relevant to the provisions and requirements of this Executive Order No. 138 are found in Article XX, Section of the Colorado Constitution, Charter Sections 2.2.1, *2.93* (D) and (E), Section 28-17 D.R.M.C. and Executive Order No. 100.

2.0 **Structure**: The Denver Shared Space Project is a collaboration of multiple City and community agencies, led by staff in the Denver Office of Strategic Partnerships, an office housed in the Agency for Human Rights and Community Partnerships. The Project is overseen by a Steering Committee and supported by a number of working committees, created to support and work toward the vision and goals of the Project.

3.0 **Definition**: Shared space is defined as two or more organizations with a public purpose co-locating office space. Shared space may also include the development of a mutually beneficial arrangement to share in other space resources for meetings, program delivery, storage, and other purposes such as back office efficiencies.

4.0 **Mission**: The Denver Shared Space Project is a nationally recognized effort designed to support the best practice creation and operation of multi-tenant nonprofit centers in Denver. The Project works to create and enhance shared spaces throughout the community, provide general resources and information to those creating or operating shared spaces, streamline City and community resources in support of shared space, and create a formal network of shared space facilities throughout the community. The Project's values include affordability and stability of office space, intentional collaboration of tenants and communities, and promoting energy efficient facilities.

5.0 **Scope:** Agencies involved may include, but are not limited to the City Attorney's Office, Community Planning and Development, Denver Public Library, Department of Finance, Department of Human Services, Human Rights and Community Partnerships, Office of Economic Development, Parks and Recreation, and Public Works.

6.0 **General Policy Statement:** Shared space is an important tool to enhance communities; ensure an appropriate combination of services to meet the needs of communities and neighborhoods; create space for local community convenings and community building activities; activate underutilized real estate spaces; bring workers into communities; eliminate food deserts in neighborhoods; enhance the economic development and overall well-being of communities; and support efficient use of resources invested in nonprofit organizations. Agencies under the authority of the Mayor will include legally permissible shared space as a considered alternative in efforts around real estate usage, community and economic development planning efforts, nonprofit facilities investments, and as a means for supporting growth and innovation in small businesses.

7.0 **Responsibilities and Potential Uses:** Opportunities to create or lay a foundation to create shared space facilities should be considered during, but are not limited to, the following activities:

  a. Long range guiding community planning and development activities including neighborhood, corridor, and station area planning efforts.

  b. Economic development and/or revitalization plans created for specific properties or areas in the City.

  c. Use of City-owned real estate for community purpose outside internal City agency occupancy.

  d. Acquisition, disposal, or leasing of real estate by the City for public purposes.

  e. Provision of feedback by City staff to developers and commercial building owners considering options around potential use of commercial space.

  f. Investment in community facilities using City funds or formula or block grant funds.

  g. Creation of Innovation Centers for small businesses consistent with the Jumpstart Economic Development Strategic Plan.

  h. Development of Denver Seeds Initiative projects aimed at growing a local urban food economy and the elimination of food deserts in neighborhoods.

8.0 **Limitations:**

  a. When exploring use of City-owned real estate for community purpose outside internal City agency occupancy, agencies should ensure that they are meeting legal requirements and honoring pre-existing obligations to donors, grant providers, bondholders and certificate holders.

    i. The Department of Finance must verify the selected property is not subject to financing through bonds or certificates of participation which make it ineligible to participate in Shared Space Project.

    ii. The agency that operates the site must verify the selected property is not subject to other grant or funding restrictions which make it ineligible to participate in Shared Space Project.

  b. Use of City space shall be pursuant to lease, permit, licenses or other agreement with the City.

  c. Shared space should be used as a tool of mutual benefit to the City and to the community. Agencies may weigh the public benefit of creating a shared space opportunity against other substantive and real revenue generation possibilities for space resources when exploring shared space options.

9.0 **Memorandum Attachments:** The procedures for implementing this Executive Order shall be defined by Memorandum Attachments to the Executive Order, which shall become a part of the Executive Order. The Denver Shared Space Project City Coordination Committee shall work with impacted City agencies to develop procedures for implementing this policy directive.

Stories from the Field

A Strategic Use
of Municipal Assets
The Arts Factory

Marietta Kozak

Arts Factory, Vancouver, British Columbia

The author thanks Elia Kirby for his help and advice with this article but, more important, for being the major driving force, as well as the other half, of this co-location project.

Vancouver, British Columbia, like many cities in North America, has had real estate prices rise precipitously in recent years, and artists, among others, are leaving the city to find more reasonable rents. In 2012, as one measure to address this situation, the Vancouver City Council released an Request for Proposal (RFP) to renovate one of the City's own buildings into a shared artist studio space. The building is in a centrally located area; it anchors a seven-acre piece of land at the western edge of the False Creek Flats, the last remaining industrial lands in the centre of the City. This project allowed the Council to show its support for local artists while making use of a derelict, unused space. It also put a placeholder on the location for at least the length of the lease, allowing for a longer, more thoughtful planning process for the area. At the same time, the nonprofit partner in the renovation, the Arts Factory Society, was able to work toward its mandate to provide and maintain secure, safe, and fully accessible artists' studios to the downtown area, and to help service local arts organisations by providing a home for the Great Northern Way (GNW) Scene Shop (EKP Ltd.).

The result of this partnership was the Arts Factory building, a co-located artist studio and office space located in the False Creek Flats of Vancouver, British Columbia. It occupies approximately 21,000 sq. ft. in a World War II–era factory building. This building has been renovated from an empty warehouse to a space that serves a minimum of fifty people daily and includes offices, fabrication shops, a paint booth, a welding area, and working studio space for twenty-five practising individual artists. It also houses a wood studio that makes furniture from locally

FIGURE 26.1 *Gallery Walk, Arts Factory, Vancouver, British Columbia.* Visitors to the Arts Factory enjoy a narrated demonstration of a ceramicist creating a new piece in a gallery. *Photo credit: Tim Matheson, courtesy of the Arts Factory.*

felled wood, a props shop that builds for the local movie industry, and the anchor and founding tenant, a scene shop that supports and builds for the nonprofit arts sector in Vancouver. Visitors can enjoy art demonstrations at the Arts Factory, as shown in Figure 26.1.

HISTORY: THE FOUNDING OF THE ARTS FACTORY

The Arts Factory grew out of the GNW Scene Shop (EKP Ltd.), a for-profit company formed in 2009 that was originally an ancillary shop of the Department of Theatre, Film, and Creative Writing at the University of British Columbia. The GNW Scene Shop was an off-campus, satellite facility that built scenery for the local professional theatre and arts community. It was funded and directed by that academic unit to take advantage of a complex of buildings that had been donated to the four, large academic postsecondary institutions in Vancouver in the mid-1990s.

This shop was housed in a large warehouse at 555 Great Northern Way (hence the name). Over a period of ten years, it became an extremely important component of the local arts community, as it was centrally located and served as the only independent shop place to build sets in an overheated Vancouver real estate market, and it provided a visible nucleus and gathering place for the technical production activities that are so often invisible by their nature.

Once the future development and activities of the now burgeoning academic campus started to become clear (including a relocation of the Emily Carr School of Art campus from Granville Island), it became evident that it would no longer be possible to stay at the Great Northern Way site. At this point, to be eligible for available infrastructure funding from all three levels of government, the company's principals formed a stand-alone nonprofit organisation (Great Northern Way Scene Shop and Arts Factory Society, known as the Arts Factory) that was volunteer-run. The Arts Factory, however, did not register as a charity—in Canada, application for charitable status is not only onerous but also very tightly regulated, and the Society and its activities would not have qualified under federal tax legislation. Thus, the Arts Factory was founded, and it had (and still has) a mandate within its founding documents to be a facility developer and lease holder for multi-tenant arts buildings, including, but not limited to, the one that is discussed here.

This establishment of the nonprofit took place at the same time that EKP Ltd. was looking for another suitable location that would allow the company to continue to support local nonprofit arts organisations and maintain its core business. By this time, the company had started constructing scenery for several regional arts organisations, including the Vancouver Art Gallery and the Vancouver Opera, as well as maintaining its relationships with other performing arts companies and corporate clients, both large and small.

Initial federal and municipal infrastructure funding for the development of a leased building for the Arts Factory came through in the winter of 2011 for a similarly sized development at a separate location. However, this location's negotiations fell through, and the board of directors of the Society was able to negotiate with the funders to hold the grant while another site was located. Having created a needs assessment and preliminary plan for the failed project proved to be crucial as that made it possible to move quickly when another opportunity arose in August 2012: an RFP from the municipal government to develop artists' studios in a vacant building owned by the City of Vancouver.

Real estate prices in the Vancouver region had been increasing at a rate in the previous ten years that made urban living difficult and independent urban art production and practice even more so. New condominium and other developments had been displacing artists from old rundown buildings at a rapid pace; at the time that the City issued the previously mentioned RFP, 70,000 sq. ft. of artists' studios in three separate locations had been lost in one month to for-profit redevelopment. Because of these displacements, the City Council had been receiving pressure from artists and artist groups to address this loss of space. Because of this pressure, the City responded by looking at its own inventory of underutilised and older buildings that might be appropriate for use as an artists' centre and chose an old box factory for this purpose at 281 Industrial Avenue. The City staff subsequently released an RFP for this location, and the Arts Factory Society's response won the proposal to redevelop and lease the building long term.

The Arts Factory won the RFP because it had a number of pieces in place:

- Initial infrastructure funding from local and federal governments.
- An anchor tenant in the GNW Scene Shop (EKP Ltd.).
- General contracting and building capabilities in EKP Ltd.
- A needs assessment with community support now in place.

- The City of Vancouver's recognition of the opportunity and need to save the GNW Scene Shop as a production pillar of the fine arts and performing arts community.

Interestingly, the building mentioned in the RFP at 281 Industrial was one that Arts Factory Society had been looking at as a potential new location for a number of reasons: it was at grade; it had a series of east–west running north-facing sky lights; it was in the centre of the city and close to major transit stops; and it was zoned light industrial, which was imperative to allow for the scene shop's business, as well as allowing for and encouraging industrial art, something that is very difficult to house in urban settings because it generates noise and dust and other things that do not blend well with residential buildings. The Arts Factory has a commitment to working with industrial artists, partly due to the difficulties in housing that type of work and partly because of the nature of the anchor tenant's work, which would have an impact on any residential or nonindustrial neighbours.

With the winning of the RFP, fundraising from other levels of government and architectural planning accelerated. The Arts Factory had been working with a real estate specialist throughout the process, and this relationship was an integral part of the project's ultimate success. The two principals in the Arts Factory were not experienced real estate developers, and their having the guidance of someone who understood the complexities of leases, real estate development, and contracts made these elements ultimately achievable. Indeed, the importance of this individual cannot be stressed enough; many nonprofits will develop locations for themselves and end up in untenable situations because of not having the right expertise to guide them through increasingly complex development activities, real estate laws, and municipal building regulations.

The Arts Factory's success also cannot be discussed without acknowledging the support of the City of Vancouver. In the most expensive city in Canada, and one of the most expensive in North America, it would have been impossible for this project to move ahead, especially with a nonprofit mandate, without the help of the municipality. The City owns the land and the building, and as its contribution to the project (and a condition outlined in the RFP), it has leased it to the Society at a below market rate, in exchange for the Arts Factory guaranteeing low rent to the users. As part of the RFP, the Arts Factory did develop a business plan that included a co-located office space that provides a stronger income stream; however, the artists spaces were always intended to provide—and to this day do provide—working studios that are affordable, safe, and compliant with building codes.

CHALLENGES TO THE ARTS FACTORY'S DEVELOPMENT

Although 281 Industrial was a building with great bones for artists' studios (e.g., high ceilings, concrete floors, very little buildout so retrofitting and wall division was much easier, as well as other elements associated with an old factory), it had been left to crumble in previous decades. The building's envelope required a great deal of work, and there was lead paint that needed encapsulating (inside) and remediation (outside)—just one of the many things that is uncovered in old structures that are about to be renovated. The lease had been negotiated to have the landlord (the City of Vancouver) responsible for the envelope and the life safety systems, while the tenant (the Arts Factory Society) was responsible to fit out the studios and any other interior renovations that were part of the Society's business plan. This arrangement proved to be one of the areas of further discussion down the road, since, as is the case in all renovations, costs exceeded projections and the work took longer than expected—in some cases, a great deal longer.

Perhaps the biggest challenge in this project was the lengthy renovation time. While construction began in 2013, the building completed its final phase of development in February of 2017. This delay obviously caused some hardships for EKP Ltd, the anchor tenant, as it was homeless as of June 2012 and had to move twice to facilitate the changed dates, at the same time as it was directing the work on the interior of the structure. It was also problematic for the Arts Factory Society, as the building's opening had to be postponed so often that there were some repercussions regarding the studios taking a long time to be available for use from the very community that the organisation was there to serve. These repercussions were primarily negative feedback and some doubts through the arts community about the ability of the Society to finish the overall development. These concerns were able to be overcome when the building actually did open, but it could have been damaging if the Arts Factory had not completely lived up to the arts community's expectations.

Working with the City during this project proved to be both very helpful and daunting. Historically, many artists will occupy buildings that are available, regardless of the state of the structure or potential violations of the building code. Because the Arts Factory is a project in a city-owned building, all codes had to be followed, which made the renovations expensive and time-consuming, as compared to other ad hoc studio spaces that many artists are used to occupying. However, this compliance made for what is now a safe, comfortable, and generous space that has many amenities and can be used for various functions as well as being working artists' studios.

Both founders of the Society had worked in the nonprofit theatre sector for the majority of their working lives, and they had a strong understanding of the necessity of transparent policies in working with specific constituencies. Therefore, a number of practical and philosophical policies were written during the development and renovation period. Because of the City of Vancouver's participation in the location, it was necessary, and indeed desirable, to uphold the city's artist studio priority as outlined in the RFP: while this was certainly the purpose in the original proposal, it was necessary to enshrine that direction in the overall founding documents and to make it the overarching direction of all decisions that were being made.

Equally important was the adherence to the City of Vancouver's green objectives, outlined in its *Greenest City 2020 Action Plan*. In the renovations that were managed by the Arts Factory, efforts were made to uphold as much green construction as possible: using recycled rubber for floor coverings, reusing as much material from the building as possible, using wood, and sourcing second-hand and locally made furnishings in cases where that was an option.

THE BUILDING'S NORMS AND PRACTICES

As the use of the building has developed, so have various policies and norms. For example, a green objective remains a part of the ongoing operations: all waste is sorted, recycling is a part of the Arts Factory's services, and a complete policy on hazardous materials and their disposal is a required addendum to the tenants' and licensees' leases.

A co-located building was envisioned from the beginning of this project. The co-location model employed at the Arts Factory utilised a range of configurations, from artist studio spaces that are contiguous, to shared facilities such as kitchens, to a co-located office space that has bookable meeting rooms and hot desks, as well as monthly rentals as shown in Figure 26.2.

FIGURE 26.2 *Coworking Space at the Arts Factory.* The design of the Arts Factory included this "hot seat" area where individuals can work. This cultural hub is committed to offering accessible studio and administrative spaces in an environment that encourages collaboration, creation, and the exchange of ideas across disciplines. *Photo credit: Milena Salazar.*

These models were adopted partly for practical reasons—the layout of the windows on the ground floor meant that the only way that everyone would have natural light was if there were no walls between the artists' spaces. Additionally, to have created partition walls would have required more hallways that would have increased common area space and decreased usable studio space. However, the co-location model was also a part of the philosophy of the founders; it was felt that synergies and synchronicities were important to the overall success of the building and its occupants and that those interactions were to be encouraged as much as possible.

It is important to note that no policies requiring co-location events or activities are a part of this project. In the surveys that comprised the needs assessment, the initial findings were that visual artists generally want to work on their own, as opposed to having a community program of events (e.g., animation.). That being said, the resident artists have banded together on their own and hosted events on their own. And, while it is true that the open studio model does require an inclusive mindset on the part of the artists who work at the Arts Factory, it is also true that this has become an important character in the building's practices. To date, the most significant intertenant conflict arose when one of the artist tenants wanted to build partition walls around their studio. The other tenants objected to this walling as being contrary to the studio's (i.e., Arts Factory) principles that were now part of their own practice.

Because this was a project in partnership with by the City of Vancouver, the philosophy of the building's ultimate uses was determined early on through the terms laid out in the RFP and lease. The philosophy was mirrored in the nonprofit goals of the Society, and the conditions attached to the funding received for the renovations by all levels of government. Currently (in the early operational period of the building), ongoing policies and procedures are developed for the Arts Factory as the needs arise and are generally around public access, tenant relations, and special events and are discussed with the three members of the building's administrative team. While there is no formal process to include the resident/tenants, they are brought into overall policy conversations and discussions.

As with many nonprofit spaces in Canada, the Arts Factory's development was implemented on a volunteer basis by two people who had other jobs and were managing the renovations off the side of their desks. Therefore, an important part of the overall operations has been the hiring of a building manager, who is an assistant to the two principals but who has assumed all the operational administration of the building.

The biggest challenges around this renovation have been the ones that plague all projects that take on the repurposing of old buildings: time and money. The longer the work takes, the more lost opportunities there are for the leaseholder. These delays also create the potential for the core constituency to become disillusioned and negative, and their complaints often do get stronger with each passing month. Because there were significant renovations taking place (all the windows were replaced in the winter of 2016–2017), there were areas of the building still underutilised three years after building began. Managing the message is a significant part of ameliorating this situation, but perhaps the best way to deal with this issue is to be able to open and rent the building.

THE PARTNERSHIP WITH THE CITY OF VANCOUVER

There are many complications in partnering with a huge organisation like the City of Vancouver. Things move at a pace that is often not as fast as one would wish, and decisions can get held up because of differing departments and priorities. This is another area where an experienced real estate consultant can help to keep the landlord–tenant relationship on track and keep the project moving at a reasonable pace.

In a city like Vancouver, with sky-rocketing real estate values, the only way that an arts or similar nonprofit community can afford to control a large amount of real estate such as the Arts Factory is to have powerful partners or lots of money. In this particular case, the City of Vancouver Council, through pressure from local artists and because of its own political priorities, made the decision to have this project move forward; it provided the real estate as a base. It also provided significant funding through its own portion of renovation grant money and a below market rent lease agreement. In doing so, it gave up the potential for a very large sum of money, as the building occupies an entire city block in the middle of a revitalising and expensive area. There is no doubt that without its substantial and significant support, this centre would never have taken shape, and the arts community's ability to remain as a presence in the centre of the City would have been greatly diminished.

At a time when real estate can be cripplingly expensive, providing below market leases on city-owned buildings and land is a strong and relatively simple tool for civic governments to use in supporting local working artists. As of this writing (February 2017), the Arts Factory is 75% occupied, and there is already a long waiting list for artist studio space, while the open office space is about to be filled as construction has just finished. Events have been held in the gallery space, and there are anywhere between fifty and seventy-five people working out of the location on any one day including the weekends. Projects between partners are taking place. These joint projects arise casually and include everything from organising group shows and events together to multiples of partners creating work together.

CONCLUSION

In a complex and relatively large project like this one, there are a few key components that help to make the end result be successful, and they largely have to do with the quality of the partnerships. The nonprofit leaders of the renovation need expert advice and assistance, most oftentimes in the area of real estate expertise; the partners (in this case the City of Vancouver and the Arts Factory) need to have similar and concurrent goals, and there needs to be patience on all sides. In this example, it was a priority of the City Council to create this centre not only because of external pressures but also because of its own stated goals to support local artists and entrepreneurs. And, as in other cities in North America, the City owned a significant amount of land in its centre and had the ability to grant that land and buildings to nonprofits to fulfil its goals. With this project, the City was very generous in providing the land and building at below market rates and the partial funding through a capital improvement grant programme that covers one-third of the Arts Factory's Tenant Improvement budget.

Perhaps the most satisfying and rewarding part of the project is the amount the building is being used and the important part the building is already playing in the local arts ecology. What was once a derelict, empty warehousing building is now literally humming with activity and fifty to seventy-five people are working in it every day, creating art and commerce. Between the Scene Shop, and the Arts Factory Tenants, over one hundred projects a year are supported, hosted, or created in the building. Art work or projects created in the Arts Factory have travelled across the globe, won arts awards, and been prominently displayed in public and private galleries. Economically, the Arts Factory hosts twenty-four self-employed individuals/businesses/artists, twenty-six full-time employees, thirty to fifty full-time and part-time jobs, and approximately 150,000 annual hours of employment of middle-wage income earners.

The model of a City and a nonprofit partnering on this type of redevelopment fulfils goals that are beneficial to many parties: it provides accessible, affordable, safe, and stable studio and work spaces for professional artists; it creates synergies between different parties that result in long-term artistic and financial benefits; it helps to stabilise and revitalise industrial spaces while keeping the flavour and use of the area intact and viable; it encourages specialised employment through the businesses that anchor the building; and it is a gathering place and hub for the local arts community and a rich resource for the public, as shown by the person engrossed in an art creation in Figure 26.3. For these reasons, the Arts Factory is a project that is highly successful and has enormous benefits to all parties: the local community, the artists, and the City.

FIGURE 26.3 *Studio Space at the Arts Factory.* Public space at the Arts Factory adds richness to individuals' lives, since it allows them to simply enjoy or to contemplate some works of the artists. At the same time, the Arts Factory helps to support the artistic community and Vancouver's cultural life. *Photo credit: Milena Salazar.*

27

Rent Support in a Volatile Market
Sobrato Centers for Nonprofits

Megan Corning, Mara Williams Low, and Kelly Costa

Sobrato Family Foundation
Silicon Valley, California

Silicon Valley is undeniably one of the most competitive and volatile real estate markets in the country. In Santa Clara and San Mateo Counties, where the current asking price for office space is as high as $9 per sq. ft. per month, there are seventy nonprofit agencies whose rent is essentially free. These agencies are housed and co-located in three commercial nonprofit centers owned and operated by the Sobrato Family Foundation; they are known as the Sobrato Centers for Nonprofits (SCNPs). The fair market value of the in-kind rent provided by these Centers is estimated at $5.4 million a year.

Formed in 1996, the Foundation has a history and reputation of supporting Silicon Valley nonprofits as the region's largest place-based funder. See Box 27.1 for a description of their philanthropic philosophy. Since its origins, Sobrato has granted $47 million through in-kind office space. The Foundation is governed and led by the Sobrato family and funded by The Sobrato Organization (TSO), the family's real estate development business. As a company that has developed and leased corporate campuses to technology giants such as Apple and Netflix, the jump into providing space to nonprofits leaned on their real estate expertise, helped utilize their largest assets, and became known as the family's philanthropic "sweet spot."

CREATING THE FIRST SOBRATO CENTER

In 2002, during a Sobrato family meeting, discussion turned toward a 108,000 sq. ft. property in the portfolio located in Milpitas. As a twenty-five-year-old, five-building, multitenant complex of small businesses, it stood in stark contrast to the

Box 27.1 Authors' Note

The Sobrato Family is committed to building a strong and vibrant Silicon Valley community through business and philanthropic leadership. By promoting access to high-quality education, career pathways, and essential human services, the Sobrato Family Foundation (SFF) seeks to make Silicon Valley a place of opportunity for all its residents.

To support these efforts, SFF is a place-based grant maker that invests exclusively in nonprofits serving those most in need in Santa Clara, San Mateo, and Southern Alameda counties. The Foundation's portfolio utilizes both cash and real estate to achieve maximum impact, providing multi-year cash grants for general operating support, strategic and responsive program grants, and in-kind office and meeting space at its three nonprofit centers located in Redwood Shores, San Jose and Milpitas. Sobratos' cumulative community investments total $314 million between 1996 and 2014.

family's typically large and sophisticated single-tenant properties. In a conversation about the property's future, Lisa Sobrato Sonsini, Board President of the Foundation, suggested that the family donate it for nonprofits to use. There was some skepticism; Milpitas was not considered a thriving hub for nonprofit work, and its location was far from any major public transit systems or concentrated urban cores.

However, similar to today's market, rents were escalating. Nonprofit organizations lacked the resources to compete with the dominating technology sector, and many agencies were struggling to even remain in the region. As Lisa recollects, she was receiving calls from several nonprofits at the time who knew Sobrato's real estate reputation and who were desperately seeking rent support: "I think there was this notion that if we developed buildings, then we should be able to give away free space." She concluded, "Since we have a Foundation, we might as well be philanthropic in *everything* that we do."[1] Lisa recalls her father's, John A. Sobrato, openness to the idea—the notion of helping the community in a way that aligned with their real estate business was appealing. And so, the first SCNP developed in response to the difficult real estate conditions for Silicon Valley nonprofits, and it began as an experiment. See Box 27.2 for a response from a tenant.

Box 27.2 Tenant Feedback

Gabrielle Miller is National Executive Director of Raising a Reader, a national nonprofit headquartered in the Redwood Shores Center, with additional warehouse space in the Milpitas location. One key benefit of the SCNPs that Gabrielle commented on is the effect of the space and location on employee retention: "These nonprofit centers are the ONLY way an organization like ours could access Class A space, and this has a domino effect. When you're already at a bit of a disadvantage in hiring the very best talent because you happen to be a nonprofit, environment *really*, really matters" (Personal communication, March 13, 2015).

At the time, the Milpitas property had some for-profit tenants and some vacancies, which the Foundation began to fill with nonprofit organizations. There was no formal application process; tenant selection was relationship-driven and conducted via word of mouth. Since the original idea was to have a balance of for-profit and nonprofit organizations coexisting in the complex, the award was an office space jackpot—nonprofits paid absolutely nothing for rent, utilities, or maintenance, and their tenancy was subsidized by their for-profit neighbors. However, as for-profit companies moved out and nonprofit tenants took their place, the ability to maintain the complex as a "break-even" enterprise—and thus increase the potential for scale—was becoming less and less feasible. According to the Foundation's Program Director and long-term staff member, Mara Williams Low, "there was a tipping point when Milpitas became 60–70% nonprofits, and it was proving to be an unsustainable operation. . . . We were investing roughly $1 million per year in operating expenses and capital repairs."[2] With the sustainability of the Center in question, the decision was made to initiate Common Area Maintenance (CAM) fees to recoup the costs of utilities, janitorial, and general maintenance. This fee was introduced during the leasing process for new nonprofit tenants, while existing tenants were given a year's notice before they had to comply with the requirement.

Like for-profit companies, nonprofits require quality meeting space for board gatherings, trainings, and events. But high rates for Silicon Valley conference facilities prohibited access for many nonprofits, and the need for conference facilities at the Centers only grew over time. Conference rooms were not a part of the Milpitas complex at the outset, but when two of the larger for-profit tenants moved out, the Foundation seized an opportunity. They renovated the now-vacant building, investing approximately $450,000 and dedicating 8,000 sq. ft. to five conference rooms, making them available fee-free—not only to tenants but also to the larger Bay Area nonprofit community as well, as shown in Figure 27.1. As the Foundation's staff totaled two at the time, they hired a part-time Conference Center Coordinator and set up a self-service registration system to help make the cost structure sustainable. Based on the demand for the rooms at Milpitas, they recognized that having similar facilities in San Jose was critical; 9,000 sq. ft. of conference space was consequently carved out during that Center's build out.

GROWTH AND CHANGES

Even with CAM charges (assessed at $0.40 per sq. ft.), the Nonprofit Center in Milpitas was an incredible deal—and in high demand. Recognizing the nonprofit community's continued need for office space, the Sobrato's identified another building in the family's portfolio that could be converted into a nonprofit hub. This one was in a prime location—near a commuter train station and light rail, and in a major city with a flourishing nonprofit sector. In 2008, the Sobrato's opened their second Center in San Jose, adding another 105,000 sq. ft. of office space for the benefit of the nonprofit community.

FIGURE 27.1 *One of Many Gatherings at the Sobrato Centers.* Sobrato Centers for Nonprofits participants at a gathering in one of the many meeting rooms available to nonprofit organizations in the nonprofit centers created by the Sobrato Family Foundation. *Photo credit: Daniel Gaines.*

While the process of converting the Milpitas Center to a fully nonprofit-occupied facility had been a gradual one, San Jose was quite the opposite; the Center was donated, renovated, and reopened less than a year after the idea was first initiated. Like Milpitas, the San Jose Center selection process was by invitation—all but three of the organizations were hand-selected by John A. Sobrato. This was done in part out of necessity; while the Milpitas units were comparatively modest, some as small as 290 sq. ft., in San Jose, the units were between 7,000 and 20,000 sq. ft. As Mara noted at the time, "the universe of organizations that could use that amount of space was very limited, and John knew who those were."[3]

In addition to evolving financial considerations, the Foundation's practices in managing the Nonprofit Centers changed greatly over time. The Centers went through several iterations of property management, originally being managed by TSO with a part-time on-site property manager who reported to the business. In 2007, the Foundation assumed responsibility and outsourced the management services. This model was not a perfect fit, as Mara pointed out:

Outsourcing became a bit of a challenge because our business is so relationship-oriented. It seemed like it was going to be a huge plus, because being a landlord is very dissimilar to being a Foundation and a grantmaker . . . but it was actually harder to manage the relationships by using an outside group that didn't really get the business of philanthropy.[4]

Finally, in 2009, the Foundation brought management in-house by hiring a property manager as staff.

The Foundation was gaining a reputation for meeting a common need in a unique way—but, so far, only in Santa Clara County. In 2009, the Foundation conducted a needs assessment in San Mateo County and the results were clear: San Mateo County nonprofits were *also* clamoring for rent relief. Unfortunately, TSO did not own property on the Peninsula that could be donated and scaled to a size suitable for nonprofit tenants. This marked a significant moment in the evolution of the Sobrato Centers and a change in the family's perspective on the program. While Milpitas (and to some extent, San Jose) was experimental in nature, the effort to identify and locate the next Center on the Peninsula signaled the Sobrato's shift to an intentional, strategic investment.

In 2011, the Sobrato family went in search of a building to buy with no intention of turning a profit on it. They found what they were looking for in Redwood Shores—a waterfront community situated halfway between San Francisco and San Jose and home to a number of major technology companies including Oracle Corporation and Electronic Arts. The two-building complex would fit the needs perfectly, allowing Sobrato to subdivide the space into multiple-sized suites for nonprofit organizations at various stages in their development. It was not available for purchase, however, so the family was faced with the decision to enter a long-term lease for a building they would then sublease rent-free. Lisa found herself asking, "If we are going to actually pay money to rent someone else's buildings to then give the space away, what does that really mean?" In answering this question, the family acknowledged how important high-quality, dependable facilities were to the community: "We're doing this because of the added value and benefit beyond the dollars."[5] With that, they took out a thirty-year lease on the building shown in Figure 27.2 with the exclusive first right to buy should the property be put on the market.

FIGURE 27.2 *Repurposing Commercial Office Space.* This Silicon Valley office building in Redwood Shores was leased for thirty years by the Sobrato Family Foundation to provide office space for nonprofits. *Photo credit: Peter Carter.*

In late 2011, and for the first time, the Foundation launched a competitive application process to fill a Nonprofit Center. They received sixty applications for twenty suites in the first month. In assessing prospective tenants, they applied the joint lessons from their earlier Nonprofit Center experiences to the process. Priority was given to fiscally sound 501(c)(3) organizations with a three-year track record, who served 50% or more of their clients in the Foundation's geographic region and whose primary mission aligned with the Foundation's funding priorities. Key to the decision-making process was the applicant's ability to use the space effectively. As they had learned earlier, a hazard to offering space at such low cost was a tendency for organizations to overestimate the amount they needed; additional square footage was requested for "just in case" scenarios, allowing prime space to sit underutilized while other organizations lingered on the waiting list.

Another lesson learned involved the difficulties in co-locating organizations that provide direct, client-based services with organizations conducting primarily administrative activities. Mara explained, "A service or drop-in center open to the public requires a very different space design than an administrative office does. . . . It is really important that the office is well-suited to the type of operations, and the type of organization."[6] With that in mind, the Foundation sought out primarily administrative office tenants for Redwood Shores, recognizing that the physical plant and geographic setting of the Center were more suited to those activities.

While providing office space, the Sobrato's deepened their investment in conference facilities, staffing each Center with a full-time coordinator and upgrading each SNCP's resources with more sophisticated technology and design features over the years. The three Centers now offer a combined 28,000 sq. ft. of conference rooms to tenants and the larger Bay Area nonprofit community for free. The evolution in the quality of both office and meeting space demonstrates the growing recognition that nonprofits need more than the substandard space they can typically afford. High-quality facilities, like those shown in Figure 27.3, allows them to compete for talent, improve staff morale, and develop greater legitimacy with partners, funders, and clients. The Sobrato family was signaling to the community that those working on social innovation, just like those working on technological innovation, deserve a clean, safe, and comfortable working environment—impossible to come by without subsidy in this booming commercial real estate market.

HELPING TO BUILD A THRIVING NONPROFIT SECTOR

With all three Centers up and running, the Foundation was able to shift focus from facilities to more community development activities, toward the goal of supporting a thriving nonprofit sector. In 2013, they invested in a social networking tool to give their tenants increased access to one another, to share information and resources, and to invite one another to events. In 2014, the Foundation launched on-site capacity-building programming for their grantees, tenant partners, and the wider Silicon Valley nonprofit community. While more than 5,000 events were being held in the Centers annually, the Foundation itself was not, until then, playing a direct role in engaging and convening the tenant community. It was a void that they felt

FIGURE 27.3 *Raising a Reader Tenant Suite.* A teddy bear awaits the arrival of children for reading time at one of the Sobrato Centers for Nonprofits. *Photo credit: Daniel Gaines.*

needed to be filled to create greater community impact and realize the full power of co-location.

Today, the Foundation supports seventy nonprofit agencies at the three Centers. There is a large range in the types of space occupied: from a 58,000 sq. ft. combination warehouse/office unit used by a mainstage production company for administrative offices, rehearsal halls, costume storage, and a sewing shop, down to a few 215 sq. ft. cubicles belonging to small organizations in a shared office space. The types of needs provided for within the Centers are as varied as the spaces themselves. Of the 286,034 sq. ft. currently occupied at the three Centers, 41% is represented by human service organizations, 24% by community benefit agencies such as non-profit capacity-building providers and arts organizations, 23% by organizations with missions in education, and 12% by health-related organizations.

Through annual tenant surveys, a recent *State of the Sector Survey* completed by the Nonprofit Centers Network (NCN), and interviews conducted by a third party, the Foundation has had the opportunity to assess the benefits of the Nonprofit Centers beyond the cumulative annual cost savings of $5.4 million for its tenants. Anecdotal benefits are featured in Box 27.3 and Box 27.4 which detail comments from tenant organization leaders. As a customized part of the *State of the Sector Survey* conducted by NCN in 2015,[7] the Foundation learned that of forty-three executive directors across the three properties, 88% believe they have better space now than they did before they moved into the Centers, despite the fact that they are paying far less. In terms of the impact on organizational capacity, 88% of executive directors reported that both stability of their costs and their overall ability to achieve organizational goals had improved; 85% of those surveyed believed the credibility of their organizations had improved, and 89% saw increases in staff morale. Among programmatic impacts, 78% reported that the size of their programs had increased, and 80% reported that the scope had improved as a result of their tenancy.

Rent Support in a Volatile Market

Box 27.3 Life Under One Roof

Phil Santora is Managing Director of TheatreWorks, a Redwood Shores tenant and mainstage production company. Prior to their SCNP location, TheatreWorks had their operations split, with administrative services housed separately from their educational programs, rehearsals, and production. Phil discussed the increased potential for collaboration and innovation by consolidating all of these in one location at the Center: "One night we scheduled an auction and country western party on the same weekend as our student-playwright marathon. We had audience members and donors line dancing in one room, and teens who had been awake 20 hours writing plays in another room—there was an amazing energy. . . . All this creativity, fun, and community engagement happening in different rooms, at the same time. You got to see cross-pollination of communities that would not normally overlap, all in one location. Getting everything under one roof has been huge" (personal communication, March 13, 2015).

The Sobrato family and Foundation staff are delighted by the benefits their Centers have provided to the nonprofit community in Silicon Valley. The SCNPs play an integral role in the Foundation's efforts to increase the effectiveness, scalability, and systemic impact of their nonprofit partners and support the development of more high-quality nonprofit leaders. The Foundation's CEO Rick Williams commented:

Box 27.4 The Importance of Rent Support

Christa Gannon, CEO and Founder of Fresh Lifelines for Youth, is an early tenant of Milpitas whose programming and model expanded from Santa Clara to San Mateo County and whose office likewise expanded to the Sobrato Center in Redwood Shores. Christa remarked on the importance of having this type of rent support that allows nonprofit leaders to concentrate on their mission and core program work, rather than the logistics of securing space: "I see my fellow CEOs struggle with securing office space and know that is a really scary thing to do. There's a huge risk that they're constantly trying to mitigate, and I don't have to waste a second of emotional energy on that. That's huge, because it frees me up to worry about other things that I can move the needle on." She also noted that access to quality space helps elevate the sector as a whole: "Nonprofits are a really important economic driver of our community . . . and yet often as a society we have expectations that, well, 'you can work out of your car.' . . . So to have a professional, well-designed, efficient office space, that's how you build a nonprofit culture that we can all be proud of" (Personal communication, March 13, 2015).

Whether the Foundation plays host to other funders and networks, or we sponsor the programming ourselves, the SCNPs are terrific platforms for cross-sector collaboration. Organizations are able to engage with others doing similar or complementary work. . . . The conference center's reservation list shows hundreds of organizations holding thousands of meetings in the Centers each year. The Valley's social sector comprises many organizations, but in truth, it really is a small community, getting more connected every day. It's a privilege to play a role in that.[8]

Despite the resource-intensiveness in the current model, the family and Foundation remain committed to operating the three Nonprofit Centers in Silicon Valley. According to John A. Sobrato, "Our family's overarching goal is to build a strong and vibrant Silicon Valley community—because we know this community well, and they tell us what they need." He concluded, "This single-region focus means that, in both our business and our giving, we've built trust and understand regional needs. The SCNPs are our family's direct response to those needs, and we're deeply committed to supporting the sector with this vital resource."[9]

NOTES

1. Sonsini, L. S. Personal communication with Megan Corning, February 10, 2015.
2. Low, M.W. Personal communication with Megan Corning, February 3, 2015.
3. Low, M.W. Personal communication with Megan Corning, February 3, 2015.
4. Low, M.W. Personal communication with Megan Corning, February 3, 2015.
5. Sonsini, L. S. Personal communication with Megan Corning, February 10, 2015.
6. Low, M.W. Personal communication with Megan Corning, February 3, 2015.
7. Nonprofit Centers Network State of the Sector survey in 2015, customized research.
8. Williams, R. N. D. Personal communication with Megan Corning.
9. Sobrato, J. A. Personal communication with Megan Corning, April 21, 2015.

PART 10

SHARED SPACE AND NONPROFIT CENTERS AS A FIELD OF PRACTICE

28 Key Lessons to Learn from Earlier Nonprofit Centers

So far, this book has focused on current best practices for 21st-century nonprofit centers. But now we take a moment to pause and gather some additional lessons for today; they are drawn from the history of buildings for multiple nonprofits established beginning in the late 19th century through the end of the 20th century. This chapter presents an historical scrapbook of some important early pioneers in the field of shared space for nonprofits. Specifically, we profile notable centers established in the United States in three particular periods of time, honor their contributions, and glean lessons from some centers' experiences in each period that are still important to learn today.

These centers' founders, whether individuals or groups, were not all alike in their points of view. Rather, they established buildings for nonprofits out of a great variety of motivations. They were driven by their commitments to more efficient philanthropy and services, the ideals of Progressivism, memorialization of a departed loved one, religious ecumenism, more social integration and services available for children and adults with disabilities and their families, preservation of historical buildings, strengthening of their state's nonprofit sector, and better physical environments for downtown communities and for local service-providers.

NONPROFIT CENTERS: INITIATIVES FROM THE LATE 19TH AND EARLY 20TH CENTURIES

Nonprofit centers are not a very new idea. They have been present in the US since at least the last part of the 19th century; and across Canada, "mission-driven shared spaces . . . have long operated in service of a variety of social and hybrid missions."[1] Like all nonprofits, they reflect major social, cultural, and political trends and the goals and efforts of founders in their respective periods of time.

Examples of early nonprofit centers can be traced back at least to America's Gilded Age, which began in the 1870s and lasted until around 1900. This period was a time of rapid economic growth and rising fortunes in various parts of the US and Canada. "In the 1870s, there were just 100 millionaires in the United States. . . . In 1892, the *New York Tribute* counted over 4,000 millionaires."[2]

At the same time, millions of people suffered from social ills, including poverty, inadequate housing and sanitation, unsafe and exploitative workplaces, and poor health, shaped, at least in part, by the beliefs and policies creating this wealth.

However, some individuals with large new fortunes were influenced by what was called the "Gospel of Wealth," named after an article entitled "Wealth" written by steel magnate and philanthropist Andrew Carnegie, which appeared in 1889.[3] It put forth Carnegie's belief about the responsibility of the new, upper-class rich, namely, self-made men like himself, to act philanthropically. For Carnegie, this perspective "obligated him to return to society what he had taken, but he was determined to do so by following the same intelligent managerial principles that had made him a rich man."[4]

Carnegie and his peers were committed to large-scale projects for the improvement of humanity (or, "mankind," as it was then called); this commitment included their newly established philanthropic foundations, as well as other new, nonprofit institutions, such as John D. Rockefeller's University of Chicago, and the large universities named after Ezra Cornell and Leland Stanford. New hospitals and libraries also were established, institutions that could improve the lives of people in the community, as well as give public prominence to a donor's name. Thus, "these institutions exemplified massive capitalist wealth being converted into public assets."[5]

At least two buildings established in the Gilded Age could be called nonprofit centers today: the United Charities Building on Park Avenue South at East 22nd Street in Manhattan's Gramercy Park neighborhood, and the nearby Russell Sage Memorial Building, on the corner of Lexington Avenue and East 22nd Street. The presence of these two buildings, along with the headquarter buildings of other nearby charities, created the moniker, "Charity Row," for the three-block stretch of East 22nd Street and Park Avenue South.[6] They were located in one of today's most desirable neighborhoods in Manhattan.

The United Charities Building, New York, New York

This first nonprofit center, an impressive structure, was established in 1892, in response to the rising costs of New York office space rented by charities.

The idea of opening a building to house several charitable organizations had first been broached in 1885, but nothing was done about this proposal until 1890, when a subscription was started by the Charity Organization Society[1] to raise funds for the erection of such a structure. A year later, John S. Kennedy, a wealthy banker involved with several charitable groups, offered to pay the entire cost of the site and building.[7]

The original site included a 121,059 sq. ft. building; later, a three-story extension (1897) and four-story addition (1915) were added. The building was used as the headquarters of four prominent charitable institutions: The Charity Organization Society, The Association for Improving the Condition of the Poor, The Children's

FIGURE 28.1 *The United Charities Building, 105 East 22nd Street, New York, New York.* This image shows individuals lining up outside this building to receive assistance during the Great Depression. Taken by an unknown photographer, it was included in *Report of the Emergency Employment Committee, New York City, October 1930–July 1931. Source: CSS Photography Archives (Item 957; Photograph MP 130). Courtesy of Community Service Society of New York and the Rare Book and Manuscript Library, Columbia University, New York, New York.*

Aid Society, and The New York Mission and Tract Society. The building is pictured in Figure 28.1.

The United Charities Building also housed other nonprofits, including some of the Progressive Era's most influential labor and women's groups.

For example, it housed the organizations of leaders like Florence Kelley and researchers like Josephine Goldmark—women who helped mold the United States government's modern role in social issues. The coalition of organizations working in the United Charities Building, for example, convinced Theodore Roosevelt to establish the federally funded United States Children's Bureau, a group instrumental in ending child labor in America while also agitating for government regulation of contracts to promote improved labor conditions.[8]

In the 1990s, the contemporary nonprofit owners faced a time of changing welfare policies and uncertain funding. They were also dedicated service providers who understood the changing demography and the ascending real estate values in their historic locale. By selling their property, they would acquire new resources and could relocate to a less-expensive neighborhood where they could pursue their missions as well—or even better.

It was sold by the long-established charities' owners in 2014 for $128 million to a real estate developer. This action was also especially timely since the overall economy was still recovering from its recent fiscal crisis. The charities departed for other locations, and by mid-2017, the United Charities Building's interior was being gutted and leased as office and commercial space.[9]

The Original Russell Sage Foundation Building, New York, New York

Another historic nonprofit center came about through one of the oldest foundations in the US, the Russell Sage Foundation. It was established in 1907 for "the improvement of social and living conditions in the United States" by a gift of $10 million from Margaret Olivia Slocum Sage (1828–1918), widow of railroad magnate and financier Russell Sage.[10] "Mrs. Sage directed the new foundation 'to pursue research and programs for the improvement of social and living conditions in the United States of America,'"[11] and to pursue its mission through a broad set of activities, including "research, publication, education, the establishment and maintenance of charitable or benevolent activities, agencies and institutions, and the aid of any such activities, agencies, or institutions already in existence."[12]

Between 1907 and 1914, in addition to its more direct charitable activities,

the Foundation sponsored early research on programs in housing, public health, working conditions, education, consumer credit, industrial relations, social surveys, and social statistics. These programs lead to legal reforms in building codes, workplace health and safety regulations, workmen's compensation and anti-usury laws.[13]

In 1912, Mrs. Sage (as she was called) decided to establish a new building to both house the foundation and its expanding research operations and to serve as a memorial to her husband. She purchased property at 120 East 22nd Street, at the corner of Lexington Avenue.

Since the new headquarters building was planned as a memorial, more money was spent on the design and construction than would have been appropriate if it had simply been built to house the offices of the charitable group. . . . [The architect] adapted the form of a Florentine Renaissance palazzo to the needs of a modern office building.[14]

The foundation's new, nine-story headquarters building was built between 1912 and 1915 and is pictured in Figure 28.2. "The nine-story building is decorated with carved panels symbolizing Service flanked by Study and Counsel, Religion, Education, Civics, Justice, Health, Work, Play and Housing."[15] The foundation continued to sponsor and support many progressive activities[16] as well as to continue its applied research, which influenced government polies in such areas as the working conditions of women.[17]

What made this elegant building a nonprofit center in these early years? The foundation's new headquarters building not only housed the offices of the Russell Sage Foundation but also the offices of other social service organizations as well. For example, it included:

FIGURE 28.2 *Russell Sage Foundation Building, New York, New York.* Now known as Sage House, this former home of the Russell Sage Foundation and associated nonprofits was built in the style of the Italian Renaissance. It is in the same Gramercy Park neighborhood as the United Charities Building, once known as Charity Row. *Photo credit: Wikipedia Commons.*

the American Association of Social Workers and the Family Welfare Association of America. The charitable organizations housed in this building received their space at no charge. The two top floors of the building housed the Social Work Library, [then] one of the finest libraries of its type.[18]

Particularly interesting for this book is the innovation the Foundation undertook in 1929; it started a nonprofit center of its own to generate some income: "the foundation decided to expand the building by erecting a wing on East 22nd Street that was to be a profitable venture with space rented to social-service organizations."[19]

Given the broad charge Mrs. Sage gave to the first trustees in 1907 when she established the Russell Sage Foundation, the interpretation of its mission evolved over the years and changed significantly in the mid-20th century, after World War II. During the years 1945 to 1948, the early activism and the past emphasis on social service organizations and related professions was put aside in favor of developing social science research that might inform policy-making and better social science methodologies. The following steps were taken; "the Foundation . . . [phased] out all existing grants and direct financial support for charitable organizations, the original building . . . [was] sold, and staffing . . . [was] reduced." It then set about getting a more relevant building and enriching neighborhood to pursue its embrace of social science research.

In sum,

> in its early years the Foundation undertook major projects in low-income housing, urban planning, social work, and labor reform. [Today,] [t]he Foundation . . . dedicates itself exclusively to strengthening the methods, data, and theoretical core of the social sciences as a means of diagnosing social problems and improving social policies.[20]

In 1949, with the new direction of the Foundation, it moved from its large, stately building to more modern headquarters, a seven-story structure originally designed by the modern architect Philip Johnson, to which adjacent offices for scholars were established. "Together, the buildings [continue to] provide excellent facilities for individual research and collegial activities."[21] The Foundation is located at 112 East 64th Street, between Park and Lexington Avenues, where it is near a variety of educational, research, and philanthropic institutions.[22]

The Foundation's original building initially was sold to another nonprofit, the Archdiocese of New York, which used it for the offices of Catholic Charities. This building was sold again in 1975. Thereafter, in 1986, it was converted into a cooperative apartment building with 166 units and became known as Sage House."[23]

However, in 2000, the original building's historic importance was publicly recognized by its formal designation as a New York City landmark.[24] As for the Russell Sage Foundation, it has continued to develop new social science programs, to produce and to collaborate on social science research, and to disseminate new research that still reflects Mrs. Sage's goal to improve social and living conditions in the US.

Lesson Learned #1

Many years later, the leaders of these two historic nonprofit centers both made the decision to sell their current building. Their decisions were based on better actualizing the current meaning of their missions. Just as Chapter 3: Mission Comes First: How to Create a Nonprofit Center, encouraged readers that "Mission Comes First" in developing a nonprofit center, so too is it relevant for nonprofits making subsequent difficult choices. Thus, a lesson based on these historical examples that can be learned is as follows.

> Lesson Learned #1: In facing important decisions for your nonprofit organization, such as whether your individual nonprofit or your nonprofit center should remain or leave its long-established building and its neighborhood, use your organization's current mission statement as a decision-making tool. The mission statement should inform the strategic direction of the organization, including its real estate plans.

The leaders of these two historic nonprofit centers both made the decision to leave their current residences *based on their missions.* The three, long-established nonprofit agencies who collectively owned the United Charities Building had been strongly identified with their historic location for decades. But times were changing. From the 1990s onward, they encountered changing social welfare policies and uncertain funding; the gaps grew between their aspirations for serving their clients and their amounts of available funding.

As the Gramercy Park real estate strongly appreciated in the first part of the 21st century, the charity's owners found that their current building was worth many millions. They ultimately decided that their headquarters *could* be in another location, and they would best follow their mission by gaining more stable and more sizeable resources to serve clients.

In contrast, the original broad mission of the Russell Sage Foundation evolved and was reinterpreted as times changed. After World War II, when conducting and strengthening social science research became its lodestar, the original landmark building was sold, and a more modern and appropriate building close to other research resources became its new headquarters to serve its current direction.

It is also important to note that the 2014 announcement of selling the United Charities building raised alarms for some New York City observers, who had been noticing the vanishing of nonprofits from the so-called "Charity Row." So, for nonprofits and nonprofit centers in such positions, there may well be public criticism of their departures from various parties. So, they should be proactive and prepare a cogent press release and information sheet; they should invoke their current mission and state clearly that in their decision-making, "Mission Comes First!"

NONPROFIT CENTERS IN THE MID-20TH CENTURY

We now jump a few decades ahead to when further experimentation occurred with such centers and look at some notable nonprofit centers developed closely after World War II. Two notable examples that still exist today are the Interchurch Center, a faith-based nonprofit center located in New York City, and the Al Sigl Community of Agencies, a nonprofit center focused on the rehabilitation of children and adults, located in Rochester, New York. Although both centers were founded over half a century ago, they continue to embrace their original missions.

The Interchurch Center, New York City

The Interchurch Center is a nineteen-story, 660,000 sq. ft., limestone-covered office building located at 475 Riverside Drive and West 120th Street in the upper part of Manhattan in New York City. The Center was built in 1958 with gifts from John D. Rockefeller Jr. and other donors, together with a consortium of religious denominations. The purpose was to encourage cooperative work among such diverse religious groups as the Orthodox, African-American, and mainstream Protestant

FIGURE 28.3 *Interchurch Center, New York, New York* A mid-20th-century building housing a variety of faith-based organizations and other nonprofits. *Photo credit: The Interchurch Center.*

denominations, and to foster the growth of ecumenical bodies such as the National Council of Churches.

The Center's current occupants include mission boards, pension boards, and other agencies of several national denominations. Expanding on its original mission of providing a collaborative environment for a community of widely differing Christian denominations and their ecumenical activities, currently the Interchurch Center is the home of over seventy organizations, which represent community development, educational initiatives, social service, and intercultural and religious exchange.

Groundbreaking occurred in November 1957, President Eisenhower laid the cornerstone in 1958, and the building was dedicated in May 1960.[25] The significant height and notable presence of the Interchurch Center on the Upper West Side of New York City is shown in Figure 28.3.

The Al Sigl Community of Agencies, Rochester, New York

The Al Sigl Community of Agencies is dedicated to the care of children and adults with disabilities and special needs. This unique, multi-tenant and multi-site organization is located in Rochester, New York, not far from the south shore of Lake Ontario.

This organization, originally called the Monroe County Center for Rehabilitation Agencies (MCCRA), was founded in 1962. It was a period in which advances in medicine and other interventions could better address needs of disabled and special needs infants, children, adults, and their families. Moreover, with the presence of the Civil Rights movement, there was growing popular attention to recognizing and securing the rights of all individuals:

By the 1960s, disability advocates saw the opportunity to join forces alongside other minority groups to demand equal treatment, equal access and equal opportunity for people with disabilities. Disability rights activists mobilized on the local level demanding national initiatives to address the physical and social barriers facing the disability community. Parent advocates were at the forefront, demanding that their children be taken out of institutions and asylums, and placed into schools where their children could have the opportunity to engage in society just like children who were not disabled.[26]

The spirit of these times was also found in Rochester, New York, in 1962. There, parents and treatment personnel planned an innovative way for rehabilitation agencies to share space while they maintained their distinct missions and programs. Their vision was that agencies would be together in a model building with fully accessible classrooms, therapy suites, and work areas adapted for each agency, as well as a therapeutic swimming pool and gymnasium open to all.[27]

With the help of the community, this vision was achieved. The Al Sigl Center proudly opened the doors of its first building in 1968 and succeeded in meeting parents' concerns to have the services needed for their children be more accessible and concentrated in one site. The center was named for Al (Alphonse J.) Sigl (1886–1966), "a widely respected newspaper man and radio personality who took his fame and put it to work for the common good."[28]

His weekday broadcast began in 1931 with this simple introduction—"Howdy Neighbors"—and became the most highly-rated noon newscast in the United States. His tremendous popularity was a result of the trust he built with his audience, his giving spirit, particularly as a champion for people with disabilities and he made sure everyone was included.[29]

Al Sigl's generosity and leadership continue to be invoked at the nonprofit center named for him.

Al Sigl Community of Agencies Today

For more than fifty years, this organization, now called the Al Sigl Community of Agencies, has co-located rehabilitation organizations that serve its target populations on six different campuses. In addition, it has provided space for other community and voluntary nonprofits that have similar values and goals.

FIGURE 28.4 *Al Sigl Center Exterior, Rochester, New York.* This is the flagship building on Elmwood Avenue. The collaborative has grown to encompass six campuses serving over 55,000 people annually. *Photo credit: Al Sigl Community of Agencies.*

This nonprofit organization has grown from serving 3,000 people with abilities in the early years to now serving over 55,000 people.[30] It works together with its six Member Agencies: CP (Cerebral Palsy) Rochester, Epilepsy-Pralid, Medical Motor Service, National Multiple Sclerosis Society–Upstate New York Chapter, Rochester Hearing and Speech Center, and Rochester Rehabilitation.[31] A photo of its main center in Rochester is found in Figure 28.4.

This Community of Agencies is now "a collaborative community network that provides cost-effective real estate, business services and philanthropic support to a growing array of independent human service agencies that serve children and adults with disabilities and special needs."[32] This multisite nonprofit center has continued to expand its knowledge and practices regarding known and newly recognized conditions that disable individuals.

One such condition is autism spectrum disorder (ASD), and there are more than 10,000 people (adults and children) diagnosed with autism in the Greater Rochester and surrounding areas.[33] In 2018, the Al Sigl Community of Agencies announced the formal incorporation of the Golisano Autism Center, a new 25,000 sq. ft. collaborative shared space[34] in which the Al Sigl Community is one of the partners. This center will conveniently provide ASD resources to children, adults, and families by co-locating and coordinating specialized autism service providers together. The Center's comprehensive model also "emphasizes collaboration among complementary, autism-focused programs in the community."[35]

Lesson Learned #2

Neither of these mid-century nonprofit centers could have been built and operated without the dedication and commitment of volunteers. They have included philanthropists, people of faith, parents dedicated to help their children, and other individuals or groups trying to improve the world. They have contributed financially and fundraised, and they have served on various committees and governing boards.

Those who seek to establish and effectively operate their nonprofit centers, must include the topic of volunteers on their to-do lists.

> **Lesson Learned #2**: Carefully plan to reach out, cultivate, and nurture volunteers for your nonprofit center.

While there are a lot of resources available on recruiting, motivating, and managing volunteers and on nonprofit governance, there are five key tasks to undertake to help obtain and maintain commitments from volunteers.

1. *Define and prepare:* Before your center begins recruiting volunteers, take the time to first consider the various types and talents of volunteers your center needs. Rank which type(s) you need most, so you can develop criteria and better focus your search. Volunteering is a two-way street, so seek to understand which individual needs (social, educational, humanitarian, professional, etc.) volunteering could meet. Also, develop clear job descriptions for volunteers' positions. Spell out their expected time commitments so that mutual expectations will be clear.

2. *Recruit and orient:* Before your creative recruitment process begins, try to develop, and later distribute clear, welcoming orientation materials before they start working. Make sure someone welcomes and orients all volunteers to help them understand their roles and become more familiar with your center's space, schedules, and rules and any events in which they can participate (such as volunteer appreciation lunches, celebrations, and possibly training sessions).

3. *Expand roles:* Once your volunteers are more familiar, reach out and encourage selected short-term volunteers to become more involved if they have additional talents. They might play additional roles, such as committee members and could provide needed expertise and continuity, especially about real estate and management.

4. *Diversify:* Reach out effectively to recruit members of various communities, including those who historically have not been asked to become involved, so a broader array of ideas and approaches to your center's work can be gained.

5. *Care and nurture:* Monitor and attend to the care and nurturing of current volunteers—find out the variety of personal benefits they get out of volunteering and try to further facilitate such experiences; make sure that your volunteers are routinely recognized, celebrated, and honored, both formally and informally.

FOUNDATION-LED NONPROFIT CENTERS IN THE 1980S AND 1990S

In this last time period, several foundations became involved in new nonprofit shared space projects for a variety of reasons detailed in Chapter 24: Partnering with Allies.

Wilson Historic District (1981–Present)

Probably the largest nonprofit center initiative in the 1980s was undertaken by the Meadows Foundation in Dallas, Texas. It owns and operates the Wilson Historic District that it restored and opened in 1981 near downtown Dallas. (This foundation-based initiative is also discussed in Chapter 24.) Today, within its twenty-two-acre campus, as many as thirty-nine Texas-focused nonprofit organizations are housed in late 19th century, restored Victorian houses and other compatible buildings,[36] creating a charming neighborhood of nonprofits in which collaboration is expected. Their rent is paid for by the Meadows Foundation, and this project is "considered a benchmark for historic preservation and a model approach to housing nonprofits."[37]

This district is a favorite stop on visitors' tours of the city, especially when it is bedecked for winter holidays. Its positive impact now and for the future has been indicated by recognition as a City of Dallas Landmark District (for which less than one hundred areas have been chosen) and by the District's Wilson Block being listed on the National Register of Historic Places.[38]

Community Service Building (1997–Present)

In the 1990s, certain community funders and foundations in Delaware were being overwhelmed by the growing number of requests they received for capital improvements and repairs. To address this situation, they considered putting them all in one building. They subsequently visited Dallas to see what Wilson Historic District offered, and that visit helped them to see the benefits of opening a nonprofit center in their own state. They went on to fund the Community Service Building, a thirteen-story high-rise in Wilmington, Delaware, that was previously owned by the DuPont Corporation. The entire building was renovated, with the project funded mostly by Longwood Foundation dollars. The center opened in 1997. It houses over seventy-five tenants, making it one of the largest US nonprofit centers. Although all the nonprofits renting in the building directly serve Delaware, they represent a wide range of missions; they include organizations focused on various kinds of education, the arts, community development, small business development, technology, and more.

Other Foundation-Based Nonprofit Centers in This Period

Other foundation-based initiatives came about in this period as well. Two illustrations include (i) the Thoreau Center for Sustainability (now called Tides Converge) and seen in Figure 28.5, which was originally developed by Tides in 1996, and (ii) the NEW Center in Ann Arbor, Michigan. (NEW is an acronym for Nonprofit Enterprise at Work) developed by the McKinley Foundation and described in Chapter 17: From Grants to Earned Income.

FIGURE 28.5 *Thoreau Center for Sustainability, (now Tides Converge), San Francisco, California.* This historic army hospital is located in the Presidio National Park and was one of the first historic buildings renovated with green design in the US. *Photo credit: Saul Ettlin.*

Lesson Learned #3

Philanthropic foundations played an active role in establishing and funding new, large nonprofit centers between 1980 and 1999. Their endeavors took nonprofit centers to a new scale; they could now be found covering rejuvenated blocks of a major city and housing scores of nonprofits in a high-rise building. In the process, some foundations in this period have become literally closer to nonprofits (as was also found more than a century ago, in the Progressive Era's United Charities Building). For example, some Delaware foundations' headquarters co-located within the Community Service Building, and as part of the renewal of the neighborhood, the Meadows Foundation relocated and built its new, Victorian-style headquarters in the Wilson Historic District, not far from the Wilson Block of nonprofits. Since this 20th-century period ended, this pattern of foundation–nonprofit co-location has been further duplicated.[39] So here's a last lesson learned from this last historic period.

> **Lesson #3**: Foundations have a long history of establishing nonprofit centers. Learn about relevant examples, and as is articulated in Chapter 24: Partnering with Allies, cultivate your local foundation community.

CONCLUSION

Pioneers from various walks of life and organizations have built attractive—and even beautiful—real estate for the specific needs of nonprofit organizations and those they serve. Their endeavors in each period also provide at least three key lessons that are still relevant to nonprofit centers today: mission-based decision-making, cultivation and nurturing of volunteers, and seeking out opportunities with philanthropic foundations.[40]

NOTES

1. Katsnelson, R. and McFarlane, E. *Knowledge in Action 1: Corporate Structures and Regulatory Context.* Denver: Nonprofit Centers Network, 2016–2017, 1. Accessed March 31, 2018. https://www.nonprofitcenters.org/canadasr1/.

2. Zunz, O. *Philanthropy in America: A History.* Princeton, NJ: Princeton University Press, 2012, 12.

3. Carnegie, A. "Wealth." *North American Review, 391,* June 1889. Accessed April 1, 2018. https://www.swarthmore.edu/SocSci/rbannis1/AIH19th/Carnegie.html.

4. Zunz, O. *Philanthropy in America: A History.* Princeton, NJ: Princeton University Press, 2012, 1.

5. Zunz, O. *Philanthropy in America: A History.* Princeton, NJ: Princeton University Press, 2012, 9.

6. Zachary, K. "Cashing Out: Nonprofits Are Raising Funds by Selling Historic Headquarters on 'Charity Row.'" *Luxury Listings NYC.* May 6, 2014. Accessed April 1, 2018. http://www.llnyc.com/ neighborhoods/gramercyflatiron-2.

7. Gramercy Neighborhood Associates, Inc. "United Charities Building 105 East 22nd Street. Last revised August 31, 1998. Accessed April 2, 2018. http://www.preserve2.org/gramercy/proposes/ext/ension/105e22.htm.

8. National Park Service, US Department of Interior. "Places Where Women Made History: United Charities Building." National Register of Historic Places Itinerary. Accessed April 2, 2018. https://www.nps.gov/nr/travel/pwwmh/ny26.htm.

9. "CL Investment Launches Leasing Campaign at 287 Park Avenue." *Real Estate Weekly.* July 3, 2017. Accessed April 2, 2018. http://rew-online.com/2017/07/03/cl-investment-launches-leasing-campaign-at-287-park-avenue/.

10. See Russell Sage Foundation. "History of the Russell Sage Foundation." 2018. Accessed April 1, 2018. https://www.russellsage.org/about/history.

11. Russell Sage Foundation. "History of the Russell Sage Foundation." 2018. Accessed April 1, 2018. https://www.russellsage.org/about/history.

12. Russell Sage Foundation. "Trust." 2018. Accessed April 1, 2018. https://www.russellsage.org/research/trust.

13. Russell Sage Foundation. "History of the Russell Sage Foundation." Accessed April 1, 2018. https://www.russellsage.org/about/history.

14. Gramercy Neighborhood Associates, Inc. "Russell Sage Foundation (Now Sage House) 122–130 East 22nd Street." Last revised August 31, 1998. Accessed March 31, 2018. http://www.preserve2.org/gramercy/proposes/ext/ension/122_130e22.html.

15. Russell Sage Foundation. "History of the Russell Sage Foundation." 2018. Accessed April 1, 2018. https://www.russellsage.org/about/history.

16. Russell Sage Foundation. "History of the Russell Sage Foundation." 2018. Accessed April 1, 2018. https://www.russellsage.org/about/history.

17. For example, in 1910, Mary van Kleeck joined the foundation's Department of Industrial Studies to study the working conditions of women. Her book *Women in the Bookbinding Trade* led to legislation banning the employment of women in factories between 10 PM and 6 AM Russell Sage Foundation. "History of the Russell Sage Foundation." 2018. Accessed April 1, 2018. https://www.russellsage.org/about/history.

18. Gramercy Neighborhood Associates, Inc. "Russell Sage Foundation (Now Sage House) 122–130 East 22nd Street." Last revised August 31, 1998. Accessed December 21, 2018. http://www.preserve2.org/gramercy/proposes/ext/ension/122_130e22.htm.

19. Gramercy Neighborhood Associates, Inc. "Russell Sage Foundation (Now Sage House) 122–130 East 22nd Street." Last revised August 31, 1998. Accessed March 31, 2018. http://www.preserve2.org/gramercy/proposes/ext/ension/122_130e22.html.

20. Russell Sage Foundation. "About the Foundation." Accessed April 1, 2018. https://www.russellsage.org/about.

21. Russell Sage Foundation. "About/Headquarters." 2018. Accessed April 1, 2018. https://www.russellsage.org/about/headquarters.

22. Adapted from the Russell Sage Foundation. "History of the Russell Sage Foundation." 2018. Accessed April 1, 2018. https://www.russellsage.org/about/history.

23. Adapted from Gramercy Neighborhood Associates, Inc. "Russell Sage Foundation (Now Sage House) 122–130 East 22nd Street." Last revised August 31, 1998. Accessed March 31, 2018. http://www.preserve2.org/gramercy/proposes/ext/ension/122_130e22.html. Also see "The Sage House at 4 Lexington Avenue-Description." *Streeteasy.com*. Accessed April 2, 2018. https://streeteasy.com/building/the-sage-house

24. New York City Landmarks Preservation Commission. "Russell Sage Foundation Building and Annex, June 20, 2000." On an Incomplete List of New York City Designated Landmarks in Manhattan from 14th to 59th Streets. Accessed April 6, 2018. https://en.wikipedia.org/wiki/List_of_New_York_City_Designated_Landmarks_in_Manhattan_from_14th_to_59th_Streets#M%E2%80%93Z.

25. This history was reviewed and approved by the Interchurch Center. Personal email from Paula Mayo, Executive Director of the Interchurch Center, to China Brotsky, January 2018.

26. Anti-Defamation League. "A Brief History of the Disability Rights Movement." Anti-Bias Education Series. 2017. Accessed April 6. 2018. https://www.adl.org/education/resources/backgrounders/ disability-rights-movement.

27. Al Sigl Community of Agencies. "Celebrating 55 Years." 2018. Accessed April 7, 2018. http://www.alsigl.org/about-us/.

28. "Al Sigl." RocWiki: The People's Guide to Rochester. Last revised April 4, 2010. Accessed April 6, 2018. https://rocwiki.org/Al_Sigl.

29. Al Sigl Community of Agencies. "Our Namesake." 2018. Accessed April 7, 2018. http://www.alsigl.org/about-us/.

30. Al Sigl Community of Agencies. "Celebrating 55 Years: Mission Statement." 2018. Accessed April 7, 2018. http://www.alsigl.org/about-us/.

31. Al Sigl Community of Agencies. "Member Agencies." Accessed April 7, 2018. http://www.alsigl.org/member-agencies/.

32. Al Sigl Community of Agencies. "Celebrating 55 Years: Mission Statement." 2018. Accessed April 7, 2018. http://www.alsigl.org/about-us/.

33. See "Golisano Autism Center to Be Built in Rochester" [Press release]. AutismUp. (Rochester, NY). May 16, 2017. Accessed April 7, 2018. https://autismup.org/news/2017/golisano-autism-center-to-be-built-in-rochester.

34. "Golisano Autism Center Incorporated." March 1, 2018. Accessed April 7, 2018. https://www.alsigl.org/news/golisano-autism-center-incorporated/.

35. "Golisano Autism Center Incorporated." March 1, 2018. Accessed April 7, 2018. https://www.alsigl.org/news/golisano-autism-center-incorporated/.

36. Meadows Foundation. "Wilson Historic District." 2018. Accessed April 7, 2018. http://mfi.org/WHD.html.

37. Meadows Foundation. "Wilson Historic District." 2018. Accessed April 7, 2018. http://mfi.org/WHD.html.
38. Meadows Foundation. "Wilson Historic District." 2018. Accessed April 7, 2018. http://mfi.org/WHD.html.
39. See, for example, the shared space at the headquarters of the Charles A. Frueauff Foundation in Little Rock, Arkansas, which started in 2007. In 2018, there are four residents (selected nonprofits or foundations). This Foundation also offers its conference room, its smaller meeting room, and a resource room to all area nonprofits.
40. See, for example, Dundjerski, M. "Foundations Offer Shelter to Charities." *Chronicle of Philanthropy.* October 2, 1997, 9–10.

29 It Takes a Network to Build a Field

Lessons of the Nonprofit Centers Network

One of the key factors in the spread of the concept of nonprofit centers in the US and Canada has been the creation and growth of the Nonprofit Centers Network (NCN), a multi-sector, binational (the US and Canada) peer learning network.[1] A look at the history, successes, and challenges of NCN provides interesting and useful lessons in both the growth and evolution of such intermediary networks and the process by which new infrastructure models develop and spread in the nonprofit sector.

HISTORY OF NCN

In the fall of 2000, Tides,[2] under the leadership of China Brotsky, at that time the Vice President for Special Projects, had already created a 150,000 sq. ft. non-profit center, the Thoreau Center for Sustainability (now Tides Converge), located in historic military buildings on the decommissioned Presidio Army Base in San Francisco. Ms. Brotsky had also made connections to the academic work on non-profit centers being conducted by Dr. Diane Vinokur-Kaplan, an associate professor at the University of Michigan. Publicity about the Thoreau Center had brought a stream of inquiries about how to create a shared space nonprofit center, coming from as far away as Boston, Cleveland, and Toronto. Ms. Brotsky proposed the idea of a national conference to respond to these inquiries. She was soon joined in the effort by Marc Kasky from Fort Mason Center,[3] another pioneering nonprofit center in San Francisco, and by Tom Sargent from the local real estate development firm Equity Community Builders, developers of the Thoreau Center for Sustainability (now Tides Converge).[4]

In the beginning, the conference, titled Collaborating for Success, followed a self-organizing model, which would lead in 2004 to the creation of NCN. The first conferences relied on donations of space and human capital for their success. Outreach was mainly word of mouth starting with an initial list of eight existing centers around the country.

The workshops were all given by volunteer presenters engaged in relevant practice—ranging from nonprofit practitioners to commercial real estate developers, banks, and foundations. The conference set the model for future conferences with inspirational visits to local nonprofit centers and the inauguration of the popular workshop—Mistakes to Avoid—given by nonprofit practitioners who had recently opened centers. Almost a hundred people attended this first conference including representatives of a variety of nonprofit subsectors from across Canada and the US.

In 2003, a second conference was held in donated space at The Interchurch Center in Manhattan, again organized by Ms. Brotsky and Tides. In the lead-up to the conference, participants called repeatedly for some kind of ongoing network that could continue the education and networking practitioners were finding so valuable.

In the same year, a key philanthropic contribution from the Omidyar Foundation provided a $50,000 grant for a business plan and an organizing meeting; this was followed by a three-year $250,000 grant to create NCN. This grant allowed the hiring of NCN's first staff person in addition to the staff time of Ms. Brotsky (which was contributed by Tides through the first crucial years of NCN's existence). The formal start-up of NCN began in 2004 under the fiscal sponsorship of Tides. A steering committee was formed whose evolving membership played a crucial role in guiding the network and furthering its peer learning model.

Since its first conference in the spring of 2001, NCN has held seven more international conferences. NCN has also organized many regional conferences and trainings,[5] as well as presentations at other conferences and events. See a photo of one of these conferences in Figure 29.1. Attendance at the events has grown by outreach and by the word of mouth referral to NCN of new projects. Conscious efforts to move the educational events around the US and Canada disseminated the shared space strategy and reached and inspired new members.

The conferences have grown in size and complexity of material covered, but they have continued their basic model of peer learning and teaching. Networking

FIGURE 29.1 *Building Opportunities Conference Plenary.* A plenary from one of the eight international conferences that the Nonprofit Centers Network (NCN) has held since 2001. *Photo credit: Nonprofit Centers Network.*

among those present is seen as a key value of the meeting, in which experiences are shared and compared. Presenters continue to donate their time and pay their own travel and conference registration. Partnerships and sponsorships have also grown and evolved, including foundations and interested businesses and professionals. The largest conference to date was held in Vancouver in June of 2015 in partnership with the Social Purpose Real Estate Collaborative of Vancouver, British Columbia.[6]

The growth of NCN required an ongoing catalyst and organizer, the role played by Ms. Brotsky and NCN staff. But it also required a group of co-founders, primarily nonprofit center practitioners from both the nonprofit and foundation communities with some representatives from the real estate sector. These co-founders saw the value of the education and networking being provided by NCN. They shared a vision of the potential of the multi-tenant, shared space real estate model to catalyze a significant improvement in the infrastructure of the nonprofit sector in the US and Canada. Both the model and NCN filled a significant need for nonprofits who were grappling with real estate uncertainties, especially in cities buffeted by the first dot-com boom, the growth of the financial sector, and rising rents. A vision of affordable, quality space for nonprofits to carry out their work and collaborate arose first in the US and then was spread by pioneers in Canada. NCN provided the knowledge and skills needed to make their vision a reality.

A Cross-Sector Network from the Beginning

From the early 2000s, one of the distinctive characteristics of NCN was its cross-sector nature and the diversity of its participants. The idea for the first conference originated with two nonprofits, a progressive developer, and an academic. The first conferences were held at a center on federal land, and NCN was made possible by seed funding from a foundation. Banks, property developers, and real estate management firms all provided expertise and financial support. There has been significant participation from the philanthropic sector in governance. This cross-sector involvement has continued throughout the life of NCN, mirroring the diverse institutions who participate in creating and operating nonprofit centers.

At the same time, the mission of NCN has been very clearly focused on nonprofit capacity building, with all involved sectors seeing the importance of quality infrastructure for the nonprofit sector to carry out its important work.

Many nonprofit centers have the participation of government and commercial entities in both tenancy and development. As NCN has grown, foundations and government agencies in the US and Canada have used its services to create charitable shared space projects and provided funding for others.

A good example is going on in Vancouver where the Social Purpose Real Estate Collaborative in Vancouver defines their scope as "property and facilities owned and operated by mission-based organizations and investors for the purpose of community benefit, and to achieve blended value returns."[7] Examples range from health clinics to office buildings, homeless shelters to art centers, and social purpose coworking spaces. The collaborative is primarily made up of local funders and city government who are interested in social investing in general and reflected it in their

FIGURE 29.2 *2015 Conference Plenary.* Social Purpose Real Estate Collaborative and other participants at an interactive plenary at the Building Opportunities International Conference in Vancouver in 2015. *Photo credit: Nonprofit Centers Network.*

name. As previously mentioned, the Collaborative was a key partner in bringing NCN's international conference to Vancouver. Figure 29.2 shows the closing plenary in Vancouver.

Evolution of the Network

Many of the early participants in NCN steering committee and staff saw their work as a way to further social change in the US by providing nonprofit organizations the quality and affordable homes they needed to further community transformation and development. Many conference attendees talked about the "movement" for shared space. The green building movement was in its early stages, and many in NCN became vocal advocates for green buildings and energy efficiency in the nonprofit sector. This was an important stage in NCN's development as this commitment contributed to a culture of members donating their expertise in furtherance of that movement. This culture set an educational approach of broad participation that has lasted to the present.

As the needs of network members expanded, NCN staff broadened their services to provide a wider variety of learning vehicles and technical assistance. Consulting, especially on feasibility studies, became an important contribution to creating new centers while also serving as a revenue stream. Consulting expanded beyond real estate to the creation of shared services programs. The NCN team authored or commissioned studies and publications of interest to the field. Regular webinars were held for members and others.

As NCN grew and matured, it reached out more broadly to institutions such as schools, churches, community foundations and United Ways. Practitioners from

FIGURE 29.3 *Networking at NCN.* Chances to talk with others in the field occur at every NCN event. *Photo credit: Nonprofit Centers Network.*

Japan and Europe attended the conferences. Hundreds of shared space projects were initiated on both sides of the US–Canada border. NCN included some of the pioneers of the coworking movement in its conferences. Workshops were presented on hybrid for-profit/nonprofit structures like B corporations and social enterprises. Publications like *Stanford Social Innovation Review* covered the concept of shared space.[8]

While Canadians have led and participated in NCN from the beginning, the concept of nonprofit shared space has taken strong hold in Canada in more recent years. In recognition of this growing trend, NCN includes several steering committee members from Canada. Multiple regional conferences have been offered throughout Canada, and now a Canadian committee guides the work there, helping to build NCN Canada. Figure 29.3 shows networking at NCN's Vancouver conference.

Facing New Challenges

The hardest challenge in diversifying NCN has been in bringing in participants from low-income communities and communities of color, including Native Nations. Accumulating sufficient resources to buy buildings is often incredibly difficult for people of color led organizations, just like getting foundation funding in general. Fewer projects are developed by these under-resourced communities, at least historically. Those that are created are often embedded in projects developed by larger, majority white-led nonprofits. Another obstacle to participation in NCN has been the financial burden of travel and taking time out of busy schedules to participate despite NCN scholarships and travel stipends. NCN continues to support building the community assets, strength, and capacity of organizations led by people of color and low-income communities through sharing real estate expertise, including prioritizing outreach to those communities.

Recent years have seen an upsurge in shared space and land projects that are led and developed by people of color, LGBTQIA+, and Native activists, often in response to gentrification and displacement. Examples include the 23rd Street Community Building profiled in Chapter 10: Who Drives Decisions, the Freedom and Movement Center being created in Oakland, California, by Legal Services for Prisoners with Children and All of Us or None and the nation's first women-led urban Native American land trust, Sogorea Te, also in California.

One of the ways NCN has evolved to meet the needs of its constituents who lack funds for travel is increased use of digital communications. Member webinars and an online resource center provide remote access to both training and the networking that is so integral to NCN. Moving beyond one-day trainings or webinars, NCN began to create nine-month experiential learning experiences where center leaders worked virtually together and with an NCN leader to experiment with innovative ways to run their centers. (See Chapter 19: The Collaboration Project, for one such learning lab.) The next virtual lab created was on evaluation.

Following the successful 2013 international conference held in Denver, NCN made the strategic decision to leave its institutional home at Tides in San Francisco and move to Denver, Colorado, which has the largest concentration of nonprofit centers in the US. NCN found a welcoming home at the Alliance for Sustainable Colorado, a leading environmental nonprofit center (see Chapter 8: The Alliance Center). The move to Denver has allowed NCN to deepen its relationships with the Denver Shared Spaces initiative (see Chapter 25: Denver's Test Kitchen) and local funders who understand the model. In addition, this move has allowed NCN to recruit staff and steering committee members from the local community of practice. This move has positioned NCN for long-term success.

The formal terminology and definition of an expanded shared spaces field is still in process. As previously mentioned, "social purpose real estate" is one term being explored, especially in Canada. This terminology is a more accurate description of who can be served by NCN. But it has not yet reached the popular parlance in the US. One very recent development is in St. Louis, Missouri, where Social Innovation St. Louis is creating a network of shared spaces anchored by a regional hub under the rubric of social purpose real estate.[9]

NCN has continued to evolve over time. See the subsequent section Stepping Outside a Niche for some of the latest developments. And look out for a possible name change for NCN after this book is published.

LESSONS LEARNED
It Takes a Network: Efficacy of a Network in Building the Field

NCN, through its consulting and trainings, has added credibility to many proposed nonprofit center projects with local funders and government officials. As an external expert, NCN and its research have been useful in convincing them that such projects have successfully served important social purposes in other cities. NCN's support for well-planned real estate projects in the nonprofit sector, backed by reliable feasibility assessments, has drawn attention from real estate developers and municipal business development agencies. Armed with viable financial models, nonprofits in many cities can now more easily find for-profit developers and project managers interested in working on their projects.

Application of some of the basic lessons taught by NCN peers can make the difference between success and costly failure for those trying to create shared space projects. Real estate is not a core competency of nonprofit organizations, and overworked nonprofit executives too often try to reinvent the wheel when embarking on a real estate purchase or a shared space project. The basic lessons NCN teaches in its Nonprofit Center Boot Camps and Conferences prepare people to take the right first steps and do the work successfully. Figure 29.4 shows participants at a site visit to an existing center in conjunction with an international conference.

As shared space projects mature, many of the same questions arise about building tenant collaboration, building operations, and financial sustainability. NCN's research, peer learning sessions, and webinars present solutions to those common problems, which can be adapted for many different kinds of projects. The Energize series of workshops acts to network center managers to share lessons and new opportunities for their shared space. NCN's model of combining developed curriculum taught by staff with peer education taught by practitioners (whether

FIGURE 29.4 *Site Visit at NCN Conference.* All international conferences and many other regional events include site visits to centers, like this one to Magnolia Place in Los Angeles, where practitioners share their experiences with visitors. *Photo credit: Nonprofit Centers Network.*

done virtually or in person) is relatively inexpensive compared to other educational models. NCN was created specifically to support various kinds of social purpose shared space projects, and it provides collective resources that are often available elsewhere only from expensive consultants. The affordability and accessibility of NCN resources have been invaluable in spreading the nonprofit center model broadly with a very small staff.

NCN realized early on that the networking at its conference was as valuable to people as the formal content. Many practitioners are relatively isolated when there are few similar projects in their area. Meeting others doing the same work provides practical advice and builds morale and spirit. Jan Williamson, the Executive Director of the 18th Street Art Center in Santa Monica California, which combined nonprofit offices with performance, gallery, and studio space, talked about the benefits of joining NCN:

With NCN I learned about long term facility planning, day-to-day facility operations and collaboration among our residents. These are basic needs that neither my staff nor I ever found through our other peer networks in the arts. The visual/performing art networks focus heavily on programs, marketing and fundraising. But at NCN, everyone is talking about how your facilities work in service to your mission, and not just as an afterthought left for the maintenance crew to deal with. This is especially important when you are dealing with adaptive reuse buildings. With NCN, we had found our people.[10]

Figure 29.5 shows networking from one of NCN's international gatherings.

FIGURE 29.5 *Networking at NCN Los Angeles Conference.* The opportunity to network with others in the shared space field is one of the most valued features of NCN events, as shown at the Collaborating for Success International Conference in Los Angeles in 2011. *Photo credit: Nonprofit Centers Network.*

Evidence of Success of NCN's Work

As part of its strategic planning process in 2013, NCN commissioned national consulting group TCC Group to carry out an environmental scan and situational analysis that provided evidence on the efficacy of NCN in both helping individual projects flourish and impacting the broader field of nonprofit real estate. They also carried out an evaluation of NCN's products and services which surveyed 117 existing centers and 116 projects to create nonprofit centers—known as emerging centers in the field.[11] Key findings included:

- NCN's trainings, consulting and other resources had a very positive impact on the success of the users' shared space projects. "NCN Users are
  - 45% more likely to achieve positive outcomes related to efficiency and effectiveness than non-NCN users. (Those who didn't access NCN resources)
  - 25% more likely to achieve cost savings outcomes than non-NCN users.
  - 18% more likely to achieve operations outcomes than non-NCN users.
  - More likely to achieve positive collaboration, governance, and financial sustainability outcomes than non-NCN users (13%, 13%, and 14%, respectively)."
- "NCN is well known and respected within its niche market—the intersection of nonprofit real estate and collaboration."
- "NCN is valued above all (*by its participants*) as a network of practitioners; the extent to which the membership is maintained, leveraged and connected drives the value of NCN."

The Role of Human Capital in NCN Growth and Development

Human capital is crucial in organizational development. This is especially true of NCN where volunteers were predominantly senior nonprofit staff and board members who could leverage networks and resources. The first dedicated NCN staff person was not hired until 2008, and staffing has never exceeded four full-time staff. By strategically leveraging the generous contributions of expertise, time, and financial resources from active members and its steering committee, NCN leaders magnified their initial seed funding and built a well-respected capacity-building organization. This has continued to the present day as new members join the rotating steering committee bringing new ideas, energy, and resources. Figure 29.6 shows NCN staff and steering committee members.

The organization was created with a multi-source funding strategy that included membership dues. This membership structure has had several important impacts. It creates a stable revenue source. Even more important, the membership model creates an ongoing sense of connection with nonprofit center practitioners and those from other sectors who also become members. One clear sign of the efficacy of this model is the very successful Ask-NCN list-serv moderated by NCN staff and open only to members. Every query receives multiple responses, and there are often exchanges of templates and documents as well as advice.

FIGURE 29.6 *NCN Steering Committee and Staff.* NCN steering committee members and staff have come from every part of the US and Canada and provide essential program content and guidance to the Network. *Photo credit: Nonprofit Centers Network.*

Community building is an essential element of NCN's success. The lessons learned by members directly inform new best practices which are disseminated through trainings, publications, and online resources. Members are encouraged to suggest workshops and webinar topics, share their successes, and volunteer their time as speakers or as NCN program or steering committee members.

STEPPING OUTSIDE A NICHE—BROADENING NCN'S SCOPE

NCN was created originally as a peer network for practitioners creating and operating multi-tenant nonprofit centers. It served to disseminate the nonprofit center strategy across the US and Canada. Through its educational and consulting work NCN helped many projects get started. Over time, the nonprofit center niche has led to new, exciting, and strategic opportunities. Beginning formally in early 2018, NCN has decided to expand in other related directions. The real estate and collaboration skills and knowledge that NCN teaches are relevant to a much broader audience, including individual nonprofits entering the real estate market as well as those creating other kinds of social purpose real estate like healthcare homes, coworking spaces, and transit-oriented development.

Similarly, as centers mature and focus on building collaboration among their tenants and partners, NCN is an important thought partner in the effort to build nonprofit and cross-sector collaboration outside of shared buildings. NCN is expanding its resources on how nonprofits can access and create shared services programs. NCN is pursuing grant-funded research into best practices to grow the nonprofit sector's knowledge base on shared resources. Bringing together "unusual suspects" continues to be a signature of NCN's work as showcased at the 2017 and 2018 Sharing Innovation programs which have highlighted academics, software developers, community loan funds, and creators of nonprofit centers explaining their collaborative and ground-breaking ideas.[12] NCN is committed to reaching a broader constituency while continuing to serve its core membership of nonprofit centers.

THE ROAD TO SUSTAINABILITY FOR AN INTERMEDIARY NETWORK

As with nearly all small to mid-size nonprofits, NCN faces challenges achieving sustainable funding. But its character causes special obstacles shared by only some nonprofits. First, as an intermediary—an organization helping the development of other organizations and not doing direct service or advocacy—it faces the challenges of all intermediaries of articulating and establishing the critical needs it is filling. Using data provided by the centers at the 2009 international conference, NCN staff computed that in aggregate, tenants of the nonprofit centers participating served hundreds of thousands of people annually. But for many national funders, this connection has felt too remote to be compelling. NCN most often receives grant funding as support for local or regional workshops providing training to a foundation's core nonprofit constituents.

Similar issues exist with foundations that provide capital funding and are interested in nonprofit real estate. Most capital funding by foundations and government, if done at all, is carried out on a local or regional level. So, while individual shared space projects can obtain local capital funding, especially at start-up, most of these funding sources do not have funding for a national intermediary like NCN as part of their funding mandate. The exception has been a number of individuals and private foundations in both the US and Canada, which have either themselves been involved in creating shared space projects as part of their overall funding strategies or are invested strategically in the collaborative models of nonprofit centers and networks. John Powers was one of the first and most loyal contributors and he continues to support NCN with funding and space at the Alliance Center. The Lodestar Foundation, with its focus on collaboration, has been one of the most important recurring funders. At various times both the Omidyar Network and The Kresge Foundation have supported NCN's network building. A recent addition has been funding from the Robert Wood Johnson Foundation to study the systems alignment between nonprofit collaboratives and social determinants of health screening tools, allowing the broader community to understand how to better use limited health resources in the US. These funders have provided crucial support to NCN as it grows. Figure 29.7 shows funders, speakers, and staff at the Los Angeles conference.

Like its members, NCN operates as a social enterprise, deriving much of its financial sustainability from earned revenue. Grants from large and small donors and foundations are still a core part of NCN's financial model; however, membership dues, training registrations, and consulting fees constitute a growing percentage of the business model. Educational events, like Nonprofit Centers Boot Camp and Energize: High Impact Shared Spaces, expand the number of practitioners equipped to establish and successfully lead shared spaces while providing a pipeline

FIGURE 29.7 *Speakers, Funders, and Staff in Los Angeles.* Speakers, funders, and NCN staff at the NCN international conference in Los Angeles in 2011. *Photo credit: Nonprofit Centers Network.*

for consulting work. NCN's growing consulting practice provides opportunities to deepen the understanding of current challenges for nonprofits across North America, while developing new tools to share with the community. For over a decade, NCN's diverse portfolio of revenue streams has enabled NCN to continue its mission, and its staff, steering committee, and members continue to find innovative ways to support this growing community.

CONCLUSION

This chapter has shown how the movement for shared space nonprofit centers has grown and become institutionalized in NCN. NCN, in turn, has augmented its staff capacity with the human capital of its members, steering committee, and supporters to continue to educate individuals and communities about the benefits of this shared space and services infrastructure model. The network character of NCN has enabled its growth by leveraging its results beyond the size of its staff and funding and poised the network to reach a new and growing constituency.

The history of NCN clearly establishes the important role intermediary organizations can play in fostering an effective but complex infrastructure model like shared space and services. The creation of NCN has led to a twentyfold increase in nonprofit centers by pollinating the model and providing peer support.

NCN is an example of a successful intermediary organization. Intermediaries[13] are critical in advancing the nonprofit sector, but philanthropy's reluctance to provide consistent support, with a few key exceptions, has often limited their effectiveness. NCN's model of multiple revenue streams, including earned revenue as well as program income and philanthropic support, has proven necessary for this growing infrastructure network to sustain itself.

Even in this new digital age, physical convenings and trainings are shown to be instrumental in fostering community and the crucial exchange of ideas. At the same time, digital technologies are now providing more accessible and affordable ways for NCN to carry out its work and reach larger and more diverse communities.

NCN continues to provide a vital resource and hub to support the development of the new nonprofit centers opening every year. It also helps deepen the shared resources model by supporting the movement toward increased collaboration, knowledge sharing and shared services that is growing in the nonprofit sector.

Like all nonprofit organizations, NCN needs to continue to change and adapt as conditions and its constituency changes. Its staff and steering committee are committed to those changes and keeping NCN relevant and strong. But, as NCN enters its fifteenth year in 2018, the ongoing stories of nonprofit centers and shared services across North America provide the reward needed to continue its work.

NOTES

1. The NCN is an excellent resource for anyone working on a shared space project and can be reached at www.nonprofitcenters.org.
2. Tides is a US-based nonprofit intermediary organization working to accelerate the pace of social change. It works with innovative partners to solve society's toughest problems. Services provided include charitable grantmaking, fiscal sponsorship, collaborative workspaces and social impact consulting.
3. Fort Mason Center in San Francisco is a large arts-oriented nonprofit center housed in a former military embarkation facility that shipped soldiers to the Pacific theaters of World War II.
4. Equity Community Builders (ECB; http://www.ecbsf.com/) provides responsible real estate development and project management services focused on urban infill, sustainable development and adaptive reuse of existing buildings in Bay Area communities. They have managed the development of over forty projects with a total value more than $1 billion for their own account or on behalf of their many nonprofit clients. See Chapter 9: A Developer's Perspective: The David Brower Center for a nonprofit center project done by ECB.
5. These training and networking events continue. See www.nonprofitcenters.org.
6. See more on the Collaborative elsewhere in this chapter and at http://www.socialpurposerealestate.net/.
7. *Social Purpose Real Estate* (SPRE) is a term coined by the Social Purpose Real Estate Collaborative, a group of funders, investors, and government representatives in Vancouver, British Columbia. http://www.socialpurposerealestate.net/about/what-is-spre. See also Social Purpose Real Estate Collaborative. "Helping Mission-Driven Organizations with Their Real Estate Needs." 2017. http://www.socialpurposerealestate.net/.
8. Butzen, J. "Shared Space Strategies: An Interview with China Brotsky." *Stanford Social Innovation Review.* March 23, 2012. "https://ssir.org/articles/entry/shared_space_strategies_an_interview_with_china_brotsky. Butzen, J. "Expand Your Nonprofit's Mission Through Co-Location," *Stanford Social Innovation Review.* January 11, 2012. https://ssir.org/articles/entry/expand_your_nonprofits_mission_through_co_location.

9. Social Innovation St. Louis. "Regional Infrastructure." 2017. https://www.sistl.org/regional-infrastructure. See also the presentation at NCN's Sharing Innovation conference at https://www.nonprofitcenters.org/sharing2017/.

10. Personal conversation with Jan Williamson, Executive Director of the 18th Street Arts Center, Santa Monica, California, November 2016.

11. The TCC Group work, including the quotes included, were accessed by China Brotsky as a steering committee member of NCN and reprinted with permission.

12. Nonprofit Centers Network. "Sharing Innovation." 2018. https://www.nonprofitcenters.org/sivideos18/.

13. Another relevant term for NCN may be "backbone organization" as it is used in collective impact initiatives. See https://ssir.org/articles/entry/understanding_the_value_of_backbone_organizations_in_collective_impact_2.

30 Thinking Forward
Trends Encouraging More Nonprofit Centers

Is the increase in the number of nonprofit centers founded in the first decade of the 21st century going to continue? In terms of growth in available shared office space, the answer is yes. Now, in the second decade of the 21st century, there are expanding opportunities in many North American cities for nonprofit organizations to obtain rentals in shared spaces. For example, coworking space for entrepreneurs and small and emerging organizations has become very popular not only in the business sector but also among nonprofit centers as well.

In addition, some recent economic and social challenges that nonprofits have faced, and to which they have tried to respond, may well stimulate more centers to be developed or replicated. Two challenges in particular—first, continuing pressures on nonprofits' budgets and, second, funders' pressures for greater efficiency—may well encourage various interested parties to establish more nonprofit centers. Such moves would help nonprofits enjoy lower shared costs and be a viable response to continuing financial challenges. So while the nonprofit sector faces these headwinds, the increase in nonprofit centers represents a positive opportunity.

ECONOMIC PRESSURES ON NONPROFIT ORGANIZATIONS
Budget Pressures

Many US nonprofits suffered from significant fiscal stress during the financial downturn and Great Recession starting in 2007.[1] Salamon, Geller, and Spence[2] noted that during those years, there was a "perfect storm" of four specific factors challenging nonprofits' finances and causing budget pressures: (i) declining revenues and endowments of funders; (ii) increased costs overall; (iii) increased competition for financial resources; and (iv) lack of funding specifically for infrastructure. Some of these factors are currently still challenges.

Declining Revenues and Endowments of Funders

The two major sources of all nonprofit revenues are government funding and philanthropic giving (including individuals, bequests, foundations, and corporations). Nonprofits surveyed in a 2009 Johns Hopkins study reported that over a third (35%)

experienced declines in government support, and 37% percent reported delays in government payments. These findings may help explain why over half of those organizations reported cash flow problems.[3] These cutbacks were especially hard for human service nonprofits with 2009 contracts and grants from the government; half (50%) had frozen or reduced employee salaries, 39% had drawn on reserves, and 38% reduced the number of employees.[4]

Overall, more charitable nonprofits closed between the recession years of 2008 to 2012 than in the prior period, 2004 to 2008, with small organizations being the most vulnerable.[5] In addition, less money was given to nonprofits by individuals during the recession,[6] and philanthropic giving—bequests, corporations, and foundations—presented an overall story of stagnation or decline in giving from 2008 to 2011.[7]

From 2014 to 2016, during improving economic times, the amount of total giving continued to rise as it has during the last half century, apart from recessionary times. In 2016, total giving to US charities (around $390 billion), "rose 2.7% in current dollars (1.4% adjusted for inflation) from [almost $380 billion] total giving in 2015."[8] However, these figures do not show greater public generosity when looked at as a share of gross domestic product (GDP) or disposable personal income. As Benjamin Soltis recently noted:

the trend line of total charitable giving as a share of GDP . . . is notable for its flatness. For the past five decades, total giving as a share of GDP has hovered around the 2 percent mark. . . . Measures of individual giving as a share of disposable personal income have also generally held around 2 percent.[9]

So, while the number of dollars given has been rising, the overall percentages in national and individual giving behavior have stayed much the same, ever since they have been measured.

Moreover, there was continuing growth of registered charitable nonprofits; between 2003 and 2013, the number of registered US public charities grew 19.5% and totaled 954,476 in 2013, as compared to only 798,988 ten years earlier.[10] Canada has also seen growth in its charitable sector over the last decade or so.[11] If this growth trend continues (even though some nonprofits will close), there probably will be a net increase in the number of nonprofits seeking funding from limited resources.

Therefore, a growing number of nonprofits will continue to seek ways to decrease their expenses, since it is unlikely that a greater percentage of GDP or disposable personal income will be donated without inspirational leadership, effective marketing, dire events, or a noticeable percentage increase in donation patterns. Thus, the lower rents of nonprofit centers may well be attractive to even more nonprofits, and the demand for their establishment will increase.

In Canada, additional trends have also arisen that negatively affect charities' finances. One is the decline in household contributions going to charities, which have a special value for registered charities:

Donations may only contribute some 11% of charities' revenue, but their value lies in their being (mostly) unrestricted, unlike most of the money provided by governments, foundations, and corporate donors. This source therefore underwrites much of the operational costs of organizations in the sector; worse, it often subsidizes the other funding sources.[12]

Prior to 2007, donations by Canadian households to charities had generally been a steady percentage of Canada's GDP, roughly just under 0.5% of GDP; however, since 2007, the level of donations has fallen noticeably to 0.439% of GDP.[13] This pattern means that something is happening in the underlying behavior of donors. One influence is that the percentage of Canadians who file taxes and also claim charitable donations has been on the decline, from 25.7% in 1997 to 22.38% in 2012.[14] Additionally, the Canadian population of those who tend to donate the most is getting older,[15] suggesting that "charities are failing to attract younger donors who are entering the workforce for the first time."[16]

Religious institutions play a very large role in the Canadian charitable sector, and they place a significant emphasis on charity; but Brian Emmett and Geoffrey Emmett also note that Canadians are becoming increasingly less religious, which might help explain this fall. Also, some other possible explanations focus on younger Canadians' attitudes:

They may also feel that charities are not doing a good job and are failing to innovate. If charities fail to innovate, people might perceive them as old fashioned and ineffective, which would make them less likely to donate. It is also possible that people feel that the tax treatment they would receive for donating is not a sufficient incentive.[17]

Although the issue of donations is important, Canadian charities still receive the majority of their funds from the government.[18] A second possible trend is that government funding for charities could be cut were the party in power to seek to reduce the role of the government in the lives of Canadian citizens, as has happened in recent years.[19]

Actual and Threatened Increased Costs Overall

Despite the recovery and improved economic conditions since the end of the recession, many nonprofits still struggle with increased costs and a very uncertain future. There is high demand by the public for many services nonprofits offer, given changing demographics and longer life spans. But their provision requires nonprofits to have necessary revenues. There are still problems with late or insufficient payments on US federal, state, and local contracts that require boards to take out interest-bearing loans to cover the nonprofit's payroll. There are also threatened cost increases in the near future for all kinds of equipment, supplies, and other budget items. There are many cost uncertainties stemming from recently passed pieces of legislation (such as US tax reform) and from policies being circulated on such topics as charitable deductions, overtime work, and adequate health insurance coverage.

Under these uncertain circumstances for nonprofit and charitable organizations, nonprofit centers, with their below-market rents, present an attractive alternative to the more expensive commercial market. Moreover, their policies that promote shared costs (e.g., for meeting space or equipment), their potential economies of scale from group purchasing and discounts, and their encouragement of collaboration all help counter rising and unpredictable costs. These characteristics of shared space are especially germane for smaller, vulnerable nonprofits, those with less than $1 million in expenses who represented more than three-quarters of reporting US public charities, as previously shown in Figure 1.2.[20]

Increased Competition for Resources

US nonprofits face competition and displacement from the private sector in areas where they had previously dominated, such as daycare, education, health, and individual and family services. There is also competition for resources from newly developed forms of social benefit corporations, such as low-profit limited liability companies (L3Cs), B corporations, and some social enterprises.[21] These corporations include for-profit or low-profit companies who wish to pursue a social or environmental mission. They may approach potential funders that have traditionally funded charitable nonprofits, making the competition for resources rise even more.

However, the emphasis on collaboration in nonprofit centers could help their tenants to work better together and present a more collective and higher profile to funders in order to compete more successfully for resources.

Lack of Resources for Infrastructure

The plight of nonprofits' infrastructure has been frequently noted in this volume, especially among those providing services to socially excluded or low-income clients. Managers of various kinds of nonprofit and charities want to meet such needs as more housing for the homeless, more spacious and safe playgrounds for children in nonprofit daycares, necessary repairs for apartments of the elderly, and better designed, accessible space and effective technologies for staff and clients. But often they have limited opportunities to obtain adequate grants, or loans with reasonable financing terms, to improve their sites, technologies, and services.

Fortunately, there are some exceptions. For example, in recent years, the New York State Government successfully allocated $120 million over fiscal years 2016–2018 to the state's Nonprofit Infrastructure Capital Investment Program. "The first $100 million allocated enabled nonprofit human services providers across the state to repair, reinforce, expand and update their physical and technological infrastructure."[22] Yet, of the 600 nonprofits who applied, only 237 received funding. The probability of adequate funding to meet this great existing need to improve nonprofit infrastructure is not high. However, if and when more funding to improve infrastructure does become available, be it via philanthropic, government, and/or private sectors, new nonprofit centers and those needing improved infrastructure may have a better chance to receive such funding, given the efficiencies of nonprofit shared space sites.

Funder Pressure to Run Nonprofits "More Like a Business"

The second trend already commenced several decades ago; there has been a continuing drumbeat to view and treat nonprofits as businesses. This trend, sometimes called "commercialism"[23] or "new public management" among public administrators,[24] does recognize the services that nonprofits provide, but it firmly underlines the need for more efficiency, innovation, and cost containment among them; it "emphasizes not the professional skills of doctors, educators and social workers [as in the past], but rather of the professional manager and his/her business-oriented skills"[25]

There is some upside to these newer management approaches; this trend creates the context to make the financial benefits of nonprofit centers more understandable and salient to some funders and investors, and it may help gain their support for investing in them. Indeed, nonprofit co-locations, shared services, and collaboration are in tune with this new context. Moreover, these approaches underline evaluation and accountability, which are necessary activities of any high-performing organization.

However, in considering the charitable nonprofit sector as a whole, this intense, competitive ethos that has pervaded it, with an emphasis on applying short-term performance metrics, runs the risk of undervaluing the contributions of some nonprofits to the public good. For instance, how can the performance of advocacy or policy nonprofits be assessed in a valid, quantitative way when they produce fewer short-term, easily obtained measures of outcomes to prove their successful performance?

Similarly, the short-term business perspective that currently characterizes many business investments and government budgets does not encourage measurement of the longer-term and qualitative outcomes that many nonprofits produce for individuals, communities, and society, for example, in education, religion, and the arts. Moreover, in at least some cases, the adoption of this short-term perspective has encouraged some nonprofits who were competing for funding to decrease or eliminate their requests for needed overhead funds—funds that could at least maintain their infrastructure.

Indeed, government, private donors, and foundations have all contributed to a phenomenon often called the "nonprofit starvation cycle," where they do not pay adequately—if at all—for overhead costs. The corrosive effects of this trend have been discussed by professionals[26] as well as empirically documented for the last twenty-five years.[27] While some headway has been made—for instance, with some foundations willing to give general support or to act more like a bank by providing program-related investments or lower-cost loans that can be used for operations and infrastructure—it remains an ongoing issue.

Specifically, this concept shows "a debilitating trend of under-investment in organizational infrastructure that is fed by potentially misleading financial reporting [caused by nonprofits competing to show they cost less to donors] and donor expectations of increasingly low overhead expenses."[28] In other words, to effectively compete for funding, nonprofits make themselves appear less expensive—and therefore more attractive to funders—by asking for less indirect costs than they actually require. This lack of needed overhead funds means that there is less money available to spend on training and escalating rents or to maintain and improve current nonprofit workplaces and their technology infrastructures.

Moreover, at least in the recent past, nonprofits faced many difficulties in accessing investment capital, which they need "to finance the facilities, technology, and innovations required to remain viable in an increasingly competitive environment."[29] For example, in 2006, Salamon and Geller found that 77% of nonprofits they surveyed reported they needed capital for acquisition/renovation of buildings or land.[30] Despite this great need, less than 40% reported they had secured funding for buying or improving these sites over the last three years.[31]

Here, nonprofit centers can be helpful to nonprofits, since they usually acquire or manage the space and its infrastructure, as well as the building's repairs. It is one less hurdle for nonprofits' executive directors and their boards.

SUMMARY AND CONCLUSION

There are at least two economic trends that may encourage the development of more nonprofit centers, given the more economical, below-market rents centers charge their nonprofit tenants and the shared space, resources, and services they provide.

One trend is the continuing and probably growing budget pressures, where there is not enough funding to cover nonprofits' needs adequately, especially in regard to maintaining and improving their infrastructure. However, some new philanthropic finance models have emerged in the US that may support more nonprofit centers, as discussed in several previous chapters. In Canada, there is growing attention to "social purpose real estate," nonprofit reuse of underutilized buildings (see Chapter 26 on the Arts Factory), and community-based models of more integrated service delivery (see Chapter 11 on Toronto's Community Hubs).

Serious financial pressures remain on the budgets of US nonprofits who must fend for funding in a period of many changes; which includes shifts from past government priorities and budget allocations, potential discouragement of charitable giving from new tax laws, and an ever-growing US federal deficit that puts downward pressures on federal, state, and local spending for social services, education, the arts, and other areas served by nonprofits. In contrast, in Canada, despite some financial pressures, there is growing appreciation of the charitable sector as a meaningful part of the economy.[32]

A second economic trend is the pressure from funders for nonprofits to be run "more like a business," with metric-measured efficiency and performance, an approach that began in the 1980s. This outlook has also been adopted by many foundations.[33] Given the current shifts in national priorities found in the US government, which do not emphasize many of the causes in which charitable nonprofits are involved, it is probable that government and other funders will continue their demands for greater efficiency among nonprofits. This prediction is especially probable because given the growth trend in the nonprofit sector, there will be continuing competition among even more nonprofits for funding from philanthropy, government, individuals, and the private sector.

These two socio-economic trends, while difficult for organizations to weather on their own, may well positively influence more nonprofit centers being developed and expanded in new and different areas in the US. Appreciation of Canadian nonprofit centers is also being promoted by the Nonprofit Centers Network–Canada, supported by the foundation Tides–Canada.[34] The efficiency of nonprofit centers, together with their business-like approach to cover their costs, will be attractive to parties that could invest in them, as well as to the nonprofits who will become these centers' tenants.

NOTES

1. A research team at Johns Hopkins University's Center for Civil Society Studies investigated the impact of the 2007–2009 economic recession on nonprofit organizations, using their nationwide sample of over 1,400 nonprofit organizations in five key fields: children and family services, elderly housing and services, education, community and economic development, and the arts. A full 80% of these nonprofits reported some level of fiscal stress during the target period of September 2008 to March 2009; moreover, close to 40% of these organizations considered the stress to be "severe" or "very severe." See Salamon, L. M., Geller, S. L., and Spence, K. L. *Impact of the 2007–09 Economic Recession on Nonprofit Organizations.* Communiqué No. 14 of the Listening Post Project. Baltimore: John Hopkins University, Institute for Policy Studies, Center for Civil Society Studies, 2009, 1. Accessed March 5, 2018. http://ccss.jhu.edu/publications-findings/?did=252.

2. See Salamon, L. M., Geller, S. L., and Spence, K. L. *Impact of the 2007–09 Economic Recession on Nonprofit Organizations.* Communiqué No. 14 of the Listening Post Project. Baltimore: John Hopkins University, Institute for Policy Studies, Center for Civil Society Studies, 2009, 4–8. Accessed March 5, 2018. http://ccss.jhu.edu/publications-findings/?did=252.

3. Salamon, L. M., Geller, S. L., and Spence, K. L. *Impact of the 2007–09 Economic Recession on Nonprofit Organizations.* Communiqué No. 14 of the Listening Post Project. Baltimore: John Hopkins University, Institute for Policy Studies, Center for Civil Society Studies, 2009, 5. Accessed March 5, 2018. http://ccss.jhu.edu/publications-findings/?did=252.

4. Boris, E. T., de Leon, E., Roeger, K., and Nikolova, M. *Human Service Nonprofits and Government Collaboration: Findings from the 2010 National Survey of Nonprofit Government Contracting and Grants.* Washington, DC: Urban Institute–Center on Nonprofits and Philanthropy, October 2010, 19, Figure 8. These authors conducted a survey of what happened during the last recession to nonprofits in human services that had received government contracts and grants. They used a national random sample of nonprofit human service organizations with more than $100,000 in expenses in eight human service program areas. They found that the recession had exacerbated financial problems faced by these human service nonprofits.

5. Dietz, N., McKeever, B., Brown, M. S., Koulish, J., and Pollak, T. H. *The Impact of the Great Recession on the Number of Charities by Subsector and Revenue Range.* Washington, DC: Urban Institute, June 23, 2014, 1. Also see Brown, M. S., McKeever, B., Dietz, N., Koulish, J., and Pollak, T. H. *The Impact of the Great Recession on the Number of Charities.* Washington, DC: Urban Institute, October 16, 2013. https://www.urban.org/research/publication/impact-great-recession-number-charities. They note: "According to NCCS (National Center for Charitable Statistics) data, the charitable nonprofit sector proved surprisingly resilient during and after the Great Recession (2008–12), with only a small increase in the percentage of organizations closing their doors as compared to the period directly before the recession (2004–08)" (Abstract, 1).

6. Reich, R. and Wimer, C. 2012. *Charitable Giving and the Great Recession.* Stanford, CA: Stanford Center on Poverty and Inequality, 2012, 3. https://inequality.stanford.edu/sites/default/files/CharitableGiving_fact_sheet.pdf. Also see a recent related study using the Panel Survey of Income Dynamics: Meer, J., Miller, D., and Wulfsberg E. The Great Recession and Charitable Giving. *Applied Economics Letters, 24*(21): 1542–1549, 2017.

7. Reich, R. and Wimer, C. *Charitable Giving and the Great Recession.* Stanford, California: Stanford Center on Poverty and Inequality, 2012, 3. https://inequality.stanford.edu/sites/default/files/CharitableGiving_fact_sheet.pdf.

8. Giving USA Foundation. *The Annual Report on Philanthropy for the Year 2014, Report Highlights.* Chicago: Giving USA Foundation, 2015, 39; Giving USA Foundation. *The Annual Report on Philanthropy for the Year 2015, Report Highlights.* Chicago: Giving USA Foundation, 2016; Giving USA Foundation. *The Annual Report on Philanthropy for the Year 2016, Report Highlights.* Chicago: Giving USA Foundation, 2017.

9. Soskis, B. *Giving Numbers: Why, What, and How Are We Counting?* Washington, DC: Urban Institute, March 2017. https://www.urban.org/research/publication/giving-numbers-why-what-and-how-are-we-counting.

10. McKeever, B. *The Nonprofit Sector in Brief 2015: Public Charities, Giving, and Volunteering* (Brief). Washington, DC: Urban Institute, October 29, 2015, 2–3, Table 1. https://www.urban.org/sites/default/files/ publication/72536/2000497-The-Nonprofit-Sector-in-Brief-2015-Public-Charities-Giving-and-Volunteering.pdf.

11. Emmett, B. and Emmett, G. "Charities in Canada as an Economic Sector" (Discussion Paper). Toronto: Imagine Canada, June 22, 2015, 15. Accessed March 9, 2017. http://www.imaginecanada.ca/sites/default/files/imaginecanada_charities_in_canada_as_an_economic_sector_2015-06-22.pdf.

12. Brodhead, T. "On Not Letting a Crisis Go to Waste: An Innovation Agenda For Canada's Community Sector." *The Philanthropist, 23*(1), 2010. Accessed March 8, 2018. https://thephilanthropist.ca/original-pdfs/Philanthropist-23-1-402.pdf.

13. Emmett, B. and Emmett, G. "Charities in Canada as an Economic Sector" (Discussion Paper). Toronto: Imagine Canada, June 22, 2015, 24. Accessed March 9, 2017. http://www.imaginecanada.ca/sites/default/files/imaginecanada_charities_in_canada_as_an_economic_sector_2015-06-22.pdf.

14. Emmett, B. and Emmett, G. "Charities in Canada as an Economic Sector" (Discussion Paper). Toronto: Imagine Canada, June 22, 2015, 25. Accessed March 9, 2017. http://www.imaginecanada.ca/sites/default/files/imaginecanada_charities_in_canada_as_an_economic_sector_2015-06-22.pdf.

15. Emmett, B. and Emmett, G. "Charities in Canada as an Economic Sector" (Discussion Paper). Toronto: Imagine Canada, June 22, 2015, 25. Accessed March 9, 2017. http://www.imaginecanada.ca/sites/default/files/imaginecanada_charities_in_canada_as_an_economic_sector_2015-06-22.pdf.

16. Emmett, B. and Emmett, G. "Charities in Canada as an Economic Sector" (Discussion Paper). Toronto: Imagine Canada, June 22, 2015, 26. Accessed March 9, 2017. http://www.imaginecanada.ca/sites/default/files/imaginecanada_charities_in_canada_as_an_economic_sector_2015-06-22.pdf.

17. Emmett, B. and Emmett, G. "Charities in Canada as an Economic Sector" (Discussion Paper). Toronto: Imagine Canada, June 22, 2015: 26. Accessed March 9, 2017. http://www.imaginecanada.ca/sites/default/files/imaginecanada_charities_in_canada_as_an_economic_sector_2015-06-22.pdf.

18. Emmett, B. and Emmett, G. "Charities in Canada as an Economic Sector." (Discussion Paper). Toronto: Imagine Canada, June 22, 2015, 26. Accessed March 9, 2017. http://www.imaginecanada.ca/sites/default/files/imaginecanada_charities_in_canada_as_an_economic_sector_2015-06-22.pdf.

19. Emmett, B. and Emmett, G. "Charities in Canada as an Economic Sector" (Discussion Paper). Toronto: Imagine Canada, June 22, 2015, 27–28. Accessed March 9, 2017. http://www.imaginecanada.ca/sites/default/files/imaginecanada_charities_in_canada_as_an_economic_sector_2015-06-22.pdf.

20. McKeever, B. "Figure 1. Number and Expenses of Reporting Public Charities as a Percentage of All Reporting Public Charities and Expenses, 2013." In *The Nonprofit Sector in Brief 2015: Public Charities, Giving, and Volunteering* (Brief). Washington, DC: Urban Institute, October 29, 2015, 4. Accessed April 3, 2018. https://www.urban.org/sites/default/files/publication/72536/2000497-The-Nonprofit-Sector-in-Brief-2015-Public-Charities-Giving-and-Volunteering.pdf.

21. For further discussion, see Salamon, L. M., ed., *New Frontiers of Philanthropy: A Guide to the New Tools and New Actors that Are Reshaping Global Philanthropy and Social Investing.* New York: Oxford University Press, 2014.

22. Shack, F. "Gov. Cuomo, Increase the Nonprofit Infrastructure Capital Investment Program." *New York Nonprofit Media*, January 31, 2018. Accessed April 4, 2018. https://nynmedia.com/knowledge/gov-cuomo-increase-the-nonprofit-infrastructure-capital-investment-program. Also see the proposed 2019 New York State Division of the Budget. "Nonprofit Infrastructure Capital Investment Program." Accessed April 4, 2018. https://www.budget.ny.gov/pubs/archive/fy19/exec/agencies/appropData/NonprofitInfrastructureCapitalInvestmentProgram.html.

23. Salamon, L. M. (Ed.). *The State of Nonprofit America.* Washington, DC: Brookings Institution Press, 2012, 18.

24. Osborne, S. P. (Ed.). *The New Public Governance? Emerging Perspectives on the Theory and Practice of Public Governance.* 1st ed. New York: Routledge, 2010.

25. Salamon, L. M. (Ed.). *The State of Nonprofit America.* 2nd ed. Washington, DC: Brookings Institution Press, 2012, 18.

26. For the original article, see Gregory, A. G. and Howard, D., "The Nonprofit Starvation Cycle." *Stanford Social Innovation Review*, Fall, 2009, 48–53.

27. Lecy, J. D. and Searing, E. A. M. "Anatomy of the Nonprofit Starvation Cycle: An Analysis of Falling Overhead Ratios in the Nonprofit Sector." *Nonprofit and Voluntary Sector Quarterly*, 44(3), 539–563, June 1, 2015. https://doi.org/10.1177/0899764014527175.

28. Lecy, Jesse D. and Searing, Elizabeth A. M. "Anatomy of the Nonprofit Starvation Cycle: An Analysis of Falling Overhead Ratios in the Nonprofit Sector." *Nonprofit and Voluntary Sector Quarterly*, 44(3), 539–563, June 1, 2015, abstract, p. 539. https://doi.org/10.1177/0899764014527175.

29. Salamon, L. M. and Geller, S. L. *Investment Capital: The New Challenge for American Nonprofits.* Communiqué No. 5 of the Listening Post Project. Baltimore: Johns Hopkins

University, Institute for Policy Studies, Center for Civil Society Studies, 2006, i. http://ccss.jhu.edu/wp-content/uploads/downloads/2011/09/LP_Communique5_2006.pdf.

30. Salamon, L. M. and Geller. S. L. *Investment Capital: The New Challenge for American Nonprofits*. Communiqué No. 5 of the Listening Post Project. Baltimore: Johns Hopkins University, Institute for Policy Studies, Center for Civil Society Studies, 2006, Appendix, Table 2:12. http://ccss.jhu.edu/wp-content/uploads/downloads/2011/09/LP_Communique5_2006.pdf.

31. Salamon, L. M. and Geller, S. L. *Investment Capital: The New Challenge for American Nonprofits*. Communiqué No. 5 of the Listening Post Project. Baltimore: Johns Hopkins University, Institute for Policy Studies, Center for Civil Society Studies, 2006, Appendix, Table 3:13. http://ccss.jhu.edu/wp-content/uploads/downloads/2011/09/LP_Communique5_2006.pdf.

32. Emmett, B. and Emmett, G. *Charities in Canada as an Economic Sector* (Discussion Paper). Toronto: Imagine Canada, June. 22, 2015, 26. Accessed March 9, 2017. http://www.imaginecanada.ca/sites/default/files/imaginecanada_charities_in_canada_as_an_economic_sector_2015-06-22.pdf.

33. Salamon, L. M. *The Resilient Sector Revisited: The New Challenge to Nonprofit America*. Washington, DC: Brookings Institution Press, 2015, 44.

34. Tides Canada. "NCN Canada publishes "Knowledge in Action" Shared Spaces Learning Series." (Media Announcement). April 20, 2017. https://tidescanada.org/media/ncn-canada-publishes-knowledge-in-action-shared-spaces-learning-series/. (Titles included in this series of three research briefs are: Knowledge in Action 1: Corporate Structures and Regulatory; Knowledge in Action 2: From Start-up To Sustainability – Emerging Business Models; and Knowledge in Action 3: Proving and Improving – Evaluation in Shared Spaces. All are available for download, free of charge, at http://tidescanada.org/about-us/reports-publications).

PART 11
CONCLUSIONS

31 Looking to the Future

In an increasingly uncertain world, many nonprofits embody a culture of empathy and caring and promote values of diversity and inclusion. As the safety net continues to erode in an era of budget cuts, the environment frays, and inequality surges, these nonprofits represent people coming together to make the world a better place. Their work, whether it is advocacy or service, arts or health, is more important than ever.

Given the growing size of the nonprofit and charitable sectors, with more than 13 million employees across Canada and the US, the over 700 nonprofit centers existing or in progress are just the beginning of creating quality, affordable work space for all nonprofits that need it.

This book describes a cutting-edge infrastructure model—the nonprofit center—which can, and is, making a difference in the effectiveness and financial sustainability of nonprofit organizations. It is a proven model that propels organizations forward toward better meeting their missions and creates positive impacts for the communities where they are located, and even society as a whole.

SO WHERE DO WE GO FROM HERE: A CALL TO ACTION

We have showed how the shared space model has propagated from a few known nonprofit centers to hundreds across the US and Canada in twenty years. What is necessary for the continued growth of this model in the next twenty years? It is to nurture allies and to invest in the continued creativity of the field.

The Role of Allies in Supporting the Field with Resources and Research

In states and provinces across North America, foundations, government agencies, for-profit developers, and the community development field have grasped the efficacy of the model and the concrete difference it can make for nonprofit organizations and those they serve. Escalation of that support—including funding, real estate expertise, and research and policy—is crucial to advance the field and propel momentum.

The many ways philanthropy supports shared space has been outlined in other chapters of this book. In particular, the support of intermediaries and local foundations has been instrumental in establishing new shared spaces. Community foundations and other funders that are active in local communities can and have played a unique role exactly because of their roots in the community. Picking an issue area like human services and providing support for a one-stop center or a shared services program for nonprofits can be transformative, as illustrated by the Community Hubs created by the United Way in Toronto (see Chapter 11: Building Community, Not Just Buildings). The leadership of organizations like the Sobrato Family Foundation is another example of how foundations can help propel this model forward (see Chapter 27: Rent Support in a Volatile Market). These institutions are leading examples of how to support local organizations not only with grant support, but through organizational capacity building. More community-based foundations should follow suit.

More research is needed on shared space and services, especially an update of the comprehensive 2011 NCN study. Support for intermediaries like NCN and the Community Development Financing Institutions (CDFIs) that support nonprofit centers can make possible that research and facilitate the peer learning that has fueled the model.

Nonprofit centers are about place and placemaking. A number of individual donors, real estate developers, corporate sponsors, and entrepreneurs have embraced this model exactly because of their commitment to their local place and the nonprofits that serve it. They've brought expertise to the field, created innovative projects, and at times given the general support and seed money that is so hard to raise for new projects. An increase in these examples would qualitatively advance the field.

Rather than retreating from the capital needs of nonprofits, governments have an important role to play in enabling the creation of new centers. First, government can provide financial support through capital grants and loans. Second, it can enable the repurposing of unused government facilities, in both high and low rent areas, for the use of shared nonprofit facilities. Specific government policies, like Denver's Executive Order 138 mandating city support of shared space, would help municipalities meet the needs of local nonprofits. (See Chapter 25: Denver's Test Kitchen for more information on Order 138.) And grants and other programs to encourage collaboration and the tackling of social issues on a collective level can be facilitated and led by the public sector.

As we've described elsewhere, the cities of Vancouver and Denver, the US National Park Service in the Presidio of San Francisco, and the Province of Ontario are examples of where this public sector support has existed. With their financial and real estate assets, cities, provinces, and states are uniquely positioned to serve in a leadership role in the shared space field.

There are also public policy changes that can create a richer environment for shared space. Changes in US tax policy that would extend the reach and amount of New Market Tax Credits, especially for nonprofits would be very helpful, as would creative use of the new Opportunity Zone program. And changes that would make it easier for nonprofits to utilize historic tax credits would be strong incentives to expand nonprofit real estate projects. In Canada, the creation and implementation of similar tax credits and the loosening of restrictions on non-profits carrying out income-producing activities would give a significant boost to the field. In both countries, adapting property tax exemptions to allow for-profit tenancy in buildings run by nonprofits would also facilitate the financing of nonprofit centers.

In the US, recent large reductions in the corporate tax rate make both charitable contributions and acquisition of tax credits potentially much less useful for tax savings by for-profit businesses and reduce resources for nonprofits. In that context, the role of philanthropy and government in supporting the nonprofit sector is magnified.

Creative Real Estate Thinking

Several real estate trends, occurring especially but not exclusively in the US, are creating opportunities that can leverage the growth of nonprofit centers. One factor in enabling centers is whether there is affordable real estate available. Outlined in the following text are three real estate opportunities and related strategies that can help provide that real estate.

Aging Buildings

Given the historical development of North America, there is a surplus of aging buildings, factories, and polluted lots in cities, older suburbs, and rural areas. They take a toll on effective land use, contribute to blight, and are costly to maintain and repair. However, they often have the advantage of being in centralized areas and near public transportation. Moreover, there is growing public attention to the need to repair aging infrastructure and nonprofit centers can harness this momentum.

While complicated, creative individuals and organizations have developed such buildings and sites into nonprofit centers, especially in cities seeking to renew their urban cores. A successful example is NEW Center, a nonprofit center built on the remediated site of a former junkyard near downtown Ann Arbor, Michigan. In Dallas, Texas, the Sammons Center for the Arts houses fourteen arts organizations and provides services and performance space for more than one hundred, all in the Historic Turtle Creek Pump Station. Old train stations have been used several times to create nonprofit centers. Evergreen Brick Works has created a demonstration hub of sustainability as a social enterprise in an old multi-building brick factory near Toronto, Ontario.

Excess Infrastructure

In gentrifying cities where light industry has been forced out or in cities with declining industries and depopulation, there may be opportunities for nonprofit centers to arise in underutilized buildings. Nonprofit arts centers, in particular, have thrived in declining industrial areas since old factories have the space and height for their needs. Fairhill Partners in Cleveland, Ohio was developed at a former US Marines Corp hospital and now serves older adults and also provides opportunities for lifelong learning and intergenerational relationships. Churches have also transformed underutilized properties to create community assets. Take, for example, the Link Center in Tupelo, Mississippi, which serves as a regional hub for arts and education organizations in a former Baptist church.

The Challenge of Finding Affordable Real Estate: Sharing Larger Spaces

In areas of rising prices and expensive rents, individual nonprofits, small businesses, and new social enterprises may lack the resources to enter the commercial market as owners or lessees. Creatively bringing these entities together to occupy larger spaces and share their financial resources has been an effective strategy in Denver, Toronto, Seattle, and elsewhere.

Each of these strategies requires real estate creativity, financing know-how, a willingness to collaborate and commitment to a social mission. Cross-sector collaborations between real estate developers, nonprofits, and government hold the key to realizing this potential.

ROLE OF PRACTITIONERS IN EXPANDING THE FIELD

What will be necessary to recruit allies and encourage growth? This book, by documenting the benefits, impact, and successful implementation of the nonprofit center model is intended to help support that growth. But just as powerfully, it is people talking to people—in local areas, at conferences and convenings, in articles, and in speeches and events that celebrate the collective accomplishments of centers—that will effectively move the adoption of this model forward.

The first twenty years have been about propagating the model center by center, executive director to executive director. Now that successful examples exist in virtually every state and province, growth could become exponential. And the most successful ambassadors are those who have done it successfully. The field of nonprofit centers needs to embrace its role as a social entrepreneur, thinking big about solutions and replication and growing the solutions that develop. It needs to expand into the arenas of shared services in their buildings and serving nonprofits beyond their buildings. The field needs to build partnerships in cross-sector real estate, including coworking and larger mixed-use developments. NCN and NCN Canada have important roles to play in this growth as field-wide representatives and advocates.

The growth of the nonprofit sector itself creates an urgency for creative solutions that include shared space and resources. Practitioners' willingness to undertake and support these collaborative, complex endeavors demonstrate the increasing sophistication of on-going efforts to make positive social change.

FINAL LESSONS

Creating a nonprofit center is a complicated process. Projects don't always succeed or they succeed initially and then may face insurmountable economic and financial obstacles. The road to success is often long and circuitous, but tenacious leaders have proven over and over that the model is achievable. Our goal is that the lessons we have laid out in this book can lead to many more successes—financially sustainable projects that create positive, long-lasting impact in their communities and in the world. The following can help insure project success.

1. *Be flexible.* There is not one rigid template for nonprofit centers. They can be adapted with great flexibility for local conditions once the basic model and process for development are understood.

2. *Find a champion.* Champions are needed to create nonprofit center projects. Are there one or several individuals who are in it for the long haul? Most successful projects have had champions who hold the vision and organize the project for the long term.

3. *Gain allies.* Once the champions spring into action, it is essential to then gather allies and reach out to the community. Going it alone can result in burnout and the loss of momentum as difficulties arise. It is important to marshal the necessary resources from allies including from philanthropy, government, the for-profit sector, and the wider community development field.

4. *Understand the numbers.* Real estate is a business, even if done for social purposes. The necessity for starting with a good business plan, sound financial projections, and a sustained focus on the budget and cash flow is crucial.

5. *Pick wisely.* Don't fall in love with a building; fall in love with your project's purpose! Make sure that the real estate you pick is affordable to build or renovate and then operate. Then design your space to reflect the mission and goals of the project.

6. *Be patient.* Projects take longer than you ever imagined, and partnerships are wonderful but time-consuming—be prepared. Patience is important. Start small and build community and supporters as you go. Can you collaborate before you co-locate, lease before you buy, or start in interim space to prove the model to local stakeholders?

7. *Don't reinvent the wheel.* Learn from those who have gone before. The Nonprofit Centers Network (NCN) is a good place to do that. Visit other shared spaces; have a tactile experience of what you are building and bring along naysayers and community advocates.

8. *Get on the same page.* Every successful project has had organizational alignment. Boards, staff, management, and key donors must support the project as a logical strategic move for the partner organizations.

9. *Make enough time.* Staff the project correctly; make sure whoever is in charge really has the needed time and focus. Developing or managing a nonprofit center is not the kind of project that can be done intermittently and on a part-time basis.

10. *Developing a nonprofit center is not a DIY project.* Get relevant expertise involved early in the process. Use professional help, starting with a good developer or project manager, an attorney, and sometimes a real estate broker. Be sure they understand and support what you're trying to do.

11. *Purpose comes first.* Finally, always remember the purpose of the center—the reason for the shared space—and who the center will ultimately serve: the staff, partners or clients, stakeholders, and constituents. The space should reflect their needs, meet their challenges, and make their lives better.

OUR VISION

Our vision is that every nonprofit has space that dignifies their work; that they've been able to leave the church basements behind, and every city has quality shared space to house and highlight the work of nonprofits; that nonprofits sit at the table in every neighborhood participatory planning process along with the people they serve and that they're involved in decisions that concern their communities; and that co-location, shared services, and collaboration magnify the impact of every issue-focused organization. Figure 31.1 embodies this ethos.

This book was written as a tribute to the many nonprofit entrepreneurs and communities who saw a need for placemaking in their community or movement and went to work, not stopping until the doors opened, the partners moved in, and the results began. They've created a path and this book is intended to invite others to follow it.

FIGURE 31.1 *Nonprofit Centers Create Hope for the Future.* Serve Denton is a nonprofit center located in Denton, Texas. One of Serve Denton's centers is The Wheeler House, a transitional housing facility managed by Giving Hope, Inc., and an affordable health clinic managed by Health Services of North Texas. This is a playground built to accompany the children living in the housing component of The Wheeler House. *Photo credit: Serve Denton.*

Acknowledgments

Like any nonprofit shared space, this book took a long time to get off the ground and many people helped, in both big and small ways. The project was launched in December 2014 as the authors were preparing to convene and attend the largest gathering to date of nonprofit centers, the 2015 Building Opportunities Conference in Vancouver, in partnership with our Canadian colleagues at the Social Purpose Real Estate Collaborative. That gathering was a culmination of more than fifteen years of work with nonprofit centers and reinforced the need to document the field of nonprofit shared space. We have many people and organizations to thank who contributed to this volume.

First, we are grateful to the nonprofit practitioners who agreed to contribute *Stories from the Field*, the real-life examples of nonprofit shared spaces. Several of the original contributors have since moved on from their posts, but these *Stories* provide a lasting testament to their excellent work. The *Stories* presented here are only a fraction of the hundreds of centers operating across North America; they provide vivid and hard-earned lessons about shared spaces. We thank them for their contributions. We would like to thank our colleagues Saul Ettlin, and Kim Sarnecki, who provided the chapter on facility operations. We also received support in finding photos and collecting needed references from many other creators of shared projects in both the US and Canada. We are proud to showcase their spaces in this book.

We are also grateful to the experts we consulted, who reviewed chapters, and who responded to our queries. Thank you to Cathy Barr and Theresa L. M. Man for their expertise on the Canadian nonprofit sector. Thanks also to Cynthia R. Rowland for her US legal expertise, Josh Simon for his keen ability to present complex financial information clearly, Roxanne Hanson for her early field leadership and excellent editing skills, and Thomas Pollak and Michelle Zhou, for their insights and data analysis about nonprofit occupancy costs.

All three authors have made countless site visits to existing nonprofit centers and emerging shared spaces. These visits, interviews, and consulting projects have informed much of our own knowledge, and we thank them for opening their organizations to us for study, observation and exchange. We hope this book is a fitting tribute to them.

This book would not be nearly as useful or beautiful without the many volunteer hours by our exceptional graphics artist, Lisa Roth, who designed our tables and charts and prepared the photos. We also want to thank our project manager, K. D. Sullivan, who gracefully shepherded the last months of the editorial process. Cristina Chan provided marketing assistance and a key content review, and Sathya Narayanan helped with the compilation of our manuscript's first draft.

We have had an exceptional editorial team working with us! Thanks first to David Follmer, founder of Lyceum Books and Principal of the David Follmer Group without whose initial belief and ongoing advice this book would not exist. Thanks to Joseph "Jay"

Conner and Jonathan Spack for their insightful reviews and practical advice. We also have appreciated the willingness to answer our many questions and the ongoing support we received from Dana Bliss, Andrew Dominello, Stefano Imbert, Denise Phillip Grant, and Sarah Butcher at Oxford University Press and Rajeswari Balasubramanian and her team at Newgen Knowledge Works.

We want to thank the staff of the Nonprofit Centers Network (NCN), the support organization that developed and housed much of the work of nonprofit center field building and facilitated the conferences and trainings where the authors met. Over the years, these people contributed their time and careers to building this field. Staff members, contributors and friends include Martha Burton, Jackie Cefola, Bruce DeMartini, Christa DeRicco, Katie F. Edwards, Saul Ettlin, LoriAnn Girvan, Jeffrey Golden, Roxanne Hanson, Lara Jakubowski, Mina Kim, Yasmine Kohli Fordham, Lynette Logan, Maria Martinez, Shantel Nilson, Tuan Ngo, Pauline Vela, and Alice Wagner. Other staff at both of NCN's institutional homes at Tides and Third Sector New England also supported the work, and we thank them. A special thanks to Katie F. Edwards, Lara Jakubowski, and Leena Waite for answering endless questions and opening NCN's research and publications archive to us.

Thank you to NCN's steering committee, both founding members and present-day leaders for their indefatigable dedication: Allison Andrachuk, Jerry Bilton, Debra Box, Martha Burton, Joseph "Jay" Connor, Katie F. Ensign, Saul Ettlin, Miriam Pena Garcia, LoriAnn Girvan, Jeff Good, Stephanie Fallcreek, Kimberly Frentz Edmonds, Michael Gathercole, Shelley Hamilton, Becky Jasso, Vicki Jay, Andy Johnston, Anne-Marie Jones, Joanne Lee, Glen Newby, Tom O'Connor, Jennifer Pedroni, Janna Six, Pat Smith, Jonathan Spack, Doug Vilsack, Mara Williams Low, Rima Zabian, Margie Zeidler, Alan Zimlicki, and Alex Zwissler.

Diane would like to thank Bowen McBeath for his contributions to her "Under One Roof" research project, publications, and conference presentations, and Christine Su, Jessica Jurek, Veronica Marie Gentile, David Dobbie, Carly E. Kingstrom, and James DeVaney for research and database assistance. Diane thanks the following for research funding: The Aspen Institute's Nonprofit Sector and Philanthropy Program, the School of Social Work and Office of the Vice-President of Research at The University of Michigan, and one of the nonprofit centers she studied.

The past years have seen so much change, both in our personal lives and in the world. Of course, in the US, our political world has been upended by the 2016 election with near-daily news of changes to laws and regulations that protect poor and marginalized peoples and the organizations that support them. These organizations are the very groups that are served by the nonprofit shared spaces in this book, and the need for them is more important than ever. These organizations, tenants, and partners in nonprofit centers remain a bright spot of hope in these tumultuous times.

Finally, in our own lives, we weathered one major knee surgery, a job change, two retirements, an emergency birth and NICU stay, and other health scares. We have also had many joys—bar mitzvahs, new and growing children and grandchildren, new grand nephews, family trips overseas, and college graduations. Along the way, this book was always with us, and we extend our gratitude and love to our families for their unwavering support.

China Brotsky + Sarah M. Eisinger + Diane Vinokur-Kaplan

Biographical Sketches of Authors

China Brotsky has over thirty-five years of experience in nonprofit management, real estate, and finance and is an international thought-leader and consultant on nonprofit center creation and development. While senior vice president of Tides, a philanthropic partner and nonprofit accelerator, China managed the restoration and development of the historic Thoreau Centers for Sustainability (now Tides Converge) in San Francisco and New York—a combined 250,000 sq. ft. of shared nonprofit space occupied by over one hundred tenants. China also co-founded and served as the first executive director of the Nonprofit Centers Network, an international peer learning network of nonprofits and their philanthropic and real estate partners. She was also the founding executive director of Groundspring.org, a nonprofit technology shared service provider. Until May 2019, she served as the Director of Operations and Finance at SumOfUs, a global digital campaign organization. China is a member of the board of directors of 350.org, the ACLU of Northern California, the Nonprofit Centers Network, and Oasis Legal Services. She is a Certified Public Accountant in the State of California. She is a native San Franciscan where she continues to live with her family.

Sarah M. Eisinger has more than twenty years of experience in the nonprofit, real estate, community development, and philanthropic fields. She currently serves as vice president in the Real Estate Department at MassDevelopment, the state economic development agency in Massachusetts. Prior to her arrival in Massachusetts, Sarah spent fifteen years in New York City, including as a real estate consultant to nonprofit organizations such as Bill T. Jones/Arnie Zane Dance Company, Elizabeth Streb's Dance Company, and Poets House. In 2011, Sarah joined the Nonprofit Centers Network (NCN) where she guided the development of shared space projects across North America. She served as executive director of NCN from 2013 to 2015 and led the organization's largest gathering of nonprofit centers, in Vancouver, BC. Sarah is a LEED Accredited Professional Building Design + Construction (LEED AP BD + C), was a Licensed NY State Real Estate Salesperson for ten years, and holds a Master's in Urban Policy and Management from the Milano School at The New School in New York. Sarah lives in Amherst, Massachusetts, with her husband, baby daughter, and stepchildren.

Diane Vinokur-Kaplan (also known as Diane Kaplan Vinokur) is Associate Professor Emerita at the University of Michigan School of Social Work where she taught various Master of Social Work courses on nonprofit management and also a doctoral seminar on Research on Nonprofits. She and Bowen McBeath published the first study of attitudes and satisfactions of nonprofit tenant organizations co-located at three large nonprofit centers in the US. Diane has served on the Board of ARNOVA, the Association for Research on Nonprofit Organizations and Voluntary Action, and is on the Editorial Board of Nonprofit and Voluntary Sector Quarterly. She also serves on the Board of NEW, Inc., a nonprofit management support organization that also includes the NEW Center, a nonprofit center with over twenty nonprofit tenants, located in Ann Arbor, Michigan. She holds a BA (cum laude) from Oberlin College and did graduate studies at the University of Michigan, where she received two master's degrees, (MA, Sociology, and MSW, Social Policy) and a PhD from the Interdisciplinary Program in Social Work and Sociology.

Biographical Sketches of Contributors

Danielle Cameron, MPH, is Chief Strategy Officer for National Health Foundation where she is responsible for developing and executing strategies to achieve the mission, communicate with stakeholders, and fund operations. Prior to her time at National Health Foundation, she held administrative positions in the senior service and childcare fields. Ms. Cameron earned her Master's in Public Health from the University of California at Los Angeles and a Bachelor of Science in Psychology from Loyola University Chicago.

Kelly Costa has been an advocate for social change as a researcher, writer, nonprofit director, and leader of large-scale initiatives for nongovernmental organizations and social enterprises since 1991. As Research and Communications Associate with the strategic advisory firm Open Impact, she has worked with the Sobrato Family Foundation since 2010. Kelly holds a Master's in Geography, Human-Environmental Studies, and a Bachelor of Science in Graphic Communications. https://www.linkedin.com/in/kellycosta.

Centre for Social Innovation (CSI) is a community, co-working space, and launchpad for people and organizations working across sectors to create a better world. With four locations in Toronto and one in New York City, CSI works to accelerate their members' success and amplify their impact through the power of collaboration. Together, CSI and its members are building a movement for people and planet.

John Clawson, Founding Principal of Equity Community Builders, LLC, brings broad expertise in all phases of the real estate development process, which includes complex financing structures combined with conventional financing, investor equity, and funding secured through New Markets and Historic Tax Credits. John earned a Master's Degree from the MIT Center for Real Estate Development and Bachelor of Architecture from Arizona State University. John serves on multiple Boards of Trustees for arts and educational organizations.

Megan Corning (BA, University of Connecticut and AmeriCorps alumna), supported the Sobrato Family Foundation's Centers for Nonprofits (2011–2015). She was first a Center Coordinator, providing onsite property management services, and later a Program Associate, assisting with the administrative and operational aspects of leasing and managing the facilities. An enthusiastic shared space proponent, Megan worked to foster community among tenants and provided creative programming throughout her time at the Sobrato Centers for Nonprofits.

Megan Devenport is Executive Director of Building Bridges, a community-driven nonprofit that equips youth with leadership skills to address the root causes of discrimination. As a community social worker, Megan's background includes direct service with young people, community-building, and advocacy. Most recently, Megan managed Denver Shared Spaces, helping nonprofits connect commercial real estate with social impact. She received her Master's in Social Work from the University of Denver and her Bachelor's in Psychology from the University of Illinois.

Lorraine Duff is the Director, Special Projects at United Way Greater Toronto. As part of the Building Strong Neighborhoods Strategy, Lorraine works with various partners to develop Community Hubs—infrastructure projects that bring vital programs and services, as well as community space to under-served neighbourhoods. Her previous twenty-five years of work includes community development, funding, and management related to social service and health sectors. Lorraine has a Master's in Social Work.

Katie F. Edwards is the Executive Director of the Nonprofit Centers Network. She holds a Master's in Public Affairs in Nonprofit Management from Indiana University, where nonprofit co-location was her research focus. Ms. Edwards has been involved with the shared space community in North America for over seven years. In 2015, Ms. Edwards oversaw the *State of the Shared Space Sector* survey, resulting in the first reports on financial health and staffing in nonprofit shared space.

Saul Ettlin is a Nonprofit Real Estate Consultant with the Northern California Community Loan Fund where he assists organizations with their space needs. Previously, he was the Collaboration + Space Manager at Tides where he helped operate their two nonprofit centers totaling 250,000 sq. ft. and home to over one hundred organizations. Saul is a seasoned nonprofit manager and is committed to strengthening organizations through shared space and collaboration. He holds a MPA from Portland State University.

Lara Jakubowski is a Senior Consultant at La Piana Consulting, She works with nonprofits to address organizational issues and partners with others for sustainable impact. She specializes in working with complex collaboratives working toward shared goals, helping them identify successful strategies and design plans for action. She was formerly the Executive Director of the Nonprofit Centers Network, Denver, Colorado, and founding Executive Director of the Mile High Community Loan Fund, an $18 million community development financial institution. She holds an MBA (Wharton School of Business, University of Pennsylvania).

Yodit Mesfin Johnson is Chief Operating Officer and Vice President of Strategy for NEW. She has overall strategic and operational responsibility for the NEW Center and all programs. As the chief program officer, she provides leadership to NEW's strategic planning process and implements new programmatic strategic initiatives including opportunities to expand NEW's impact through partnerships with NEW Center's tenants. She is a nationally recognized leader in business development, non-profit management, and social entrepreneurship.

Marietta Kozak, along with Elia Kirby, manages and developed the Arts Factory in Vancouver, a 23,000 sq. ft. co-located artist studio space. She has been running non-profit theater companies in the city since 1980, and is currently the General Manager of a local performance company, Mortal Coil, as well as financial manager for the Great Northern Scene Shop, a local theatrical scenic building shop.

William Leddy, FAIA, is a founding Principal of Leddy Maytum Stacy Architects in San Francisco. Leddy believes that architecture has an important role to play in leading our communities toward a just, sustainable future for all. His firm has received over 140 design awards and is one of only two firms in the nation to have received ten or more AIA COTE Top Ten Green Project awards. Leddy Maytum Stacy Architects was the 2017 recipient of the National AIA Firm Award.

Mara Williams Low is the Program Director of Sobrato Family Foundation, Silicon Valley's largest place-based grantmaker. She leads the Foundation's operations, grantee capacity building efforts, its impact and learning function, and its three nonprofit centers, which house and support seventy nonprofit tenants with in-kind rent and fee-free conference space. She holds a BA in English from UC Berkeley.

Jessie MacKinnon was Vice President of Programs and Partnerships at The HSC Foundation for sixteen years until she retired in 2016. There she served as Chief Operating Officer of the Foundation's National Youth Transitions Center, a shared space nonprofit building in Washington, DC, guided by a national collaborative of organizations serving youth with disabilities. She has over thirty years of experience in marketing and communications, survey research and analysis, and program development in the nonprofit and for-profit sectors.

Glen Newby is the CEO of New Path Youth and Family Services, the lead organization for mental health services in Simcoe County, Ontario. Under his twenty-year tenure as President and CEO of New Path Foundation, Glen established the two Common Roof™ multitenant nonprofit centers in Orillia and Barrie, which now serve over 10,000 clients annually. Glen holds an MSW from Wilfrid Laurier University, a management degree from Queen's School of Business, and is also past Steering Committee Co-Chair of Nonprofit Centers Network based in Denver.

John Powers and Janna Six co-founded the Alliance for Sustainable Colorado in 2004 to develop and operate the 40,000 sq. ft. Alliance Center in downtown Denver near the Capitol. Throughout, they have been members and supporters of the Nonprofit Centers Network, a tenant in the Alliance Center. Currently, Powers serves on the Alliance and other nonprofit and foundation boards. Six is a volunteer for the Alliance and is the Executive Director of the Prentice Foundation.

Stacy Ratner is the founder of Open Books and co-founder of the Chicago Literacy Alliance, both located in Chicago. Previously, she helped take four tech startups from idea through national rollout and $30 million in committed venture capital. Stacy holds degrees in literature and law (Brandeis University, Boston College Law School) and will receive her MBA from Northwestern University's Kellogg School of Management in 2018. The Literacenter, featured in this publication, received the Library of Congress's Best Practices in Literacy Award in 2016.

Lisa Roth is a graphic designer, producing print materials and websites for social movements, nonprofits, and individuals. Lisa is also a lifelong social justice activist, actively opposing racial and gender prejudice, and is a founder of the John Brown Anti-Klan Committee and the San Francisco Dyke March. See her work on http://www.lisarothgrafix.com and contact her at lisa@lisarothgrafix.com.

Kim M. Sarnecki formerly served as Director of Administration and Real Estate for Tides, overseeing collaborative space for social ventures in San Francisco and New York City. Tides is a philanthropic partner and nonprofit accelerator working for shared prosperity and social justice. Kim received her BA in Anthropology and Sociology from Kenyon College, and her MA in Cultural Anthropology and Social Transformation from the California Institute of Integral Studies.

Jonathan Spack served as CEO of TSNE MissionWorks (previously Third Sector New England) for thirty-four years. Under his tenure, TSNE became a national leader in fiscal sponsorship and social purpose real estate. He spearheaded TSNE's acquisition/development of the NonProfit Center, a focal point of Boston's social justice activity. Jonathan also co-founded the National Network of Fiscal Sponsors and the Nonprofit Centers Network. He holds a Bachelor's and Master's in Human Services Management from Brandeis University and a JD from NYU Law School.

Thaddeus Squire is founder and Chief Commons Officer of CultureWorks Commons Management and its supported organizations, CultureWorks Greater Philadelphia and CultureWorks Greater Houston. Mr. Squire holds degrees in history, musicology, and orchestral conducting from Princeton University and Leipziger Universität and the Hochschule für Musik und Theater "Felix Mendelssohn Bartholdy" (both in Leipzig, Germany). His lifelong interests in complex systems have led his work to focus on the dimensions and dynamics of resource sharing, with an emphasis on the nonprofit fields of arts and heritage.

Megan Yonke is a passionate community development advocate with over ten years of experience supporting partners and clients in business development, program management, and policy planning and implementation. At Radian|Placematters, she supported community-serving organizations, both for- and nonprofit, in finding space to thrive and enhance their services to disadvantaged communities. She has a Master's in Urban and Regional Planning from the University of Colorado–Denver. She left Radian in 2018 to become a Housing Development Officer at the Denver Office of Economic Development.

Index

Tables, figures and boxes are indicated by an italic *t*, *f* and *b* following the page number.